A history of the Canadian Pacific Railway

To
MY PARENTS

A HISTORY OF

The Canadian Pacific Railway

BY HAROLD A. INNIS

———————

with a foreword by Peter George

David & Charles : Newton Abbot

© 1971 University of Toronto Press, Toronto and Buffolo
First Published 1923
New Impression 1972
ISBN 0 7153 5520 1

Reproduced and Printed in Great Britain by
Redwood Press Limited
Trowbridge & London for
David & Charles (Publishers) Limited
Newton Abbot   Devon

Foreword

PROFESSOR Innis' *A History of the Canadian Pacific Railway*, first published in 1923, represents the most significant scholarly contribution to Canadian transportation history dealing with Canada's first transcontinental railroad. Thoroughly researched and carefully documented, the book discusses in painstaking detail all aspects of CPR construction and operation to 1921.

With the reprinting of the *History*, it is an interesting and instructive exercise to re-read Innis' book together with recent studies by Albert Fishlow[1] and Robert Fogel[2] on the relations between railroads and economic development in the nineteenth-century United States, and to compare the methodological foundations underlying the older and newer studies as well as the nature of their findings. The "scientific" approach which is currently in vogue among economic historians is epitomized by the work of Fishlow and Fogel: these "new" economic historians emphasize the explicit use of economic theory to construct and test hypotheses about the developmental role of the railroad. Innis' method, on the other hand, was descriptive and narrative, relying exclusively on descriptive statistics and qualitative argument, and employing little formal economic theory, even though he apparently was concerned to study the CPR from "a scientific point of view."

The treatment of topics of traditional interest to economic

[1] Albert Fishlow, *American Railroads and the Transformation of the Ante-Bellum Economy* (Cambridge, Mass., 1965).
[2] Robert W. Fogel, *The Union Pacific Railroad: A Case in Premature Enterprise* (Baltimore, 1960) and *Railroads and American Economic Growth: Essays in Econometric History* (Baltimore, 1964).

historians, such as the significance of railroads in economic growth, has changed primarily because the methodological basis of economic history has changed. Certainly, no contemporary economic historian desiring to analyse the impact of the CPR on Canadian economic development would be likely to write the kind of book that Professor Innis did. Yet he would refer to the *History* time and again for detailed information about CPR construction and operations and about documentary sources, and because he would be struck by the continued relevance of the questions posed by Innis. Insights and hypotheses, although frequently implicit, abound in Innis' *History*.

I

Although a lengthy summary of the *History* need not be given here, it may be worthwhile to outline briefly some of Professor Innis' main conclusions. He began by describing the political and economic factors culminating in the entry of British Columbia into Confederation and the commitment of the Canadian government to build a Pacific railway (chaps. I and II, *passim*), and concluded that the CPR was a necessary condition of Canadian political and economic development (pp. 74, 96, 277). From the inception of the project, "liberal" subsidies were essential to induce private promoters to undertake construction of the railroad (pp. 101, 277–8) and, during 1881 to 1885, the CPR Company was obliged to make repeated calls on the government for financial assistance (pp. 108–27) before construction of the mainline was completed in November, 1885.

Upon completion of the mainline, the Company was, because of its financial structure, in a promising position (pp. 270–4, 292). However, the subsequent profitability of the Company's operations was attributed primarily to the initiative of management in expanding the road and developing freight traffic, which contributed to the growth of operating revenues and spread overhead costs associated with unproductive stretches of track (pp. 129 ff.). Branch lines were constructed, especially in the west, and land and freight and passenger rate policies were employed by the Company to promote rapid settlement of the west and the subsequent development of freight traffic (chaps. IV and V, *passim*), although western complaints that the profits of the railroad have been extracted largely from western pockets were justified (pp. 268–9, 293–4). Elevators were constructed at strategic shipment points to expedite the movement of grain (p. 134), and locomotive- and car-shops and general repair shops were established in Montreal and Winnipeg to improve the Company's capacity to add to and maintain plant and equipment (p. 134).

The CPR Company proved to be very profitable, earning large surpluses over operating expenses and fixed charges and paying high dividends to its shareholders (chaps. IX and X *passim*, and p. 292). Moreover, the CPR made a significant contribution to Canadian economic growth (p. 294) and to Canadian political and economic integration (p. 277).

Many of Innis' conclusions about the CPR have been incorporated into Canadian historiography. There has been no comprehensive examination of the developmental role of Canadian railroads similar to those completed with United States data by Fishlow and Fogel; in particular, the economic history of the CPR remains much as Innis left it. Yet, it is interesting to compare Innis' method of assessing, and conclusions about, the profitability of CPR investment and the developmental impact of the CPR with those of Fishlow and Fogel, and this writer's[3] recent study of government subsidization of the CPR. Finally, Innis' method and findings can be related to some recent suggestions about directions which new research efforts might take in determining the impact of the CPR on the growth of the Canadian economy.

II

Professor Innis concluded that the CPR Company was profitable (in accounting terms) after examining data on the railroad's operating revenues and operating expenses, fixed charges, and dividend rates (chaps. IX and X, *passim*). This procedure can be compared with that adopted by Fogel in his study of the Union Pacific Railroad, which involved a major reinterpretation of its financial history and developmental impact.[4]

---

[3] P. J. George, "Rates of Return in Railway Investment and Implications for Government Subsidization of the Canadian Pacific Railway: Some Preliminary Results," *Canadian Journal of Economics*, I (Nov., 1968), 740–62.

[4] In many ways, the Union Pacific was the American counterpart of the CPR: it was the first American transcontinental, it was heavily subsidized by the federal government, and it generated the Credit Mobilier scandal of 1873. However, the Union Pacific, unlike the CPR, was continually beset by financial difficulties after its completion.

The general interpretation, in American historiography, of the cause of the financial problems of the Union Pacific had centred around the charge that the promoters of the railroad were guilty of profiteering during its construction, and that their profiteering weakened it financially to an extent that rendered bankruptcy inevitable. Fogel first re-examined the charge of "profiteering" and, given his estimate of "justifiable" profits to the promoters, concluded that these charges were much exaggerated. Moreover, the financial difficulties of the railroad were found to result primarily from its financial structure and particularly from its large bonded debt, and in part from the government's provision of financial assistance in the form of bonds. Secondly, and more significantly, the financial problems of the Union Pacific were found to have disguised the *economic* profitability of the project, compared with its failure according to *accounting* concepts of profitability. Fogel's calculation of the "private rate of return," computed from data on net earnings and costs of construction, demonstrated that the project was *ex post* very successful by economic criteria and could have been built by private enterprise unaided. However, under prevailing economic conditions and expectations, the railroad probably would not have been constructed without government assistance. In such circumstances, the government's decision to intervene appears economically rational, judged by the high "social rate of return" (about 30 per cent between 1870 and 1879) attaching to the project.[5]

The Union Pacific was unprofitable in accounting terms yet profitable in economic terms. Innis' conclusion that the CPR was profitable (by accounting criteria) leaves unanswered the question – was the CPR profitable by economic criteria? And, what role did the subsidy received by the Company play in determining accounting profitability? When Innis wrote that the CPR received "liberal" subsidies (pp. 101, 277–8), was he

[5] On occasion, "private rate of return" is used synonymously with "internal rate of return." The numerator in the "social rate of return" calculation is equal to the net earnings of the railroad plus the "unpaid benefits" – "the increase in national income brought about by the road but which failed to be reflected in the company's net earnings." Fogel, *The Union Pacific Railroad*, 98. The economic theory of rent formed the basis for estimating the "unpaid benefits" which accrued from the opening up of lands through which the railroad was constructed.

not hypothesizing that the CPR received "excessive" subsidies? To conclude that subsidies were "liberal" or "excessive"
formally requires the specification and testing of a hypothesis
about the amount of subsidy necessary to induce Company
construction of the CPR. In fact, my own study, suggested by
Fogel's work on the Union Pacific, was concerned with determining the economic profitability of the CPR, and testing
hypotheses about the necessity and amount of subsidies
awarded to the CPR Company by the Canadian government.

From the inception of the CPR project, the government was
concerned that a private company be organized to build the
railroad, a decision which for private investors depended solely
on economic considerations, not on a state of political urgency.
If potential investors had believed that the railroad would be
profitable, then they could have built it without subsidy. In
fact, private enterprise never seriously considered building the
CPR without the financial assistance of the government.
Anticipated profits were too small in view of the considerable
risks attached to the project. The CPR represented, in Fogel's
terminology, "premature" enterprise.[6] An extremely large
amount of capital was required for construction costs, and
earnings were likely to be small for several years after the
completion of the railroad before traffic was sufficient to yield
profits.

Even if the railroad had to be built for political reasons, there
remain questions of the necessity and appropriate amount of
subsidy to induce Company construction. Data on construction
expenditures and reported Company net earnings were employed to calculate private rates of return on CPR investment
for the first decade of operation, 1886 to 1895, the levels of
which suggested that the CPR was unprofitable in *economic*
terms. The calculated private rates of return were then used to
compute *ex post* "required" subsidy.[7] Secondly, the value in

---

[6] "Premature, that is, when the measuring rod of its maturity and practicability was the willingness of unaided private enterprise, guided solely
by the search for profits, to undertake the project." Fogel, *The Union
Pacific Railroad*, 18. Innis also emphasized the great risk associated with
Pacific railroad investment (p. 77).

[7] "Required" subsidy was defined as "that capital grant payable by the
government in 1885, sufficient in amount to allow Company net earnings to
yield the normal rate of return on privately contributed capital." George,
"Rates of Return," 759.

1885 of subsidies paid to the Company was estimated (including estimated values of railroad constructed by the government and turned over to the Company, of cash subsidies, of the land grant, of tax exemptions, and of the remission of import duties on construction materials). *Ex post*, it was found that the Company was awarded "excessive" subsidies.[8] A complete answer to the question of whether the CPR was excessively subsidized would require examination of the *ex ante* situation governing the bargain made between the Company and the government in the autumn of 1880, but such an examination was not feasible with the available data.

Whereas the political basis of the government's decision to subsidize the construction of the CPR may be accepted without hesitation, the relevance of the economic grounds for that decision remains to be established. The subsidy was justified economically on the assumption that the railroad was likely to yield large social returns on investment but only low levels of private income to the Company. These anticipated social returns were comprised of the "unpaid benefits" of the railroad.[9] It was expected that the CPR would reduce transportation costs, both for passengers and freight, and stimulate the development of the industrial and financial sectors of the economy. However, the railroad was likely to effect an increase in national income primarily by opening the lands of the western prairies to settlement and, to a lesser extent, by opening northern Ontario and British Columbia for mining and lumber production. In fact, Innis argued that the CPR Company had to build branch lines in order to increase traffic on the main line: increased traffic depended on increased population, and increased population depended on extending branch lines (pp. 130, 143-7).

Canadian economic historians have tended to complement the indisputable assumption that the CPR was a political necessity with claims of its great contribution to the magnitude

---

[8] The minimum estimates of "excessive" subsidy in 1885 were $61 million, $40 million, and $34 million when the market rate of return on investment was assumed to be 6, 8, and 10 per cent respectively. *Ibid.*, 761. The conclusion that subsidies were "excessive" was reinforced by the direction of biases in the estimates of the value of subsidies actually paid to the Company and in the estimates of *ex post* "required" subsidy, which imply that the estimates of *ex post* "excessive" subsidy are lower bounds.

[9] See n. 5 above.

and pattern of Canadian economic growth after 1885.[10] However, the techniques of modern economic analysis have not yet
been applied to analysing the economic significance of CPR
investment. Previous studies of the railroad, Innis' *History*
included, have been essentially descriptive, and have been, to a
considerable extent, based upon the implicit assumption that
the "economic benefits" of the railroad were "substantial"
(p. 294, for example). In fact, the validity of this assumption
remains to be tested by the calculation of the social rate of
return on CPR investment.

Although the extent of the CPR's contribution to Canadian
economic development and the economic efficiency of government intervention in CPR construction are as yet untested,
Fishlow and Fogel have analysed the developmental impact of
railroads in the United States and attempted to quantify the
benefits to the economy of railroad construction and operation.
Both writers began with the predictions of economic theory
that the railroad could offer direct benefits through lowering
the real cost of transporting commodities and passengers compared with alternative carriers, and indirect benefits through
induced responses or linkage effects in those industries which
employ railroad services as inputs (forward linkage) or produce
inputs for use in the railroad sector (backward linkage).

Both Fishlow and Fogel measured direct benefits accruing
from the railroad sector. With this calculation, Fogel was
expressly concerned to examine systematically the undisputed
acceptance in American historiography of the "axiom of
indispensability"[11] – the implicit assumption that the nineteenth century United States economy lacked a viable transport
alternative to the railroad (that is, that direct benefits were
"large"). The contribution of the railroad to the American

[10] For example, in reviewing Innis' *History*, O. D. Skelton wrote: "There
has been no factor in the economic development of Canada in the past fifty
years so significant as the Canadian Pacific Railway." *Canadian Historical
Review*, x (June, 1923), 180. This conclusion would be valid in economic
terms only if the social rate of return on CPR investment had been calculated and found to be greater than the social rate of return on all alternative
investment projects during the fifty-year period.
[11] The "axiom of indispensability" is discussed in Fogel, *Railroads and
American Economic Growth*, 1–16. The "axiom" received perhaps its finest
enunciation in an article by Leland H. Jenks, "Railroads as an Economic
Force in American Development," *Journal of Economic History*, IV (May,
1944), 1–20.

economy in 1890 was the "social savings"[12] estimated to accrue
from the shipment of freight via the inter-regional and intra-
regional railroads. Railroad "social savings" amounted to
approximately 4.7 per cent of gross national product in 1890.[13]
Fogel pointed out that, although the railroad was the most
efficient form of transportation open to the economy, the data
failed to "establish a *causal* relationship between the railroad
and either the regional reorganization of trade, or the change
in the structure of output, or the rise in per capita income, or
the various other strategic changes that characterized the
American economy of the last century . . . [and the evidence
failed even to] establish the weaker proposition that railroads
were a *necessary* condition for these developments."[14]

[12] "Social savings" is defined as "the difference between the actual level
of national income in 1890 and the level of national income that would have
prevailed if the economy made the most efficient possible adjustment to the
absence of the . . . railroad." Fogel, *Railroads and American Economic
Growth*, 20. For a discussion of the concept, see 20–9 and 52–8.
  Here, Fogel has made use of a "counterfactual conditional," that is, a
comparison between what actually happened and what *would* most likely
have occurred in the absence of the railroad. In order to determine what
would have happened, the economic historian must deduce the "counterfactual" with the aid of a theoretical model. As Fogel has suggested, one
difference between the "old" and "new" economic history lies not in the
frequent use of counterfactual propositions in the "new," but in the extent
to which such propositions, implicit in more traditional studies, have been
made explicit and tested empirically. See R. W. Fogel, "The New Economic
History: Its Findings and Methods," *Economic History Review*, Second
Series, xix (1966), 653–6, and A. H. Conrad and J. R. Meyer, "Economic
Theory, Statistical Inference and Economic History," in Conrad and
Meyer, *The Economics of Slavery* (Chicago, 1964), 23–4.
[13] Fogel, *Railroads and American Economic Growth*, 223. Marc Nerlove,
"Railroads and American Economic Growth," *Journal of Economic
History*, xxvi (March, 1966), 112–15, takes Fogel to task: "instead of asking
whether the contribution of railroads to American economic growth was
great or small *in toto* and absolutely, we should ask whether it was great or
small at the margin and relatively. That is to say, we should ask whether
the marginal social return . . . was greater, equal or less as compared to the
marginal social return on other forms of investment." *Ibid.*, 112. Nevertheless, Nerlove's calculations (based upon admittedly shaky data) confirm
Fogel's conclusions regarding the impact of railroads. (In any event, in
correspondence with Nerlove, Fogel has questioned the use of the marginal
concept as the sole criterion of "contribution" in this context.)
[14] Fogel, *Railroads and American Economic Growth*, 15. (My italics.) In
fact, Fogel demonstrated that adaptation of the economy to a non-rail
transportation technology was feasible. The loss of the railroad in 1890
would have lowered the area of commercial agricultural land by 24 per cent.
An improved internal navigation system would have reduced the loss to
7 per cent of 1890 acreage; allowing for improvement of country roads as
well, only 4 per cent of 1890 commercial agricultural acreage would have
been withdrawn from cultivation in the absence of the railroad. *Ibid.*, 91–
110.

In his *American Railroads and the Transformation of the Ante-Bellum Economy*, Albert Fishlow calculated that "social savings" attributable to the railroad in 1859 amounted to 4 per cent of gross national product.[15] Direct benefits from the railroad sector yielded a social rate of return on railroad investment of about 15 per cent prior to 1860,[16] and direct and indirect benefits together gave a social rate of return estimated to lie between 20 and 30 per cent.[17] Fishlow admits that such high rates of return do not imply that the railroad was indispensable to American economic growth. Canals and roads might have been improved in the absence of the railroad. Nevertheless, Fishlow confirms for 1859 Fogel's finding that the railroad was the most efficient transport medium among available alternatives. Interestingly enough, Fogel and Fishlow disagree about the *degree* of importance in United States development of the railroad's embodiment of low real costs of transportation.

Some of the most interesting aspects of Fishlow's and Fogel's work lie in their attempts to assess the indirect effects of the railroad sector. Fishlow, for example, examines the popular belief that railroads were constructed "ahead of demand" in the American mid-west, and uniquely influenced the spatial distribution and timing of movement of factors of production.[18] The alleged importance of derived demands from the railroad sector to the manufacturing sector is examined by both writers.[19]

Fishlow's examination of the "construction ahead of demand" hypothesis represents a deliberate attempt to determine whether or not the railroad played a *causal* role in the growth of population and commercial agriculture in the midwest between 1848 and 1860. He rejects the ideal-type sequence of zero population (frontier density of 2 to 6 persons per square mile) – railroads – population and economic development, as unrealistic. Rather, he develops an ingenious restatement of the

---

[15] Fishlow, *American Railroads*, 52. Fishlow suggests that a more plausible estimate than Fogel's of "social savings" in 1890, based on extrapolation of his results for the pre-1860 period, would be in the range of 10 to 15 per cent of gross national product. *Ibid.*, 61.

[16] *Ibid.*, 54.

[17] *Ibid.*, 305.

[18] *Ibid.*, chap. 4.

[19] Fogel, *Railroads and American Economic Growth*, chaps. 4, 5; Fishlow, *American Railroads*, chap. 3.

hypothesis so that it can be tested empirically with the data at hand. He deduces three implications of "construction ahead of demand." First, to argue that a railroad was built "ahead of demand" implies that investors expected the railroad to be unprofitable over some period of time. The existence of government subsidies to the railroad company is a test of *ex ante* expectations about the profitability of railroad investment.[20] Secondly, "construction ahead of demand" implies that excess capacity will exist on the railroad in the early years of operation. Thus, *ex post* net operating revenues will be too low to yield the market rate of return on investment in the early years, but will rise over time as increases in the demand for railroad services occur with increased settlement. Finally, he suggests that the population density of areas into which railroads were built can be used as a proxy for traffic demand.

Fishlow's hypothesis is, then, that "construction ahead of demand" has not occurred if railroads did not receive government aid,[21] were profitable from the beginning of operations, did not show an upward trend in net earnings, and were built into areas of considerable prior settlement. In fact, Fishlow's data refute "construction ahead of demand" in the case of mid-western railroads. Instead, he finds that railroads were built sequentially from high-population-density areas to areas of lower density, suggesting a rational exploitation of profit opportunities. However, refutation of the "construction ahead of demand" hypothesis does not necessarily imply that railroads did not "cause" western settlement, since settlement appears to have occurred in *anticipation* of railroad construction and led, in turn, to the emergence of profitable railroad investment opportunities.[22]

[20] "Mixed enterprise" (subsidized private enterprise) and public works projects are consistent with "construction ahead of demand," and unaided private enterprise projects consistent with "waiting demand." However, the existence of *ex ante* subsidies is not sufficient to indicate that the project was premature; investors might have sought subsidies from government in order to raise profits above market levels on mature projects. The existence of a subsidy indicates only that investors expected to earn *at least* the market rate of return on investment with the subsidy.

[21] An exception is local government aid, since the existence of local governments presupposes established population and, hence, "waiting demand." In any case, most local government aid to railroads in the midwest was in the form of loans which required repayment, not outright grants.

The importance to American industrial development of the input demands of the railroad sector has frequently been emphasized. W. W. Rostow, for example, has claimed that railroads were the decisive element in economic growth in the United States, Canada, and other countries. In particular, he argued that the development of the coal, iron and steel, and engineering industries were dependent upon the initial construction and subsequent maintenance and expansion of the railroad sector.[23]

Can the dependence of the industrial sector on the railroad sector be measured? With the data available, it was possible for Fishlow and Fogel to estimate the railroad sector's consumption of coal, lumber, machinery, and transportation equipment products in the pre-Civil War period, and thereby to test Rostow's contention that railroads were a "leading sector" in the American "take-off" of 1843–60.

Fogel found that railroad demand for iron products averaged 17 per cent of total domestic output of iron products from 1840 to 1860, rising from low levels in the 1840s to about 25 per cent from 1854 to 1860.[24] Railroad direct demand for coal and lumber was negligible before 1860, and railroad purchases from the transportation equipment and machinery industries were only a small part of their total sales. In 1859, railroad direct purchases amounted to only 2.8 per cent of value added in manufacturing and, if all the indirect effects of railroad input requirements were accounted for, at most 3.9 per cent of manufacturing value added.[25]

Fishlow reported similar findings. For example, railroad requirements amounted to about 20 per cent of domestic iron consumption in the 1850s,[26] and railroad consumption of coal

[22] However, "anticipatory settlement" is consistent with factors other than expectations of railroad construction. Densely populated areas might arise in advance of the railroad because of the existence of non-rail transportation systems (for example, location on a navigable waterway) or simply because land is not homogeneous (for example, earlier settlement of land of relatively great fertility). Moreover, the question remains whether density of population at the date of completion of the railroad is the appropriate measure of "anticipatory settlement," or whether the density of population at the date of chartering of the railroad should be employed.
[23] *The Stages of Economic Growth* (Cambridge, Eng., 1960), 55.
[24] Fogel, *Railroads and American Economic Growth*, 131–4.
[25] *Ibid.*, 140–6.
[26] Fishlow, *American Railroads*, 141. Whereas Fogel concludes that rail-

and lumber products was a small part of total output. Moreover, Fishlow agrees with Fogel that railroad demands were not
very important to the machinery industry. Contrary to
Rostow's contention that the machinery industry developed
because of railroad demands, the rapid growth of the domestic
locomotive industry can be explained by the earlier existence
of general machine shops and skilled labour which shifted into
railroad work. Railroads had their greatest impact on the
machinery industry through the development of extensive
repair shops.[27]

The work of Fishlow and Fogel puts a new perspective on the
validity of some of Innis' conclusions about the CPR's role in
Canadian economic development. Innis concluded that the
CPR had important direct and indirect effects on the Canadian
economy, but his discussion of these effects was distinctly
impressionistic. His argument that the CPR was politically
necessary can be readily accepted, but it is intuitively more
difficult to accept his claim that the CPR was economically
necessary. A necessary condition of western agricultural expansion was low real costs of transportation, not *the* CPR.
Given the assumption of the political necessity of CPR construction, the embodiment of low real costs of transportation in
the CPR follows. However, it is possible to imagine western
Canadian economic development occurring in a non-railroad
setting (for example, with earlier development of the motor
vehicle and highway expansion, or with the extension of
navigable waterways within the west) or on the basis of branch
lines from American railroads.[28]

Again, Innis argued that CPR expansion was necessary to
generate increased traffic and improve the Company's profit
position. After Fishlow, this argument can be recast into more

road derived demands for iron were relatively unimportant, Fishlow
argues that Fogel's calculations actually support Fishlow's conclusion that
there was "a large and increasing role for railroad demands in the development of the iron industry in the 1850's." *Ibid.*, 149.

[27] *Ibid.*, 149–56.

[28] One might also consider testing hypotheses about the actual route of
the CPR, ranging from conjectures about the reasons why the Company
chose the "southern" route through the prairies rather than the "northern"
route, to general agreement that an all-Canadian route increased construction costs above, for example, the alternative route through the United
States mid-west proposed by the Grand Trunk Railway.

modern terminology, since Innis was implying that the CPR represented "construction ahead of demand"; the Innisian sequence of branch lines – population inflows – agricultural output – freight traffic can be regarded as the hypothesis of a supply-induced shift in demand for railroad services that Fishlow examined in the United States mid-west. And, moreover, the CPR would appear to fulfil Fishlow's three conditions of "construction ahead of demand." It received government subsidies, its net operating revenues were low over the first years of its operation and trended upwards thereafter, and it was constructed through areas of low population density.

Another dimension to "construction ahead of demand" has been suggested by Charles Studness[29] with respect to the timing of CPR construction. Studness has implied that more rapid completion of the railroad from Winnipeg to Fort William in the 1870s would have significantly reduced the preference of migrants for the American western agricultural frontier over Manitoba and southern Saskatchewan, and accelerated the development of Canada's wheat economy. Furthermore, he has suggested that the government's land policy also retarded western settlement: the withholding of odd-numbered sections of land from homesteading for railroad endowment is alleged to have increased farm making costs in the Canadian west, and consequently to have inhibited rapid settlement in the 1870s and 1880s. Slow progress on CPR construction in the 1870s and the railroad land grant system had social costs (which presumably are quantifiable) to Canada.

Innis did offer some interesting comments on east-west economic relations in Canada. He suggested that the history of the CPR exemplified the "acquisitive" attitude of eastern Canada towards the west (pp. 268–9, 293–4), concluding that "western Canada has paid for the development of Canadian nationality" (p. 294). The "Innis link" implies that the CPR and the protective tariff were closely connected, the tariff protecting east-west traffic on the CPR and Canadian manufacturers at the expense of western farmers (p. 293).[30] Was

[29] C. M. Studness, "Economic Opportunity and the Westward Migration of Canadians during the Late Nineteenth Century," *Canadian Journal of Economics and Political Science*, XXX (Nov., 1964), 570–84.
[30] H. A. Innis, *Essays in Canadian Economic History*, edited by Mary Q. Innis (Toronto, 1962), 72, 150, 207.

Innis not arguing, at least implicitly, that western incomes would have been higher without the CPR and the "artificial" economic incorporation of the west into Canada? Indeed, V. C. Fowke has hypothesized that, because of the tariff, the CPR was an expensive alternative to American railroads.[31]

Fowke's impressions about the effect of the tariff on the real incomes of prairie dwellers brings to mind a similar hypothesis about incomes earned in wheat farming. If constraints on the use of American railroads to ship wheat had been lifted, what would have been the effect on the farm price of wheat in western Canada? It should be possible to calculate the "social savings" to the prairie economy attributable to the CPR by comparing real costs of transportation via the CPR with those of the next most efficient alternative. Government intervention into the Canadian freight rate structure through the Crow's Nest and Manitoba Agreements might be expected to have biased CPR rates downwards compared with American rates. If American railroads were more efficient, "social savings" from CPR investment would be negative, and the downward bias in CPR rates would ensure that the estimated "social savings" would represent a lower bound on the cost of the CPR to the west. Conversely, if the CPR was more efficient, estimated "social savings" would be positive and an upper bound on the direct benefits to the west from the CPR. A test of this hypothesis would require specification of collection points, alternative transportation routes, and markets for wheat and for goods moving into the west.

III

Over the past decade, economic theory and statistical methods have been skilfully employed in assessing the contribution of the railroad to United States economic development. Since completion of the pioneering studies by Fishlow and Fogel, there exist bounded estimates of the direct contribution of the railroad sector to the gross national product of the United

---

[31] V. C. Fowke, *The National Policy and the Wheat Economy* (Toronto, 1957), 69. By contrast, W. A. Mackintosh, in his *The Economic Background of Dominion-Provincial Relations* (Toronto, 1964), 145, argued that western farmers' real incomes were not reduced by the tariff up to 1930 because the west was settled after the tariff was implemented, and the cost of the tariff was presumably discounted in the price of land. Furthermore, it is possible that western farmers have experienced windfall gains with the long-run slightly downward trend of the tariff. See John Dales, "Introduction" to Mackintosh, *Economic Background*, 9.

States through the lowering of real costs of transportation. Moreover, their studies contain careful analyses of the nature and extent of the indirect effects of railroads on the agricultural and manufacturing sectors. Apart from their findings, the essential contribution of these studies has been the formulation and testing of explicit hypotheses about the railroad's contribution to American economic development, and their introduction into a literature which had previously contained only impressionistic accounts of the railroad's significance.

However, the reassessment of the role of the railroad in Canadian economic growth has not yet progressed very far. There has been no attempt to calculate the social rate of return on CPR investment, or "social savings" attributable to the railroad. Nor has there been a formal attempt to test the "construction ahead of demand" hypothesis, although it seems clear that the CPR did represent "premature" enterprise and its subsidization and early operating experience were consistent with Fishlow's criteria. Finally, no close examination of the indirect benefits accruing to the Canadian economy from CPR investment has been undertaken. Apart from the recent analysis of government subsidies to the CPR, no findings have been presented by practitioners of the "new" economic history in Canada to confirm or challenge Innis' interpretation of the developmental role of the CPR. This is perhaps doubly unfortunate, since Innis himself felt a "sense of the incompleteness" of the *History*.[32]

Was the CPR profitable? Did it influence Canadian industrial development? Did it contribute greatly to Canadian economic growth? For Professor Innis, the answer to these questions was unequivocally "yes" (p. 294): "The Canadian Pacific Railway as a vital part of the technological equipment of western civilization, has increased to a very marked extent the productive capacity of that civilization. It is hypothetical to ask whether under other conditions production would have been increased or whether such production would have contributed more to the welfare of humanity." Hypothetical? Perhaps, but certainly not uninteresting.

PETER J. GEORGE
McMaster University

[32] H. A. Innis, *The Fur Trade in Canada* (Toronto, 1956). The phrase is contained in the author's Preface to the first edition, dated June, 1929.

Preface

In this study an attempt has been made to trace the history of the Canadian Pacific Railway from an evolutionary and scientific point of view. Obviously, no conclusions can be reached in the matter of recommendations since no attempt is made to state a definite objective. Objectives are being formulated, and the interest has been in the process of their formulation. No claim is made as to the merits or demerits of this method of approach. Protest may be anticipated, especially in view of the character of existing treatises on the subject and on related topics. Much has been written in description and in appraisal of the personalities concerned, and the subject lends itself in a very striking way to this method of treatment. These studies have been useful for the preparation of this history in their material rather than in their conclusions.

At this point, grateful thanks are expressed to Prof. C. W. Wright, of the University of Chicago, to members of the Department of Political Science of the University of Toronto, to my sister, Mrs. M. Malcolm, and to numerous others for assistance in many directions. Above all, acknowledgment is made of the aid and encouragement of my wife in all the stages of preparation.

Contents

A HISTORY OF
THE CANADIAN PACIFIC RAILWAY

I

Introduction

THOUGH almost two centuries and a half elapsed between the date of the earliest attempt to discover the North-West Passage and the completion of the Canadian Pacific Railway in 1885, both occasions were landmarks in the spread of Western civilization over the northern half of North America. This spread of civilization was dependent on the geographic characteristics of the area and on the character and institutions of the people involved. The rapidity and direction of the growth of civilization were largely dominated by the physical characteristics, the geological formations, the climate, the topographical features, and the consequent flora and fauna which these conditions produced. Topographical features which determined to a large extent the character of the drainage basins,[1] and consequently of the rivers, were of primary importance. The largest [2] basin is drained by rivers flowing into Hudson Bay—

[1] *Atlas of Canada,* 1915, p. 22.

[2]

Basin				Area.
Atlantic.	.	.	.	554,000 sq. miles
Hudson Bay .	.	.	.	1,486,000 ,,
Pacific .	.	.	.	387,300 ,,
Arctic .	.	.	.	1,290,000 ,,
Total	.	.	.	3,717,300 ,,

Compiled from *Canada Year-book,* 1919, pp. 85–6.

1

the Nelson River, the Churchill River and the Saskatchewan rivers extending westward from 1,000 to 1,500 miles and draining practically the whole of the central plains of Canada. The next largest basin is drained by rivers flowing into the Arctic Ocean—the MacKenzie River extending over 2,000 miles. The St. Lawrence River and the Great Lakes drain the southern portion of Canada as far west as the head of Lake Superior. Territory west of the Rocky Mountains is drained by several short rivers flowing into the Pacific Ocean. Access to the interior by exploration and later by settlements was gained, therefore, from three directions—from the south by the St. Lawrence, from the north by Hudson Bay, and from the west by rivers of the Pacific drainage basin. The heights of land as boundaries to drainage basins were to some extent boundaries to exploration and to a large extent boundaries to settlement. Early civilization was confined by these limits to three distinct areas. The Canadian Pacific Railroad was tangible evidence of the growth of civilization beyond these boundaries.

Within each area geographic characteristics important with respect to the spread of civilization differed widely. In the St. Lawrence drainage basin, with the exception of territory along the north shore of the river and of Lake Ontario and Lake Erie, the geological [1] formation is chiefly Laurentian, consisting of granite and granite gneiss. Proceeding south-east along the St. Lawrence, the normal annual temperature [2] as shown during the years 1888-1907, gradually rises, and going north to Lake Superior rapidly declines. In the same direction the number of hours of sunshine increases. The rainfall generally decreases, though with variation, south-east along the St. Lawrence, the

[1] *Atlas of Canada*, 1915, pp. 10, 12.

[2]

	Normal Degrees of Temp. F.	Annual Hours of Sunshine	Rainfall	Snowfall	Total Precipitation
	1888–1907				
Quebec . .	38·7	1,712	27·17	132·9	40·46
Montreal . .	42·3	1,805	29·37	122·7	41·64
Kingston . .	43·7	1,989	24·01	74·8	31·49
Toronto . .	45·5	2,048	25·28	61·0	31·38
Port Arthur .	35·7	—	19·01	44·5	23·46

Compiled from the *Canada Year-book*, 1919, pp. 166-7.

snowfall persistently declines and total precipitation generally declines. North of Lake Superior snowfall, rainfall and consequently total precipitation decline rapidly. The northern drainage basin with the exception of territory in the more immediate vicinity of Hudson Bay which is largely dominated by Laurentian formation, consists of a vast tract of fertile territory gradually rising as it approaches the Rocky Mountains. The normal annual temperature [1] is slightly lower than that of Lake Superior, but remains fairly consistent throughout the plain, rising toward the mountains. The number of hours of sunshine declines slightly toward the centre of the plain. Rainfall, snowfall and total precipitation decline rapidly in the central plain and rise in the west. On the Pacific coast, the cordillera ranges are dominant. The normal annual temperature [2] is higher than in any other part of Canada, and the rainfall and total precipitation are greater. Snowfall is consequently less and the hours of sunshine fewer than in the central plain. It was with these regions that early explorers searching for a new route to the Orient came in contact. Settlements came in the wake of exploration and, taking root, grew up and flourished to no small extent under the influence of the particular characteristics of the areas involved.

A. THE PACIFIC COAST

Encouraged by the offer of a government reward [3] to the finder of a north-west passage from the west, Captain

	1888–1907 Normal Degrees of Temp. F.	Annual Hours of Sunshine	Rainfall	Snowfall	Total Precipita- tion
[1]					
Winnipeg . .	34·9	2,178	15·62	51·9	20·81
Battleford. .	34·4	2,101	11·05	27·4	13·79
Edmonton .	36·7	—	14·18	40·2	18·20
					Ibid.
[2] Vancouver . .	49·1	1,815	57·88	23·2	60·20
					Ibid.

[3] An act of 18 Geo. II, offering a reward of £20,000 to the person or persons being subjects of His Majesty who should discover a north-west passage through Hudson Strait to the western and northern ocean of America was amended in 16 Geo. III, chap. 6, offering the reward for the discovery of " any northern passage " for vessels by sea between the Atlantic and Pacific Ocean.

James Cook [1] discovered Vancouver Island in 1778. The account of the voyages, published in 1784, was of significance in the emphasis placed on the fur trade [2] as well as on the geographic discoveries. [3] Following the publication of the account came a scramble of interests to share in the profits. [4] Englishmen [5] from China and India, and later from England, were followed by representatives [6] of other nations. The resulting competition led inevitably to disputes between individuals of the same nationality [7] but, also, of more importance, between individuals of different nationalities. Out of this situation came appeals to the home Governments and such difficulties as those illustrated in the Nootka Sound Controversy [8] between Spain and England.

The direction of the attention of various nations towards new territory was not the only result of such competition. Of more immediate importance was the beginning of settlement which accompanied the establishment of posts

[1] Cook, James, *A Voyage to the Pacific Ocean* (1788 edition), vol. II, p. 229 ff.

[2] " One of our sailors disposed of his stock alone for eight hundred dollars . . . and a few of the best skins . . . produced a hundred and twenty dollars each. . . . The total amount of the value . . . obtained for the furs of both of our vessels . . . was not less than two thousand pounds sterling. The benefits that might accrue from a voyage to that part of the American coast where we obtained them, undertaken with commercial views, will certainly appear of sufficient importance to claim the public attention." Detailed instructions for such proposed ventures accompanied this suggestion. Cook, James, op. cit., vol. IV, p. 245 ff.

[3] An account of earlier voyages is important in an attempt to appraise the contributions of Captain Cook. See Greenhow, Robert, *Memoir, Historical and Political, on the North-West Coast of North America*, pp. 22–75.

[4] Some conception of the profitableness may be obtained from the following : Captain. Hanna's voyage, 1785–6, brought over £20,000. Dixon, G., *A Voyage Round the World, but More Particularly to the North-West Coast of America, performed in 1785, 1786, 1787 and 1788*, pp. 315–16. Captain Portlock and Dixon representing the King George's Sound Company netted nearly £50,000 (*ibid.*, p. 303).

[5] Captain Hanna sailed from China (*ibid.*, p. xvii.). Captains Lorie and Guise were fitted out in India in 1786 (*ibid.*, p. 317). Captain Berkley was the first to sail from England in the same year (*ibid.*, p. 289).

[6] Captain Kendrick and Captain Gray representing the United States sailed from Boston, Sept. 30, 1787, and Martinez from Spain reached Nootka in May, 1789. Greenhow, Robert, op. cit., p. 97.

[7] A very elaborate account of one particular dispute is given. Meares, John, *Voyages made in the years 1788 and 1789 from China to the North-West Coast of America*. Footnotes, pp. xxiv.–xxxviii.

[8] For a complete history, see Manning, W. R., The Nootka Sound Controversy, *Annual Report of the American Historical Association*, 1904.

by the traders [1] and which became essential in connexion with the long ocean voyages. The history of the early settlement was closely bound up with the fur trade. Nootka Sound, because it offered " greater facilities for obtaining water and provisions as well as for repairs than any other harbour in that part of the ocean," [2] was the earliest centre of importance. But the dependence of Nootka on the fur trade was a source of weakness as well as a source of strength. Under the pressure of competition new areas more strategic for the conduct of the fur trade were found and Nootka disappeared.

Following the achievement of Alexander MacKenzie in crossing the Rockies and reaching the Pacific [3] in 1793, increased competition came from the east. The appreciation of the United States authorities of the value of this area was evinced in the Lewis and Clark expedition [4] of 1804. Determination of the North-West Company [5] to secure a larger share of the fur trade of the district occasioned the dispatch of Simon Fraser in 1806. The territory acquired by this invasion of interests coming overland

[1] John M'Key, the surgeon of the Lorie and Guise expedition, was as far as is known the first European to live among the natives " to ingratiate himself . . . so that if any other vessels should touch there he might prevent them from purchasing any furs." Dixon, G., op. cit., p. 232.

[2] Greenhow, R., op. cit., p. 90.

[3] MacKenzie, Alexander, *Voyages from Montreal through the Continent of North America to the Frozen and Pacific Oceans*, p. 349.

[4] The imperialistic nature of the expedition is evident in the wariness of Jefferson in attempting to lull all suspicion on the part of other interests. In the confidential message to Congress asking for the necessary funds, he states : " The appropriation of two thousand five hundred dollars ' for the purpose of extending the external commerce of the United States,' while understood and considered by the executive as giving the legislative sanction, would cover the undertaking from notice and prevent the obstructions which interested individuals might otherwise previously prepare in the way." And in the instructions to Lewis : " Your mission has been communicated to the ministers here from France, Spain and Great Britain—and such assurances given them as to its objects as we trust will satisfy them." " The object of your mission is to explore the Missouri River and such principal streams of it as by its course and communication with the waters of the Pacific Ocean may offer the most direct and practicable water communication across the continent for the purposes of commerce." Coues, Elliott, *History of the Expedition under the Command of Lewis and Clark*, vol. I, pp. xx.–xxvi.

[5] M. Fraser recut l'ordre de traverser les Montagnes Rocheuses par le Nord et d'établir des relations avec les sauvages de ces régions jusqu'alors inexploitées. Masson, L. R., *Les Bourgeois de la Compagnie du Nord-Ouest*, p. 29.

from the east was consolidated by the establishment of posts and the beginnings of settlement at the heads of lakes and the forks of streams [1] where furs could be collected most advantageously and where supplies of such food as fish [2] and agricultural produce [3] could be obtained most easily. Such vigorous prosecution of the fur trade necessitated an outlet on the Pacific coast. This explained the race [4] between the North-West Company and the Pacific Fur Company,[5] representing the Astor interest, for the occupation of the mouth of Columbia River. It also explained the difficulties incidental to the war of 1812, in which the former company wrested Astoria [6] from the Americans.

Nor did the effects on settlement of the competition of the fur trade cease after the victory of the North-West Company in 1813, or after the amalgamation of that company with the Hudson Bay Company in 1821. Imperialism became aggressive. Upon the insistence of the United States, Astoria (renamed Fort George by the English) was restored [7] in 1818, and an indefinite compromise [8] was reached regarding the occupancy of territory on the Pacific coast. In the race for territory, Russia made declarations [9] favourable to the Russian American

[1] The establishment of Fort McLeod at McLeod Lake, of Fort St. James at Stuart Lake, of Fort Fraser at Fraser Lake and of Fort George at the junction of the Stuart River and the Fraser River by Simon Fraser in 1806-7 (see Morice, Rev. A. G., *The History of the Northern Interior of British Columbia*, pp. 54-71), and Kootenæ House on the head waters of the Columbia River below Windermere Lake (*David Thompson's Narrative*, edited by J. B. Tyrrell, p. 375), Kullyspell House at Lake Pend d'Oreille (*ibid.*, p. 410), and Saleesh House near the mouth of Ashley Creek in Montana (*ibid.*, p. 418) by David Thompson.

[2] Harmon, Daniel Williams, *A Journal of Voyages and Travels in the Interior of North America*, pp. 205-6.

[3] *Ibid.*, p. 202, p. 248 and p. 267.

[4] Irving, Washington, *Astoria*, pp. 73-136.   [5] *Ibid.*, p. 69.

[6] Cox, Ross, *The Columbia River*, vol. I, p. 189 ff.

[7] Greenhow, Robert, op. cit., p. 167.

[8] After a long period of negotiation, the convention of 1818, which stated " that all territories claimed by the United States or by Great Britain between the Rocky Mountains and the Pacific should with their harbours, bays and rivers be free and open for ten years to the vessels, subjects or citizens of both nations," was indefinitely continued in 1827, either party being, however, at liberty after Oct. 20, 1828, to annul and abrogate the engagement on giving due notice of twelve months to the other (*ibid.*, p. 185).

[9] An imperial ukase, issued Sept., 1821, declared the whole west coast of North America north of the 51st parallel to belong exclusively to Russia (*ibid.*, p. 176).

Fur Company which led to complications [1] with Great Britain and the United States, and the conventions of 1824 and 1825. Restoration of Astoria to the United States and the growing demand of the fur trade for supplies in the nature of agricultural products [2] made it necessary for the Hudson Bay Company to select a new site for its post. Accordingly it built Fort Vancouver [3] in 1825, and in the same year laid down a definite agricultural policy. [4] In 1828, French-Canadian servants of the company were encouraged to settle in Oregon, [5] and in 1836, products [6] of the soil were of considerable importance. Additional stimulus was given to these efforts in the agreement of 1839, concluding a dispute [7] with the Russian American Fur Company, in which the Hudson Bay Company [8] was obliged to furnish 2,000 ferragoes (120 lb. each) of wheat annually for ten years at 10s. 9d. per ferrago, as well as quantities of other products.

The development of agriculture prepared the way for immigration and in turn was encouraged by immigration. [9] The truce of joint occupancy involved in the indefinite

---

[1] The convention with the United States was terminated in 1824 and with Great Britain in 1825, both of which made the extreme southern limit of Russian territory, latitude 54 deg. 40 min. (*ibid.*, p. 180).

[2] Bancroft, H. H., *History of the North-West Coast*, vol. II., pp. 436-7.

[3] Holman, F. V., *Dr. John McLoughlin*, p. 28.

[4] *Ibid.*, p. 43.

[5] *Ibid.*, p. 42.

[6]

Wheat	.	.	.	.	8,000	bushels
Barley	.	.	.	.	5,500	,,
Oats	.	.	.	.	6,000	,,
Peas	.	.	.	.	9,000	,,
Potatoes		.	.	.	14,000	,,

In addition there were ten acres of fruit trees (*ibid.*, p. 28).

[7] The treaty of 1825 between Russia and Great Britain provided full navigation of streams crossing Russian territory in their course from British possessions to the sea. The *Dryad*, a Hudson Bay Company boat, was refused this right by the Russian Company in 1838 and the English company claimed damages. After an appeal to the home Governments, the Hudson Bay Company waived its claims in return for a lease from the Russian company of all their territory between Cape Spencer and latitude 54 deg. 40 min., for which it paid an annual rental of 2,000 land otter skins and supplied the Russians with provisions. Bancroft, H. H., *History of Alaska*, p. 555 ff.

[8] Bryce, G., *Remarkable History of the Hudson Bay Company*, App. E, p. 494.

[9] " Dr. McLoughlin furnishing these immigrants with food and clothing, and also farm implements and seed wheat. . . . He also loaned cattle." Holman, F. V., op. cit., p. 75.

compromise reached between Great Britain and the United States was an incentive to American immigration. An increase in American population strengthened the position of the United States in the final division of the area and at the same time hastened the date of division. Growth of the fur trade meant increased attention to agriculture for supply purposes, and routes of the fur traders were blazed trails for the earliest settlers. With the opening of routes by fur companies immigration was inevitable. Following the prosecution of trade by the early American companies,[1] missionaries first came with the expedition of Nathaniel Wyeth,[2] in 1834. Dissatisfied [3] with their progress, Jason Lee, a prominent missionary, took advantage of the increasing attention of Congress [4] to this area, by a campaign throughout the eastern states in 1838, urging the necessity of settling Oregon.[5] The activity of the United States Government [6] and the wave of emigration [7] which began in 1842 bore tribute to his success. With settlement, issues [8] arose as to land and law, a provisional government [9] was set up, the truce of joint occupancy disappeared, and in the dispute of 1846 American supremacy was assured.[10]

The treaty of 1846, which gave to United States territory south of the 49th parallel, was only a landmark in the inevitable progress of settlement, and decline of the fur trade. The forces responsible for growth of settlement in Oregon continued, indeed became more powerful in the growth of settlement in British Columbia. Expansion of the fur trade and establishment of posts west of the

[1] American fur companies by no means ceased with the Astoria disaster. See Greenhow, R., op. cit., p. 75.
[2] Wyeth's Journal of the second expedition. *Sources of the History of Oregon*, vol. I, p. 221 ff.
[3] Bancroft, H. H., *History of Oregon*, vol. I, p. 167.
[4] *Ibid.*, ch. xiv.
[5] The memorial of the settlers signed by ten missionaries on March 16, 1838, urged the United States Government to take formal possession, as did also information furnished to Congress by Lee in 1839 (*ibid.*, p. 169 and p. 173).
[6] The *Lausanne* sailed with missionaries and settlers from New York aided by money from the United States Secret Service funds (*ibid.*, p. 177).
[7] Holman, F. V., op. cit., pp. 69–83.
[8] Bancroft, H. H., op. cit. p. 459.
[9] *Ibid.*, ch. xii.
[10] Wilson, J. R., The Oregon Question, *Quarterly of the Oregon Historical Society*, vol. I, Sept., 1900, p. 251.

Rocky Mountains, which made necessary an outlet on the
Pacific at the mouth of the Columbia River, and which
made inevitable the growth of settlement in that region,
were also responsible for the efforts made to discover the
shortest routes to the interior from that outlet. The
impossibility of navigating the Lower Fraser and the
difficulty of transporting supplies overland from the east
led to the establishment [1] of Fort Alexander in 1821 as
a supply depot for posts tributary to Fraser River, and to
the growth of Kamloops [2] at the junction of the North and
South Thompson Rivers, as a stopping-place for supplies
coming overland from Okanagan on the Columbia River.
And with the new route came establishment [3] of new posts.

New posts, whether devoted to fur trading [4] and yet
engaged in production of supplies, or devoted wholly to
production of supplies to meet the demands of expanding
trade, were, as ever, promoters of settlement. The increased attention to agriculture, and the growth of shipping
resulting from the expansion of the fur trade along the
northern coast led to a search [5] for a new centre farther
north from Fort Vancouver. The site chosen [6] was Camosun
Harbour on Vancouver Island, and in 1843 Fort Victoria
was established. [7]

[1] Morice, A. G., op. cit., p. 119.
[2] The Okanagan River was explored first by David Stuart, a representative of the Pacific Fur Company, in 1811. Ross, Alexander, *Adventures of the First Settlers on the Oregon or Columbia River*, p. 145 ff. He
established a post at Kamloops in 1812 (*ibid.*, p. 201). The North-West
Company, however, " followed hard at his heels " (*ibid.*, p. 206). See also
Franchere, G., *Relation d'un Voyage à la côte du Nord-Ouest*, p. 99. Fort
Colville was also established in 1825 to handle increasing trade down the
Columbia. Bancroft, H. H., *History of the North-West Coast*, vol. II, p. 469.
[3] A fort on Lake Babine, 1822. Morice, A. G., op. cit., p. 122. Fort
Connolly near Bear Lake in 1826 (*ibid.*, p. 131). Fort Chilcotin somewhat
later (*ibid.*, p. 210).
[4] Salmon was obtained at Fort Babine (*ibid.*, p. 122). Also at Fort
Langley. Bancroft, H. H. (*ibid.*, p. 487). Sheep and cattle grazing was
carried on at Fort Nisqually (*ibid.*, p. 525), and horses were bred for transport service at Fort Kamloops. Bancroft, *History of British Columbia*,
p. 136.
[5] James Douglas explored the whole coast and submitted a report on
July 12, 1842. Scholefield, E.O.S., *British Columbia from the Earliest
Times to the Present*, p. 460.
[6] The possibility of attracting whalers to the new port (Bancroft,
ibid., p. 85), and the unsettled boundary dispute (Coats, R. H., and
Gosnell, R. E., *Sir James Douglas*, p. 175) were additional considerations
but of secondary importance.
[7] Bancroft, H. H., *ibid.*, p. 292 ff.

Growth of settlement in British Columbia as in Oregon involved the attention of the home authorities. The attention of Great Britain, which had been occupied with the long series of disputes and treaties with other nations, characteristic of the period preceding the Oregon treaty, was attracted to the territory by the unfortunate results of bitter competition between the North-West Company and the Hudson Bay Company leading to the amalgamation of 1821. The limitation to twenty-one years and other restrictions,[1] made in the grant of 1821, which gave to the amalgamated company the right to exclusive trade with the Indians in parts other than those already taken, were evidences of awakened interest, and precedents for further regulation. As a result of the growth of settlement in Oregon, and of increased attention to the region occasioned by numerous disputes, the appeal of the company for a renewal of the grant in 1837[2] found the Government more alert to the situation.[3] Renewal[4] was made with the condition of a nominal rental, of the right to annex any part of the territory, and of the right to revoke the charter before the limit of twenty-one years had been reached. Finally, the Oregon controversy which became particularly prominent after 1842[5] was responsible for even greater vigilance,[6] and its settlement in 1846 thoroughly aroused the British Government to the necessity of more energetic interference. The growth of settlement, with the consequent disappearance of the fur trade, was the force underlying the growing interest of the British authorities.

[1] These restrictions pertained to the carrying out of Act 1 and 2, Geo. 4, c. 66, enacted for the purpose of regulating the fur trade and establishing a criminal and civil jurisdiction within certain parts of North America. *Papers Relating to the Hudson Bay Company*, 1842–70, p. 21 ff.

[2] The grant did not expire until 1842, but North-West Company interests had been purchased and a new grant was made (*ibid.*, p. 11).

[3] Correspondence between the Government and the company (*ibid.*, p. 18 ff.

[4] *Ibid.*, pp. 9–11.

[5] *Correspondence relative to the negotiations of the question of disputed right to the Oregon territory on the North-West Coast of America subsequent to the Treaty of Washington of Aug. 9, 1842.*

[6] Lieuts. Warre and Vavasour were sent in 1845 to report on steps necessary to render the posts in Oregon territory safe against attack (Scholefield, E. O. S., op. cit., p. 452), also the *America*, under Capt. Gordon, arrived at Victoria in 1845, and several ships of war in 1846. See excerpt from Roderick Finlayson's manuscript (*ibid.*, pp. 454–5).

The Oregon treaty served to consolidate the victory of settlement over the fur trade, and in narrowing the arena of the struggle prepared the way for further conquest. The Hudson Bay Company was obliged to limit activities to British territory, and Fort Victoria, the new head-quarters, received additional stimulus.[1] Columbia River, no longer a highway through British territory over which supplies and furs were carried from interior posts, was gradually abandoned, and surveys and new roads [2] were made to the interior by way of the lower Fraser River. These changes also made necessary increased shipping facilities which gave greater incentive to the search for coal and stimulated the mining industry.[3]

Growth of settlement caused by expansion of the fur trade, and stimulated by the Oregon treaty, was further increased [4] as a result of gold discoveries in California in 1849, and as a result of the awakened interest of the home authorities. Anxiety of the British Government to promote settlement had increased, and was manifest in the regulations [5] carefully included in the grant of Vancouver Island to the company made on January 13, 1849, and in the

[1] In July, 1846, "about 160 acres are cultivated with oats, wheat, potatoes, turnips, carrots and other vegetables, and every day more land is converted into fields." Seemann, Berthold, *Narrative of the Voyage of H.M.S. "Herald,"* vol. I, pp. 102–3. April 8, 1847. "The establishment is very large and must eventually become the great depot for the business of the Company." Kane, Paul, *Wanderings of an Artist*, p. 209.

[2] The imposition of duties on Hudson Bay Company goods made this inevitable. Anderson made surveys from Kamloops to Fort Langley in 1846 and 1847. Fort Yale was established in 1848 on the Fraser River and brigades came overland from the interior. In the next year, however, a new route was laid out by way of the Coquihalla River and Fort Hope was established at its mouth. Bancroft, H. H., op. cit., pp. 160–177.

[3] Fort Rupert was established in 1849 to develop coal deposits, but it was superseded by Fort Nanaimo in 1851 (*ibid.*, pp. 192–7).

[4] The lucrativeness of the supply business more than offset the loss through the desertion of men (*ibid.*, pp. 182–3).

[5] "That this present grant is made to the intent that the . . . Company shall establish a settlement . . . of resident colonists . . . and shall dispose of all lands . . . at a reasonable price . . . and that all monies which shall be received by the company for the purchase of such land . . . (after deduction of such sums by way of profit as shall not exceed a deduction of 10 per cent.) . . . be applied towards the colonization . . . of the island. That this present grant is made upon this condition that if the . . . Company shall not, within the term of five years . . . have established a settlement . . . it shall be lawful for us to revoke this present grant." Scholefield, E. O. S., op. cit., App., p. 679.

provisions [1] for the administration of justice on the island
made in the same year. But the growth of settlement
increased the opposition of the fur trade. Immediately [2]
the Oregon treaty had been signed, the company entered
into diplomatic [3] negotiations leading to the grant of
Vancouver Island. It became apparent, [4] after the grant

[1] Scholefield, E. O. S., op. cit., App., pp. 680–1.
[2] " The Hudson's Bay Company having formed an establishment on
the southern point of Vancouver's Island . . . are anxious to know
whether they will be confirmed in possession of such lands, as they may
find it expedient to add to those which they already possess." Letter
from Sir J. H. Pelly to Earl Grey, Sept. 7, 1846. *Copy of correspondence
between the Chairman of the Hudson's Bay Company and the Secretary of
State for the Colonies relative to the colonization of Vancouver's Island*, p. 3.
[3] The correspondence is amusingly diplomatic. The question as to
the company's capacity to hold land is answered, and " This, however,
is a matter of small importance compared with the colonization of such
parts of the territory." . . . " It would be a superfluous task to enter
into a detail of the reasons which render the colonization . . . an object
of great importance ; I shall merely submit whether that object . . .
might not be most readily and effectually accomplished through the
instrumentality of the Hudson's Bay Company." . . . In response to a
request for a draft of the grant to be made, "I beg leave to say
that if Her Majesty's Ministers should be of opinion that the territory
in question would be more conveniently governed and colonized (as far
as it may be practicable) through the Hudson's Bay Company, the
Company are willing to undertake it and will be ready to receive a grant
of all the territories . . . situated to the north and west of Rupert's
Land." . . . With Earl Grey's protest to such willingness " I proposed
a grant which might appear extensive, but I did this not with the view
of obtaining for the Hudson's Bay Company any advantage " . . . but
" because I was persuaded that the colonization would be much more
successfully conducted under the auspices of the company." . . . And
on the same day a more lengthy letter to the same effect. " I am very
glad to learn that your Lordship is exceedingly anxious for the colonization
of Vancouver's Island." . . . "I fear, my Lord, you will think me
prolix." Criticism made in the House of Commons and outside the House,
such as "*An examination of the charter and proceedings of the Hudson's
Bay Company with reference to the grant of Vancouver's Island*," by J. E.
Fitzgerald, was met and anticipated by propaganda such as "*The Hudson's
Bay Territories and Vancouver's Island, with an exposition of the chartered
rights, conduct and policy of the Honourable Hudson's Bay Corporation*,"
by R. M. Martin, *ibid.*, pp. 4–13.
[4] The attitude of the company was clearly demonstrated in evidence
given in *The Report from the Select Committee on the Hudson's Bay Company*,
1857. Land was sold at the prohibitive price of £1 per acre, and every
purchaser was required to bring out five labourers from England, while
in Oregon land was free. Minutes of Evidence, p. 287. Settlements
were obliged to pay 300 per cent. on the cost price of goods (*ibid.*, p. 288),
while the competition of private individuals was impossible (*ibid.*, p. 200).
Richard Blanshard, the Governor of Vancouver Island by the appointment
of the British Government in 1849, was obliged to resign in 1850, since
he received no salary, and living expenses totalled £1,100 per year (*ibid.*,
p. 288). A memorial signed by all the settlers protesting against the
company's monopoly might be cited as further evidence (*ibid.*, p. 293).

had been made, that the terms were much better adapted to further the company's policy of hostility to settlement than to meet the demands of the British Government for colonization.

Expansion and consolidation of the fur trade in the interior, which stimulated the growth of Fort Vancouver, and the desirability of gaining access to territory along the northern coast, not tributary to the Columbia River, had still other results. There came the demand for ships to carry supplies and furs from Fort Vancouver to England, and from new posts to be established along the coast to Fort Vancouver. With it came the growth of the Hudson's Bay Company's fleet,[1] and the expansion of the fur trade [2] along the coast.

The penetration and development of the fur trade in the territory north of the Columbia River had been delayed by the geographic features of the country, but such delay made no less inevitable the growth of settlement accompanying the fur trade, which so largely characterized the history of the settlement of Oregon. The resistance of the company was doomed to failure. Though settlement was delayed,[3] the delay made the protests of settlers more effective and the further investigation and activity of the home authorities more imperative. James Douglas, the successor of Blanshard as Governor of Vancouver Island, was instructed [4]

[1] A list of boats arriving each year from 1819 to 1840 is given in Bancroft, H. H., *History of the North-West Coast*, vol. I, p. 341. . . . In 1845 three vessels in the company's service plied between London and the north-west coast. Bancroft, *History of British Columbia*, p. 120. In 1837 the company had six armed vessels on the north-west coast. Letter from George Simpson to J. H. Pelly. Feb. 1, 1837. *Papers relating to the Hudson's Bay Company*, 1842–1870, p. 70. The *Beaver* was the first steam vessel to arrive at Fort Vancouver in 1836. McCain, C. W., *History of the ss. "Beaver,"* p. 20.

[2] Fort Langley was established on the lower Fraser in 1827. Bancroft, H. H., *History of the North-West Coast*, vol. II, p. 481. Fort Nisqually, near Nisqually River, on a direct overland line between Fort Langley and Fort Vancouver in 1833 (*ibid.*, p. 524), Fort Simpson at the mouth of the Nass River in 1831 (*ibid.*, p. 623), Fort McLoughlin on Millbank Sound in 1833 (*ibid.*, p. 625), with the lease of the territory of the Russian-American Company, Fort Durham on the Tako River in 1840 (*ibid.*, p. 647) Fort Stikeen on the Stikeen River in the same year (*ibid.*, p. 646).

[3] In 1857 there were not more than 250 or 300 white men in the island, the greater number of which were servants of the Hudson Bay Company. There were no free settlers. *Report from the Select Committee on the Hudson's Bay Company*, Minutes of Evidence, p. 192.

[4] *Copies or extracts of any dispatches that have been reserved by Her*

in a dispatch of February 28, 1856, from the Secretary of State " to call together an Assembly," and on February 5 of the following year a select committee [1] was appointed " to consider the state of those British possessions in North America which are under the administration of the Hudson's Bay Company, or over which they possess a licence to trade." Progress of the fur trade in the development of transportation routes to the interior was a stimulus to further settlement. With the opening of routes into the interior came news of gold discoveries in the Upper Columbia region in 1856,[2] the rush of immigrants in the following years,[3] the necessity of government, and the adoption of the select committee's report,[4] as shown in the Act [5] to provide for the government of British Columbia in 1858. As in Oregon, so it was in Vancouver Island and in British Columbia—the fur trade had paved the way for settlement, and for its own disappearance.

The direction and progress of settlement were greatly influenced by the gold rush to the tableland between the Upper Columbia and the Thompson and Fraser Rivers, known as the Coteau region.[6] The Fraser River route from the coast to this territory being shorter [7] than the Columbia River route was generally followed, and demand [8]

Majesty's Secretary of State for the Colonies on the subject of the establishment of a representative assembly at Vancouver's Island, p. 3.

[1] *Report from the Select Committee on the Hudson's Bay Company,* p. ii.

[2] *Copies or extracts of correspondence relative to the discovery of gold in the Fraser's River District in British North America,* p. 5.

[3] " Crowds of people are coming in from all quarters. The American steamer *Commodore* arrived from San Francisco with 450 passengers, and the steamer *Panama* with 750 passengers." Dispatch from Governor Douglas to the Right Hon. Lord Stanley, M.P., June 19, 1858. *Papers relative to the affairs of British Columbia,* Pt. I, p. 18.

[4] " Your committee are of opinion that it will be proper to terminate the connexion of the Hudson's Bay Company with Vancouver's Island. . . . Means should also be provided for the ultimate extension of the colony over any portion . . . to the west of the Rocky Mountains." *Report from the Select Committee on the Hudson's Bay Company,* p. iv.

[5] *Papers relative to the affairs of British Columbia,* Pt. I.

[6] *Copies or extracts of correspondence relative to the discovery of gold in the Fraser River District in British North America,* p. 8.

[7] From the mouth of the Fraser River to Fort Thompson (Kamloops), 150 miles. From Dalles at mouth of the Columbia River to Kamloops, 487 miles. Macdonald, D. G. F., *British Columbia and Vancouver's Island,* pp. 105-9.

[8] Victoria was particularly favourable to the improvement of communication along the Fraser River, thus becoming " a depot and centre

for improvements on the route was consequently great. Failing to enlist the support of the home Government,[1] the colony, to avoid difficulties of the upper Fraser, first, determined upon and completed [2] a route by way of Harrison Lake, Lake Lillooet, Lake Anderson and Lake Seton to a point on the Upper Fraser near the Great Falls, and later constructed a road along the river.[3] The mining industry stimulated, and was stimulated by, construction and improvement of roads. The accessibility of the upper Fraser and the disappearance of claims in the older regions led to a northerly search, and to the discoveries along the Quesnel River in 1859,[4] and in the Cariboo territory [5] in 1860 and 1861. There followed the construction of a main road from Lillooet to Clinton in 1861, to Alexandria in 1863, and from Yale to Clinton in the same year,[6] as well as the opening of trails to neighbouring districts.[7] So, too, the road east from Hope to Similkameen constructed in 1860,[8] the improvement of routes to the Upper Columbia region,[9] and the disappearance of claims, led to the search along the Kootenay River and the discovery on Wild Horse Creek in 1863 [10] and further north at Big Bend [11] in

of trade for the gold districts." *Copies or extracts of correspondence relative to the discovery of gold in the Fraser River District in British North America,* p. 13.

[1] " The admonitions—that British Columbia should look to her own exertions for success—must not pass unheeded ; but a practical exemplification of that advice must be exhibited." Dispatch from the Duke of Newcastle to Governor Douglas, Oct. 28, 1859. *Papers relative to the affairs of British Columbia,* Pt. III, p. 105.

[2] *Ibid.,* Pt. II, p. 46. Improvements were continually being made such as to make it the important thoroughfare of the country. *Ibid.,* Pt. IV, p. 23.

[3] Roads along the Fraser River from Yale to Lytton were constantly being pushed forward. A pack road from Derby (near Langley) to Lytton was completed in 1860 (*ibid.,* Pt. III, p. 50). See also *ibid.,* Pt. III, p. 17, p. 29; Pt. IV, p. 53.

[4] *Ibid.,* Pt. III, p. 50.

[5] *Ibid.,* Pt. IV, p. 50.

[6] Scholefield, E. O. S., op. cit., vol. II, pp. 101-3.

[7] Trails were broken as far north as Lake Stuart and Lake Babine. Morice, A. G., op cit., pp. 315-16.

[8] Moberly, Walter, *The Rocks and Rivers of British Columbia,* p. 33.

[9] A very good description of the various routes involved is given in the *Handbook to the Gold Regions of the Fraser's and Thompson's Rivers* by Alexander C. Anderson. *Papers relative to the affairs of British Columbia,* Pt. I, App. 2, p. 79.

[10] Bancroft, H. H., *ibid.,* p. 523.

[11] Scholefield, E. O. S., op. cit., p. 234.

1865. These discoveries were followed by extension of the Dewdney trail [1] from Princeton along the Similkameen River and near the boundary line to Wild Horse Creek, and by the construction of a route [2] overland from Cache Creek on the Cariboo trail, by boat to Seymour at the head of Shuswap Lake, and again overland to the Columbia River.

Development of transportation facilities incidental to expansion of the fur trade hastened, and was rapidly hastened by, the gold rush. The interaction was evident in every phase of economic development. The gold discoveries and the continued output [3] magically increased settlement. Immigrants, made enthusiastic by glowing accounts,[4] came in thousands.[5] Agriculture was stimulated.[6] Foreign trade rapidly increased.[7] Shipping [8] consequently

[1] The trail from Hope to Similkameen. *Ibid.*, p. 233.

[2] *Ibid.*, pp. 237–8.

[3] Value of yearly production :

1858	. . 705,000	1865	.	. 3,491,205
1859	. . 1,615,070	1866	.	. 2,662,106
1860	. . 2,228,543	1867	.	. 2,480,868
1861	. . 2 566,118	1868	.	. 3,372,972
1862	. . 2,656,903	1869	.	. 1,774,978
1863	. . 3,913,563	1870	.	. 1,336,956
1864	. . 3,735,850			

—*Year-book of British Columbia*, 1897, p. 196.

[4] *The Times* correspondent wrote several articles the effect of which is very well described in *British Columbia and Vancouver Island*, by John Emmerson. See also Hazlitt, W. C., *British Columbia and Vancouver Island ;* Ballantyne, R. M., *Handbook to the New |Gold Fields ;* and Cornwallis, K., *The New El Dorado.*

[5] " About 10,000 foreign miners in Fraser's River." Dispatch from Governor Douglas to Rt. Hon. Lord Stanley, M.P., Aug. 19, 1858. *Papers relative to the affairs of British Columbia*, Pt. I, p. 27. The number was subject to considerable fluctuation, but it was estimated there were " 15 to 20,000 whites and Chinese." Harvey, Arthur A., *Statistical Account of British Columbia*, p. 9.

[6] " In 1866 enough wheat was produced near the mines to meet the entire consumption of flour for the present season." *Ibid.*, p. 16 ; see also Macfie, M., *Vancouver Island and British Columbia*, ch. vi., xi.

[7]

	Imports		Exports	
	B. C.	Van. Id.	B. C.	Van. Id.
1860	 1,286,945	—	.. 57,000	—
1861	 1,444,400	2,083,055	.. 63,430	—
1862	 2,800,840	3,721,885	.. 61,385	—
1863	 2,174,265	3,986,480	.. 94,020	197,895
1864	 2,497,765	3,714,210	.. 99,865	396,045
1865	 2,489,670	2,971,485	.. 167,380	601,270

The most important customer was the United States. *Ibid.*, p. 19. They consisted of almost every variety of goods, but chiefly food-stuffs. Pemberton, J. D., *Vancouver Island and British Columbia*, pp. 67–68.

[8] *British Columbia, Report of the Hon. H. L. Langevin*, p. 144 ff.

flourished. Coal-mining [1] received a decided impetus. The direction and strength of economic activity was shown in the growth of Victoria [2] opposite the mouth of the Fraser River, and in the development of towns [3] along transportation routes to the interior.

With the gold discoveries, and the rapid development of the country which they occasioned, renewed interest was given to the search for a shorter route [4] between British Columbia and the older countries than by Cape Horn, by the Isthmus of Panama, or overland by San Francisco. The construction of roads in the interior became links [5] in an ultimate overland route through British territory, and the home authorities, aware [6] of the advantages of such a route, gave encouragement.[7] The trails of the fur traders

[1] Sales of coal by mines,

1861	..	14,600 tons	1866	..	25,155 tons
1862	..	18,690 ,,	1867	..	31,239 ,,
1863	..	21,394 ,,	1868	..	44,005 ,,
1864	..	28,632 ,,	1869	..	35,802 ,,
1865	..	32,819 ,,	1870	..	29,843 ,, *Ibid.*, p. 13.

[2] Macfie, M., op. cit., pp. 65–6.
[3] New Westminster. Mayne, R. C. *Four Years in British Columbia and Vancouver Island*, p. 72; Fort Hope (*ibid.*, p. 95); Yale (*ibid.*, p. 96); Lytton (*ibid.*, p. 109); Kamloops—Bancroft, H. H. (op. cit., p. 458); Port Douglas, Lillooet, Port Pemberton and Port Anderson. Mayne, R. C. (op. cit., pp. 130–7). Barkerville—Laut, A. C., *The Cariboo Trail*, p. 46.
[4] Mayne, R. C., op. cit., pp. 356–7.
[5] "We hope to complete the last section of a pack road from Derby to Lytton. . . . From Lytton a natural pack road exists leading to Red River settlement, by the Coutannais Pass, through the Rocky Mountains, and from thence following the valley of the Saskatchewan; . . . a settler may then take his departure from Red River in spring with cattle and stock and reach British Columbia . . . in course of the autumn following. This is no mere theory, the experiment having been repeatedly made by parties of Red River people travelling to Colville . . .; so much so, indeed, that the whole distance from Lytton to Red River, with the exception of the Coutannais Pass, may be safely travelled with carts. If the Canadian Government would undertake to open a road from Red River to the borders of Lake Superior, which really presents no formidable difficulties, the connexion between British Columbia and Canada would be complete, and the whole distance might, I think, be travelled on British soil." Governor Douglas to the Duke of Newcastle, Oct. 18, 1859. *Papers relative to the affairs of British Columbia*, Part III, p. 68. In connexion with the construction of the road east of Kamloops in 1865 Moberly discovered Eagle Pass. "I blazed a small cedar tree and wrote upon that, 'This is the Pass for the Overland Railway.'" Moberly, W., op cit., p. 44.
[6] A new route was suggested by various writers: Cornwallis, K. (op. cit., pp. 66–72); Hazlitt, W. C. (op. cit., pp. 229–40); Ballantyne, R. M. (op. cit., pp. 51–4).
[7] Sir E. Bulwer Lytton in a speech on the Act providing for the Government of British Columbia in 1858 stated, "I do believe the day will come

lent feasibility to the project.   In 1862 Viscount Milton and
Dr. Cheadle successfully completed a journey across the
continent by way of St. Paul, Fort Gary, Yellowhead
Pass, and the Thompson and Fraser Rivers to Victoria,
and contributed [1] to the discussion of the subject carried
out by imperialistic writers. [2]   The difficulties of such a
scheme were underestimated.   The British Columbia Overland Transit Company proposed [3] in 1862 as a result of the
enthusiasm disappeared [4] after the issue of its prospectus.
Alfred Waddington's petitions [5] to the House of Commons
in the interests of British Columbia in 1868 were also
unsuccessful.   Formal encouragement was limited to
moral support.

Canada, the eastern terminus of the proposed route, was
more vitally concerned.   The interest [6] in British Columbia,
aroused by the gold discoveries, became more pronounced
with the later developments.   The Overland expedition [7]

and that many now present will live to see it when one direct line of
railway communication will unite the Pacific and the Atlantic." *Canada
and its Provinces*, vol. XXI. p. 148.
   [1] Milton; Viscount, and Cheadle, W. B., *The North-West Passage by Land*.
   [2] A partial list of such literature : Forbes, C., *Vancouver Island : Its
resources and capabilities as a colony*, p. 46 ff.   Pemberton, D. (op. cit.,
pp. 84–125) ; Mayne, R. C. (op. cit., pp. 353–69) ; Macfie, M. (op. cit.,
pp. 334–77).
   [3] The prospectus included several features.   It anticipated legislative,
colonial and governmental postal subsidies and promised a guarantee of
6 per cent. on a capital of £500,000 in 50,000 shares of £10 each.   The
terms of subscription were £1 per share on application, and £1 10s. on
allotment with no further call except by consent of a general meeting
of shareholders.   Application had been made to British Columbia and
to the Canadian Government for local charters.   The route was that
indicated by Governor Douglas from Lytton to Red River following the
Saskatchewan valley.   The necessary equipment for passenger and freight
traffic consisted of carts, horses and log shanties.   Convoys were to be
used.   The journey from Lake Superior to British Columbia was to
occupy twelve days, arrangements were made with the Grand Trunk to
forward passengers to Detroit, and steamers and stage coaches were
provided for the journey to Red River.   The fares were to be £20 per
adult from St. Paul.   Emigrants were to be sent out from England.   A
revenue of 30 per cent. was anticipated.   *Globe*, April 25, 1862.
   [4] Some conception of the cool reception given the company may be
obtained from letters printed in MacDonald, D. G. F., op. cit., p. 401–17.
   [5] The first petition was presented May 29, 1868, by Waddington, and
the second on July 3 by Viscount Milton, in which he emphasized " the
advantages of an overland communication."   Begg, A., *History of British
Columbia*, p. 378.
   [6] The Canadian House solicited the aid of the Imperial authorities in
establishing government in British Columbia in 1858.   *Legislative Council*,
July 23, 1858.
   [7] McNaughton, Margaret, *Overland to Cariboo*.

organized in Canada crossed the continent by way of St.
Paul, Fort Gary, Fort Edmonton and Tête Jaune Cache
in 1862. Additional zeal on the part of Canada for an
overland route was occasioned by the possibilities of
American aggression. The Western Union Telegraph Company constructed [1] several miles of line in British Columbia
in 1865 in an attempt to link Europe with America by an
overland cable through Alaska and Russia. Of more
importance, a bill [2] was introduced in the House of Representatives in 1866, to provide for admission of " the
states of Nova Scotia, New Brunswick, Canada East and
Canada West, and for the organization of the territories
of Selkirk, Saskatchewan and Columbia." The purchase of
Alaska in 1867, and the Northern Pacific project [3] gave
further cause for anxiety. Canada was generally interested. [4]

The rapid development of British Columbia, the resulting
encouragement of the British authorities, and Canadian
interest in the proposed route, made possible a definite
project. The depression [5] which followed the exhaustion
of the more important mines, its peculiar effects on the
character of immigrants attracted by the gold rush, and

[1] Whymper, Frederick, *Travel and Adventure in the Territory of Alaska*,
p. 68.
[2] 39th Congress, 1st session, H. R. 754, July 21, 1866.
[3] " The opening by us first of a North Pacific Railroad seals the destiny
of British possessions west of the 91st meridian. Annexation will be but
a question of time." *Report of U.S. Senate on Pacific Railroads*, February
19, 1869, p. 1363.
[4]   OTTAWA, *January* 28, 1870.
MY DEAR BRYDGES,—
   It is quite evident to me not only from this conversation, but from
advices from Washington, that the United States Government are resolved
to do all they can short of war to get possession of the western territory,
and we must take immediate and vigorous steps to counteract them.
One of the first things to be done is to show unmistakably our resolve
to build the Pacific Railway. . . . It must be taken up by a body of
capitalists and not constructed by the Government directly. Canada
can promise most liberal grants of land in alternate blocks and may perhaps
(but of this I cannot speak with any confidence) induce Parliament to
add a small pecuniary subsidy. No time should be lost in this and I
should think that we had made a great stride if we got you to take it up
vigorously. . . . The thing must not be allowed to sleep, and I want
you to address yourself to it at once and work out a plan. Cartier and
I will talk it over after conference with you and push it through.
                              Yours faithfully,
                              JOHN A. McDONALD.
Pope, Sir Joseph, *Correspondence of Sir John MacDonald*, pp. 124-5.
[5] Scholefield, E. O. S., op. cit., p. 225 and p. 278.

the dissatisfaction [1] of the people of Vancouver Island, with the increasing prominence of the mainland, and with the union of the two colonies in 1866 all were additional factors explaining the importance attached to a road to Canada. On March 18, 1867, a resolution [2] was unanimously adopted by the Legislative Council asking Governor Seymour "to take measures without delay to secure the admission of British Columbia into the Canadian Confederacy." The forwarding of the resolution was delayed by the hostility of office-holders, and in protest the citizens of Victoria at a meeting on January 27, 1868,[3] "amidst the wildest enthusiasm," supported [4] the Legislative Council resolution and asked "that an essential condition to such admission should be the construction by the Dominion Government, within two years, of a transcontinental wagon road, connecting Lake Superior and the head of navigation on the Lower Fraser." The movement gained in strength with the death of Governor Seymour,[5] and with the diplomatic [6] appointment of Governor Musgrave, who was favourable to the union. With further encouragement of the home authorities,[7] a delegation was dispatched [8] to Ottawa to arrange the terms of union. Canadian enthusiasm aroused by the agitation of Waddington [9] for the construction of a transcontinental road generally sanctioned

[1] Scholefield, E. O. S., op. cit., p. 245.
[2] Copy of a report of a committee of the Honourable the Privy Council approved by His Excellency the Governor-General in Council on March 6, 1868. *Correspondence respecting the Northwest territory including British Columbia*, p. 10.
[3] Memorial of the citizens of Victoria to His Excellency the Governor-General and the Honourable Queen's Privy Council of Canada (*ibid.*, p.13).
[4] *Ibid.*, p. 9.
[5] Governor Seymour was largely responsible for the delay. *Ibid.*, p. 10.
[6] Sir John A. MacDonald was influential in securing the appointment of a governor favourable to union. See letter quoted in *Canada and Its Provinces*, vol. XXI, p. 172.
[7] Dispatch from Earl Granville to Governor Musgrave, August 14, 1869. *British Columbia Sessional Papers*, 1881, pp. 139–40.
[8] Scholefield, E. O. S., op. cit., p. 293.
[9] Attention was drawn to the possibility of a transcontinental road by an application for a charter for "The Canada Pacific Railway," notice of which appeared in the *Canada Gazette* of October 12, 1869 (p. 185). It was proposed to build a road from Minnesota over the plains of Saskatchewan to Yellowhead Pass at a cost of £20,000,000. Waddington claimed the scheme originated with Mr. Burpee, a Canadian engineer, and that it was compiled from his own notes, the purpose being to attract the attention of the public. See Bancroft, H. H., op. cit., p. 644.

the terms proposed, and Canada was pledged to the commencement of the construction of a railway within two
years and to its completion within ten years.[1]

The character of civilization which developed in British
Columbia was therefore an important factor in determining the character of the terms of union. Geographic
features were of particular significance. The navigability
of the Columbia River determined the direction of the
routes of the early fur traders. The early trading posts
and the inevitable beginnings of settlement were located
at the junctions of rivers and the heads of lakes. Growth
of settlement at the mouth of the Columbia River, due
to the expansion of the fur trade in the interior, aroused
national jealousies, and led to the controversy which was
settled by the cession of Oregon to the United States.
Moreover, it drove back the fur trade. With the new
boundary line it became necessary to find new routes
to the interior and to explore the lower Fraser. With
new routes, Victoria and settlements along the Fraser
came into prominence. Of more importance, came the
discovery of gold, the rush of immigration, the changes
in government, the hectic economic development, the
construction of roads and the discovery of other routes
along the lakes and rivers, the renewed interest of Canada
and Great Britain, and the entry of British Columbia
into the union. The direction, the extent, and the character
of the development of civilization in British Columbia,
were determining factors in the attitude of British Columbia
toward the terms of union, just as they were determining
factors in her attitude toward the fulfilment of those
terms.

B. THE HUDSON BAY DRAINAGE BASIN

The growth of civilization in the great central plain
east of the Rocky Mountains to which Hudson Bay affords
access, was also important as a condition leading to union.
In an effort to discover a north-west passage from the east,
benefiting by knowledge gained in the voyage of Fro-

[1] Appendix A.

bisher [1] in 1578, and in the voyages of Davis [2] in 1585 and later years, Henry Hudson [3] entered Hudson Strait and sailed into Hudson Bay in 1610. Immediately, attempts [4] were made to find a passage westward out of the bay. With these attempts came beginnings of trade in furs. [5] In 1670, partly in compensation [6] for the failure of the attempts, and partly as evidence of the growing importance of the fur trade [7] on the North American continent, a charter was granted to the " Governor and Company of Adventurers of England trading into Hudson Bay."

The beginning of settlement in the great central plain known as the North-West was dominated, therefore, as in Oregon and British Columbia, by demands of fur trade. Vessels sailing under the auspices of the Hudson Bay Company followed the eastern coast of Hudson Bay to the southern extremity, and, later, turned northward along the western coast establishing posts [8] at the mouths of

[1] " Being persuaded of a new and nearer passage to Cathay than by Capo de Buona Speranca which the Portuguese yearly use . . . he began . . . with his friends to confer and laid a plain plot to them that that voyage was not only possible by the north-west but also . . . easy to be performed." Hakluyt, R., Voyages of Elizabethan Seamen to America, ed. Payne, E. J., p. 64.

[2] " I am assured the (passage) must bee in one of foure places or els not at all." Hakluyt, R., The Principall Navigations, etc., vol. XII, p. 247.

[3] See Henry Hudson the Navigator, ed. Asher, G. M. ; also Burpee, L. J., The Search for the Western Sea, p. 9 ff.

[4] In 1613 Button sailed along the western coast of the bay to Port Nelson. Burpee, L. J., op. cit., p. 44 ff. He was followed by Baffin in 1615 (Fox, Luke, North-West, p. 149), and later by Fox and James (Burpee, L. J., ibid., p. 47 ff.).

[5] As early as Davis's voyage furs were of considerable importance. Master Davis to William Sanderson (Merchant) London. " They have brought home five hundred seales skinnes and an hundred and fortie halfe skinnes and pieces of skinnes " (Hakluyt, R., The Principall Navigations, etc. Ibid., p. 247.

[6] " Whereas our dearly beloved cousin Prince Rupert (and others) have at their own great costs and charges undertaken an expedition for Hudson's Bay in the north-west parts of America for the discovery of a new passage into the South Sea and for the finding of some trade for furs, minerals and other considerable commodities. . . ." His Majesty's Royal Charter to the governor and company of Hudson's Bay. Report from the Committee appointed to inquire into the state and condition of the countries adjoining to Hudson's Bay and of the trade carried on there, together with an Appendix. Reported by Lord Strange, April 24, 1749, p. 237.

[7] See particularly the negotiations of Radisson, Voyages of Peter Esprit Radisson (Prince Society), p. 11 ff.

[8] " The year 1667 when Zachariah Gilliam—passed through Hudson's Streights, and thence southward—where is a river, afterwards called Prince Rupert's River. He had a friendly correspondence with the

rivers giving access to the interior. Establishment of posts at the mouths of rivers as strategic points for prosecution of the fur trade, and consequent development of trade with the interior,[1] occasioned the competition of the French, who attempted to divert furs to the St. Lawrence. As a result of this competition, forts [2] were constructed at important points, and harried attacks [3] were made on Hudson Bay Company posts, which only ceased with the treaty [4] of Utrecht. Persistence of the French and penetration, largely under the direction of La Verendrye, of the great central plain as far as the Rocky Mountains by Lake Superior and the Winnipeg River, or the southern gateway, was accompanied by the construction of forts [5]

natives, built a fort, named it Fort Charles." Oldmixon, J., *The British Empire in America*, vol. I, p. 544. "In the year 1682 Mr. Bridger embarked for Port Nelson where a factory was to be established and a fort built " (*ibid.*, p. 559) ; "In the preceding year (1683) the chief factory was removed from Rupert's to Moose-Sebee . . . which has ever since been called Albany River; where a fort was built, a factory settled" (*ibid.*, p. 560). "There is an island in the bottom of the bay called Hay's Island where a factory had been settled." Another settlement mentioned is at New Severn (*ibid.*, p. 561). The Prince of Wales Fort was not strongly established at the mouth of the Churchill River until 1733. See Robson, J., *An Account of Six Years' Residence in Hudson's Bay*, 1733–36 and 1744–47, p. 9.

[1] York Fort, September 8, 1690. "This summer I sent up Henry Kelsey . . . into the country of the Assinae Poets . . . to call encourage and invite the remoter Indians to trade with us." *Report from the committee appointed to inquire into the state and condition of the countries adjoining to Hudson's Bay and of the trade carried on there.* App., p. 275.

[2] 1684(Du Lhut) "¡Il me reste à vous mander que tous les Sauvages de Nord ont beaucoup de confiance en moy et c'est ce qui me fait vous promettre qu'avant deux années il ne descendra pas un Sauvage chez les Anglois à la Baye d'Hudson . . . toutes les nations . . . m'ont promis d'estre le printemps prochain au fort que j'ay fait faire à la Rivière à les Manne dans le fond du Lac Alemipigon " (Nipigon). Margry, P., *Découvertes et Etablissements des Français dans l'Ouest et dans le sud de l'Amérique Septentrionale*, vol. VI, p. 51.

[3] "The French began to be afraid all the Upland Indians might be drawn down to the Bay . . . wherefore they resolved to drive the English out of all their places in the bottom of the bay." Oldmixon, J., op. cit., p. 561 ; see *ibid.*, ff.

[4] Art. X, XI. Treaty of Utrecht. *Ibid.*, p. 567.

[5] La Nöue established a post at the mouth of Kaministiquia River in 1717 (*ibid.*, p. 504 ff.). La Jemeraye under the direction of La Verendrye established Fort Saint Pierre on Rainy Lake in 1731 (*ibid.*, p. 586). La Verendrye built Fort Saint Charles on Lake of the Woods in 1732 (*ibid.*, p. 587). His son built Fort Maurepas at the mouth of the Winnipeg river in 1734 (*ibid.*, p. 588). Ascending the Assiniboine, Fort La Reine was built in 1738 (*ibid.*, p. 590). Fort Dauphin was constructed on Lake Manitoba in 1741 (*ibid.*, p. 594). Forts were built on the Red River, at the fork of the Red River and the Assiniboine, and at the mouth of the Pasquia (Saskatchewan) River but were abandoned (*ibid.*, p. 617).

at the heads of lakes, the mouths of rivers, and along waterways giving access to the interior. This effective control of the fur trade on the part of the French made necessary the construction of posts [1] and the undertaking of journeys [2] to the interior on the part of the Hudson Bay Company.

After the conquest of Canada, English traders followed the routes to central Canada discovered by the French. The disastrous effects [3] resulting from aggressiveness of these individual traders led to establishment [4] of the North-West Company in 1783. Competition [5] from this company, increased in 1794 by the Jay Treaty,[6] which restricted territory of the North-West Company by transferring several of its posts to the United States, and necessitated the adoption of more northerly routes, was a further stimulus [7] to the efforts of the Hudson Bay Company from the north and occasioned an increase in the number of posts [8] by both companies at competitive points and in

Fort Bourbon was situated at the mouth of the Saskatchewan River (*ibid.*) ; Fort la Jonquiere was established in 1751 (Il fit partir dix hommes en deux canots, lesquels remontèrent la rivière du Paskoya jusque la montagne de Roche, où ils firent un fort), *ibid.*, p. 642. Fort a la Corne was built on the Saskatchewan in 1753. Burpee, L. J., *Search for the Western Sea*, p. 281 ; also Bell, C. N., *Trans. No. 17 Manitoba Hist. and Sci. Soc.*, 1885, p. 17.

[1] " A fort . . . called Henly House which is 150 or 200 miles up the River (Albany) . . . the governor erected that fort to prevent the French trade who never traded there before that season." *Report from the Committee on the state of Hudson Bay*, 1749, p. 221.

[2] Journal of a Journey by Anthony Hendry to explore the country inland and to endeavour to increase the Hudson's Bay Company trade A.D. 1754-5. *Proceedings and Transactions of the Royal Society of Canada*, 3rd series, vol. I, 1907, p. 321, ed. Burpee, L. J.

[3] MacKenzie, A., *A General History of the Fur Trade from Canada to the North-West*, p. 12.

[4] *Ibid.*, p. 21, also Atcheson, Nathaniel, *On the Origin and Progress of the North-West Company*, p. 7.

[5] MacKenzie, A., *Voyages from Montreal through the Continent of North America to the Frozen and Pacific Oceans*, p. 14.

[6] Atcheson, Nathaniel, *ibid.*, p. 28.

[7] Hearne made successive journeys to the interior in the years following 1769 (Hearne S., *Journey from Prince of Wales Fort in Hudson's Bay to the Northern Ocean*, especially p. xxxv. ff.) and in 1774 established Cumberland House on the Saskatchewan (*ibid.*, p. 266) as a reply to the aggressiveness of Frobisher, who intercepted trade going to Hudson Bay by a fort on the Saskatchewan River near the site of Fort Poskoyac and by Fort la Traite on the Churchill River. Masson, L. R., *op cit.* I, p. 14. See also Davidson, G. C., *The North-West Company*, pp. 35-6.

[8] Fort Athabasca was built by Peter Pond in 1778, " sur la Rivière à la Biche, à quarante milles de sa décharge." Masson, L. R., op cit., p. 14. Fort aux Trembles as well as another fort on the Assiniboine River were

more remote regions. Rapid expansion of the fur trade occasioned by such competition led to improvement [1] of the shortest possible routes and to the growth of settlement at strategic [2] points for the handling of furs

in existence prior to 1780 (*ibid.*, p. 17). Pine Fort was built about eighteen miles below the junction of the Souris and Assiniboine River in 1785. Coues, E., *New Light on the Early History of the Greater North-West*, p. 296. Fort Esperance was built on Qu'Appelle River, a branch of the Assiniboine, in 1787. Masson, L. R., op. cit., p. 274. Fort Resolution was built on Upper Slave Lake in 1787 and Fort Providence on the north side of the Lake in 1789 (*ibid.*, p. 30). Fort Chipawean was built near Lake Athabasca to take the place of Fort Pond in 1788. A fort was built on Peace River in the same year. MacKenzie, A., *Voyages in North America*, p. 129. The increased aggressions of the Hudson Bay Company became more noticeable about this period. Descending the Albany River Osnaburg House was built in 1786. Masson, op. cit., vol. II, p. 244. Mention is made of Manchester House and of Hudson's House on the Saskatchewan River in 1787 and 1788. *David Thompson's Narrative*, ed. by J. B. Tyrrell, p. lxv. Buckingham House on the North Saskatchewan is mentioned in 1793, also South Branch House on the South Saskatchewan (*ibid.*, pp. lxvi.–lxvii.). Fort George was established by the North-West Company in the same locality in 1791. Masson, L. R., op. cit., II, p. 17. Lac d'Orignal Fort was established on Beaver River two years earlier (*ibid.*, p. 14). A fort farther up the Peace River was built in 1792. Mac-Kenzie, A., op. cit., p. 135. Toward Lake Athabasca the Hudson Bay Company established a post at Ile la Crosse in 1791 near the North-West Company's posts at that point. Coues, E., op. cit., vol. II, p. 580. They forced the North-West Company to abandon Pine Fort by the establishment of Souris River Fort in 1793. Masson, L. R., op. cit., I, p. 271. Brandon House was established in 1794. Coues, E., op. cit., p. 298. In retaliation the North-West Company built Assiniboine House in the same vicinity in 1795 (*ibid.*). Proceeding up the North Saskatchewan Fort Augustus was built by the North-West Company in 1794-5. Tyrrell, J. B., op. cit., p. lxxviii. Edmonton House farther up the river was built by the Hudson Bay Company in 1795 (*ibid.*, p. 432). Fort Carlton is given the date 1797. Coues, E., op. cit., p. 490. Rocky Mountain House was built in 1799. Tyrrell, J. B., op. cit., p. xlvi. Southward the North-West Company built a fort at the mouth of the Pembina River in 1797. See Burpee, L. J., op. cit., p. 385, and Tyrrell, J. B., op. cit., p. lxxv. Nearer the Hudson Bay district Fairford House was built on the Churchill River in 1795 (*ibid.*, p. lxx.), but apparently abandoned in favour of Bedford House the following year (*ibid.*, pp. 133-4). Under the stress of competition from the X Y Company from 1801 to 1804 (Masson, L. R., op. cit., I, p. 77) several other forts were built—Chesterfield House on the South Saskatchewan in 1805. Masson, L. R., *ibid.*, II, p. 30. Posts were established by the North-West Company at Moose River and Charlton Island on Hudson Bay (*ibid.*, I, p. 80). Other posts were established at various competitive points. See Davidson, G. C., op. cit., pp. 89-91.

[1] Yonge Street from Toronto to Georgian Bay was largely used by the North-West Company at that time. The company supplied funds for the improvement of the road—contributing as much as £8,000 in one single payment. *History of Toronto and the County of York*, vol. I, Pt. II, p. 16. Under the pressure of the same traffic a canal was built at Sault Ste Marie in 1798 for the passage of bateaux and canoes. Capp, E. H., *The Annals of Sault Ste Marie*, pp. 117-19.

[2] An interesting description of such points and particularly of Grand Portage is given in MacKenzie, A., *A General History of the Fur Trade*, p. 55 ff.

and supplies. Consequently, head-quarters were removed from Grand Portage to Kaministiquia [1] (later known as Fort William) [2] in 1801 as a result of the discovery [3] of a route from Rainy Lake to Lake Superior, which avoided the difficulties of Grand Portage. At about the same time, an ill-fated [4] suggestion was made by Alexander MacKenzie proposing [5] the formation of the Fishery and Fur Company, " to open and establish a commercial communication through the continent of North America between the Atlantic and Pacific oceans to the incalculable advantage and furtherance of the Pacific Fishery and American fur trade of Great Britain." [6]

The necessity of increasing settlement to furnish supplies [7] and to handle traffic—considerations involved in expanding trade—was a factor favourable [8] to the grant of land by

[1] Masson, L. R., op. cit., I., p. 47. The growth of settlement in Fort William is well described in Franchere, G., op. cit., p. 269 ff.

[2] Ibid.

[3] Masson, L. R., ibid., p. 46.

[4] The scheme necessitated the granting of legal rights by the Hudson Bay Company (Sir Alexander MacKenzie to Lord Hobart, Jan. 7, 1802, Canadian Archives Report, 1892, p. 148), and in view of the competitive situation was consequently impossible. Sir Alexander MacKenzie to John Sullivan, Oct. 25, 1802, ibid., p. 150.

[5] It was proposed " by these waters that discharge themselves into Hudson's Bay at Port Nelson " . . . " to carry on trade to their source at the head of the Sascatchiwine River which rises in the Rocky Mountains not eight degrees of longitude from the Pacific Ocean. The Columbia River flows also from the same mountains and discharges itself likewise in the Pacific in latitude 46° 20'. Both of them are capable of receiving ships at their mouths and are navigable throughout for boats." MacKenzie, Sir Alexander, Voyages from Montreal, etc., p. 410.

[6] Sir Alexander MacKenzie to Lord Hobart, Jan. 7, 1802 (Canadian Archives Report, 1892).

[7] At Grand Portage " for which purpose several milch cows are constantly kept." MacKenzie, A. (A General History of the Fur Trade), p. 75. Fort du Bas de la Riviere " Cet établissement avait plutot l'air d'une métairie que d'un post de commerce." Franchere, G., op. cit., p. 262.

[8] " Of late years this expense (provisions exported from England), has been so enormous that it has become very desirable to try the practicability of raising provisions within the territory itself. . . . With these views the company were induced in the year 1811 to dispose of a large tract of their lands to the Earl of Selkirk." Statement Papers relating to the Red River Settlement, 1819, p. 4. The significance of this statement is appreciably lessened in view of its date, Feb. 14, 1815, which admits the possibility of its controversial character, especially in view of the fact that the Earl of Selkirk possessed £40,000 out of a total of £105,000 of the Hudson Bay Company when the grant was made. (See "Coltman's Report," ibid., p. 152.) The motives of the Earl of Selkirk have been subject to controversy. Even such a sympathetic appreciation of his patriotic efforts as is shown in Martin, Chester, Lord Selkirk's Work in Canada, p. 190, admits " without a doubt Selkirk felt justified in advoca-

the Hudson Bay Company to Lord Selkirk for colonization purposes, and to the establishment of settlement at the Forks of Red River.   On the other hand, severity [1] of competition, more pronounced because the step appeared [2] to be a direct blow at the North-West Company, made settlement almost impossible.[3]   But difficult as such attempts [4] at settlement were, the demands of the situation were ultimately such as to favour a permanent establishment,

ting his scheme among his relatives as an ultimately remunerative investment.   Selkirk would have been the last to affirm or even admit that his projects for proprietary colonization were economically unsound."   In a description of a more successful venture on Prince Edward Island, the Earl of Selkirk states :   " The settlers . . . were allowed to purchase in fee simple and to a certain extent on credit ;   from 50 to 100 acres were allotted to each family at a very moderate price, but none was given gratuitously. . . .   Every assistance they received was a loan after due scrutiny into the necessity of the case and under strict obligations of repayment with interest."   Selkirk, Earl of, *Observations on the present state of the Highlands of Scotland with a view of the causes and probable consequences of emigration*, pp. 204-5.   Criticism of the methods involved may be found in Strachan, John, *A Letter to the Right Honourable the Earl of Selkirk on his settlement at the Red River near Hudson's Bay.*

[1] The loss of life in the tragedy of Seven Oaks, the destruction of property, and the hopeless litigation were incidental to the struggle of the period.   See *Papers relating to the Red River Settlement*, 1819.   McDonnell, A., *Narrative of Transactions in the Red River Country*.   Pritchard, John, *Narratives respecting the aggressions of the North-West Company against the Earl of Selkirk settlement.   The Report of the Proceedings connected with the Disputes between the Earl of Selkirk and the North-West Company at the Assizes at York*, 1818.   *The Report of the Proceedings at a Court of oyer and terminer appointed for the investigation of cases from the Indian Territories*, 1819, and more partial statements *The communications of Mercator*, and *Claims of the Hudson's Bay Company*, 1817.   See also Davidson, G. C., *The North-West Company*, p. 118 ff.

[2] The scheme was regarded in general as injurious to the fur trade, and in particular as hostile to the North-West Company, since it was looked upon as " a nursery of servants for the Hudson's Bay Company," as an excuse for bringing out more emigrants to carry out a policy of aggression, as an attempt to reduce the price of supplies and to make the Indians independent of them, and as a denial of their rights to the territory granted—a serious consideration, since the nature of the grant was such as to cut off the communication of the North-West Company between Fort William and the Athabasca territory, as well as the Assiniboine terrirory.   (See map, Plate I, *Papers relating to the Red River Settlement*, 1819).   " Coltman's report."   *Papers relating to the Red River Settlement*, 1819, pp. 153-4.

[3] The hardships of the settlers, involving at times the complete disappearance of the settlement, are very well described by Donald Gunn, who arrived in 1813.   Gunn, Donald, and Tuttle, C. R., *History of Manitoba*.

[4] About 70 reached Red River in August, 1912 (*ibid.*, p. 73), about 20 in 1813 (*ibid.*, p. 76), about 90 in 1814 (*ibid.*, pp. 194-5), about 100 in 1815 (*ibid.*, p. 133).   See also Bryce, G., op. cit., p. 213.   Several French families arrived from Canada in 1818.   Ross, A., *The Red River Settlement—Its rise, progress and present state*, p. 48.   In 1821 about 170 Swiss colonists were sent out.   Gunn, D., and Tuttle, C. R., op. cit., p. 218.

and the very ferocity of competition, making amalgamation [1] necessary, unavoidably involved an increase [2] in population. Increase in population left settlement none the less subject to exigencies of the fur trade. Amalgamation of the companies brought the decline of Fort Alexander [3] (Bas de la Riviere) and Fort William,[4] formerly important, because they were situated on the main route of communication of the North-West Company, and the growth of Fort Douglas [5] at the confluence of the Red and Assiniboine Rivers, the centre of the southern fur territory. In a more active capacity the Hudson Bay Company exercised the power of monopoly in regulating affairs of the settlement by dictating the price of land [6] and of commodities,[7] by subsidizing enterprises [8] calculated even in failure to redound to its own advantage, and by countenancing tyrannical practices.[9]

[1] For terms of the amalgamation see Davidson, G. C., op. cit., App. p. 305 ff.

[2] The De Meurons, part of a Swiss regiment which the Earl of Selkirk had taken with him for the purpose of restoring order in the territory, were given land in the vicinity of Fort Douglas. Gunn, D., and Tuttle, C. R., op. cit., p. 199. Again, " the number of servants employed by the contending parties was triple the number required in quiet . . . times, and more especially when the business came to be managed by one firm. . . . The influx of families from the fur trade in 1822 and the following summer exceeded in number those who represented the original colonists brought in from all quarters by his Lordship " (ibid., pp. 225–6).

[3] Keating, W. H., Narrative of an Expedition to the Source of St. Peter's River, Lake Winnipeek, Lake of the Woods, etc., performed in the year 1823. Vol. II, p. 81.

[4] Ibid., p. 171.   [5] Ibid., p. 61.

[6] The price of land in 1829 was raised from 5s. per acre to 7s. 6d. (Gunn, D., and Tuttle, C. R., op. cit., p. 260), in 1833 to 10s. 6d. per acre, and in 1834 to 12s. 6d. (ibid., pp. 282–3).

[7] " First 33⅓ per cent. was added to the prime cost ; then on that amount 58 per cent., which became the selling price " (ibid., p. 223). See also tariff of reduced prices for agricultural produce (ibid., p. 260).

[8] The Buffalo Wool Company, the experimental farm of Hayfield, the Tallow Company and the sheep speculation were particular instances (ibid., ch. VI–X). See Ross, A., op. cit., p. 219.

[9] The manner of carrying on trade—the settlers " pay and are paid in handkerchiefs, etc. . . . and if they make a fortune it must be all in clothes. . . . These poor people have thus been reduced to the level with the savages without sharing their advantages or enjoying their independence." Beltrami, J. C., A pilgrimage in Europe and America, leading to the discovery of the sources of the Mississippi and Bloody River. Vol. II, pp. 353–4. " The only good thing I see in the matter (the sale of land) is that they give me a salary of twenty-five pounds for keeping their accounts." Simpson, Alexander, The Life and Travels of Thomas Simpson, the Arctic Discoverer, p. 94. A very good statement of the company's attitude may be found in Gunn, D., and Tuttle, C. R., op. cit.

Friction between the company and the settlers was the
natural result of such regulations. Of necessity the breach
widened with increase in population and particularly
with increase in the number of half-breeds—the larger
and more unsettled portion.[1] The consequent increase
in agricultural products and in the returns of the annual
buffalo chase began to exceed the company's demand,[2]
and there arose the cry of the settlers for a wider market.
The margin of the company's profits on goods sold to the
settlers occasioned the growth of a petty trading class[3]
of importers independent of the company. Demand for
imports caused the growth of trade[4] with Americans along
channels previously opened by early purchases of grain
by the colony. The ʼmonopoly of the company became
subject to increasing strain. In the widening of the breach,
the company displayed greater activity[5] in defence of its

[1] Ross, A., op. cit., p. 166.
[2] The number of carts for buffalo trips steadily increased.

| 1820 | . . | 540 | 1830 | . . | 820 | 1840 | . . | 1,210 |
| 1825 | . . | 680 | 1835 | . . | 970 | | | |

Ibid., p. 246. See also pp. 115, 116.

[3] A feature of the high prices was further effective. " At the year
1834 . . . a ready-money system was introduced (goods not supplied on
credit as formerly). The distress and confusion of this system had
lasted for several years when a few private individuals resolved on importing for themselves. . . . At length every man who could muster
twenty shillings became an importer " (ibid., pp. 155–6).

[4] " In 1847 there were no less than 102 English importers in the colony,
and nearly as many more from the United States . . . whose united
invoices amounted to £11,000 sterling, exclusive of the Company's outfit "
(ibid., p. 395).

[5] The management of Lord Selkirk's colony was more actively assumed
in 1826 (Simpson, A., op. cit., p. 94), and an even more strategic advance
was made in the direct purchase of the colony in 1834. Martin, Chester,
op. cit., App., p. 223. In the same year the Council of Assiniboia, consisting largely of company officials, was organized (Gunn, D., and Tuttle,
C. R., op. cit., pp. 288–9). Resolutions were adopted imposing an import
duty of 7½ per cent., and an export duty of an equal amount. Provision
for their imposition was made in the establishment of a volunteer corps
(see a copy of a partial list, Begg, A., History of the North-West, vol. I,
pp. 236–7). In 1839 the company appointed Judge Thom, and under
his direction a proclamation was issued in 1844, providing a censorship
of the business letters of the settlement (ibid., p. 257), and a clause was
included in all land titles prohibiting the owner from dealing in furs
(see copies of deeds, Appendix to the report from the Select Committee
on the Hudson's Bay Company, pp. 361–2 and 371–2). In 1845 a duty
of 20 per cent. particularly on all imports over £50 by fur traders was
imposed. It was further made possible to prohibit fur traders from
handling goods, and middlemen were forbidden to handle furs (see extracts from minutes of meeting of the Governor and Council of Rupert's
Land, June 10, 1845, ibid., p. 373). The company further refused to
carry goods for agitators. (Begg, A., op. cit., p. 265.) The appearance

monopoly. The settlement became increasingly discontented, and, with every evidence of aggressiveness on the part of the company, unrest became more marked, although violence was generally forestalled by the company's concessions.[1]

Another phase of the struggle between the settlement and the monopoly of the company came with the attempt of the settlement [2] to secure redress from the British Government, which, though temporarily unsuccessful, contributed to produce far-reaching results. Energetic correspondence [3] of Mr. A. K. Isbister in behalf of the settlers failed to [4] secure definite results from the Govern-

of the 6th regiment shortly afterwards was regarded with suspicion. (They were sent out under secret instructions. *Report of Select Committee on Hudson's Bay Company*, p. 169).

[1] In 1834 the Larocque incident was settled by a money payment. (Gunn, D., and Tuttle, C. R., op. cit., pp. 284–5.) The institution of flogging was abandoned through the fear of a demonstration such as had followed the punishment of Louis St. Dennis, in 1836 (*ibid.*, p. 292). The trial of Regis Laurent, whose house had been forcibly broken open and his furs seized, and the trial of William Sayre in 1849 for trading in furs, aroused such determined opposition that the company was virtually obliged to concede free trade (*ibid.*, pp. 304–5). As a result of this pressure, the price of land was reduced from 12s. 6d. to 7s. 6d. (*ibid.*, p. 286), and the import duty was also reduced from 7½ per cent. to 5 per cent. and to 4 per cent. Begg, A., op. cit., p. 254.

[2] A memorial was submitted on Feb. 17, 1847, signed by Mr. A. K. Isbister and others and accompanied by a petition signed by 977 names. See instructions for the guidance of the memorialists. Copy of Memorial and petition from inhabitants of the Red River Settlement, complaining of the government of the Hudson's Bay Company, and reports and correspondence on the subject of the Memorial. *Papers relating to the Hudson's Bay Company*, 1842–70, pp. 86–90.

[3] The correspondence covers several pages (*ibid.*). See also Papers relating to the legality of the powers in respect to territory, trade, taxation and government claimed or exercised by the Hudson's Bay Company on the continent of North America, under the charter of Charles II or in virtue of any other right or title (*ibid.*).

[4] " Lord Grey is of opinion . . . that the charges you have brought against the Hudson's Bay Company are groundless " (letter from B. Hawes to A. K. Isbister, June 14, 1847). Copy of Memorial and Petition, etc. (*ibid.*, p. 50). " Lord Grey has arrived at the conclusion that there are no grounds for making any application to Parliament on the subject of the oppression alleged by you " (letter from B. Hawes to A. K. Isbister, Jan. 23, 1849, *ibid.*, p. 113). As further evidence of the Government's lassitude—after a resolution had been passed by the House of Commons asking for an inquiry as to the legality of the company's rights (Papers relating to the legality of the powers, etc., *ibid.*, p. 3), and it had been ascertained that the company's rights did "properly belong to them," but that a competent tribunal should be appointed to consider the rights more carefully (*ibid.*, p. 7)—the Government made no provision for such a tribunal, but practically obliged Mr. Isbister to drop the matter by insisting that he should bear the responsibility and the expense of the undertaking (*ibid.*, pp. 13–4).

ment, which was apparently satisfied by diplomatic [1] assurances [2] of the company, but it undoubtedly contributed to a growing feeling of dissatisfaction with the company's administration. Increase [3] in settlement and

[1] " Some of the settlers have of late been carrying on a clandestine trade in furs. . . . The injury thus done the company's trade, though considerable, is but one, and that the least, of the evils resulting from this practice. The persons engaged in it are diverted from the cultivation of the soil, etc. . . . The perusal of the above-mentioned documents will, I trust, satisfy your Lordship that the allegations of the memorialists are groundless " (letter from Sir J. H. Pelly, Bart., to Earl Grey, April 24, 1847, *ibid.*, p. 21). In answer to an intimation that a further inquiry would be conducted ". . . that if your Lordship will let me know the particular points on which you require further information, I shall be most ready to co-operate with you " (Sir J. H. Pelly, Bart., to Earl Grey, June 21, 1847). At Sir J. H. Pelly's suggestion the memorialists were persuaded to submit the matter in dispute to the award of Earl Grey (*ibid.*, pp. 105–6). Earl Grey, relying upon information afforded by Col. Crofton (*ibid.*, pp. 101–2) and Major Griffiths (*ibid.*, pp. 110–12), two officers of the 6th regiment both of whom were Governors of the colony (Begg, A., op. cit., p. 269), and belonged to a regiment regarded with suspicion by the settlers, decided very strongly in favour of the company (letter from B. Hawes to A. K. Isbister, Jan. 23, 1849. Copy of Memorial and petition, etc., *ibid.*, p. 113).

[2] In the application for the renewal of the grant made in 1837, a year later than that of the organization of the Assiniboia Council and five years before the existing grant expired, the righteousness of the Company's activities was effectively paraded and Mr. (afterwards Sir) J. H. Pelly emphasized very strongly the statements of Mr. George Simpson as to the exceptional work of the company in promoting the interests of Red River Settlement. " It will be seen that Red River Settlement has advanced rapidly in population and improved since 1821 . . . and there is a prospect that at no very distant period a considerable export trade in the articles of wool, flax, etc., will be established from that settlement " (copy of the existing charter or grant by the Crown to the Hudson's Bay Company, and correspondence on the renewal of the charter, etc., *ibid.*, p. 14, see also pp. 12–17). " It has become necessary to establish a more regular form of government and administration of the laws than heretofore. These measures are now in progress, and it is estimated that the attendant expenses will exceed £5,000 per annum, which will be borne by the company, although they might with great propriety call on Her Majesty's Government to relieve them from that charge " (letter from the Governor of the Hudson's Bay Company to the Lords of the Committee of Privy Council for trade. Feb. 7, 1838, pp. 25–6).

[3] Some conception of the character and growth of the settlement may be gained from the following statistics of 1849 :

Families	1,052
Total population	5,291
Houses	745
Horses	1,095
Oxen	2,097
Cows	2,147
Pigs	1,565
Sheep	3,096
Ploughs	492

Land cultivated at 2 bushels of wheat per acre, 6,392. Compiled from Appendix to *Report from the Select Committee of the Hudson's Bay Company*, p. 363.

its demands for a wider market, and growth of trade with the United States—results of the accessibility of the route by way of the Red River to St. Paul—made this dissatisfaction [1] more pronounced. Although the Red River Settlement had suffered from the neglect of the British Government, it had not entirely escaped notice,[2] and with the signs [3] of American imperialism, more serious in view

[1] " Nous sommes près de la ligne territoriale ; nous pourrions nous ranger sur le territoire voisin : nous y sommes invités." Petition of settlers to Queen Victoria. Copy of Memorial and Petition from Inhabitants of the Red River Settlement, etc. *Papers relating to Hudson's Bay Company*, 1842–70, p. 5. See also accompanying memorial (*ibid.,* p. 3). About 1846 a petition was sent to the American Government desiring it to annex the Red River territory, and promising them assistance against the Hudson's Bay Company. *Report from the Select Committee on the Hudson's Bay Company*, p. 132.

[2] The Government had occasion to intervene because of the crimes resulting from the severity of the competition in the fur trade in an Act 43 Geo. III, c 138 " for extending the jurisdiction of the courts of justice in the provinces of Lower and Upper Canada to the trial and punishment of persons guilty of crimes and offences within certain parts of North America, adjoining to the said Provinces ; " in 1st and 2nd Geo. IV, c. 66 " for regulating the fur trade and establishing a commercial and civil jurisdiction within certain parts of North America " ; and in the management of the Selkirk difficulties, shown in the " *Papers relating to the Red River Settlement*, 1819," particularly in the issue of the proclamation demanding peace (*ibid.*, pp. 71 and 94). Further evidence of interest is shown in the limitation of the grant of 1821 to 21 years, and in the insistence throughout the correspondence leading to the grant of 1838, and in the grant that " nothing herein contained shall extend or be construed to extend to prevent the establishment by us . . . of any colony or colonies, province or provinces . . . or by annexing any part of the aforesaid territories to any existing colony or colonies by us " (copy of the existing charter or grant by the Crown to the Hudson's Bay Company, etc., *Papers relating to the Hudson's Bay Company*, 1842–70, see pp. 19 and 29, see also above, p. 10).

[3] The growth of imperialism which led to the cession of Oregon in 1846 served to arouse Great Britain to the dangers of further aggression. The activities of the United States in the territory south of the Red River assumed greater significance. Following the Louisiana purchase in 1803, the United States dispatched Lieut. Z. M. Pike to visit Minnesota in 1805 (see Coues, Elliot, *Expeditions of Zebulon M. Pike*, vol. I). Lewis Cass was given permission to undertake a similar exploring tour in 1820. (Schoolcraft, H. R., *Summary Narrative of an Exploratory Expedition to the Sources of the Mississippi River in* 1820, p. 31). Major S. H. Long was sent in 1823 in charge of a party " to the point of intersection between Red River and the forty-ninth degree of north latitude, thence along the northern boundary of the United States to Lake Superior. The object of the expedition is to make a general survey of the country " (Keating, W. H., op. cit., p. 3). On March 3, 1849, a bill was passed organizing the Territory of Minnesota, and in 1858 Minnesota was admitted to the Union (Neill, E. W., *The History of Minnesota*, pp. 492 and 628). Of significance also was the proposal of Mr. Whitney, an American engineer, to build a road from Lake Michigan to California. Congress was asked for a grant of thirty miles of land on each side of the

of the rapid western development of the United States, a more active interest was assumed.

The fact that the fur trade and the company's monopoly were irrevocably opposed to settlement, as was evident in the Isbister correspondence, and in the difficulties of British Columbia, began to be appreciated. Propaganda[1]

line. It was proposed to sell the first ten miles, then to build the road, and sell the next ten miles—the road being built as settlement advanced. The whole was to be completed in fifteen years (*The Times*, Sept. 21, 1849). He expressed the belief further that a Pacific road could be built only through Canada because of better country, lower gradients and shorter distance (*Leader*, May 12, 1858).

[1] A road from Halifax to Fraser River was advocated in 1849. The purpose of the scheme was to link up the whole English race, and to furnish Great Britain a soil for her population and a market for her labour. The road was to be built by convicts and Indians, aided by local labour, and at an estimated cost of £150,000,000. England, the Hudson's Bay Company and the North American provinces were to furnish the necessary capital, and the management of the road was to be vested in fifteen directors, three representing Great Britain, and an equal number representing the Hudson's Bay Company, Nova Scotia, New Brunswick and Canada (Smyth, Carmichael, *Employment of People and Capital of Great Britain in her own colonies*). Following Smyth, Wilson, F. A., and Richards, A. B., *Britain Redeemed and Canada Preserved*, 1850, impressive statements were made as to the imperialistic advantages, and a very elaborate scheme was worked out. The road was to be built at a cost of £1,500 per mile, and the capital was to be raised by the saving of the poor rate due to the emigration and relief from the surplus population (*ibid.*, p. 4), by the increase in the value of the land served by the railroad, and by the revenue from the road (*ibid.*, pp. 318-9). The line was to be divided into seven sections of 400 miles each (*ibid.*, p. 31).

Miles.

No. 1 Atlantic division running from Halifax to Quebec 400
,, 2 Quebec division from Quebec to Tamiscaming Lake 400
,, 3 Lake division, from Tamiscaming to Lake St. Anne 400
,, 4 Central division from Lake St. Anne to Fort Gary 400
,, 5 Prairie division from Fort Gary to Saskatchewan River 400
,, 6 Mountain division, from Saskatchewan across the Rocky Mountains, by the Devil's Nose to Upper Arrow Lake 400
,, 7 Pacific division from Upper Arrow Lake to New Georgia Gulf 400

Total length . . . 2,800

It was proposed to employ 20,000 convicts (*ibid.*, p. 200), guarded by a legion of 5,000 men. The convicts were later to be settled on the island of Anticosti. In addition, about 6,000 able-bodied paupers were to be enrolled and apportioned to the various divisions (*ibid.* p. 218). The military precision was further elaborated in detail as to the equipment, plans of barracks, convict prisons, retreat of women for each station, block buildings, etc. (p. 557), and in the number of farmers, carpenters, shoemakers, and other necessary tradesmen (*ibid.*, p. 248). Even greater stress was placed on the imperialistic advantages of such a road

which had been carried on by imperialistic writers in the insistence on the benefits of a transcontinental road also had its effect. The necessity of renewing to the Hudson's Bay Company, the grant which expired in 1859, offered an opportunity to investigate the whole situation, and finally [1] the Select Committee of 1857 was appointed, and at the same time, Captain Palliser was dispatched [2] to explore the territory in question.

Prospect of relief of Red River Settlement from the monopoly of the company as a result of these activities was much more promising. Although Captain Palliser pointed out the difficulties of establishing communica-

(Synge, M. H., *Great Britain One Empire*, 1852). Various distances were compared with an obvious conclusion.

From England	To Sydney Miles	Days		To New Zealand Miles		To Hong Kong Miles
By Central America	12,491 to 13,920	63 to 65	.	11,336 to 12,765	.	13,720 to 15,760
By the Cape of Good Hope	12634 to 14,655	70 to 80	.	13,789 to 15,810	.	13,330 to 14,530
By the Indian route	11,727 to 13,425	62 to 66	.	12,882 to 14,580	.	15,590
By British America	11,600	44	.	11,058	.	11,490

Ibid., p. 57.

The route was, moreover, carefully outlined. 1. Water communication to the head of Lake Huron (or existing land routes, or mixed). 2. Railroad portage (for a short time) round the falls of St. Mary. 3. Water communication to the first impediment in the navigation of the Kamenis Toquoih. 4. Railroads thence to Rainy Lake, past the several impediments using the chain of lakes for water communications. 5. Water communication to the head of the Lake of the Woods. 6. Railroad to the head of the navigation of Rat River. 7. Water communication to the rapids of the Saskatchewan. 8. Railroads round the rapids of the Saskatchewan. 9. Water communication to the foot of the Rocky Mountains. 10. Passage of the mountains and descent to the Pacific upon the same plan. The road was to be built gradually and every advantage taken of the navigation facilities of the country (*ibid.*, p. 87). The road was to be financed by grants of land (*ibid.*, p. 104).

[1] The resolution adopted by the House of Commons in 1849 asking that means should be taken to ascertain the legality of the powers claimed by the Hudson's Bay Company was a preliminary step, although no definite action resulted. Papers relating to the legality of the powers, etc. *Papers relating to the Hudson's Bay Company*, 1842–70, p. 3.

[2] Palliser, Captain. *The journals, detailed reports and observations relative to the exploration of that portion of British North America which in latitude lies between the British boundary line and the height of land or watershed of the northern or frozen ocean respectively, and in longitude between the western shore of Lake Superior and the Pacific ocean during the years* 1857, 1858, 1859, 1860, p. 4.

tion [1] between Canada and the settlement, he strongly
favoured [2] the formation of a British colony extending from
the Red River to British Columbia, and in this other members of the expedition substantially [3] concurred.

Canada was even more seriously concerned than Great
Britain with the possibilities of American imperialism,
and with the growth of trade between Red River Settlement and the United States. The invitation [4] of the Colonial
Secretary on December 4, 1856, to Canada to present her
case before the Select Committee [5] met " with great satisfaction," and almost immediately it was arranged [6] that
Chief Justice Draper should be appointed as a delegate.
The activity of Canada was further evident in the instructions [7] given to the delegate, and in the generally able
manner [8] in which the case was conducted. A peti-

[1] " I cannot recommend the Imperial Government to countenance or
lend support to any scheme for constructing or forming a thoroughfare
by this line of route either by land or water, as there would be no immediate advantage commensurate with the required sacrifice of capital,
nor can I advise such heavy expenditure as would necessarily attend
the construction of any exclusively British line of road between Canada
and the Red River Settlement " (*ibid.*, p. 6). " I think there can be no
other means of access to be recommended save those via the United
States." Further papers, etc., 1860 (*ibid.*, p. 5).

[2] " I cannot see any object in limiting a new colony . . . and feel
decidedly in favour of annexing not only the Saskatchewan, but also
the Swan River district . . . and so establish one great border line from
the new colony of British Columbia up to the Red River Settlement.
. . . The whole would thus include a territory of 240,000 square miles.
. . . I have no hesitation in stating that no obstacles exist to the construction of a railway from Red River to the eastern base of the Rocky
Mountains . . . I have no hesitation in expressing my conviction
that it is impossible for the Hudson's Bay Company to provide a government to meet the exigencies of a growing colony " (*ibid.*, pp. 4–5).

[3] Lieut. Blakiston, emphasizing the advantages to the settlement of
communication with Canada, suggested a further search for a route from
a port on the north shore of Lake Superior to the Red River. Papers
relative to the exploration, etc., 1859 (*ibid.*); see also Further Papers,
etc., 1860 (*ibid.*, pp. 57–8).

[4] *Correspondence, Papers and Documents of dates from* 1856 *to* 1882
*inclusive, relating to the Northerly and Westerly boundaries of the Province
of Ontario,* 1882, p. 2.

[5] *Ibid.* [6] *Ibid.*, p. 3.

[7] " It is especially important that Her Majesty's Government should
guard any renewal of a licence of occupation . . . or any recognition
of rights by the company by such stipulation as will cause such licence
or such rights not to interfere with the fair and legitimate occupation
of tracts adapted for settlement " (*ibid.*, pp. 3–5).

[8] See Memorandum of Chief Justice Draper, May 6, 1857 (*ibid.*, pp.
37–40), and particularly the Final Report of Chief Justice Draper, respecting his mission to England (*ibid.*, pp. 51–59).

tion [1] from the Board of Trade of the City of Toronto to the
Legislative Council dated April 20, 1857, was forwarded
to the Select Committee, and in response to a petition [2] from
Red River settlers presented on May 22, 1857, the province
appointed a select committee, which collected evidence
unfavourable [3] to the company, and likewise presented it
to the same body. Finally an expedition [4] was dispatched
to the North-West in the same year for the purpose of
gathering information on its possibilities. The report
of the Select Committee favouring the annexation [5] of the

[1] The petition stated in part " . . . they humbly submit that a renewal
of such licence of exclusive trade is injurious to the interests of the
country so monopolized, and in contravention of the rights of the inhabitants of Canada." *Appendix to report from the Select Committee
on the Hudson's Bay Company*, p. 435.
[2] The petition was signed by 575 inhabitants and asked " that such
measures may be devised and adopted as will extend to us the protection
of the Canadian Government, laws and institutions " (*ibid.*, p. 439).
[3] The committee was composed of five Honourable gentlemen, and the
report consisted of evidence given by three men, Mr. Allan McDonnell,
Mr. George Gladman and Mr. William MacD. Dawson, all of whom were
hostile to the company, and all of whom spent considerable time in the
discussion of the territorial rights and of the possibilities of communication between Canada and the Red River (*ibid.*, pp. 385–402).
[4] The expedition was placed in charge of Mr. George Gladman, on July
22, 1857. " Le premier objet de l'expédition est de faire une étude
complète du pays compris entre le Lac Supérieur et la Rivière Rouge dans
le but de trouver sur le territoire Anglais la route la plus facile et la
meilleure pour communiquer du lac aux établissements de la Rivière."
*Rapport sur l'Exploration de la Contrée située entre le Lac Supérieur et
les établissements de la Rivière Rouge*, 1858, p. 6. Mr. S. J. Dawson
was appointed as engineer (*ibid.*, p. 10), and Professor H. Y. Hind as
geologist and naturalist (*ibid.*, p. 15). In 1858 the expedition was divided
into two sections, one under Professor Hind " to procure all the information in your power respecting the Geology, Natural History, Topography
and Meteorology of the region " . . . " lying to the west of Lake Winnipeg
and Red River and embraced . . . between the River Saskatchewan and
Assiniboine as far west as ' South Branch House.' " Hind, Henry Youle,
*Narrative of the Canadian Red River exploring expedition of 1857, and
of the Assiniboine and Saskatchewan exploring expedition of 1858*, vol. I,
p. 269. The other was headed by Mr. Dawson (*ibid.*, p. 267). The results
of Hind's work are well described (*ibid.*, vol. I and II), and that of Dawson
is presented in Dawson, S. J., *Report on the Exploration of the country
between Lake Superior and the Red River Settlement, and between the latter
place and the Assiniboine and Saskatchewan.*
[5] " Your committee consider that it is essential to meet the just and
reasonable wishes of Canada to be enabled to annex to her territory such
portion of the land in her neighbourhood as may be available to her for
the purposes of settlement, with which lands she is willing to open and
maintain communications, and for which she will provide the means of
local administration. Your committee apprehend that the districts
on the Red River and the Saskatchewan are among those likely to be
desired for early occupation. Your committee trust that there will be
no difficulty in effecting arrangements as between Her Majesty's Govern-

Red River and Saskatchewan districts to Canada was a tribute to these activities.

The report proved but an incident in a struggle which, since it involved the life of the monopoly and of the fur trade, was destined to be prolonged. It was followèd by suggestions of the British authorities as to machinery with which the proposals could be carried out. The company succeeded in checking progress in this direction by a resort [1] to the charter, although some advantage was

ment and the Hudson's Bay Company, by which these districts may be ceded to Canada on equitable principles, and within the districts thus annexed to her the authority of the Hudson's Bay Company would of course entirely cease." *Report from the Select Committee on the Hudson's Bay Company,* 1857, pp. iii.–iv.

[1] The history of the correspondence presents the case in more detail. The Imperial authorities on December 4, 1856, intimated to Canada the advisability of presenting its case before the Select Committee (*Correspondence, Papers and Documents of dates from 1856 to 1882 inclusive relating to the Northerly and Westerly boundaries of the Province of Ontario,* 1882, p. 2). The Canadian authorities replied on January 17, 1857, and stated the desire " to urge the importance of ascertaining the limits of Canada in the direction over which the Hudson's Bay Company claim jurisdiction," (*ibid.*). Accordingly, the whole question of the company's rights was submitted to the Solicitor-General and the Attorney-General, June 9, 1857 (Appendix to the *Report from the Select Committee on the Hudson's Bay Company,* p. 402). It was stated after a careful argument, " We cannot but feel that the important question of the boundaries of the territory of the Hudson's Bay Company, might with great utility as between the company and Canada be made the subject of a quasi-judicial inquiry. But this cannot be done except by the consent of both parties, namely Canada and the Hudson's Bay Company," July, 1857 (*ibid.*, p. 404). The Judicial Committee of the Privy Council was suggested by the Imperial authorities (July 15, 1857), and the suggestion was accepted by the Hudson's Bay Company (July 18, 1857). The whole correspondence with the company related to boundaries, but it was feared that Canada would insist also upon the question of the charter's validity. After the Select Committee's report had been received, with this fear in mind, the Imperial authorities (Jan. 20, 1858), suggested " the appointment of a Board of Three Commissioners, one to be nominated by the province of Canada, one by the company, and one by Her Majesty's Government . . . to consider and report on . . . the amount of pecuniary compensation which may become justly payable to the company in consequence of such contemplated annexation " (*Correspondence, Papers and Documents of dates from* 1856, etc., pp. 60–61). To this again the company agreed, Jan. 21, 1858 (*ibid.*, p. 62). The Canadian Parliament according to expectations (Aug. 3, 1858), asked that the question be submitted " without restriction as to any question Canada may present on the validity of the said charter " (*ibid.*, p. 68). At this the company, Oct. 12, 1858, refused to be " a consenting party " (*ibid.*, p. 72), and despite the threats of Sir E. Lytton, Nov. 3, 1858 (*ibid.*, p. 73), they remained of the same opinion (*ibid.*, p. 74). To carry out the threats Canada was urged to obtain a writ of *scire facias* to repeal the charter, Dec. 22, 1858 (*ibid.*, p. 76). To this it was answered (April 29, 1859), that " Canada ought not to be called upon to litigate the question of the validity of the charter claimed by the company, inasmuch as such portion

gained by the Government, since the issue became clearly
defined.[1] Canada, impressed with information which had
been gathered by Hind [2] and Dawson,[3] continued the
offensive. In 1858, the North-West Transportation,
Navigation and Railway Company was incorporated [4]
with powers to establish communication from one or more
points on the shore of Lake Superior to any point in the
interior " within the limits of Canada." The boundaries
of Canada being of a controversial character, this company
undertook to make arrangements giving it power to conduct
operations on territory beyond Canadian jurisdiction.
The Act of Incorporation was therefore amended [5] in
1859 to enable it to unite with another company to be
formed in England for a similar purpose. In addition

of Territory as the charter covers is not part of Canada and is, if the
charter be invalid, subject to Imperial and not provincial control "
(*ibid.*, p. 87).

[1] " It is . . . right to notice that the territories mentioned as those
that may probably be first desired by the Government of Canada, namely
the Red River and Saskatchewan districts, are not only valuable to
the Hudson's Bay Company as stations for carrying on the fur trade,
but that they are also of peculiar value . . . as being the only source
from which the company's annual stock of provisions is drawn ; . . .
the ultimate loss of these districts will most probably involve the . . .
company in very serious difficulties, and cause a great expense in conducting their trade " (letter from J. Shepherd to Rt. Hon. H. Labouchere.
Jan. 21, 1858). Copies of correspondence that has taken place between
the Colonial Office and the Hudson's Bay Company, or the Government of
Canada, in consequence of the report of the Select Committee on the
affairs of the company which sat in the last session of Parliament (*Papers
relating to Hudson's Bay Company*, 1842–70, pp. 5–6).

[2] " It is a physical reality of the highest importance to the interests
of British North America that this continuous belt can be settled and
cultivated from a few miles west of the Lake of the Woods to the passes
of the Rocky Mountains, and any line of communication whether by
wagon road or by railroad passing through it will eventually enjoy the great
advantage of being fed by an agricultural population from one extremity
to the other " (Hind, H. Y., op. cit., vol. II, p. 234).

[3] The possibilities of a route from Fort William to Fort Gary were
examined, and it was estimated that with some improvements the land
carriage would be reduced to $131\frac{1}{2}$ miles, leaving $367\frac{1}{2}$ miles of navigable
river, and that " the journey from Lake Superior to Red River might
be performed in about three days." With an additional outlay Fort
Gary might be brought within five days' journey of Toronto. He
pointed out the advantages of this route over the St. Paul and Pembina
route, and the fact that trade would be transferred to Canada, that the
gold regions of British Columbia would be brought within reach, and
that the whole territory would be colonized (Dawson, S. J., op. cit., p. 29).

[4] 22 Vic. c. 122, 1858. See MacDonnell, Allen, *The North-West Transportation Navigation and Railway Company : Its Objects.*

[5] 22 Vic. c. 97, 1859.

the name was changed to the " North-West Company,"
and power given to construct a telegraph line. The Act
expired [1] through non-user.

The disappearance of this enterprise and the attitude [2]
of the company towards the attempts of Canada to establish
a postal service with Red River, made apparent the strength
of the Hudson's Bay Company in withstanding attempts
at colonization by its insistence upon territorial rights.
But antagonism of the company, and the prominence of
the British Columbia goldfields at that time, served to
arouse Canadian authorities to even greater activity.
In 1862 they tried to take advantage [3] of an Imperial Act [4]
which provided for organization of the Saskatchewan
territory.   In a more direct manner [5] they attempted to
secure the co-operation of the Hudson's Bay Company.
The Imperial authorities refused [6] to interfere with territory
under the company's jurisdiction, and the Hudson's Bay
company again made abundantly clear [7] the cause of their
resistance.   An appeal was made to the authorities,[8] but

[1] *Journals of the Legislative Assembly of Canada*, 1861, p. 77.
[2] " Arrangements were made within the last four years for postal
service with Red River, but the want of territorial rights at Red River
and along the greater part of the route defeated the plans of the Canadian
Government and after a very considerable outlay the line had to be
abandoned."   The Provincial Secretary to the Governor of the Hudson's
Bay Company, April 15, 1862. *Sessional Papers, Canada,* 1862, vol. 22,
No. 29, p. 1.
[3] *Ibid.*, No. 31, p. 12.
[4] Imperial Act 22 and 23 Vic. c. 26.
[5] " I am commanded by His Excellency the Governor-General to state
that the Canadian Government have decided at once to establish steam
and stage communication to the extreme limit of the territory under their
government and are ready to unite with the Hudson's Bay Company in a
mail service and post route to British Columbia."   Provincial Secretary
to Governor of Hudson's Bay Company, April 15, 1862. *Sessional Papers,*
op. cit., No. 29, p. 2.
[6] The Act " contained an enactment in the concluding section that it
should not be applicable to territories heretofore granted to the Hudson's
Bay Company."   The Colonial Secretary to the Governor-General, April
16, 1862 (*ibid.*, No. 31, p. 2).
[7] " The Red River and Saskatchewan valleys, though not in themselves
fur-bearing districts, are the sources from whence the main supplies of
winter food are procured for the northern posts, from the produce of
the buffalo hunts. A chain of settlements through these valleys would
not only deprive the company of the above vital resource, but would
indirectly in many other ways so interfere with their northern trade as
to render it no longer worth while prosecuting on an extended scale."
Governor of Hudson's Bay Company to Provincial Secretary, April 16,
1862 (*ibid.*, No. 29, p. 3).
[8] *Ibid.*, No 31, p. 2.

in Great Britain largely because of activities [1] of the company it was unsuccessful.[2] Finally, an Act [3] was passed in the same year incorporating the North-West Navigation and Railway Company with power to establish communications " within the Northern and Western limits of Canada," and to " unite with any company formed or to be formed in England for the purposes aforesaid."

The primary issue was the claim of the Hudson's Bay Company to the North-West territory which was in substance a question of fur trade or settlement. This was as evident in later as it was in earlier developments. In 1861 Mr. E. W. Watkin was dispatched [4] by the Grand Trunk Railway directorate to retrieve that company from the difficulties of the period. The appointment was of significance, since he was favourable [5] to the extension of railway communication to the Pacific, and since British authorities were sympathetically cognizant [6] of his view-

[1] ". . . Between Fort William and the heights of land, the natural difficulties of the country will make road-making a very expensive business, while the soil . . . will offer no inducement to settlers. . . . Beyond Red River to the base of the Rocky Mountains, the line will pass through a vast desert, in some places without wood and water, exposed to the incursions of roving bands of Indians and entirely destitute of any means of subsistence for emigrants. . . . With regard to a telegraphic communication it is scarcely necessary to point at the prairie fires, the depredation of natives and the general chapter of accidents as presenting almost insurmountable obstacles. . . . I have thought it my duty thus slightly to sketch the difficulties. . . . The Governor at Red River Colony has instructions to make grants of land to settlers on easy conditions, without any restrictions as to the company's right of exclusive trade." The Governor of the Hudson's Bay Company to the Colonial Secretary, May 19, 1862 (*ibid.*, pp. 3–4).
[2] " Although it is not in the power of Her Majesty's Government to grant assistance from imperialistic funds for carrying out the object which the Canadian Government has in view, there would be every desire on their part to co-operate in any well-devised scheme. . . . I would direct your Lordship's attention to the facilities for the acquisition of land which the Hudson's Bay Company announce." The Colonial Secretary to the Governor-General, June 3, 1862 (*ibid.*, p. 3).
[3] 25 Vic. c. 67.
[4] Watkin, Sir E. W., Bart., M.P., *Canada and the States, Recollections,* 1851–1886, p. 11.
[5] . . . "To work it (the Grand Trunk Railway) so as to produce a great success in a few years can only in my opinion be done in one way. . . . That way . . . lies through the extension of railway communication to the Pacific " (*ibid.*, p. 14).
[6] " He (the Duke of Newcastle) authorized me to say, in Canada, that the Colonial office would pay part of the cost of surveys ; that these works must be carried out in the greatest interests of the nation and that he would give his cordial help " (*ibid.*, p. 65).

point, and of its difficulties.[1] With further encouragement,[2] he was in a position in the following year to submit
a proposal [3] for the construction of a telegraph line and a
common highway between Canada and the Pacific, to
Canadian delegates who sought Imperial support for the
Intercolonial railway and who had only hoped to impress [4]
upon the authorities the urgency of the Pacific project.
But although negotiations [5] were conducted with every

[1] The Duke of Newcastle had strenuously endeavoured to make some
arrangements with the Hudson's Bay Company but with no success (see
Begg, A., op. cit., pp. 331–2).

[2] Ibid., p. 81.

[3] The proposal was to the effect " that upon a Governmental guarantee
of interest at the rate of 4 per cent. a sum of five hundred thousand
pounds would be immediately raised for the purpose of constructing
at once a telegraph line and a common highway for carrying the mails
and the traffic between Canada and the Pacific." Memorandum by
Honourables Messrs. Sicotte and Howland to His Grace the Duke of
Newcastle, December 11, 1862. Sessional Papers, Can. 1863, No. 14.

[4] Ibid.

[5] The delegates replied to the proposal that subject to minor provisions
they were " of opinion that the Canadian Government will agree to give
a guarantee of interest at the rate of 4 per cent. upon one-third of the
sum expended, provided the whole sum does not exceed five hundred
thousand pounds, and provided also that the same guarantee of interest
will be secured upon the other two-thirds of the expenditure by Imperial
or Columbia contributions " (Watkin, E. W., to Hon. L. V. Sicotte and
W. P. Howland. December 17, 1862, ibid.). In anticipation of difficulty
with the Imperial Government, which might insist that British Columbia
should bear a larger portion of the responsibility, they refused to guarantee
a higher rate of interest as Mr. Watkin suggested but proposed guarantee
of interest even on one-half the capital (Messrs. Sicotte and Howland
to Mr. Watkin, December 20, 1862, ibid.). According to expectation
the Imperial authorities decided they could not " apply to Parliament
to sanction any share in the proposed subsidy " and " that without a
submarine Transatlantic telegraph the proposed line in America will be
of comparatively small value to the Imperial Government " and finally
" the Duke of Newcastle is prepared to recommend that British Columbia
and Vancouver Island shall pay the sum of £10,000 per annum as their
share of £20,000 (being at the rate of £4 per cent on a capital of £500,000).
Letter from the Duke of Newcastle to Mr. E. W. Watkin, March 5, 1863.
(Watkin, E. W., op. cit., p. 114.) As an alternative it was then suggested
" that the Imperial Government should agree to give a grant of land of
some reasonable extent, also that portion of the territory lying between
the Hudson's Bay Territory and British Columbia which belongs to the
Crown, provided a telegraphic and road communication passes through
any portion of that territory (Mr. E. W. Watkin to the Duke of Newcastle,
March 27, 1863, ibid., p. 112) and to this the Duke of Newcastle agreed
(ibid., p. 111). Accordingly the heads of proposals were submitted by
Mr. Watkin to the Duke of Newcastle, April 28, 1863 (Sessional Papers,
Canada, 1863, No. 31), and with minor objections were accepted on
May 1, 1863 (ibid.). An important clause of the proposals stated, " . . .
and the Hudson's Bay Company shall . . . within the territories belonging
to them grant to the company such land . . . and all such rights as
may be required." In accordance with the attitude of the Hudson's Bay

hope of success, insistence of the Canadian Government upon facilities for settlement made accomplishment of the scheme impossible.

Persistence of the Canadian authorities, encouraged by the British Government and by the continued appeals [1]

Company the Governor on being approached expressed a violent opinion on the matter. "What! sequester our very tap root. Take away the fertile lands where our buffaloes feed! Let in all kinds of people to squat and settle and frighten away the fur-bearing animals they don't kill and hunt. Impossible!" (Watkin, E. W., op. cit., p. 120). Nothing daunted, they bought out the Hudson Bay interests hostile to the project on July 3, 1863 (*ibid.*, pp. 120–7). Mr. Watkin was immediately (July 6, 1863,) dispatched by the new interests to report on "the possibility of commencing operations for an electric telegraph " (*ibid.*, p. 153). Agreements were drawn up looking toward the establishment of telegraphic communication between the Atlantic and Pacific through arrangements with the Montreal Telegraph Company and the United States telegraph companies and the construction of a line from Pembina to Fort Gary, to Jasper House and Fort Langley (for copies, see *ibid.*, pp. 174–8), and some of the material was ordered (*ibid.*, p. 178). Such ardour was not supported by the Hudson's Bay Company (*ibid.*, p. 188). Canadian authorities were less enthusiastic (*ibid.*, p. 173), and on February 18, 1864, they definitely pointed out that they would not be "likely to receive benefits corresponding to the cost of constructing a line of telegraph " . . . "unless at the same time the fertile valleys and plains of the Great North-West are made accessible to Canadian settlers and to European emigrants . . . unless ' The Atlantic and Pacific Transit and Telegraph Company ' are prepared to undertake the construction of a road, *pari passu*, with the telegraph line, the committee cannot . . . recommend acceptance of the heads of proposal." *Sessional Papers*, Can. 1864, No. 62, p. 2.

[1] See petition of Malcolm McLeod, April 24, 1862. Copy of all petitions that have been addressed to Her Majesty or to Her Majesty's Government from the inhabitants of the Red River district or other settlements or districts within the boundaries of British territories in North America from 1860 up to the present time (*Papers relating to the Hudson's Bay Company*, 1842–70, pp. 3–4). Of more significance was the *Memorial of the People of Red River Settlement* January 21, 1863, and the resolutions adopted January 22, 1863. The advantages and facility of establishing communication between the Red River and Lake Superior were especially stressed, and to ensure further activities Mr. Sandford Fleming was asked to represent their interests in Canada and England. Finally the *Memorial* was accompanied by remarks of Mr. Fleming pertaining to the whole question. He elaborated upon the agricultural possibilities of the country, stressed the dangers of American expansion and emphasized the advantages of the route by Lake Superior.

	Rail	No. of Miles Water	Stage	Total
Toronto to Fort Gary by Detroit, Chicago, St. Paul .	810	688	290	1,788
Toronto to Fort Gary by Detroit, Milwaukee, St. Paul	618	788	290	1,696
Toronto to Nipigon Harbour and by proposed route to Fort Gary	95	723	232	1,050
In favour of proposed route over shorter American route .	523	65	58	646

of Red River Settlement, eventually met with success. The position of the Hudson's Bay Company was very much weakened with the reorganization engineered by Mr. Watkin which occasioned the disappearance of the old interests in 1863. Sir Edmund Head, formerly Governor of Canada and head of the newly organized company, was favourably inclined toward a complete sale of the company's territory to the Crown and started negotiations [1] with that end in view. This step was characteristic of the general attitude [2] of new interests in the company which greatly increased the growing uneasiness [3] of the settlers

Such an advantage was possible with the construction of only 232 miles of common stage road, one dam and a small set of wooden locks. He proposed the construction of a telegraph along the line of a future railway. This was followed by a substantial road built as settlement warranted and estimated to reach Fraser River in thirteen years. This in turn was supplanted by a railroad when the population had increased sufficiently. The scheme was made more complete with the suggestion as to the construction of colonization and concession roads for the purpose of opening up the country. Such a proposal it was argued would avoid a heavy initial expenditure which would be necessary with the immediate construction of a railroad. *Sessional Papers*, Can. 1863, No. 83.

[1] On November 11, 1863, the following proposals were suggested : (1) An equal division of the portion of the territory fit for settlement between the company and the Crown with inclusion of specified tracts in the share of the former. The company to construct the road and the telegraph. (2, 3 and 4) The Crown to purchase such of the company's premises as should be wanted for military use and to pay to the company a net third of all future revenue from gold and silver. To these suggestions the Duke of Newcastle offered counter-proposals dated March 11 and April 5, 1864 : (1) The company to surrender to the Crown their territorial rights. (2) To receive one shilling for every acre sold by the Crown but limited to £150,000 in all, and to fifty years in duration whether or not the receipts attained that amount. (3) To receive one-fourth of any gold revenue but limited to £100,000 of adjacent land for every lineal mile constructed of road and telegraph to British Columbia. The company agreed March 14 and April 13 in the main, but asked that the amount of the payments within fifty years be either not limited or else placed at £1,000,000 and that they should be granted 5,000 acres of wild land for every 50,000 acres sold by the Crown. On December 7, 1864, they suggested an alternative of £1,000,000. *Journals of Legislative Assembly*, 1865, pp. 49–52.

[2] The company, still favourable to a policy of promoting settlement, continued its exertions in favour of a telegraph by dispatching in 1864 Dr. Rae and Mr. Schwieger on a journey through the North-West territory to ascertain the practicability of a route (Hargrave, J. J., *Red River*, pp. 331–2).

[3] In 1859 the *Nor'-Wester*, the first newspaper, was established and it assumed an important place in the campaign against the company (*ibid.*, p. 145). A climax came in 1863 with the forcible release from prison of the Rev. Mr. Corbett, who had been sentenced under the company's jurisdiction (*ibid.*, pp. 284–8). " The position of those in authority is so disagreeable I have had great difficulty in persuading the magistrates

and lost to it the interest and affection of the wintering partners[1] who were more directly affected by a loss of the fur trade.

The aggressiveness of Canada continued.[2] Further negotiations[3] with the Imperial Government led to the visit of Hon. George Brown in 1864, and settlement of the North-West territories was a feature[4] included in the programme of the Confederation delegates in the following year. Evidences[5] of American Imperialism, as shown particularly in the offer of Anglo-American capitalists[6] to

to continue to act "(A. G. Dallas to E. W. Watkin, August 17, 1863. Watkin, E. W., op. cit., p. 249).

[1] The wintering partners conducted the fur trade of the company and a deed poll or agreement was made, as to the profits, with the shareholders in England. News of the reorganization of the company caused considerable alarm (Hargrave, J. J., op. cit., pp. 297-8. Watkin, E. W., op. cit., p. 145, also pp. 191-2). A suggested rearrangement of the deed poll (*ibid.*, pp. 155-63) was wisely abandoned (Bryce, G., op. cit., p. 452. See *Sessional Papers*, 1867-8, No. 19, pp. 6-11).

[2] " I have considered it advisable to open a correspondence with the Imperial Government with a view to arrive at a precise definition of the geographical boundaries of Canada. . . . Such a definition of boundary is a desirable preliminary to further proceedings " (Speech from the Throne, February 19, 1864. *Journals of Legislative Assembly*, 1864, pp. 2-3).

[3] In reply to the statement of the Canadian authorities declining to accept the heads of proposals suggested by Mr. E. W. Watkin the Imperial authorities, July 1, 1864, asked that a duly authorized person should be sent over from Canada to negotiate " with a view of accepting the government of any portion of the territory " (*Journals of the Legislative Assembly*, 1865, vol. 25, pp. 45-6). To this it was stated, November 11, 1864, that although they urged the settlement of the territory " the Committee are of the opinion that the negotiations will be advantageously left in the hands of the Imperial Government." Nevertheless, Mr. Brown left for England on November 16 (*ibid.*, pp. 47-8). Mr. Brown regarded the company's demands for the purchase of their rights as " utterly untenable " and particularly since the reorganization of 1863 had meant an increase in capitalization from £1,000,000 to £1,500,000 (*ibid.*, pp. 52-3).

[4] *Ibid.*, p. 8. The Imperial Government agreed to guarantee a loan to purchase all the territory east of the Rocky Mountains and north of the Canadian lines from the company to be transferred to Canada (*ibid.*, p. 12).

[5] A Bill " for the admission of the states of Nova Scotia, New Brunswick, Canada East and Canada West and for the organization of the territories of Selkirk, Saskatchewan and Columbia," July 2, 1866, 39th Congress, 1st Session H. R. 754, occasioned considerable alarm. See also letter from Governor of Hudson's Bay Company to Colonial Secretary, July 17, 1866. *Sessional Papers*, 1867-8, No. 19, pp. 14-15.

[6] A request from Mr. McEwen, January 18, 1866, to the company as to possible arrangements of purchase met with a favourable reply, January 24, 1866. The Imperial authorities warned the company of the existing understanding with Canada, February 20, 1866, to which the company retorted that " the possibility of losing a favourable opportunity may become a very grave one in a pecuniary point of view " (March 1, 1866). Canada asked (June 22, 1866) that the company should be restrained from

purchase the territory of the Hudson's Bay Company, proved a decided stimulus to further activity. The British North America Act included provisions [1] for the annexation of the North-West territory and the first Parliament on December 12, 1867, adopted resolutions [2] strongly advising transference of the jurisdiction and control of the region to Canada, and presented an address embodying these resolutions to the Imperial authorities.[3] Confident in the success of such enterprise, the Canadian Government proceeded [4] to construct a road from Fort William according to the suggestions of Mr. S. J. Dawson in 1859, and actually completed the first section of six miles.[5]

Attempts at colonization evident in the efforts of Canada to establish communication between Red River and Lake Superior were not favourably regarded. The appearance of the Canadian authorities [6] in 1868, for the purpose of building a road from Fort Gary to Lake of the Woods, and at the same time of providing relief to the Red River settlers, whose harvests had been destroyed by grass-hoppers, by paying for the construction with provisions, was the occasion of a protest [7] from the company.

selling any of the territory and intimated that action would be taken as soon as the union was formed (*Sessional Papers, ibid.*, pp. 3–5, 11–13). It ought to be added that the Canadian delegation, February 8, 1869, stated "that the only overtures . . . which the company had received were not merely encouraged but suggested and concocted by prominent members of the company . . . with a view . . . to negotiation and the stock market " (*Sessional Papers*, 1869, No. 25, pp. 21–2).

[1] Imperial Act 30–1 Vic. c. 3, Article XI, sec. 146.
[2] *Journals House of Commons*, 1867–8, vol. I, pp. 66–7.
[3] *Ibid.*, pp. 67–8. An additional report of the Privy Council, December 28, 1867, adopting a memorandum of the Minister of Public Works which urged the necessity of immediate action was also forwarded by the Imperial authorities. *Sessional Papers*, 1869, No. 50, p. 23.
[4] On June 14, 1867, the Commissioner of Crown Lands recommended the expenditure of £55,900, which would open 120 miles of the route from Lake Superior to Red River. The recommendation was adopted on June 18, 1867. *Sessional Papers*, No. 19, pp. 20–1.
[5] Report of Superintendent of Colonization roads October 4 and December 22, 1867, *ibid.*, pp. 23–25 and supplementary return, pp. 1–2.
[6] *Sessional Papers*, 1869, No. 25, p. 12.
[7] Governor McTavish in letters to the company dated October 10 and November 11, 1868, did not express undue enthusiasm as to the arrival (*ibid.*, p. 11). As a result the company objected in that " the Committee cannot but look upon this proceeding as a most unusual and improper one. . . . This trespass will be an actual encroachment on the soil of the company " (Deputy-Governor of Hudson's Bay Company to Colonial Office, December 22, 1868. *Ibid.*, p. 10). " Their objection is not to

The Hudson's Bay Company had ample reason to protest against Canadian activity.   Sir Edmund Head anticipated [1] and questioned [2] the assumption of Canada that the company's rights vested in its charter should be submitted to the protection of " courts of competent jurisdiction." The Imperial authorities recognized the force of this contention implicitly [3] by the passing of an Act [4] arranging for transfer of the " requisite powers of government and legislation."   It was evident that cancellation could only be secured by purchase.   To this end negotiations continued. [5]   Canada anxiously [6] requested the privilege of sending delegates and upon their arrival in England after a long series of proposals [7] and counter-proposals both

the road's being made, but to its being undertaken by the Canadian Government as a matter of right " (Governor of Hudson's Bay Company to Colonial Office, February 2, 1869. *Ibid.*, p. 13).

[1] A letter was written January 15, 1868, to the Colonial Secretary prior to the receipt of the Canadian resolutions. *Journals of House of Commons*, 1867–8, pp. 368–9.

[2] This was true of the letter of January 15. 1868, but more particularly of a letter of January 25, 1868, written after the Canadian resolutions had been received. The point at issue related to the sixth resolution, " The Government and Parliament of Canada will be ready to provide that the legal rights of any corporation . . . within the same shall be respected and placed under the protection of courts of competent jurisdiction." In the earlier letter it was insisted that such inquiry should be referred to the judicial committee of the Privy Council, and the second letter protested "that before any incorporation of Rupert's Land or the North-West territory with Canada, the rights of private property vested in the company and the exact limits of such rights should be ascertained, acknowledged and efficiently protected by law" (*ibid.*, pp. 370–3).

[3] " They desire, however, to pay due regard to the interests of Her Majesty's subjects already concerned in the territory " (the Under-Secretary to the Deputy-Governor of the Hudson's Bay Company, April 23, 1868. *Ibid.*, p. 374).

[4] Rupert's Land Act, 1868, 31–2, Vic. c. 106.

[5] The Colonial Secretary to the Governor-General. *Sessional Papers*, No. 25, 1869, p. 1.

[6] See copies of telegrams. *Ibid.*, pp. 3–4.

[7] On May 13 the company proposed that they should surrender all the territory with a reservation of 6,000 acres around each post other than the Red River Settlement at 1s. per acre. That the Government should pay one-quarter of the sum received for gold and silver with a limitation of £1,000,000. That the company should have the right to select 5,000 acres of land free out of every 50,000 acres, such land to be free from taxation. To objections raised by the Imperial authorities they modified their proposals October 27, 1868. Land-tax exemption limited to twenty years. Lands purchased by the company not to be reckoned in the free grants. Free grants surveyed at the company's expense. Lands for churches, roads or schools exempted from shilling payment. In fertile belt land granted around posts reduced to 3,000 acres. In response the Imperial authorities proposed December 1, 1868:

Canada and the company agreed to accept the terms
proposed by the Imperial authorities as a solution to the
apparent deadlock. With minor adjustments,[1] these terms
were finally incorporated in a deed [2] of surrender, signed
November 19, 1869.

The continual and protracted struggle [3] of settlement

Land about posts further limited. Company received one-fourth land
receipts. Company given five lots of not less than 200 acres in each township. Tax exemption until wild lands surveyed and marked. Upon
payment to company of £1,000,000 for gold and silver right of company
to share of land receipts ceased. On January 15, 1869, the company
defended its proposals but added, " if the Canadian Government were
prepared to complete the purchase of the territory at once . . . it would
conduce to a more satisfactory result." This letter was submitted to the
Canadian delegates and in a reply of February 8, 1869, after a great deal
of argument, it was stated that the Canadian Government would not
pay more than £106,431, a sum arrived at on the basis adopted in the
reorganization of the company. The company regarded this (February 26,
1869) as an impossible suggestion and advised the creation of a crown
colony and relied upon the co-operation of the Government " in protecting
the settlement from any trespass or interference on the part of Canada."
Recognizing the deadlock the Imperial authorities suggested the following
proposals on March 9, 1869. The company to surrender all rights on the
payment of £300,000 by the Government of Canada. The land in the
vicinity of posts not to exceed 50,000 acres. Free grants of land made
not in excess of one-twentieth of land set out. *Sessional Papers*, 1869,
No. 25, pp. 5-33.
  [1] Protests were embodied in a series of resolutions adopted by the
company and transmitted to the delegates on March 12, 1869. The
delegates refused to consider these protests, March 13, 1869. The company
largely reasserted its position on March 16, 1869, and evidences of a
better feeling characterized the reply of the delegates, March 18, 1869.
A word from the Imperial authorities, March 9, 1869, was formally and
sympathetically acknowledged by the Canadian authorities, March 27.
In minor adjustments memoranda, dated March 22 and March 29, were
adopted by the Canadian delegates and by the company (*ibid.*, pp. 33-9).
Resolutions were adopted by the Senate and the House of Commons
of Canada accepting the arrangements of the delegates (*Journals House
of Commons*, 1869, pp. 150-2) and embodied in an address to the throne
(*ibid.*, pp. 153-5). An Act " for the temporary government of Rupert's
Land and the North-Western Territory when united with Canada " 32
and 33 Vic. c. 3, 1869, was assented to June 22, 1869.
  [2] " The Canadian Government shall pay to the company the sum of
£300,000 sterling when Rupert's Land is transferred to the Dominion of
Canada. The company to retain all the posts or stations now actually
possessed and occupied by them, . . . may at any time within fifty years
after . . . acceptance of the said surrender claim in any township or
district within the fertile belt in which land is set out for settlements
grants of land not exceeding one-twentieth part of the land so set out."
Statutes of Canada, 1872, pp. lxxvii.-lxxxiii.
  [3] The petitions of the Red River settlement were supplemented by
appeals from settlements beyond the jurisdiction of the Council of Assiniboia. A memorial of the inhabitants of Portage la Prairie settlement
of June 1, 1867, urged the necessity of British law and protection and
on June 10, 1867, resolutions were adopted asking that the case should be
presented to the Imperial authorities and to the Canadian authorities.

against the fur trade had apparently ended. Actually it became more violent. Negotiations had been conducted and closed by London officers of the company with slight regard to wishes of the wintering partners, who were directly dependent upon profits of the fur trade. They had been made suspicious through reorganization of the company in 1863, and became increasingly alert [1] to dangers of the policy of London officials. This dissatisfaction of the wintering partners accompanied, if it did not encourage, [2] the unrest of the half-breeds who were likewise dependent for their livelihood on the fur trade, and who were equally alert to possibilities of its destruction. Finally the sale of land and the change of government, executed without reference to their interests by the company with which they had struggled for every concession, appeared to leave no alternative but a protest determined even to the point of violence.

On July 10, 1869, Col. J. S. Dennis was dispatched [3] by the Minister of Public Works for Canada, to survey the territory preparatory to transfer. Trouble with the half-breeds was anticipated, [4] but surveys were prosecuted

Copy of all petitions that have been addressed to Her Majesty's Government from the Inhabitants of the Red River district or other settlements, etc. *Papers relating to the Hudson's Bay Company*, 1842-70, pp. 8-10. A letter was addressed to the Canadian Government, January 17, 1868, asking for admission to the Dominion and threatening to annex to the United States if refused (*ibid.*, p. 10). These petitions were consistent with the earlier petitions of the Red River Settlement and with the "memorial of the undersigned merchants, traders, etc., loyal inhabitants of that part of Rupert's Land the Red River Settlement" January 17, 1867, asking to be included in the Canadian confederation and stating the advantages of a route from Lake Superior to British Columbia (*ibid.*, pp. 5-6).

[1] "This change (1863) has been made without our consent on the supposition that our interests would be unaffected. Such a supposition is . . . untenable. The wintering partners represent the fur trade . . ." (Letter from Chief Factor, James Anderson, to Mr. D. A. Smith, Willson, Beckles, *The Life of Lord Strathcona and Mount Royal*, p. 134). "We must be prepared not to receive very much sympathy from the new shareholders or the new Board " (Mr. D. A. Smith to Mr. Barnston. *Ibid.*):

[2] The influence of the company has been subject to controversy. The Canadian authorities accused the company of negligence if not complicity. Report of a Committee of the Privy Council Canada, December 16, 1869. *Sessional Papers*, 1870, No. 12, p. 142. Beckles Willson, a partisan of the company, admits and excuses their negligent attitude, Willson, Beckles, op cit., p. viii; and p. 167.

[3] *Sessional Papers, ibid.*, No. 12, N p. 1.

[4] " In the meantime the French half-breeds . . . (say 3,000 souls) are

until they were ordered to stop [1] by a party under Louis
Riel on October 11. As a further preparatory step, Hon.
Wm. McDougall, was appointed [2] Lieutenant-Governor
of the North-west Territories on September 29, 1869,
with instructions [3] to report on the whole situation, and to
take immediate steps " for the extension of the telegraph
system from the territory to Pembina and for its connexion
at that place with the system of the American Telegraph
Company." He was forbidden to proceed to Fort Gary [4]
and on November 2, 1869, was escorted [5] beyond the
boundary to the American side.

Faced with opposition Canada immediately notified [6]
the Imperial authorities, and placed upon them the responsibility [7] of securing order. Although the Imperial
authorities declined [8] to accept these views and the argument continued, the Canadian Government took active
measures to meet the situation. Mr. D. A. Smith was
dispatched as a special commissioner [9] with sufficiently
elastic instructions [10] to handle the questions involved,
as were also, though with less authority,[11] Mr. Thibault

likely to prove a turbulent element " (J. S. Dennis to Minister of Public
Works, August 21, 1869, *ibid.*, pp. 5–6). " I have again to remark the
uneasy feeling which exists in the half-breeds and Indian element "
(August 21, 1869. *Ibid.*, p. 7).
  [1] Memorandum of facts and circumstances connected with the active
opposition by the French half-breeds in this settlement to the prosecution
of the government surveys (J. S. Dennis, October 11, 1869. *Ibid.*, No. 12a,
p. 7).
  [2] *Ibid.*, pp. 4–5.   [3] *Ibid.*, pp. 2–3.
  [4] " Le Comité National des Métis de la Rivière Rouge intime à Monsieur
Wm. McDougall l'ordre de ne pas entrer sur le territoire du Nord Ouest
sans une permission spéciale de ce Comité. Par ordre du Président John
Bruce, Louis Riel, Secrétaire " (October 21, 1869). *Ibid.*, p. 11.
  [5] *Ibid.*, p. 15.
  [6] *Ibid.*, No. 12a, p. 138.
  [7] " Canada cannot accept transfer unless quiet possession will be given "
(Telegram Governor-General to Colonial Secretary, November 26, 1869.
Ibid., p. 137).
  [8] " It has never been hinted that the company is to be bound to hand
over its territory in a state of tranquillity " (The Colonial Secretary to
the Governor-General, November 30, 1869. *Ibid.*, p. 140). To this
Canada replied, " The obvious reason why no express stipulation to that
effect was made was, that it was assumed that the company had both
the right and the power to hand over the territory " (Report of a Committee of the Honourable the Privy Council, December 16, 1869. *Ibid.*,
p. 142).
  [9] *Ibid.*, p. 49.
  [10] Secretary of State to Mr. D. A. Smith, December 10, 1869. *Ibid.*, p. 48.
  [11] Secretary of State to Mr. Thibault, December 4, 1869. *Ibid.*, pp. 45–6.

E

and Colonel de Salabery. At a late date [1] Bishop Taché was added to the list. The success of these measures was evident in the growth of a feeling of unity [2] in the settlement, and in the dispatch on March 22, 1870, of delegates by Red River Settlers to Ottawa to present their demands. [3] The Canadian Government in response passed the Manitoba Act, [4] which was accepted by the settlement, and which brought difficulties to an end. After a long controversy, payment [5] was made to the Hudson's Bay Company, and with later adjustments [6] the Province of Manitoba was formally admitted to the Dominion of Canada.

As a precaution against further trouble, troops were dispatched by the Canadian Government [7] with Imperial sanction. [8] Construction of the road from Fort William to Fort Gary, which Canada had persistently continued, [9]

[1] Secretary of State to the Very Reverend the Bishop of St. Boniface, February 16, 1870. *Ibid.*, p. 128.

[2] Report of Very Rev. J. B. Thibault, March 17, 1870. *Sessional Papers, ibid.*, No. 12*xx*, pp. 1-3 ; also Report of Donald A. Smith, *ibid.*, No. 12*x*, pp. 1-10, and appendix, pp. 10-13.

[3] These demands were in part—the establishment of a province, two representatives in the Senate and four in the House of Commons, no liability for public debt of Canada before entry, payment of £80,000 annually by Dominion to Province, properties, rights and privileges respected, no interference of rights due to Hudson's Bay Company bargain, steam communication between Lake Superior and Fort Gary guaranteed within five years, Public works undertaken at expense of Dominion, etc. *Correspondence relative to the Recent Disturbance in the Red River Settlement,* 1870, pp. 130-1.

[4] 33 Vic. 3 assented to, May 12, 1870.

[5] Receipt was finally acknowledged, May 11, 1870. *Correspondence relative to recent disturbances,* etc., p. 214.

[6] Orders in Council Rupert's Land and the North-west Territory, June 23, 1870. *Statutes of Canada,* 1872, pp. lxxiii.-lxxxiii.

[7] *Correspondence relative to recent disturbances, etc.,* p. 162.

[8] The Imperial authorities sanctioned the advance of troops on conditions—

  1. Canadian authorization to pay £300,000 to Hudson's Bay Company at once.

  2. Imperial authorities to pay expense of British troops only not exceeding 250 and Canadian Government the rest at least 500 trained men.

  3. Canadian Government to accept the decision of Imperial authorities on all disputed points of the Settler's Bill of Rights.

  4. Military arrangements to be to the satisfaction of Imperial military authorities.

Telegram from Colonial Secretary to Governor-General, April 23, 1870. *Ibid.*, p. 177.

[9] Previous to suspending operations on the Fort Gary section of the road because of the disturbances twenty-nine miles had been opened for

received additional stimulus [1] with the transport of the expedition. The arrival of the troops at Fort Gary, and the possibilities of the road,[2] from a commercial and military standpoint, made the appearance [3] of Lieutenant-Governor Archibald, on September 2, 1870, a significant omen in the establishment of peace and order at Red River Settlement, and in the disappearance of the rule of the Hudson's Bay Company, and the régime of the fur trade.

The entrance of the province of Manitoba into the Dominion of Canada, marked another victory of settlement over fur trade. The settlement [4] which grew up, dominated in character and in location by demands of the fur trade, and which increased under the favourable conditions peculiar to the Red River Territory, after a long struggle, broke the bonds of monopoly of the trade which had given it birth. The establishment of posts at points geographically and technically strategic for the handling of furs and supplies, as shown in the growth of Fort Alexander, of Fort William (as well as in their subsequent decline with the amalgamation of the companies and the abandoning of the Lake Superior route), and of Fort Gary, was a tribute to the

carriage travel and sixteen miles had been surveyed in advance. *Sessional Papers*, 1870, No. 12, pp. 18–30. On the Lake Superior section a report of Mr. S. J. Dawson, dated May 1, 1869, was submitted recommending the construction of a road from Lake Superior to the navigable waters of the Summit region, forty miles ; the improvement of the lake region from the terminus of the road to the north-west angle of the Lake of the Woods, 311 miles ; and the construction of another road from the north-west angle to Fort Gary, ninety miles, at an estimated cost of $247,700. Later the roads would be supplanted by railroads and the lake region improved by canal locks at an estimated cost of $5,800,000 (*ibid.*, pp. 32–55). On June 9, 1869, the author of the report was directed to start work on the forty miles of road proposed (*ibid.*, p. 31). On March 26, 1870, the length of road practicable to horses and waggons was twenty-five miles, and to oxen and carts, thirty-five miles (*ibid.*, p. 72). The interest of private enterprise might also be noted in the extension of the time limit to 1870 for the commencement of operations for the North-west Navigation and Railway Company (31 Vic. c. 87).

[1] The work of the soldiers was of inestimable value in constructing the road. See Dawson, S. J., Report on the Red River Expedition of 1870. *Sessional Papers*, 1871, No. 47, pp. 1–31, especially p. 16, also Wolseley, Field-Marshal Viscount, *The Story of a Soldier's Life*, vol. II, p. 189.

[2] The route was opened for the conveyance of emigrants in 1871, although about 400 settlers had passed over it prior to that date. *Sessional Papers*, 1875, No. 37, p. 11.

[3] *Sessional Papers*, 1871, No. 20, p. 9.

[4] Population of Manitoba, 11,960. Half-breeds, 9,840. *Sessional Papers*, No. 20, 1871, p. 92.

influence of geographic features, as was also the growth of trade [1] between the Red River Settlement, and the United States by the Red River. The physical characteristics which conditioned the growth of trade with America, and which gave to the development of the United States a more threatening character were responsible simultaneously for the development of interest [2] on the part of Canada and of Great Britain and for the consequent activities which led to the purchase of the North-west territories by Canada. Politically the North-west Territories were united to Canada but geographically there remained a discrepancy to measure the seriousness of which requires a study of the position of Eastern Canada.

C. ON THE ST. LAWRENCE

Acceptance of the terms of union by Eastern Canada implied a pronounced development of civilization in the St. Lawrence drainage basin. It remains to examine more closely the character of that development in order to understand the difficulties involved in fulfilment of the terms. Discoveries of Columbus, in search of a short cut to the Orient, had turned the attention of Europe westward. As a result [3] Cabot sailing from England reached the northeast coast of the North American continent in 1496. The discovery of the Newfoundland fisheries [4] on this voyage, and the profitableness [5] of this trade led to a race of fisher-

[1] A very rough estimate from January 1 to November 1870, values the imports into the North-west territories via Pembina from Canada and England at over $100,000 and from the United States at over $250,000. *Ibid.*, p. 44.

[2] " We intend to be liberal both in money and land, as it is of importance to settle that country at once " (Sir John A. MacDonald to Sir John Rose, April 17, 1872, Pope, J., *Memoirs of the Right Honourable Sir John Alexander MacDonald*, vol. II, p. 189).

[3] See a copy of Letters Patent granted to the Cabots by Henry VII (R. O. Pat. 4 Ed. VI, p. 6) 1496. Bland, Brown and Tawney, *English Economic History*, pp. 400–2.

[4] " They affirm that the sea is full of fish that can be taken not only with nets but with fishing baskets . . . and this . . . is told by the Messer Joanne. And . . . his partners say they can bring so many fish that this kingdom will have no more business with Islanda and that from that country there will be a very great trade in fish " (Raimondo di Soncino to the Duke of Milan, December 18, 1497, cited in Weise, A. J., *The Discoveries of North America to the year* 1525, p. 193).

[5] Prowse, D. W., *A History of Newfoundland from the English Colonial and Foreign Records*, p. 19 (footnote).

men of various nationalities [1] to the new field. Effective
prosecution of the fishing trade necessitated arrangements
and accommodation [2] on the shore for winter residents,
as well as for the conduct of operations characteristic of
dry fishing. [3] Need for suitable harbours for these purposes
brought about the establishment of posts at St. John's,
and at other points along the coast of Newfoundland.
Beginnings of settlement on the shore stimulated the
growth of trade with the Indians, [4] and these settlements
served as bases for extension of fishing and discovery
of new territory. The incentive supplied by the scramble [5]
for territory, and for the North-west passage, resulted in
the success of Cartier in distinguishing the straits of Belle
Isle from the maze of inlets characteristic of the eastern
Newfoundland coast, in discovering [6] the mouth of the
St. Lawrence, and in penetrating [7] the interior as far as
Hochelaga (Montreal).

Biscayan whaling expeditions [8] and fur traders followed
the route opened by this voyage, and began to found a
settlement at Tadousac, [9] a point strategically located
at the mouth of the Saguenay River on the St. Lawrence.
Movement toward the interior continued slowly, [10] partly

[1] *Ibid.*, pp. 3–23, 43 ; also Biggar, H. P., *The Early Trading Companies
of New France*, pp. 18–20.
[2] " From a very early period a few crews were left behind every winter
to cut timber for building cook-rooms, stages, trainvats, wharves " (Prowse,
D. W. *Ibid.*, p. 159).
[3] Denys, N., *Description and Natural History of the Coasts of North
America* (Champlain Society), pp. 268–77, 331–6.
[4] A very good discussion is given in Biggar, H. P., op. cit., pp. 28–32.
" Notices of this fur trade are found scattered through the records of
almost the whole of the sixteenth century " (*ibid.*, p. 29).
[5] Stephen Gomez was dispatched from Spain in 1524. Prowse, D. W.,
op. cit., p. 43. Robert Thorne was sent trom England in 1527 (*ibid.*, pp.
38–9), and Master Hore in 1536 (*ibid.*, pp. 41–2).
[6] In the first voyage (1534) Cartier missed the mouth of the St. Lawrence
river. Michelant, H. and Rame, A., *Relation Originale du voyage de
Jacques Cartier au Canada en* 1534. Several explorers had been equally
unfortunate previous to his visit. See Biggar, H. P., op. cit., pp. 1–5.
[7] D'Avezac, *Bref récit et succinte narration de la navigation faite en
MDXXXV et MDXXXVI par le Capitaine Jacques Cartier aux îles de
Canada Hochelaga, Saugenay et autres*, p. 22.
[8] Prowse, D. W., op. cit., pp. 47–9.
[9] Biggar, H. P., op. cit., pp. 27, 29.
[10] Cartier in the second voyage kidnapped several of the Indian chiefs.
D'Avezac, op. cit., pp. 40–44. His reception on his third voyage in 1541
under Monsieur Roberval's direction was distinctly hostile. Hakluyt,
R., *Principall Navigations*, vol. III, pp. 235–6. This enmity toward the

because of climatic difficulties evident in the unsuccessful attempt [1] at colonization of M. de Roberval. Although demands of the fur trade led to the establishment of settlement for the handling of supplies and furs, the navigability of the St. Lawrence, the proximity to such bases of supply as Newfoundland and Europe, and the impossible coast-line of the upper St. Lawrence largely militated against the success of colonization schemes. [2] On the other hand, continued activity in the fur trade stimulated competition [3] and intensified nationalistic jealousy, [4] making necessary further attempts to establish settlements and to regulate the trade. Along the exposed coast-line of the outlying regions, competition (incidental to the wealth of fisheries and furs) between commercial and national interests made settlement unusually difficult. [5]

French continued and proved to be a serious obstacle. Biggar, H. P., p. 32.

[1] Lescarbot, Marc, *The History of New France* (Champlain Society), vol. II, p. 181.

[2] Marquis de la Roche under French authority given in 1578 (Rame, A., op. cit., pp. 5–10) set sail with three hundred men in 1584, but the voyage met with disaster in shipwreck. Hakluyt, R., op. cit., p. 26. Another attempt was made by the same gentleman under authority given in 1598 (Lescarbot, Marc, op. cit., pp. 196–201) to colonize Sable Island which also ended disastrously (*ibid.*, vol. I, pp. 44–5). In 1599 Pierre Chauvin and François Grave, under a trading monopoly of ten years in which they agreed to take out fifty colonists a year, made a voyage to Tadousac and left sixteen men. Laverdiere, C. H., *Œuvres de Champlain*, Tome III, p. 43 (according to the copy in the Toronto Public Library Tome V is bound with Tome III. This reference would be Tome V, p. 43). The monopoly, due to the protests of the French merchants, was revoked in 1602 (Rame, A., op. cit., p. 12 ff.) with no tangible colonization results. Arrangements were then made with various merchants from Rouen and St. Malo for colonization (*ibid.*, pp. 15–21 ff.). Pont Gravé and Champlain in 1603 explored the St. Lawrence (Laverdiere, C. H., op. cit., ch. VI), also the Gaspe peninsula and Acadia, to which regions under a monopoly granted to Sieur de Monts and other traders (Lescarbot, Marc, op. cit., pp. 211–16, 221–3) a colony was sent in 1604. *ibid.*, pp. 227–40. Settlement was established on the inhospitable St. Croix Island on the Bay of Fundy (*ibid.*, pp. 240–2) and removed across the Bay to Port Royal in 1605 (*ibid.*, p. 280). The monopoly, subject to inroads from other merchants (Biggar, H. P., op. cit., pp. 63–4) was revoked in 1607, the support of Sieur de Monts withdrawn and the colony returned to France. Lescarbot, M., op. cit., pp. 351–3.

[3] A monopoly granted to Captain Jaunaye and Jacques Nouel was protested against by other merchants and revoked. Rame, A., *Documents inédits sur le Canada*, pp. 10–11 ; also Biggar, H. P., op. cit., p. 34.

[4] See Hakluyt, R., Discourse on Western Planting written in the year 1584. *Documentary History of the State of Maine*, vol. II, pp. 102–3.

[5] M. de Poutrincourt made a further attempt to establish a colony at Port Royal, sailing in 1610 (*ibid.*, vol. III, p. 35). A succession of Jesuit priests attempted to start a colony farther south at the mouth

It was not until the establishment of a colony at Quebec, in 1608, by Champlain,[1] at a point on the St. Lawrence particularly well-fortified and strategically located for the conduct of the fur trade,[2] that settlement gained a continuous foothold in Eastern Canada. Accessibility of the St. Lawrence made the establishment of posts in the interior largely unnecessary.[3] It also occasioned such ruinous competition,[4] that monopoly was essential, and, with the strategic location of Quebec,[5] gave this monopoly effective control. This tendency toward concentration of settlement at Quebec was not favourable to rapid growth. Its numerical weakness, its value from the standpoint of control of the interior, and its location near the mouth of the St. Lawrence made the increasing competitive pressure [6] characteristic of the outlying coast-line particularly dangerous. The capture of Quebec in 1629 and its possession until 1632 by the English were results.

of the Penobscot River but were routed by the English (*ibid.*, p. 64). This led to a further attack on Port Royal and to its destruction by fire in 1613 (*ibid.*, p. 66). The later history of this whole region is largely a narrative of attacks and counter-attacks.

[1] Laverdiere, C. H., op. cit., Tome II, ch. III, IV, p. 148 ff.

[2] The colony was established under a monopoly granted by the French Government with no stipulations as to colonists. *Ibid.*, pp. 136–7.

[3] Trade was carried on at strategic rendezvous from year to year, generally determined upon after a consultation with the tribes concerned and usually at the mouth of a river tributary to the St. Lawrence. In 1610 it was arranged at the mouth of the Richelieu. Laverdiere, C. H., op cit., Tome II, p. 210 ff. In the following years it was generally held at the mouth of the Ottawa, the Lachine Rapids. *Ibid.*, p. 242 ff., p. 290 ff.

[4] As evidence of the evils of competition, see *ibid.*, Tome II, pp. 217–18, 224, 240, 242, 245, 252–3, and particularly 283–4.

[5] The difficulties of enforcing the monopoly granted to Sieur. de Monts in 1604 which pertained to the whole mainland coast (Biggar, H. P., op. cit., p. 54) are a contrast to the efficiency of the monopoly including only the St. Lawrence valley which was given earlier to Chauvin, *ibid.*, p. 44, and later to the friends of Champlain. *Ibid.*, pp. 101–6.

[6] In 1621 Sir William Alexander was given a grant under the English Crown of the peninsula between the Gulf of St. Lawrence and the Atlantic Ocean (Slafter, E. F., *Sir William Alexander and American Colonization*, Prince Society, pp. 127–48), and after considerable difficulty (*ibid.*, pp. 197–202) established a colony in 1626 (Slafter, 1628) at Port Royal (Biggar, H. P., op. cit., p. 142; see also Murdoch, Beamish, *A History of Nova Scotia or Acadia*, vol. I, p. 66). The French under Biencourt held at least Port Lomeron near Yarmouth as well as other forts (De Saint-Père, Rameau, *Une Colonie Féodale en Amérique L'Acadie* (1604–1881), pp. 67–8). Lord Ochiltrie established a post with fifty colonists in 1629 in Cape Breton (Biggar, H. P., op. cit., p. 43). This was destroyed and replaced by the French in the same year (*ibid.*, p. 147). The French gained control in 1632 by the Treaty of St. Germain en Laye.

But eventually the expansion of the fur trade and the penetration to the interior which it involved occasioned a demand for the establishment of posts [1] farther up the river. Contact with new tribes of Indians gave new zeal to missionaries, who planted, at such rendezvous of the traders as Three Rivers [2] and Montreal,[3] chapels which served to encourage more permanent establishments for the fur trade. Further recognizing the dangers of nationalistic and commercial competition, France attempted to encourage settlement in the regulation of the fur trade as shown in the stipulations [4] with regard to colonization in the charter of the Company of New France, in 1627.

The expansion of settlement in the interior brought difficulties. Proximity of the St. Lawrence River and its southern tributaries to the sources of the Hudson River brought the fur trade of the French into competition with the trade of the Dutch and later with that of the English, conducted from Albany.[5] The fierceness of this competition was evident in the pro-Dutch aggressiveness of the Iroquois, who raided French settlements,[6] persecuted French missionaries,[7] and literally exterminated the Huron nation.[8] As a result the French were seriously

[1] Champlain sought " un lieu propre pour la situation d'une habitation " at the Lachine Rapids in 1611 (Laverdiere, C. H., Tome II, p. 242, also p. 283). In 1616 he promised the Indians to build a fort at the same place (ibid., Tome III, p. 104).

[2] The first mass was celebrated July 26, 1615 (Le Clerq, F. C., First Establishment of the Faith in New France (Shea), vol. I, p. 91). The first mission was established in 1617 (see Sulte, B., Histoire de la Ville des Trois Rivières et de ses environs, pp. 35-7). A fort was built in 1634. (Jesuit Relations and Allied Documents, vol. IV, p. 261).

[3] Sieur de Maissoneuve arrived at Montreal with about forty men under the auspices of the Society of " Notre Dame de Montreal " on October 14, 1841 (De Casson, Dollier, Histoire du Montreal, Mémoires de la Société Historique de Montreal, IV, p. 33).

[4] The monopoly granted in 1614 was revoked in 1620 as a result of the neglect of the colonies' interests and a new charter granted to De Caens, (Laverdiere, C. H., Tome III, pp. 326-7) and again because of negligence the monopoly was revoked and a new charter granted in 1627 with ample and explicit stipulations for colonization. (Collection de documents relatifs à la Histoire de la Nouvelle France, vol. I, pp. 64-71).

[5] In 1624 under the auspices of the Dutch Fort Orange was built near the site of Albany. (Documents Relative to the Colonial History of the State of New York, vol. I, p. 149). The English took possession in 1664 (ibid., vol. II, p. 250).

[6] Charlevoix, P. F. X., History and General Description of New France (Shea, vol. II, p. 96, p. 138).   [7] Ibid., p. 221 ff.

[8] See discussion, Canada and its Provinces, vol. I, pp. 68-71.

hampered and restricted [1] in the conduct of the fur trade to the territory north and north-west of the St. Lawrence. The energies of settlement were necessarily directed toward defence.[2] Harassed further with the liquor traffic [3] and other features [4] pertaining to severity of competition, slow progress [5] was inevitable. The attempt of France to increase settlement through the Company of New France failed, and in 1662 its charter was surrendered.[6]

More strenuous efforts were necessary if the country was to be held in the face of the increasing competition characteristic of the mainland,[7] and of the interior. More

[1] Trade was re-established with the Hurons and Ottawas who had been scattered to the north-west in 1656 by the Ottawa River (*ibid.*, pp. 270-2), but even then it was conducted with considerable difficulty (*ibid.*, ff.).

[2] Fort Richelieu was built at the mouth of the Sorel River in 1642 (Charlevoix, P. F. X., vol. II, p. 133). The history of the period is generally characterized by Indian raids.

[3] *Ibid.*, vol. III, pp. 53-5. See also the history of the period.

[4] In 1644 the Company of New France abandoned the fur trade to the settlers in return for an annual quit-rent of one thousand beaver skins (*Edits Ordonnances Royaux Déclarations et Arrêts du Conseil d'état du Roi concernant de Canada*, vol. I, pp. 28-9).

[5] The available statistics for the period illustrate the slight growth and the concentration of the whole population at strategic points.

1635	Marriages	Births	Deaths
Quebec . . .	3 ..	4 ..	3
Three Rivers . . .	— ..	— ..	10
1660			
Quebec . . .	14 ..	62 ..	16
Three Rivers . .	— ..	15 ..	8
Montreal . . .	10 ..	36 ..	23

—*Census of Canada*, 1870-1, vol. V, pp. 174-7.

[6] *Edits*, etc. (pp. 30-1).

[7] After the restoration of Acadia to the French in 1632 the territory was divided into three districts under separate jurisdiction. The competition between these districts was also a feature of the geographic characteristics of the region and complicated national competition. The French captured in 1633 a Plymouth trading house at Machias (*Winthrop's Journal, Original narratives of early American History*, vol. I, p. 113) and in 1635 Pentagoet on the Penobscot River (*ibid.*, p. 157). In the meantime the district under Raziliy and later Charnise had a settlement at Port de la Heve on the south coast of Nova Scotia which was transferred to Port Royal. La Tour in charge of another district was strategically located at Fort St. Jean at the mouth of the St. John River. Charnise laid siege to Fort St. Jean in 1643, but with the aid of Bostonians (*ibid.*, vol. II, p. 130) La Tour defeated him (*ibid.*, p. 136). In 1645 Charnise captured the fort. On his death in 1650 Le Borgne came into possession, but the widow of Charnise returned Fort St. Jean to La Tour. In 1654 the English captured Port Royal, Fort St. Jean and other French forts. In 1667 it was ceded again by the English to France. See Charlevoix, P. F. X., op. cit., vol. III, pp. 129-35, especially the footnotes ; also Denys, N., op. cit., pp. 97-103.

direct control of the colony [1] was assumed and measures taken to increase the size of the settlement.[2] Troops [3] were despatched, forts were constructed at strategic localities,[4] and attacks made on Iroquois and English [5] territory. The trade of the Iroquois was cut off by the establishment of strategic [6] posts. North and north-west, such aggressiveness was equally in evidence.[7] The English

---

[1] In 1664 the colony was granted to the West India Company but the first posts were filled by the French Government, (*Edits, etc.*) and the charter was revoked in 1675. *Ibid.*, pp. 74-8.

[2]

Province of Quebec	Marriages	Births	Deaths
1660	24	113	47
1665	74	178	54
1670	122	311	85
1675	30	404	49
1680	65	386	100
1685	80	419	130
1690	104	510	181

The number of " territorial circumscriptions " increased from 5 to 19. *Census of Canada*, 1870-1, vol. V, pp. 176-80.
See measures adopted to increase population. *Edits, etc.*, pp. 67-8, pp. 73-4.

[3] In 1665 companies of the Carignan Salieres regiment arrived. *New York Colonial Documents*, vol. IV, pp. 25-6.

[4] Fort Sorel replaced Fort Richelieu at the mouth of Sorel River. Fort Saint Louis (Chambly) and Fort St. Teresa were built farther up the same river (*ibid.*, pp. 82-3).

[5] Two expeditions were sent in 1666, the later one with considerable effect (*ibid.*, pp. 88-91). Schenectady (*N.Y. Col. Doc.*, vol. III, p. 693), Salmon Falls (*ibid.*, vol. IX, p. 471) and Casco Bay were attacked and destroyed in 1690 (*ibid.*, vol. III, p. 720).—

[6] In 1672 Fort Cataracqui was built (*ibid.*, p. 76).   In 1678-9 a fort was built at Niagara (Gravien, Gabriel, *Découvertes ét établissements du Cavelier de la Salle de Rouen dans l'Amérique du Nord*, pp. 93-4).   In the same year La Salle reached Lake Michigan and built Fort Miami at the mouth of Lake Joseph (*ibid.*, p. 123), and in 1680 Fort Crevecoeur was established on the Illinois River (*ibid.* p. 146) and Fort St. Louis in 1683 on the same river (*ibid.*, p. 212).   In 1686 Denouville ordered the construction of a post between Lake Erie and Lake Huron (Margry, P., op. cit., vol. V, p. 23).   A strong post was built at Detroit in 1701 (*ibid.*, p. 187).

[7] Radisson and Groseilliers built a fort on the shore of Lake Superior in 1661 (*Radisson's Voyages* (Prince Society), pp. 194-6) which is generally agreed to have been at Chequamegon Bay (*Parkman Club Papers*, No. 2, p. 20).   The Jesuits were instrumental as ever in constructing permanent establishments at strategic fur trade rendezvous. La Pointe at Chequamegon Bay was established in 1665 (*Jesuit Relations and Allied Documents*, vol. I, p. 33) and later at St. Ignace (Michilimackinac), at Sault Ste Marie, at Green Bay and at St. Joseph's on Lake Michigan (*ibid.*, p. 35).   Dulhut built forts on the northern shore of Lake Superior and prepared the way for the advance into western Canada. An overland attack of the French on the English forts in Hudson Bay in 1686 (Valois, J. M., *Histoire du Chevalier D'Iberville*, ch. II) and a naval expedition in 1697 under D'Iberville against the same forts were further evidences of aggressiveness (*ibid.*, pp. 177-202).

and the Iroquois retaliated with raids upon French settlements, with destruction of forts [1] and a constant warfare
on the French fur trade. [2]

These activities and the accessibility of the St. Lawrence
drainage basin explained the rapidity of the French discoveries to the south-west, as shown in the exploration of
the Mississippi followed by the establishment of posts
from the mouth of the St. Lawrence to the mouth [3] of the
Mississippi. This expansion tended to direct the energies
of settlement toward the fur trade and consequently French
civilization in North America was characterized by a lack
of concentration other than at points strategic for the
conduct of that trade. On the other hand, the inaccessibility of the interior because of the Alleghany Mountains
and the lack of advantageous water-routes explained the
relative neglect of western exploration on the part of the
English colonies. The English pressing north-west around
the Alleghany Mountains were directly opposed by the
French pressing south-west by the Great Lakes and the
Mississippi River and later by the Ohio River. With increasing national and commercial competition [4] on the

[1] The raids and warfare were features of the whole period. See particularly the massacre of Lachine in 1690. *New York Colonial Documents*,
vol. IX, p. 435.

[2] Numerous ambushes and wars upon the French-Indian allies were
constantly being made. " We knocked the Twightwies (Miamis) and the
Chutaghicks (Illinois) on the head because they had cut down the trees
of peace. . . . They have hunted beavers on our lands, they have acted
contrary to the customs of all Indians, for they left none of the beavers
alive, they killed both male and female " (Speech of Garrangula, an Onan-
doga chief, in 1684. Smith, Hon. W., *The History of the late Province of
New York from its Discovery to the Appointment of Governor Colden in* 1762,
vol. I, p. 67).

[3] A fort was built at the mouth of the Mississippi in 1699 by D'Iberville
(Margry, P., op. cit., vol. IV, p. 284). Another fort was built " dix huit
lieues avant dans la rivière " in 1700 (*ibid.*, p. 364). Mobile was established in 1702 (*ibid.*, p. 515). New Orleans was constructed in 1717 (*ibid.*,
vol. V, p. 550) and became the chief centre in 1722 (*ibid.*, p. 641). Fort
Chartres north of Kaskaskia River was built in 1720 (Ogg, F. A., *The
Opening of the Mississippi*, p. 219).

[4] The region continued to be the scene of continuous activity. In
1673, seven years after the agreement of 1667, the English took Pentagoet
and Fort Gemesie (St. John) (Charlevoix, P. F. X., op. cit., vol. III, p.
188). Again there were raids in 1680 and the seizure of posts (*ibid.*, pp.
210–11), and in 1690 Port Royal and Chedabouctou were captured (*ibid.*,
vol. IV, pp. 156–60). An unsuccessful attack was also made on Quebec
in the same year (*ibid.*, p. 184 ff.). Port Royal was retaken by the French
in 1691 (*ibid.*, p. 215). Similar activities characterized the Newfoundland

outlying coast, and with increasing competition [1] arising
from the expansion of the English colonies north-west along
the Hudson, a struggle [2] for supremacy was inevitable.
The struggle [3] proved the weakness of the French position.
The English broke the long line of communication between

coast (*ibid.*, p. 244 ff.). In 1694 in retaliation the French and the Indians
destroyed several English villages on the main coast (Murdoch, Beamish,
op. cit., vol. I, pp. 211–13). After a long series of struggles, Port Royal
was captured by the English again in 1710 (*ibid.*, p. 315). In 1713, with
the Treaty of Utrecht, Acadia remained English and Cape Breton French
(*ibid.*, p. 332 ff.). Louisburg was consequently selected and fortified by
the French (*N.Y. Col. Doc.*, vol. X, p. 225). Difficulties continued as
shown in the destruction of Norridgework in 1724 (*ibid.*, vol. IX, p. 937).
An excuse for increased activity came with the declaration of war between
France and England in 1744, and in 1745 Louisburg was captured by the
English (Lincoln, *The Correspondence of William Shirley*, vol. I, p. 239),
but again returned to the French in 1748 (Murdoch, Beamish, op. cit.,
vol. II, p. 123). As a movement of consolidation, Halifax was established
in 1749 (*ibid.*, p. 137). On the northern coast in 1750 a fort was built
at Beaubassin. The French retaliated with the construction of fort
Beausejour on the opposite coast (*ibid.*, p. 179). Beausejour was captured
in 1755 (*ibid.*, p. 269). The conquest of the English along the coast was
completed with the fall of Louisburg in 1758 (*Journal of John Knox*,
Champlain Society, vol. III, App., p. 191).

[1] Partially as evidence of such increasing tension the continual raids
may be cited as instanced in the massacre of Deerfield in 1704 (*N.Y. Col.
Doc.*, vol. IV, p. 1083), and at other places by both colonies.

[2] In 1722 a fort was built at Oswego at the mouth of Oswego River
on Lake Ontario by the English (Smith, Hon. W., op. cit., vol. I, p. 216),
and as a counter-move the French strengthened Fort Niagara in 1726
(*ibid.*, p. 233). Fort St. Frederick at Crown Point on Lake Champlain
was constructed shortly afterwards by the French (*ibid.*, pp. 245–6).
In 1749 Celoron under French instructions took possession of the Ohio
valley (Margry, P., op. cit., vol. VI, p. 666 ff.). Shortly afterwards forts
were built at Presque Isle (*N.Y. Col. Doc.*, vol. X, p. 256) near the
southern shore of Lake Erie, farther south Fort La Boeuf and at the
junction of French Creek and Alleghany River Fort Machault (*ibid.*,
Hulbert, A. B., *Historic Highways of America*, vol. III, pp. 74–9). The
English under Major Washington protested in a visit to Fort La Boeuf
but with no satisfaction (Margry, P., op. cit., pp. 728–31). The establishment of Fort Du Quesne at the junction of the Alleghany and Ohio Rivers
precipitated the struggle (*ibid.*, p. 732).

[3] The defeat of the English at the forks of the Ohio and Monangahela
Rivers in 1754 (*Journal of Colonel George Washington*, edited by Toner,
J. M., p. 18) and at Fort Necessity (*ibid.*, p. 156) led to Braddock's unsuc-
cessful attack on Fort Du Quesne in 1755 (*A Review of the Military Operations in North America from 1753 to 1756*, p. 33 ff.), to the partially successful
attack of Johnson on Crown Point and the failure of the expedition under
Shirley to take Fort Niagara, and to the capture of Oswego on Lake
Ontario (*ibid.*, p. 136) and Fort William Henry on Lake George by the
French (*Knox Journal, ibid.*, vol. I, pp. 67–8). In 1758 the attack on
the flank brought about the fall of Louisburg, of Fort Frontenac (*ibid.*,
vol. III, pp. 149–150), of Fort Du Quesne (*ibid.*, vol. I, p. 297) and of
Fort Niagara (*ibid.*, vol. III, p. 242), but Ticonderoga at the centre
remained intact. The superiority of English naval power which proved
effective at Louisburg caused the fall of Quebec in the following year
(*ibid.*, vol. II, pp. 131–2).

French establishments in the capture of Fort Frontenac and occasioned the fall of posts to the west. The strength of a concentrated force brought about the downfall of the flanks at Louisburg and of the centre at Quebec.

Cession of Canada [1] to England in 1760 closed a chapter in the history of colonial expansion. Settlement in the New England colonies previously barred by the Alleghany Mountains and the national ambitions of France moved steadily forward with the conclusion of the struggle. [2] English fur traders, long held back by strategic posts of the French, pushed rapidly into new territory. The Indian wars in the struggle with Pontiac, though in part an aftermath [3] of the concluded struggle, were also a phase [4] of continued westward expansion.

Growth of settlement, of which the cession of Canada and the conquest of the Indians were results and of which they were in turn [5] causes occasioned an increasing antagonism to regulations of the English colonial policy which eventually terminated in the American revolution. Restrictions [6] which became increasingly heavy on the expanding trade and commerce of the colonies and which were

---

[1] Articles of Capitulation, September 8, 1760 (Shortt, A., and Doughty, A. G., *Documents Relating to the Constitutional History of Canada, 1759–1791*, pp. 21–9 ; Treaty of Paris, February 10, 1763 (*ibid.*, pp. 97–125).

[2] See Stone, William L., *The Life and Times of Sir William Johnston, Bart.*, vol. II, p. 138 ff.

[3] The French influence among the Indians of the more remote interior continued to be very strong (*ibid.*, pp. 134–6). There was also the impossible attitude of the English traders well described in Rogers, R., *Ponteach or the Savages of America, a tragedy* ; also Stone, W. L., op. cit., vol. II, pp. 136–7. See *Canada and Its Provinces*, vol. III, p. 56 ff. ; also Marquis, T. G., *The War Chief of the Ottawas*, pp. 1–10 ; Burton, C. M., ed. *Journal of the Pontiac Conspiracy*, 1763.

[4] The appearance of the settlers was of crucial importance (Stone, W. L., op. cit., vol. II, pp. 138, 142 ff.). The war witnessed the fall of all the posts except Detroit, Niagara and Fort Pitt (*ibid.*, pp. 191–2). Peace was virtually concluded in 1765 (*ibid.*, p. 261).

[5] See Bartlett, W. H., *The History of the American Revolution*, p. 281.

[6] The situation was appreciated by Montcalm as early as 1759. "I know them well . . . all these English colonies would long ago have thrown off the yoke . . . if the fear of seeing the French at their doors had not proved a bridle to restrain them. . . . But once let Canada be conquered . . . and on the first occasion when Old England appears to touch their interests, do you imagine . . . that the Americans will obey ? " (Letter quoted, *ibid.*, p. 275). The protests of the Otis speech, later the agitation against the Stamp Act, and finally the Boston Port Bill and the Massachusetts Bay Bill led to war. See Frothingham, R., *History of the Siege of Boston.*

particularly burdensome on such ports as Boston grew
more serious as a result of regulations [1] prohibiting the westward movement of settlement and reserving the Ohio valley
for the fur trade and the Indians.   In the final struggle the
naval supremacy of Great Britain, which had been effective
through the accessibility of the St. Lawrence valley in the
capture of Quebec, was effective in holding that point.[2]
On the other hand, the relative inaccessibility of the
territory under the control of the English colonies made
naval supremacy of little avail.   The treaty of Versailles of
September 13, 1783, concluded the struggle of the colonies
for the removal of barriers [3] restricting westward expansion.

[1] Ostensibly to pacify the Indians the King's Proclamation of October 7,
1763, expressly provided "that no governor . . . of our colonies . . .
do presume to grant warrants of survey or pass patents for any lands
beyond the heads . . . of any of the rivers which fall into the Atlantic
from the west or north-west . . . and we do hereby forbid all our loving
subjects from making any purchases or settlements whatever . . . of
any of the lands above reserved. . . .   And we do further strictly . . .
require all persons whatever who have . . . seated themselves upon any
lands . . . above described . . . forthwith to remove themselves from
such settlements " (Hart, A. B., and Channing, E., *American History
Leaflets*, No. 5, p. 14).   A project of Franklin's in 1765 to establish a
new colony in the Illinois country met serious objections from the Government, and not until 1772 was a petition granted.   The Lords Commissioners
for Trade and Plantations favoured the earlier principles adopted of
" confining the western extent of settlements to such a distance from the
sea coast as that those settlements should be within the reach of the
trade and commerce of this kingdom " and within " the exercise of that
authority . . . conceived to be necessary for the preservation of the
colonies in due subordination to and dependence upon the mother country."
Lastly the Quebec Act of 1774 extended the boundaries of Quebec to
include the Ohio valley as far as the Mississippi. (Shortt, A., and Doughty,
A. G., op. cit., p. 402).   It was the occasion of widespread and pronounced
discontent.   See Hinsdale, B. A., " Western Land Policy of the British,"
Ohio Archæological and Historical Publications, vol. I, p. 207 ff. ; also
Sparks, Jared, *The Works of Benjamin Franklin*, vol. IV.

[2] The valley of the Hudson River was geographically strategic in the
conduct of the war.   The early capture of the route by the Americans
was of significance in the rapid conquest of the whole of Canada except
Quebec.   The effectiveness of British naval supremacy at this point
occasioned the defeat of the Americans and the later attempts of the
British to penetrate to the Hudson River by Oswego and the Mohawk
valley and by Lake Champlain.   Again the naval supremacy of the British
was effective in the capture of New York and of other coast towns.   The
attempts to penetrate the Hudson by New York and by other routes as
well as to penetrate the interior by other rivers were unsuccessful, since
long lines of communication were constantly exposed to the attacks of
Americans.   See Semple, E. C., *American History and its Geographic
Conditions*, pp. 49–50 ; also Greene, F. V., *The Revolutionary War and
the Military Policy of the United States*.

[3] The new boundary line ran through the centre of Lakes Ontario,
Erie, Huron and Superior (Shortt, A., and Doughty, A. G., op. cit., pp.

The westward movement gained in momentum with the removal of political barriers. It spread north of the St. Lawrence valley, and particularly with the United Empire Loyalists' [1] settlements [2] began to appear in the territory north of Lake Ontario and Lake Erie. Anxious as to the outcome of this movement in the United States, Great Britain in addition adopted measures to encourage [3] the settlement of that area. Meanwhile settlement [4] in the lower St. Lawrence valley necessarily hampered by conflicts characteristic of the long struggle was at last favoured by peace.

But peace was of short duration. With continued westward expansion in the United States the St. Lawrence valley

491–3). Under the continued pressure of western expansion (Roosevelt, T., *The Winning of the West*, vol. IV) the western boundaries were more carefully set down in the Jay Grenville treaty of 1794 (MacDonald, W., *Select Documents of the History of the United States*, pp. 116–17).

[1] Loyalists emigrated to the Upper St. Lawrence and the Bay of Quinte to the number of almost 4,000 persons ; to the Niagara district about 100 persons, and to the territory farther west a smaller number. In 1791 it was estimated that there were 10,000 persons in the country above Montreal. See Wallace, W. S., *The United Empire Loyalists*, pp. 104–10.

[2] A very interesting description of the beginnings of settlement in Upper Canada is given in *Canada and Its Provinces*, vol. XVII, pp. 13–99.

[3] Under Imperial direction grants of land and various privileges were given to the Loyalists (Shortt, A., and Doughty, A. G., op. cit., pp. 494–5 ff.). The Constitutional Act of 1791 was designed largely to meet the demands of the English settlers (*ibid.*, p. 694 ff.). The necessity of settlement was also urged in later instructions (*ibid.*, 1791–1818, p. 33 ff.).

[4]					Marriages		Births		Deaths
1700	.	:	.	.	172	..	907	..	350
1710	.	.	.	.	189	..	1,023	..	315
1720	.	.	.	.	207	..	1,341	..	426
1730	.	.	.	.	382	..	1,910	..	1,173
1740	.	.	.	.	406	..	2,420	..	941
1750	.	.	.	.	619	..	2,974	..	1,879
1760	.	.	.	.	821	..	3,449	..	2,563
1770	.	.	.	.	699	..	4,738	..	3,336
1780	.	.	.	.	931	..	6,180	..	2,895
1790	.	.	.	.	1,137	..	6,825	..	4,212
1800	.	.	.	.	1,606	..	10,080	..	4,701

The number of " circumscriptions " during the period increased from twenty-four to forty-three (*Census of Canada*, 1871, vol. V, p. 182 ff., and compiled from registers kept by the Roman Catholic Church). The population has been estimated :

1676	.	.	.	8,415	1,714	.	.	.	26,904
1688	.	.	.	11,249	1,759	.	.	.	65,000
1700	.	.	.	15,000	1,784	.	.	.	113,000
1706	.	.	.	20,000	1,825	.	.	.	450,000

Bouchette, J., *The British Dominions in North America*, vol. I, p. 347.

became increasingly [1] coveted as an outlet to the sea. Among a number of other causes the advantages of its possession led to the war of 1812. The growth of settlement in Upper Canada and in Lower Canada and the effectiveness [2] of British naval supremacy which was evident in earlier struggles, proved sufficient to frustrate the effort of the Americans to loosen British control.[3]

The conclusion of peace was favourable to the expansion of settlement [4] in Upper Canada and in the Western states.[5] This expansion, which had been largely determined by the waterways and particularly by the St. Lawrence system, occasioned the further development of trade and commerce [6]

[1] Although difficult to establish with documentary evidence, the possibilities of Canada were undoubtedly important as factors leading to the declaration of war. The struggle was in large part another phase of western expansion. The immediacy of the attacks upon Canada with the beginning of the conflict and the boasts of such American leaders as Clay and Jefferson were of a suggestive character (Thompson, D., *History of the late War between Great Britain and the United States of America*, p. 34 ; see also a very good discussion, Wood, W., *The War with the United States*, pp. 4–19 ; and Wood, W., *Select British Documents of the Canadian War of* 1812 (Champlain Society), vol. I, pp. 1–3).

[2] The stubbornness of the defence which characterized the efforts of the Canadians during the early years of the campaign was finally successful with the co-operation of the British navy in the reinforcement of troops, the blockade and the attacks on the American coast (Wood, W., *The War with the United States*. Semple, E. C., op. cit., pp. 130–146).

[3] The Treaty of Ghent, December 24, 1814. MacDonald, W., op. cit., p. 192 ff.

[4] Population of Upper Canada:

1811	.	.	.	.	77,000 according to Bouchette
1824	.	.	.	151,097
1825	.	.	.	158,027
1826	.	.	.	163,702
1827	.	.	.	176,059
1828	.	.	.	185,526
1832	.	.	.	261,060

Board of registration and statistics, appendix to the first report, 1849, p. 10.

[5] Population of Western States:

	1800	1810	1820	1830
Illinois.	—	12,282	55,211	157,445
Indiana	5,641	24,520	147,178	343,031
Michigan	—	4,762	8,896	31,639
Ohio	45,365	230,760	581,434	937,903

—*Statistical Abstract of the United States,* 1919, p. 30.

[6] *Principal articles imported from Upper Canada into Lower Canada by St. Lawrence :*

	Ashes bls.	Wheat bus.	Flour bls.	Beef bls.	Pork bls.
1830	9,745	252,330	92,584	1,936	10,935
1831	10,482	409,975	85,026	1,020	12,643

which necessitated the improvement of those waterways by the construction of canals. Activity in this direction was increased by national and commercial rivalry.[1] Settlement also had its effect upon the development of other means of communication [2] and these in turn promoted settlement.

Increased trade of Upper Canada occasioned further demand for improvements on the St. Lawrence. These demands for improvements on a common waterway on the part of Upper Canada and the trading interests necessitated the co-operation of Lower Canada since Montreal by virtue

Principal articles imported from U.S. into Montreal by St. Lawrence :

	Ashes bls.	Wheat bus.	Flour bls.	Beef bls.	Pork bls.
1830	. 15,375	—	36,781	77	2,868
1831	. 18,112	2,646	42,000	1,541	3,910

Lake Erie to Lake Ontario, 1831 :

Staves (no.)	Ashes bls.	Timber ft.	Wheat bus.	Whisky bls.	Flour bls.	Boards (ft.)	Pork bls.
137,318	3,250	28,500	275,101	1,795	41,116	987,888	12,739

Lake Ontario to Lake Erie, 1831 :

Mdse. (cwt.)	Salt (bls.)
23,734	14,182

Bliss, H., *The Colonial System*, p. 129–131.

[1] The Erie Canal was begun in 1818 and completed in 1825. The Ohio canal between Lake Erie and the Ohio River, and the Oswego canal joining Lake Ontario and the Erie Canal were completed in the same decade (MacTaggart, J., *Three Years in Canada*, vol. II, pp. 237–40). Under Canadian jurisdiction the Lachine canal begun in 1821 was completed in 1824 (*ibid.*, vol. I. p. 236). The Welland canal was begun in 1825 and partially opened in 1829. *Ibid.*, vol. II, pp. 144–5). The Rideau canal begun in 1826 was not completed till 1832. *Ibid.*, vol. I, p. 104.

[2] The roads from 1813 had been opened with the encouragement of the British authorities for the development of settlement, for purposes of defence and in response to the demands of the fur trade. Consequently a road was built along the shore of the Detroit River and Lake St. Clair directly westward following the Thames River and continuing to the extreme end of Lake Ontario. Connexions were made with Lake Erie by two parallel branches to Port Talbot and the mouth of the Lynn River. Branching at Lake Ontario on the south it followed the southern shore of Lake Ontario to the Niagara River and on the north the northern shore of the Lake, continuing along the north shore of the St. Lawrence River to Montreal. For the fur trade Yonge St. had been extended to Lake Simcoe in 1794 and an alternative route provided from the northwest (*History of Toronto and the County of York*, vol. I, Pt. II, p. 13 ; see Chewett, Wm., *Map of the located districts in the province of Upper Canada*, 1813). In 1825 several roads had been built south of the main road from Lake St. Clair to Lake Ontario. The Niagara peninsula was a network of roads, as was also the territory north of Lake Ontario served by Yonge St. All the territory north of the road to Montreal more readily accessible to settlement was liberally covered with roads. See Chewett, J. G., *Map of the province of Upper Canada in 1825* ; also Bouchette, J., op. cit., vol. I, pp. 75, 90, 97, 205, 308.

of strategic location controlled [1] the collection of such an important source of revenue as the customs duties for both provinces and since the necessary improvements [2] were partly within its jurisdiction. Conflict in Lower Canada between new trading interests averse to customs duties and other agrarian interests averse to land duties [3] complicated by racial controversies [4] and by constitutional struggles [5] which culminated in the rebellion of 1837 made such co-operation impossible. The resulting delay in improvements not only hampered [6] the development of Upper Canada, but also aggravated other difficulties [7] incident to the growth of settlement. The rebellion [8] which followed led to the investigation of Lord Durham, to his famous report, and to the Act of Union which solved the problem by uniting the two provinces.

The removal of these difficulties made possible the prosecution of necessary improvements on the St. Lawrence. The work was stimulated by growing recognition of the value of the river as a highway for increasing trade of the rapidly expanding western states and of its possibilities [9] as a link

[1] " The financial relations between these two provinces are a source of great and increasing dispute " (Durham, Earl of, *Report on the Affairs of British North America* (ed. Lucas), vol. II, p. 142).

[2] " For the whole of the works in the Upper Province when completed would be comparatively if not utterly useless without the execution of similar works on that part of the Saint Lawrence which lies between the Province line and Montreal. But this co-operation the Lower Canadian Assembly refused or neglected to give " (*ibid.*, p. 90).

[3] *Ibid.*, pp. 35–50.

[4] " I found a struggle not of principles but of races " (*ibid.*, p. 16).

[5] " It was inevitable that such social feelings must end in a deadly political strife " (*ibid.*, p. 45). " The defects of the colonial constitution necessarily brought the executive Government into collision with the people " (*ibid.*, p. 71).

[6] Resolutions of Upper Canada Commons House of Assembly, February 26, 1838. *Further copies or extracts of correspondence relative to the affairs of Lower Canada and Upper Canada*, pp. 177–8.

[7] The burden of the system of land grants and of the numerous irregularities became increasingly heavy, with the growth of settlement (*ibid.*, vol. III, App. A, pp. 1–12).

[8] *Ibid.*, vols. II and III.

[9] As early as 1829 a canal route through " the great inland seas of Canada " had been suggested to open up the country and " to shorten the navigation between Europe and Asia " (MacTaggart, J., op. cit., vol. II, p. 322), and it had been optimistically written " when the steam-packet line is established between Quebec and London as it soon will be we may come and go between China and Britain in about two months. The names at the stages will be London, . . . Quebec, Montreal, Kingston Port Dalhousie, Port Maitland, Erie, Huron, Superior, Rocky Mountains.

in a chain of waterways extending even to the Pacific and was vigorously prosecuted.[1] The result of these exertions and of encouraging legislation [2] was a rapid increase in the trade of the lakes.[3]

Unfortunately [4] abolition of the preference to Canadian

Athabaska, Nootka and Canton " (*ibid.*, vol. I, p. 169). In 1835 Sir John Smyth in the *Christian Guardian* suggested the possibilities of a short and direct line from New York to Montreal, thence to Toronto, the Mississippi, the Rocky Mountains and the Columbia River in developing the western trade as well as trade with India and China. Ten years later as a result of the rapid expansion of the western states, of the growth of the Red River Settlement and of the more promising situation in Canada after the Union, he elaborated on the earlier proposal. A line was advocated from London to China by way of the British colonies and Chicago. Other roads calculated to develop traffic were advocated as feeders. With Toronto as a centre, a road was projected from Lake Superior to Winnipeg and from Winnipeg connecting with the road to Columbia River, and another road north of the Chicago route by boat across Lake Michigan to Milwaukee and connecting with the main road. As a military caution a line was proposed north of Lake Huron and Lake Superior to unite with the Lake Superior-Winnipeg route (Smyth, Sir John, *Railroad Communication*; see also Bonnycastle, R. H., *Canada and the Canadians in 1846*, vol. I, pp. 138–40).

[1] Welland Canal was enlarged after 1842 (*Report of the Chief Engineer of Canals*, 1880, pp. 7, 8). St. Anne lock on the Ottawa was built in 1843 (Kingsford, W., *The Canadian Canals*, p. 37). Galops canal and Iroquois canal were completed by 1846. Rapide Plat canal and Farrans Point canal were built in 1844–7 (*ibid.*, p. 57). Cornwall canal was completed in 1843 (*ibid.*, p. 56). Beauharnois canal was built in 1842–5 (*ibid.*, p. 52), and the Lachine canal enlargement begun in 1843 was completed in 1848 (*ibid.*, p. 71); see also *Canada and its Provinces*, vol. X, pp. 508–28.

[2] In 6 Geo IV c. 64, Canada was given preferential treatment in the imposition of a duty on wheat of 5s. per quarter at all times, and in 1827 the Act was favourably amended so that the 5s. rate applied only when wheat was below 67s. This preference, since American produce passing through Canada was admitted as Canadian produce, favoured the shipment of grain from the United States by the St. Lawrence. As the result of further Canadian agitation more extensive preference was granted in the Canada Corn Bill of July 12, 1843. In consideration of a duty of 3s. per quarter imposed by Canada on American wheat, the duty imposed by Great Britain on Canadian wheat was reduced to 1s. per quarter and the duty on flour made equivalent to the duty on wheat (*Journals of the Legislative Assembly of the Province of Canada*, 1843, pp. 16–17). Further, an Act was passed in 1846 (9 Vic. c. 1) " to encourage the transport of foreign produce through the canals of this province," providing for the bonding of foreign wheat and maize for exportation. To offset the abolition of the Corn Laws by Great Britain in 1846 to 1849 which withdrew the preference, and the effects of an Act passed by the United States in 1846 extending the bonding privilege to Canadian produce, and consequently tending to divert Canadian produce over American routes, Canada urged the abolition of the British Navigation Acts and this was accomplished in 1849. See discussion *Canada and Its Provinces*, vol. V, p. 189 ff.; also Lucas, Sir Chas., *Historical Geography of the British Colonies*, vol. V, p. 195 ff.

[3] "Hitherto (1855) the imports and exports of the lakes have more than doubled every four years " (Hogan, Sheridan, *Canada*, p. 24).

[4] The removal of the preference of the Corn Laws was an additional

products in Great Britain resulting from the repeal of the Corn Laws occasioned the diversion of trade by Oswego [1] on Lake Ontario to New York and the Atlantic coast. This diversion of trade stimulated and was stimulated by the agitation which culminated in the Reciprocity Treaty of 1854.

These disappointing results of this diversion, particularly to Montreal and Quebec, led, with the continually increasing traffic [2] and constantly growing recognition [3] of the possibili-

factor provoking the Annexationist Manifesto of 1849 (Allin, C. D., and Jones, G. M., *Annexation, Preferential Trade, and Reciprocity*, pp. 106–14).

[1] The completion of the railroad from Ogdensburg to connexions with the coast in 1850 gave Oswego an additional advantage (Andrews, I. D., *Report on the Trade and Commerce of the British North American colonies and upon the trade of the great lakes and rivers*, p. 23).

	1850		1851	
Exported to and through	Flour (bls.)	Wheat (bus.)	Flour (bls.)	Wheat (bus.)
Buffalo . .	19,244	66001	10,860	101,655
Oswego . .	260,872	1,094,444	259,875	670,202
Ogdensburg .	32,999	—	30,609	18,195
Lake Champlain . .	90,998	192,918	11,940	626
Montreal and Quebec .	280,618	88,465	371,610	161,312

Ibid., p. 359.

[2] The exports and imports of Chicago are an excellent index :

	Imports		Exports
1842	664,347	..	659,305
1843	971,849	..	682,210
1844	1,686,416	..	785,504
1845	2,043,445	..	1,543,519
1846	2,027,150	..	1,813,468
1847	2,641,852	..	2,296,299
1851	24,410,400	..	5,395,475

Shipment of Grain :

	Bus.		Bus.
1852 . .	5,873,141	1855 . .	16,633,700
1853 . .	6,412,181	1856 . .	21,583,221
1854 . .	12,932,320	1860 . .	31,256,697

—Bross, W., *The Toronto and Georgian Bay Ship Canal*, p. 7.

[3] The expansion of the western states as illustrated in the Oregon dispute of 1846 and the growth of the Red River Settlement and British Columbia, particularly in view of the increasing knowledge of the country, were factors emphasizing the advisability of a route through British territory. It was proposed in 1851 after a review of the possible advantages of a road to the Pacific that the Government should sell land sixty miles wide from Lake Superior to the Pacific at a reduced rate to a company in consideration of the settlement of the country and the consequent gradual construction of the road. "When ten miles of the road shall have been completed . . . a patent shall issue to the company for the first half of the road or five miles." The scheme was evidently borrowed from

ties of a route to the Pacific, to the encouragement [1] and
vigorous projection of geographically strategic railroads.[2]

Mr. Whitney (McDonnell, A., " Observations upon the construction of a
railroad from Lake Superior to the Pacific," *Journals of the Legislative
Assembly*, 1851, App. UU). A petition was presented to the House asking
for a charter (*Journals of the Legislative Assembly*, p. 40) and referred
to the railway committee which stated " that the scheme ought not to
be regarded as visionary or impracticable," but that it " had no evidence
. . . of the capacity of the petitioners to commence or prosecute the
undertaking," and consequently reported " such application is premature."
It indulged a hope that " the Imperial Government will be led to entertain
the subject as one of national concern and to combine with it a general
and well-organized system of colonization " (*ibid.*, App. UU). The geographically strategic location of Toronto on a direct route from Lake
Huron to Lake Ontario shown in the early construction of a road to
Lake Simcoe and Georgian Bay made it particularly susceptible to the
prospects of traffic developed in the north-west. Agitation against the
Hudson's Bay Company began in the *Globe* at almost the same time (Lewis,
John, *George Brown*, p. 213 ff.) and the advantages of a road occasioned
considerable discussion. See an article " The Great North-West, 1852,"
in Sandford Fleming's *Scrap Book*. The directness of the route from
Toronto in its accessibility to the north-west was also advantageous for
the grain trade of the western states which followed the Great Lakes.
Consequently the northern railway was built to Collingwood on Georgian
Bay in 1855. The completion of the road, the evidences of American
expansion, the gold rush of British Columbia and the difficulties leading
to the appointment of the Hudson Bay Committee in 1857 led to vigorous
agitation (see an article in the *Globe* elaborating on the competitive advantages of the route via Collingwood to the Atlantic, August 28, 1856), to
the resolutions of the Toronto Board of Trade in condemnation of the
Hudson's Bay Company, December, 1856, and to the energetic activities
of Toronto and Canada in the following years. To offset the activities
of Toronto in directing traffic along the route, via Collingwood, to the
Atlantic, Hon. A. N. Morin with seven members of Parliament and ten
laymen petitioned for a charter to build a road from Portland to Montreal,
to Ottawa, along the north shore of Lake Huron crossing the river at
Sault Ste Marie, and along the south shore of Lake Erie to the Great
Bend of the Missouri and the Pacific. The petition included a proposal
for an agreement with an American company, but there were no tangible
results (*Canadian Parliamentary Journals*, 1854-5, vol. I, p. 447, and
Morin, A. N., and others, *Petitions praying for a charter by the name of
Northern Pacific Railway Company*, Quebec, 1854. 1st Session, 5th
Parliament, 18 Vic. 1854).

[1] See discussion of provincial assistance, *Canada and Its Provinces*,
vol. IV, p. 391 ff.

[2] The Great Western directly west from Suspension Bridge to Windsor
completed in 1854 was an important link connecting with American roads.
The Northern from Toronto on Lake Ontario to Collingwood on Georgian
Bay, completed in 1855, was a direct route supplementing the roundabout
water-route by Lake Huron and Lake Erie. The Grand Trunk west from
Sarnia to Montreal was completed in 1856 and extended to Portland
(Maine) and to Quebec and Rivière du Loup in 1860. (Trout, J. M. and
Edw., *The Railways of Canada for* 1870-1, p. 35). The importance of the
extension of this line to the maritime provinces was evident in the agitation
of Quebec. (See an editorial debate between the *Quebec Chronicle*, urging
the expenditure of money for provincial defence, and the *Intercolonial
and the Toronto Globe*, emphasizing the necessity of opening up the west,
especially *Globe*, November 15, 1861, March, 12, 1862; *Leader*, June 12, 1862.)

Results were scarcely more promising, and the shorter distance to the Atlantic coast by Oswego continued to prove effective. In addition traffic was drawn by the Great Western [1] and American roads through Niagara peninsula. The Grand Trunk to Portland and Rivière du Loup was in difficulty.[2]

These failures to divert the increasing traffic of the western states and of Upper Canada through Canadian territory occasioned further activity in the renewal [3] of an agitation for access to a Canadian port on the Atlantic open to winter

[1] " It . . . has enjoyed a success scarcely paralleled in the railroad history of America " (Hogan, Sheridan, op. cit., p. 101). It must be added that the intense competition of American lines later brought the road into difficulties.

[2] " In 1861 the line was embarrassed with a floating debt of over twelve millions of dollars and was absolutely without credit " (Trout, J. M. and E., op. cit., p. 82). For a description of the effect of through traffic on the company's fortunes and for a general discussion of the company's situation see *Report of the Commission appointed to inquire into the Affairs of the Grand Trunk Railway*, 1861, p. 36 ff. The long branch to Rivière du Loup depending upon the construction of the Intercolonial for a connexion with the Atlantic seaboard was a decided drawback (Trout, J. M. and Edw., op. cit., p. 79).

[3] In 1832 a wagon road was proposed " from Quebec to the harbour of St. Andrews " to bring the exports of the provinces to the Atlantic " with more speed, regularity and security " and " at all seasons of the year " (Fairbairn, H., *The United Service Journal and Naval and Military Magazine*, Pt. II, 1832, p. 209). In 1836 resolutions favourable to a road were adopted by New Brunswick, Nova Scotia and Lower Canada. The St. Andrews and Quebec Railroad Company was incorporated, and with Imperial support, surveys were made in the same year. To this the State of Maine objected successfully on the ground of the unsettled boundary and proceedings were terminated (Fleming, Sandford, *The Intercolonial*, p. 8 ff.). The settlement of the boundary dispute in the Ashburton treaty of 1842 furnished additional evidence of the energetic efforts of the State of Maine to prevent the construction of the road (*ibid.*, pp. 38–9). In 1846 another attempt was made in the incorporation and survey of the Halifax and Quebec railway (*ibid.*, p. 45 ff.). Considerable enthusiasm was aroused as evidenced in Howe's famous statement on May 15, 1851 : " I believe that many in this room will live to hear the whistle of the steam-engine in the passes of the Rocky Mountains and to make the journey from Halifax to the Pacific in five or six days " (Longley, J. W., *Joseph Howe*, p. 135). But the rivalry of St. John and Halifax as possible termini and the refusal of an Imperial guarantee to the St. John or " Valley " route brought the negotiations to a close (Fleming, Sandford, op. cit., p. 53). They were resumed in 1857 and after considerable persistence on the part of the colonies an Imperial guarantee was given in 1867 (*ibid.*, p. 59 ff.). The colonial situation was aptly described as follows : " Increasing wealth and intelligence with their consequent demand for a large field of action . . . have led to the removal of some of the principal impediments in the way of . . . intercourse : yet those very facilities only make more vexatious the remaining obstacles to a perfect union " (Hamilton, P. S., *Observations upon a union of the colonies of British North America*, 1855, pp. 10–11).

navigation. Arousal of nationalistic anxiety [1] consequent to American expansion, increasing recognition of the possibilities of a route to the Pacific,[2] and development of the maritime provinces [3] gave strength to the agitation, which

[1] The American Civil War, particularly the " Trent affair," was generally recognized as an important factor in the success of the colonies in securing aid for the Intercolonial (Watkin, E. W., op. cit., p. 86 ff.) and in bringing about Confederation. See Colquhoun, A. H. U., *The Fathers of Confederation*.

[2] The subject had become of general interest (see an article McGee, T. D., " To Red River and the Pacific, via Victoria Bridge, June 15, 1861," *Canadian News*, October 31, 1861 ; *Leader*, November 4, 1861 ; a report of Sandford Fleming's address, Port Hope *Weekly Guide*, December 25, 1858 ; an extensive pamphlet—*Pacific Railway Claims of St. John, N.B., to be the Atlantic terminus*, 1858, Smith, T. T. Vernon). The Duke of Newcastle in a letter May 6, 1863, referring to a dispatch to Canada regarding the North-West Transit, " I added words which (without dictation) will be understood as implying ' No Intercolonial, No Transit ' " (Watkin, E. W., op. cit., p. 133). The negotiations of the period carried out by Mr. Watkin with regard to the Hudson's Bay Company cannot be considered without reference to the Grand Trunk (*ibid.*, p. 14). Definite expression was given by Canada in the 69th resolution of the Quebec conference in 1864. " The communications with the North-Western territory and the improvements required for the development of the trade of the great west with the seaboard are regarded by this conference as subjects of the highest importance to the Federated Provinces, and shall be prosecuted at the earliest possible period that the state of the finances will permit " (Pope, Joseph, *Confederation documents, hitherto unpublished*, p. 52, and in Section XI, Act. 146. British North America Act providing for the admission of western provinces (*ibid.*, p. 282).

[3] The retarding influence of the geographic characteristics of the maritime provinces prior to the treaty of Paris in 1763, in which the exposed mainland, the wealth of fisheries and the strategic location at the mouth of the St. Lawrence made the competitive struggles about the region inevitable, ceased with the dominance of the English. The same characteristics conditioned a rapid increase in immigration when peace was established, the New England states contributing to the accessible shores of the Bay of Fundy, and Great Britain to the eastern and northern shores of the territory (Ganong, W. F., " A Monograph of the origins of settlements in the province of New Brunswick," *Proceedings and Transactions of the Royal Society of Canada*, 1904, Section II, p. 49). For a similar reason New Brunswick and the shores of the Bay of Fundy received the largest contributions of United Empire Loyalists (*ibid.*, p. 70), and the exposed character of the area made effective the British naval supremacy in the Revolution as well as in the war of 1812. Settlement followed the numerous rivers and inlets of the region (*ibid.*, p. 71), but with the increased immigration (*ibid.*, p. 75) following the cessation of privateering which the peculiar character of the coast-line encouraged during the wars, there followed the construction of roads to the interior (*ibid.*, p. 89). The increase in population in Nova Scotia :

1818	82,053
1828	123,848
1851	276,117
1861	330,857

(Compiled from Haliburton, T. C., *An Historical and Statistical Account of Nova Scotia*, vol. II, pp. 276-7, and *Census of Nova Scotia*, 1862, p. 7.)

72 HISTORY OF THE CANADIAN PACIFIC RAILWAY

bore fruit in Confederation and in construction of the Intercolonial railway.[1] Largely in retaliation to the activity evident in these measures and in further legislative efforts [2] tending to divert the increasing traffic of Canada and of the western states through Canadian channels, the reciprocity treaty was abrogated by the United States in 1866. The abrogation gave further stimulus to intercolonial trade and to union and in turn to development of communication with the North-West bespoken in the purchase of the Hudson Bay Territory and in the admission of British Columbia and Manitoba to the Dominion.

A study of the events following the admission of British Columbia to the Dominion which involved the acceptance of terms obligating Canada to the construction of a road to the Pacific within ten years is facilitated by a review of the developments leading to the assumption of the obligation and an estimate of the strength of the third and last abutment of a Canadian transcontinental bridge.

Wealth of fisheries in the territory adjacent to the Banks of Newfoundland occasioned the early establishment of settlement, but national and commercial competition inci-

And in New Brunswick:

1824	74,176
1834	119,457
1840	156,162
1851–2	193,800
1860–1	252,047

(Hatheway, C. L., *The History of New Brunswick*, p. 81 ; and Monro Alexander, *New Brunswick, with a brief outline of Nova Scotia and Prince Edward Island*.)

and consequently in trade, further led to the construction of railroads. In Nova Scotia a railroad across the province from Halifax to Truro and to Windsor was completed in 1858 and to Pictou in 1867, and in New Brunswick in consequence of the Quebec agitation a road was built from St. Andrews to Canterbury in 1858 and to Richmond in 1862 (Trout, J. M. and E., op. cit., p. 36). A railway was also opened from St. John to Shediac in 1860 (Fleming, S., op. cit., p. 56).

[1] Provision was made for the construction of the road in the B. N. A. Act, Sec. X, Act 145 (Pope, Joseph, op. cit., p. 282).

[2] Of such a nature were the increasing duties imposed by Canada on United States manufactured articles (see the yearly changes 1855–9, Haynes, F. E., *The Reciprocity Treaty with Canada of 1854*; *Publications of the American Economic Association*, vol. III, No. 6, p. 49) and the reduction and abolition of tolls on the Canadian canals (*ibid.*, p. 54). For a concise discussion of the situation, see Hopkins, J. Castell, *Canada : An Encyclopædia of the Country*, p. 346 ff. Canada's expenditure on the transportation improvements to divert traffic over her own territory was met by revenue received from increased duties designed to the same end (*ibid.*).

dental to such wealth seriously hampered its growth. The maze of rivers and inlets characteristic of the region facilitated the beginnings of settlement but delayed exploration and discovery of the St. Lawrence River and the interior. Accessibility of the St. Lawrence to the interior to a large extent conditioned the rapidity of exploration of the St. Lawrence basin, of the Ohio River and of the Mississippi by the French, and together with its climatic severity determined the importance of the fur trade and consequently the slow growth of settlement. Relative inaccessibility of the area south of the St. Lawrence retarded exploration and led to the growth of settlement along the coast. The southwesterly direction of the St. Lawrence basin and the northerly direction of the Hudson River and the routes to the interior leading around the Alleghany Mountains provoked the conflict between English and French, the result of which was determined by the consolidation and superiority of the English settlements and the accessibility of the St. Lawrence which gave effectiveness to British naval supremacy. Steady growth of English settlements conflicted with the restrictive policy of British control of the St. Lawrence as it had with the French. Maintenance of British control on the St. Lawrence because of naval supremacy, and success of the colonies on land because of the ineffectiveness of naval supremacy in less accessible territory were the results of this struggle. Westward expansion, successful in the removal of barriers interposed by the French and the British, gaining access to the rivers characteristic of the middle of the continent, proceeded rapidly, and contributed to the development of Upper Canada and of the western states. Trade resulting from this expansion increased pressure upon the St. Lawrence, in which the question of control became a contributing cause of the war of 1812, and which necessitated the improvement of transportation facilities to the Atlantic coast. In the competitive struggle for this trade, Canada's handicap of distance to the coast, and the disastrous results, compelled improved facilities. The nationalistic dangers of western expansion contributed to the force of this factor and there followed the Intercolonial, Confederation and the admission of British Columbia to the Dominion.

74 HISTORY OF THE CANADIAN PACIFIC RAILWAY

The apparent weakness [1] of Canada as the important
abutment to a transcontinental bridge was not offset by
the strength of the remaining abutments. The hectic and
relatively slight growth of British Columbia and the relative
unimportance of the Red River settlement could not avail
in a task of such immensity. In each of the three areas
roughly included in the drainage basins concerned, civilization had developed almost alone. It had grown and ex-
panded beyond the boundaries set by topographical features.
Politically these sections were united but economically the
barriers proved to be of a character which tested severely
and almost to the breaking-point the union which had been
consummated. Political union rested upon pillars the
weakness of which bespoke difficulties before the economic
obligation essential to such union could be fulfilled.

[1]

	Population
Ontario	1,620,851
Quebec	1,191,516
New Brunswick	285,594
Nova Scotia	378,800

Compiled from *Census of Canada*, vol. VI, 1870–1.

II

From National to Economic Union (1870–1880)

The disparity between political union and the economic development necessary for fulfilment of the essential terms was immediately reflected in the controversial character [1] of the debates, leading to acceptance of the terms by the Canadian Parliament, which insisted upon safeguards against excessive taxation. The policy of the Government, as embodied in the Act [2] providing for execution of the terms,

[1] The House of Commons was by no means unanimous in the support of the terms of union. Despite the constant and well-directed assurance of the Government that "it was not the intention of the Government to construct the road, but it would be undertaken by companies to be assisted mainly by land grants. (Hear, hear.) It was not the intention of the Government to burden the exchequer much to obtain this railway." (Hear, hear.) Speech of the Hon. Sir Geo. E. Cartier, *House of Commons Debates*, 1871, vol. II, p. 662), an amendment " that the further consideration of the question be postponed for the present session of Parliament " was lost only on a vote of 75 to 85 (*Journals of the House of Commons, Canada*, 1871, p. 163). To make its position even more secure in the House of Commons, the Government adopted a resolution specifically stating, " That the railway should be constructed and worked by private enterprise and not by the Dominion Government ; and that the public aid to be given to secure the undertaking should consist of such liberal grants of land and such subsidy in money or other aid not increasing the present rate of taxation, as the Parliament of Canada shall hereafter determine " (*ibid.*, p. 266). This attitude was apparently understood to some extent by British Columbia. " Ten years was not put into the terms of union as an absolute limit but simply as a bona fides that the Government would commence the road and carry it on to completion as quickly as could be without injury to the interests of the country " (speech of Mr. Carrall, one of the delegates from British Columbia appointed to arrange the terms of union. *Senate Debates*, 1876, p. 153). " If they had said twelve or eighteen years that time would have been accepted with equal readiness, as all that was understood was that the line should be built as soon as possible " (speech of Mr. Trutch, another of the delegates. *Sessional Papers*, 1875, No. 19, p. 25).

[2] The preamble to the Act restated the resolution " that the public aid to be given . . . should consist of such liberal grants of land and such subsidy in money or other aid, not increasing the present rate of taxation." " And it was the intention of the Government not only to carry it out in spirit but to the letter. (Hear, hear.) " (Speech of the Hon.

75

was carefully planned to avoid additional expense to Canada, and it proposed to meet the expenses of construction of the road from land grants. Additional evidence of disparity was found in the energetic [1] and successful efforts of the Government to secure an imperially guaranteed loan, and in the appearance of a clause permitting the possibility [2] of private enterprise sharing in the coveted traffic of the western

Sir Geo. E. Cartier, *House of Commons Debates*, 1872, p. 172.) The Act provided for the construction and operation of the road by "one company having a subscribed capital of at least ten million dollars " and a deposit with the Receiver-General of 10 per cent. of the capital. Of most importance, it provided for a land grant not to exceed fifty million acres to be granted "in blocks not exceeding twenty miles in depth, on each side of the railway alternating with other blocks of like depth, on each side thereof to be reserved by and for the Dominion Government, for the purposes of this Act, and to be sold by it, and the proceeds thereof applied towards reimbursing the sums expended by the Dominion under this Act. . . . Provided that, so far as may be practicable, none of such alternate blocks of land . . . shall be less than six miles nor more than twelve miles in front on the railway, and the blocks shall be so laid out that each block granted to the company on one side of the railway shall be opposite to another block of like width reserved for the Government on the other side of the railway." The sums to be expended by the Dominion referred to "aid in money to be granted . . . not exceeding thirty millions of dollars " (35 Vic. c. 71).

[1] Efforts were made in respect to demands for compensation for damage occasioned by the Fenian raids. Canada urged that Great Britain should insist upon payment by the United States, since it was claimed that more prompt action on the part of that country would have lessened the damage sustained (*Sessional Papers*, No. 26, 1872, p. 2). The United States refused to consider these claims, and on the ground of expediency they were dropped by Great Britain (p. 11). As a result Canada claimed that Great Britain was responsible for the payment of compensation and suggested that such compensation should take the form of a guarantee for a loan of £4,000,000 for the construction of a Pacific railroad (*Correspondence with the Government of Canada in connexion with the treaty of Washington*, p. 3). Great Britain replied by offering to guarantee a loan of £2,500,000 (*ibid.*, p. 15), and to this Canada reluctantly consented (*Further correspondence with the Government of Canada in connexion with the appointment of the joint High Commission and the treaty of Washington*, p. 1). In addition Canada asked that an existing Imperial guarantee for £1,100,000 for the construction of fortifications should be increased to £1,500,000 and—since the settlement of difficulties with the United States made fortifications unnecessary—transferred to the guarantee for the construction of the Pacific railroad, making a total of £4,000,000 imperially guaranteed for that purpose (*Further correspondence with the Government of Canada in connexion with the treaty of Washington*, pp. 3, 5–6). Great Britain objected to the increase of £400,000, but agreed to the transfer (*ibid.*, pp. 6–7). To this Canada again agreed and the final negotiations found her in possession of an imperially guaranteed loan of £3,600,000 (*ibid.*, pp. 7–8).

[2] Section 16 of the Act provided for construction and working of branch lines from the railway " to some point on Lake Superior in British territory " and to some point on the line between the Province of Manitoba and the United States of America (*ibid.*).

states, and consequently ensuring the attractiveness and success of the policy. The policy in the face of a task which involved the construction of a railroad through barriers, the magnitude [1] of which was only beginning to be known, to unite the sparsely settled districts of British Columbia and Red River to Canada, necessitated dependence upon American traffic and American interests.

The importance of dependence on the traffic of the western states was evident in the disastrous termination of the two more concrete proposals [2] encouraged by the Government's

[1] Surveys conducted under the auspices of the Government were of an illuminating character. On April 10, 1872, surveys between Mattawa and Nepigon Bay had been completed with one exception and between Nepigon Bay and Fort Gary with two breaks. No practicable line could be found for a distance of one hundred miles east from the River Nepigon (Fleming, Sandford, *Progress Report on the Canadian Pacific Railway, Exploratory Survey*, p. 9). One line through the Rocky Mountains to the Pacific had been found practicable (*ibid.*, p. 12) ; but " a great deal still remains to be done " (*ibid.*, p. 10). Another report was made on January 26, 1874. Seven distinct routes had been found available through the Rocky Mountain district, but a choice was still unwarranted because of insufficient information (Fleming, Sandford, *Exploratory Survey Canadian Pacific Railway*, p. 34). Three practical routes had been found north of Lake Superior (*ibid.*, p. 27 ff.). The reports were optimistic as to the possibilities of a road, but at the same time eloquent of the difficulties to be surmounted. See also Grant, G. M., *Ocean to Ocean*. It was estimated by Sandford Fleming that the road would cost $100,000,000 (speech of Alexander MacKenzie, *Globe*, May 13, 1874).

[2] The proposals and suggestions pertaining to the construction of a road to the Pacific continued to be made and became more numerous. A wooden railway was advocated from Lake Superior to Red River. The cost of the railway and of the stations and rolling-stock was to be paid from land sales (Foster, John, *Railway from Lake Superior to Red River Settlement*, also *Descriptions of a Wooden Railway*). On March 17, 1870, a petition for an act of incorporation of the Canadian Pacific Railway and Navigation Company with power to construct a railway from Ottawa through the Red River territory . . . to the Pacific Ocean at Bute Inlet and also for assistance in a grant of wild lands was presented to the Canadian Parliament (*Journals of the House of Commons, Canada*, 1870, p. 82), but received little further notice (*ibid.*, p. 10). A similar fate was met (*ibid.*, 1871, p. 153) by a petition of Alfred Waddington and William Kersteman praying for an act of incorporation of the Canada Pacific Railway (*ibid.*, p. 139). The petitioners included several Americans (*Report of Royal Commissioners*, 1873, pp. 99-100), and the petition was based on a route carefully selected by Waddington.
Estimate of length of road :

						Miles
Mattawan to Fort Gary	.	.	.	.	.	985
Plain of the Saskatchewan	.	.	.	.	.	985
Rocky Mountains	.	.	.	.	.	52
British Columbia	.	.	.	.	.	570
Ottawa to Fort Gary	.	.	.	.	.	1,180
Montreal to Pacific	.	.	.	.	.	2,777

policy. In the acts of incorporation of both companies [1] stress was placed on connexions with the railways of the United States designed to secure a share of the traffic of the western states. The existence of two companies, the Interoceanic with head-quarters at Toronto and the Canada Pacific with head-quarters at Montreal, bore witness to competition [2]

Nature of Country	Level miles	Rolling miles	Poor miles
Valley of Ottawa . . .	—	70	—
Montreal Valley . . .	69	—	30
Clay level country . . .	250	—	—
Lawrentides north of Lake Superior	20	30	63
Neepigon and Black Sturgeon district	41	25	—
Height of land to White Mouth River	—	—	335
Great Western Plain . .	1,012	—	—
Great Western Plain (approach to Rocky Mountains) . . .	—	25	—
Valley of Assiniboia . . .	—	30	—
Rocky Mountains to Cache .	—	—	80
Bald or Gold Range beyond .	—	—	116
Along Horsefly Lake and River.	—	20	—
Chilwater Plain . . .	152	—	—
Cascade Range	—	—	84
	1,544	200	708

Miles
Rich and cultivable territory 1,744
Grazing timberland, mountainous 723

Waddington, Alfred. *Sketch of Proposed Line of Overland route,* 1871. The proposals favoured by the Government were incorporated as the Interoceanic Company (35 Vic. c. 72) and the Canada Pacific Company (35 Vic. c. 73).

[1] Clause 3 of both Acts provided for construction of branch lines "from the main line to the River St. Mary at some point on Neepigon Bay or Thunder Bay and from or near Winnipeg River to the Lake of the Woods and from Fort Garry or Winnipeg to Pembina or to any other point on the south boundary line of the Province of Manitoba, and from any point on the main line in British Columbia to any point on the boundary line of that province so as to connect with the railway system of the United States of America and to construct a railway bridge across the said River St. Mary and across Johnson's Straits." Clause 35 also provided that the Directors of the company "generally may enter into such agreements as will secure uniform and complete railway connexion with the system of railways now or hereafter existing in Canada or the United States."

[2] The failure of Canadian attempts to direct American traffic over Canadian territory had more serious consequences for Montreal than Toronto, since the north-easterly direction of the St. Lawrence increased the distance to the seaboard at Montreal, and traffic went by Niagara and Oswego. For Toronto, situated farther west, this diversion of traffic was less serious. Montreal had early urged the advisability of a railroad west to Lake Huron which would offset this handicap (see petitions Morin, A. N., and others, and the Canada Central Railway, Trout, J. M. and Edw., op. cit., p. 170). The Northern Colonization Railway, incorporated in 1869, to be constructed from Montreal to Ottawa and westward to

between geographically strategic localities for this traffic. Hon. D. L. MacPherson, head of the Interoceanic Company,[1] and others connected with the Grand Trunk were interested in promoting a steamship line from Portland to Europe. Sir Hugh Allan, head of the Canada Pacific Company, alarmed [2] at the prospects of diversion of traffic from his steamship line, energetically prosecuted the construction of railways westward to strengthen control of traffic. This activity in turn aroused the hostility of the Grand Trunk.[3] Finally the strength of American influence,[4] inevitable be-

connect with the Canada Central Railway, was a further step on the part of Montreal to secure more direct control of the traffic (*ibid.*, p. 147). Competition between Montreal and Toronto made necessary the choice of an eastern terminus of the Pacific road on or near Lake Nipissing (clause 1, 35 Vic. c. 71). "We have been obliged to place the terminus far from your city and also from Toronto for political reasons on account of the ambition of Toronto and Montreal (DeCelles, A. D., *Sir George Etiennes Cartier*, p. 52). For a similar reason the acts of incorporation were almost identical.

[1] The Canada Pacific Railway organized on June 21, 1872, with Sir Hugh Allan as president (*Correspondence relative to the Canadian Pacific Railway*, 1874, p. 32). For a full list of the fifty directors, see *ibid.*, p. 37. The Interoceanic Company elected Hon. D. L. MacPherson as President on June 20, 1872 (*ibid.*, p. 42). For a full list of directors, see *Railroad Gazette*, vol. IV, p. 287.

[2] Sir Hugh Allan had about $3,000,000 invested in sea-going steamers alone (evidence of Hon. J. J. C. Abbott, *Correspondence relative to the Canadian Pacific Railway*, 1874, p. 229).

[3] Evidence of Sir J. A. MacDonald, *Report of the Royal Commissioners*, 1873, p. 116. See also a pamphlet *Railway interests of the city of Montreal*, 1872," printed by the Gazette Printing House, the medium of Sir Hugh Allan, urging the subscription of $1,000,000 for the Northern Colonization Railway by the City of Montreal.

[4] The Northern Pacific was particularly interested in securing direct communications with Boston, and since the President had an interest in the Central Vermont a Canadian road was a geographically strategic link. These interests favoured the Montreal route as the most direct, and an acquaintanceship with Sir Hugh Allan quickly ripened (Smalley, E. V., *History of the Northern Pacific Railroad*, p. 134). Jay Cooke, financier of the Northern Pacific, was also anxious to secure control of the Canadian proposal to prevent construction in the North-west and consequently competition with the Northern Pacific for capital and emigration in England and Europe (Oberholtzer, E. P., *Jay Cooke, Financier of the Civil War*, vol. II, p. 349). Americans first approached the Government with respect to the road at the invitation of Mr. Waddington, but the proposal, as has been stated, was regarded as premature (evidence of Sir J. A. MacDonald, *Report of the Royal Commissioners*, 1873, pp. 99–100). Sir Francis Hincks, a member of the Cabinet, gave the names of these American gentlemen to Sir Hugh Allan, though not with the Government's approval. On October 5, 1871, in company with Mr. Smith and Mr. McMullen of Chicago and others, Sir Hugh Allan arrived in Ottawa to arrange a definite proposition, but the Government declined to go further than to receive propositions (*ibid.*). Relations between Sir Hugh Allan and the American interests continued (*ibid.*, pp. 190-1),

cause of the importance of American traffic, and the conse-

and on December 23, 1871, an agreement was drawn up in New York. They agreed to form a company under a charter secured by Sir Hugh Allan, Charles M. Smith and Geo. W. McMullen from the Canadian Parliament. Of the $10,000,000 stock Smith and McMullen agreed to subscribe $4,500,000, and the other parties the remainder, the latter to pay 10 per cent. of the whole $10,000,000 to Jay Cooke & Company to the credit of the Canadian Pacific Railway on its organization, to be used as the directors determined. On organization of the company no further assessments should be made on the stock without the consent of nine-tenths of all outstanding stock of the company at some regular or special shareholders' meeting. The Canada Land and Improvement Company was to be incorporated for the purpose of constructing the railway, and for the purchase and sale of lands, and the interests of the parties were to be in the same proportion as in the C.P.R. All contracts for construction were to be let to this company and it was to be allowed the use of the railway during construction without charge. Its capital was to be $1,000,000 and profits arising from construction were to be used to reimburse the parties subscribing $5,500,000 for the $1,000,000 paid by them as a 10 per cent. instalment of the Railway stock with interest thereon at the rate of 7 per cent. A majority of the stock in both companies was to be held by a trustee selected by the subscribers until the road was built, or until two-thirds of the stockholders terminated the trust —the stock to be voted by the trustee " as he shall be directed to vote by the owners of a majority thereof." After the payment of $1,000,000 by the parties referred to, profits were to be divided among stockholders in proportion to shares held. If the Canadian Parliament failed to organize the Land and Improvement Company provision was made that it should be organized in the United States. No money over $100,000 was to be drawn from the funds of the proposed company unless by consent of two-thirds of the stockholders. The essential conditions of the charter were to be a $15,000 per mile subsidy, and a land grant of 20,000 acres per mile except for the road from Fort Gary east to a junction with the section proposed to be built from Lake Nipissing to the Sault Ste Marie, on which the land grant was 25,000 acres per mile, the payments to be absolute on the completion of each section of twenty miles, and the only forfeiture in case of failure to complete the road within the time limit was to be the right to finish the uncompleted portions. Subscribers : J. Cooke & Co., $1,000,000 ; D. McLaren, $500,000 ; W. B. Ogden, $637,500 ; J. Gregory Smith, $500,000 ; G. W. Cass, $637,500 ; H. R. Payson, $175,000 ; Thos. A. Scott, $500,000 ; F. E. Canda, $175,000 ; C. J. Canda, $150,000 ; R. D. Rice, $250,000 ; Frederick Billings, $30,000 ; A. H. Barney, $230,000 ; Wm. G. Fays, $230,000 ; T. H. Canfield and W. Windowa, $180,000 ; S. Wilkinson, $750,000 ; W. Hinckman, $50,000 ; Allan, Smith and McMullen each $1,450,000 (*Correspondence relative to the C.P.R.*, p. 215).

With this agreement Sir Hugh Allan approached Mr. Brydges, Hon. D. L. MacPherson and other influential men to secure their co-operation (*ibid.*, p. 52 ff.). The Hon. D. L. MacPherson objected to a proposal in which seventeen-twentieths of the capital was subscribed by Americans, even though of the eleven directors six were to be British subjects resident in Canada. He pointed out further that all the members of the board were directors of the Northern Pacific Railway including the President and Vice-President, and refused to join it (evidence of the Hon. D. L. MacPherson, *ibid.*, p. 111 ff.). Mr. Brydges, one of the three Canadian directors of the Grand Trunk, also refused to become a member (*ibid.*, p. 54). These difficulties made necessary more strategic plans. A supplemental contract was made with the American interests, giving Sir Hugh

quent stubbornness [1] of the struggle between the companies

Allan greater freedom and permitting him to secure more funds. Dated, March 28, 1872. They agreed to take $35,000,000 in money and 50,000,000 acres of land, the money to be paid pro rata per mile as constructed, each mile to be counted as 1/2,500th part of the whole line to be built, and the land at the rate of 20,000 acres per mile. Sir Hugh Allan was given power to accept a reduction to $33,000,000 and 50,000,000 acres of land, while a committee of five, J. Gregory Smith, Sir Hugh Allan, G. W. McMullen, Geo. W. Cass, and Wm. B. Ogden, were given authority to accept $30,000,000 and 50,000,000 acres of land. This committee was also given power to make assessments for the general purposes of the company, but not exceeding one and a half per cent. of the amounts agreed to be subscribed by them to the stock of the Company. These assessments were to be considered as part of the $1,000,000 agreed to be paid in the contract of December 23, 1871. The Committee was authorized to take action which it deemed necessary. Signed Jay Cooke & Company, J. Gregory Smith, B. P. Cheney, R. D. Rice, T. H. Canfield, A. H. Barney, G. W. Cass, D. McLaren, F. Billings, W. Windowa, H. R. Payson, F. E. Canda, C. J. Canda, S. Wilkinson, W. B. Ogden, W. Hinckman, H. Allan, C. M. Smith, G. W. McMullen (*ibid.*, p. 257).

With these funds " on a calm review of the situation I satisfied myself that the whole decision of the question must ultimately be in the hands of . . . Sir George E. Cartier . . . who is the salaried solicitor of the Grand Trunk Railway to which this (railroad) would be in opposition. . . . I . . . proceeded to subsidize the newspapers . . . I . . . called on many of the inhabitants. I visited the priests. . . . This succeeded so well that " . . . " he then agreed to give the contract as required " (*Report of the Royal Commissioners*, 1873, pp. 205-6). Sir Hugh Allan's success was temporary. The Government proceeded to form a new company of which Sir Hugh Allan was president. In order to lull all suspicions raised by the Interoceanic Company in its protests against American connexions (evidence of Hon. A. C. Campbell, *ibid.*, p. 84 ff.), every effort was made to exclude American interests. The directors were carefully chosen (*ibid.*, p. 105 ff.). The Act (corresponding in the main to the earlier Acts), provided that no shares were transferable within six years without the consent of the Government and the directors, nor after six years unless with the consent of the directors. The company was required to keep a stock register and a bond register. Each director was required to be a British subject and a holder of at least 250 shares of stock. The President and a majority of the directors were further required to be residents of Canada. Provision for branches to the St. Mary's River and to the boundary in British Columbia were significantly absent (*Journals of the House of Commons*, 1873, p. 55 ff.). Sir Hugh Allan had found it necessary to write, " Dear Mr. McMullen," on October 24, 1872, informing him that, " Public sentiment seems to be decided that the road shall be built by Canadians only " (*Report of the Royal Commissioners*, 1873, p. 209).

[1] Hostility between the companies and failure of the Government to secure an amalgamation were facts particularly eloquent as to the character of the interests at stake. The Government was obliged to confine its attempts to securing an amalgamation, since offer of the charter to either company would alienate the other company's support (evidence of Sir John A. MacDonald, *ibid.*, p. 102). Its intimation to both companies expressing the desire that they should amalgamate met different receptions. (*Correspondence relative to the C.P.R.*, p. 32 and p. 43). The Canada Pacific Company expressed its willingness to comply with the Government's wishes (*ibid.*, p. 33), and the Interoceanic Company replied that amalgamation was impossible. The Canada Pacific Company was under suspicion as to its relationships with Northern Pacific interests and it

to secure the charter, led to the tragic breakdown [1] of the whole policy. In the events incidental to competition between Sir Hugh Allan and Montreal, and the Grand Trunk and Toronto, to secure the charter, the latter appealed to national sentiment in a demand for the exclusion of American interests. As a result of compliance with the demand, there developed the Pacific Scandal,

was stated that a company not pre-eminently national could not hope to secure money in the British market. American control was interested in the retardation of North-Western Canada (*ibid.*, p. 43). The Canada Pacific Company protested against the charges implied and denied any connexion with foreign interests. In the draft charter it had proposed a Board of Directors exclusively British, while the Interoceanic Company had proposed only a majority of British directors. The plan of amalgamation proposed that a majority of the new directors should be agreed upon between the two companies and the Government, and this it was urged would effectively prevent American dominance (*ibid.*, p. 34 ff.). The Interoceanic Company objected that there was little protection in the plan of amalgamation proposed. It refused to accept the denial of connexion with American interests and pointed to the lack of public support afforded the Canada Pacific (*ibid.*, p. 46). The Government intervened with an expression of confidence in Sir Hugh Allan (*ibid.*, p. 38), but the Interoceanic Company remained obstinate, and insisted that amalgamation would weaken public support (*ibid.*, p. 51). Impending elections made necessary renewed efforts (evidence of Sir John A. MacDonald, *ibid.*, p. 174). A conference was held and details arranged, but the Hon. D. L. MacPherson persistently refused to agree to Sir Hugh Allan becoming President of an amalgamated company (*ibid.*, pp. 114-15). The other directors of the Interoceanic Company were eventually persuaded, but the President remained obdurate on the ground of control of American interests (evidence of Hon. A. C. Campbell, *ibid.*, pp. 158-9).

[1] On April 2, 1873, a motion was made in the House of Commons charging that Sir Hugh Allan had been in agreement with American interests (*Report of the Royal Commissioners*, 1873, p. iii.). On April 8, Sir John A. MacDonald moved that a committee be appointed to investigate the charges (*ibid.*, p. iv.). On July 3, a series of letters and telegrams written by Sir Hugh Allan to American interests was published in the *Montreal Herald* (*Correspondence relative to the C.P.R.*, 1874, p. 52 ff.). On the following day, Sir Hugh Allan published an explanatory statement in the *Montreal Gazette*, admitting the agreement with American interests, but denying the charge that the Government knew of its existence. The McMullen correspondence followed in the *Montreal Herald* and gave additional light on the situation. The exclusion of American interests by the Government and consequently the suspending of negotiations on Sir Hugh Allan, had led to demands of Americans on Sir Hugh Allan (*Correspondence relative to the C.P.R.*, p. 66), and despite all precautions (*ibid.*, p. 259) the correspondence appeared in the newspapers. Consequently the corporation was hampered in its efforts to raise capital in England (*ibid.*, p. 233). A Royal Commission was appointed on August 14, 1873, to take the place of the Committee (*Report of the Royal Commissioners*, 1873, p. vi.). It presented the evidence to Parliament on its opening on October 23, and after a two weeks' debate, Sir John A. MacDonald resigned on November 5. For a defence of Sir John A. MacDonald's position throughout the episode, see Pope, *Memoirs of the Right Honourable Sir John Alexander MacDonald*, vol. II, chap. 23, pp. 161-96.

the failure of Sir Hugh Allan's programme and the downfall of the Government. The dependence of private enterprise on American traffic was significant indeed of Canadian
inability to meet the terms of the contract.

As a result of increasing knowledge and appreciation of
the character and magnitude of the task, and of the inability
of Canada, reflected in the persistent refusal to bear an
increase in taxation, and in the events of the Pacific Scandal,
to perform the task, a change in the policy [1] of construction
was necessary. The policy enunciated by Alexander Mac-
Kenzie, the new premier of Canada, in 1874,[2] proposing the
utilization of the enormous stretches of water communication
between the Rocky Mountains and the eastern terminus, and
embodied in the Act [3] of the same year, providing for the

[1] Sandford Fleming as government engineer undoubtedly understood
the situation. "I feel satisfied . . . after giving the matter careful
consideration that it would be best during the next two years or so to
carry on initiatory and desirable works directly by the Department of
Public Works" (Memorandum, September 29, 1874. *Sessional Papers*,
No. 48cc, 1882).

[2] Address to the electors of Lambton, January, 1874, MacKenzie,
Alexander ; also his speech introducing the Act of 1874 (*Globe*, May 13,
1874).

[3] A branch was proposed from the Eastern terminus to some point on
Georgian Bay to take advantage of Lake Superior. Provision was made
for construction of a telegraph line as soon as the railway had been located.
It provided for contracts for construction of subsections under the super-
intendence of the Department of Public Works. " The total sum to be
paid to the contractors . . . shall be ten thousand dollars per mile . . .
and no further sum . . . but interest at the rate of four per cent. per
annum for twenty-five years from the completion of the work·on a sum
. . . for each mile . . . shall be payable to the contractors and guarantees
shall be given . . . and the tenders for the work shall be required to state
the lowest sum per mile on which such interest and guarantees will be
required. That a quantity of land not exceeding twenty thousand acres
for each mile—shall be appropriated to alternate sections of twenty square
miles each along the line of the said railway . . . each section having a
frontage of not less than three miles nor more than six miles . . . and
that two-thirds of the quantity of land so appropriated shall be sold by
the Government at such prices as may be . . . agreed upon (with) . . . the
contractors, and the proceeds thereof . . . paid . . . for the contractors,
. . . the remaining third to be conveyed to the contractors. Each . . .
subsection . . . shall be the property of the contractors . . . and shall be
worked by . . . such contractors under such regulations as may . . . be
made by the Governor in Council. . . . In every contract . . . the Government . . . shall reserve the right to purchase . . . the said railway . . . on
payment of a sum equal to the actual cost of the said railway . . . and
ten per cent. in addition thereto "(37 Vic., c. 14). Further provision for
expenses of construction were made in an Act appropriating $2,500,000
out of the sum guaranteed by the Imperial authorities and providing for
this sum a sinking fund of 1 per cent. per annum and $1,500,000 out of a
sum to be raised without an Imperial guarantee (37 Vic., c. 2).

gradual construction of the road and for settlement of the country, was a result.

This change implied modification [1] of the terms of Union with British Columbia and evoked vigorous protests [2] from the people of the province who were unusually petulant as a result of the legacy of impatience inherited from the period of the gold discoveries and the consequent hectic development. Appeal [3] was made to the Imperial authorities and the Earl of Carnarvon was agreed upon as an

[1] The province had earlier shown signs of impatience at the delay in construction, but these were more pronounced as a result of MacKenzie's policy. As an evidence of good faith the Dominion Government passed an order in council on June 7, 1873, that " Esquimault . . . should be fixed as the terminus of the Canadian Pacific Railway and that a line of railway be located between the harbour of Esquimault and Seymour Narrows," and recommended that British Columbia be asked to transfer to Canada a strip of land twenty miles in width along the eastern coast of Vancouver Island between Esquimault and Seymour Narrows (*Correspondence respecting Canadian Pacific Railway Act so far as regards British Columbia*, 1875, p. 51). The province replied on July 25, objecting to the conveyance of the land until the line of railway was defined, but agreeing to make a reservation (*ibid.*). On September 20 the Dominion Government was asked to complete the surveys (*ibid.*, p. 55). Alexander MacKenzie, in a speech at Sarnia on November 25, 1873, tactlessly declared his intention of securing a modification of the terms of Union. On February 19, 1874, Mr. J. D. Edgar was sent by the Canadian Government to British Columbia to arrive at some basis of agreement. He was definitely instructed to insist that the construction of the road within the time set was an impossibility, and to point out that the terms did not require construction to Victoria or Esquimault and that the terms were only assented to by Canada to secure election pledges (*ibid.*, p. 31). He suggested that the Dominion Government would (1) Commence at once and finish as soon as possible a road from Esquimault to Nanaimo, (2) Spare no expense in settling as rapidly as possible a line to be followed by the railway on the mainland, (3) Make at once a wagon road and line of telegraph along the whole length of the railway in British Columbia, and continue the telegraph across the continent, (4) The moment the surveys and road on the mainland were completed, spend the minimum amount of $1,500,000 annually upon the construction of the railway within the province (letter to Attorney-General from J. D. Edgar, May 8, 1874, *ibid.*, p. 36). The Provincial Premier at once asked for Mr. Edgar's credentials (*ibid.*, p. 38). Mr. Edgar was recalled (*ibid.*, p. 61), and on June 8 the announcement made that the terms were withdrawn (*ibid.*).

[2] A protest was made on November 22, 1873 (*ibid.*, p. 57) and again on February 9, 1874, to the Dominion Government against the infraction of the terms of Union (*ibid.*, p. 58). Little satisfaction was obtained, since the Government replied that construction was impossible until the line had been located (*ibid.*, p. 60).

[3] In answer to a telegram of June 11, 1874, from British Columbia to the Earl of Carnarvon, stating that a delegate was to be sent to appeal against Canada's bad faith, Carnarvon ventured to act as arbitrator (*ibid.*, p. 24). To this British Columbia agreed on August 3 (*ibid.*, p. 69) and Canada on July 23 (*ibid.*, p. 72).

arbitrator.   The   arbitration   award [1]   expressed   in   the
Carnarvon terms was favourable to Canada and generally

[1] The cases of both parties were carefully presented.   As a preliminary
Mr. Walkem, the representative of British Columbia (*ibid.*, p. 63), in a
memorandum of June 15, 1874, reviewed the whole situation, emphasizing
the loss to British Columbia occasioned by delay of the project and the
very evident negligence of Canada in not fulfilling the terms as shown,
particularly in the policy embodied in the Canadian Pacific Railway Act of
1874 (*ibid.*, p. 39 ff.).   Mr. MacKenzie, on the other hand, insisted that
it was regarded as essential to the contract that the rate of taxation should
not be increased and that the terms were directory and not mandatory.
He reviewed the Edgar proposal and on the basis of Mr. Edgar's report
(*ibid.*, p. 29 ff.) pointed out that the intense interest of British Columbia
was due to the enormous personal benefits to be derived by a population
of 8,576 from vast construction expenditure (*ibid.*, p. 27 ff.).   In a dispatch
on July 23 greater stress was placed on the impossibility of constructing
the road by 1881 (*ibid.*, p. 72 ff.).   To this Mr. Walkem replied with
reference to the whole situation and particularly to the Edgar proposals—
(1) Nothing was being done by the Dominion Government towards commencing a railway from Esquimault to Nanaimo ; (2) That the surveying
parties on the mainland were numerically weak and that no guarantee
had been given as to the speedy prosecution of the surveys ; (3) That a
wagon road was not desired and it would be useless to people of British
Columbia and that even the telegraph proposed would not be made until
the route of the railway was settled ; (4) That the time of completion of
the surveys was very remote and that an expenditure of $1,500,000 was
insufficient.   Further by section 11 of the Canadian Pacific Railway Act,
1874, the House of Commons could reject at any time the contract for a
section of the railroad and prevent continuous construction—obviously
a direct charge against the good faith of the Dominion Government (*ibid.*,
p. 74).   The Dominion Government answered on September 17, 1874—
(1) The Dominion had no engagement to build a railway from Esquimault
to Nanaimo, notwithstanding the Order in Council of June 7, 1873, fixing
the terminus at Esquimault ; (2) That the surveys were being pushed with
the utmost expedition ; (3) A wagon road was one of the proposed terms
of the Union made by the British Columbia Legislature—it was a part of
railway construction and the declaration that British Columbia did not
desire it was made to lessen the value of the proposals to that province ;
(4) Nothing had occurred to justify the suspicion that by section 11 of
the Canadian Pacific Railway Act the House of Commons would prevent
continuous construction (*ibid.*, p. 80 ff.).   As a basis of agreement the
Earl of Carnarvon proposed—(1) That the Esquimault-Nanaimo section
should be begun at once ; (2) That the surveying parties should be greatly
increased in strength on the mainland and that a definite considerable
minimum amount should be expended ; (3) The wagon road to be abandoned and a telegraph line postponed until the road was located ; (4)
That an annual minimum sum of $2,000,000 should be expended on the
railway in British Columbia and that the road should be completed by
1890 (*ibid.*, p. 74).   The Dominion Government objected to the suggestions, particularly the increase of the annual minimum expenditure, the
increase in the size of the engineering force which involved duplication,
and the fixed limit of time for completion.   It promised to agree that
the territory west of Lake Superior should be completed to afford connexion with the existing lines of railway either by the United States or by
Canadian waters and to build the telegraph line as soon as possible (*ibid.*,
p. 80 ff.).   On October 31 Mr. Walkem finally presented the case of British
Columbia in a very lengthy review of the history of the controversy (*ibid.*,
p. 85 ff.).   On November 17 the Earl of Carnarvon gave his decision—

a recognition of the impossibility of fulfilling the terms of Union, and a justification of the new policy.

Operations were begun on portions of the route strategically located for settlement of the country.   An attempt was made to continue and improve the Dawson route,[1] from

(1) That the railway from Esquimault to Nanaimo should be commenced and completed as soon as possible ; (2) That the surveys on the mainland should be pushed with the utmost vigour ; (3) That the wagon road and telegraph line should be immediately constructed ; (4) That $2,000,000 should be the minimum expenditure on railway works within the province from the date at which the surveys were sufficiently complete to enable that amount to be expended on construction ; (5) That on or before December 31, 1890, the railway should be complete and open for traffic from the Pacific seaboard to a point on the western end of Lake Superior at which it would be connected with the existing line through a portion of the United States and also with navigation on Canadian waters (ibid., p. 92).

[1] This road, built to facilitate the transfer of the Red River expedition, continued open (Sessional Papers, No. 37, 1875).   Previous to its opening about 2,000 people had gone over the route of whom about 400 were settlers (ibid.).   After the opening 244 emigrants had been conveyed over the route to December 31, 1871 (ibid., No. 64, 1872), and 2,739 passengers, of whom 805 were emigrants, to October, 1873 (ibid., No. 37, 1875).   The fare was decreased from $25 in 1871 to $15 in 1872 and $10 in 1873 (ibid.).   In 1874 considerable improvement was effected (ibid., No. 39, 1875, p. 1 ff.) and a contract was made with W. H. Carpenter and Co.   A bonus of $75,000 was given by the Government to keep open a line of transportation for passengers and freight.   Passenger stages and freight wagons were to be run at least three times per week, the passengers to be conveyed in ten to twelve days and freight in fifteen to twenty days. The rates were carefully scheduled to encourage traffic.

THUNDER BAY TO FORT GARY

Passengers with 200 lb. Baggage	$10.00
Passengers under 14 yrs. with 100 lb. . .	5.00
Children under 3 yrs.	free
Freight, securely packed, per 100 lb. . . .	2.00
Household furniture (owner's risk) per 100 lb. . .	3.00

Machinery, horses, cattle, sheep, etc., at special rate.
Meals 30 cts.

WAY PASSENGERS AND FREIGHT

Land—Thunder Bay to Shebandowan—45 miles.
     North-West Angle of Lake of the Woods to Fort Gary—95 miles.

Passengers per mile	5c.
Freight per 100 lb. per mile	1½c.

Water and Portages—

Passengers per mile	2c.
Freight per 100 lb. per mile	½c.
Passengers Thunder Bay to Fort Francis .	$7.00 (ibid.)

In that year 2,000 to 2,500 passengers were carried, the majority during the first two or three weeks of the season (House of Commons Debates, vol. 1, 1875, p. 448).   In 1875 the number decreased to 1,800 or 1,900. The amount of freight in that year was only less than 2,000,000 lb. (Sessional Papers, No. 71, 1876).   The following year the road was abandoned after an expenditure of an annual average of $220,000 during the six years of its operation (House of Commons Debates, vol. 11, 1876, p. 452).

In order to make available the water stretches between Lake Superior

Lake Superior to Red River for the use of settlers. Surveys were prosecuted [1] particularly in British Columbia [2] to

and Red River work was commenced on Fort Francis Canal on Rainy River in 1875 (*Report of the Canadian Pacific Railway Royal Commission Evidence*, vol. I, p. 330). It was planned to make available 200 miles of navigable water between Kettle Falls and Rat Portage for steamboats of moderate draught. After an expenditure of $200,000 the work was abandoned (*House of Commons Debates*, vol. III, 1877, p. 1324 ff.).

[1] Reports appeared as the progress of surveys made possible definite decisions as to location. The choice of Yellowhead Pass gave a definite objective for a line from Lake Superior. The report of the surveys of 1877 located a satisfactory line from the standpoint of the various factors affecting the success of the road from Lake Superior to Tête Jaune Cache (Fleming, S., *Report on Surveys and preliminary operations on the Canadian Pacific Railway up to January*, 1877, p. 88). In 1878, Burrard Inlet was recommended as a terminus (Fleming, S., *Report Canadian Pacific Railway*, 1879, p. 17) and adopted by an order in council of July 13, 1878 (*Sessional Papers*, No. 19, 1880, p. 22). Dissatisfaction in British Columbia with this terminus led to a suggestion that another route should be surveyed (Fleming, S., op. cit., p. 18). A resolution was adopted on May 10, 1879, providing for further explorations in the Peace and Pine River districts (*House of Commons Debates*, 1879, p. 1895). Permission was also given to locate a new line from the Red River westward (*ibid.*). The British Columbia survey failed to reveal a better route than that to Burrard Inlet and it was chosen again on October 4, 1879 (Fleming, S., *Reports and Documents in reference to the Canadian Pacific Railway*, 1880, p. 6). A new line by Birdtail Creek was adopted for the route from the western boundary of Manitoba to the Saskatchewan on January 22, 1880 (*ibid.*, p. 24). Surveys over the whole line had been conducted with considerable energy and reported in a presentable manner, with the result that a great deal of information about the country had been gained and disseminated. They were conducted with a loss of thirty-eight lives. To June 30, 1880, surveys had cost $4,166,687.77 (*Report of the C.P.R. Royal Commission, Conclusions*, vol. III, p. 107).

[2] Geographically it was necessary to locate the line in British Columbia. Upon its location depended the choice of a pass through the mountains and upon this choice depended the location of the line to Lake Superior. The task was particularly difficult and tedious delays occasioned further protests from British Columbia. The attitude of the Province was one of insistence upon rapid prosecution. The Carnarvon terms could not settle the difficulty. The inability of Canada was constantly reflected in protests against an increase in taxation. " A road with less than ten people per mile " ; " 10,000 people asked Canada to build a line costing $200,000,000 " ; " Infatuation in the extreme to build 2,700 miles of road without increasing the taxation." A resolution that the Government should proceed vigorously with construction in British Columbia was defeated 154 to 7 (*House of Commons Debates*, vol. II, 1876, p. 879 ff.). The Esquimault and Nanaimo Railway Bill introduced in 1875 to build a road according to the Carnarvon terms was defeated in the Senate. " I opposed that bill . . . chiefly because it was part of the Carnarvon terms which I did not believe could be fully carried out consistently with the taxation resolution " (speech of Hon. Edward Blake, quoted Willison, J. S., *Sir Wilfrid Laurier and the Liberal Party*, p. 380). Compensation for delays in construction to the extent of $750,000 offered by the Dominion Government was rejected (*Journals of the Legislative Assembly of the Province of British Columbia*, p. 13 ; see also *Letters of Britannicus, Pacific Railway*, 1876). A motion was presented in the provincial Legislature providing for severance of political connexions with Canada, but had no

secure early location of the line preparatory to construction
of sections of permanent railroad and of telegraph line.[1]
To improve the communication between Red River and
Canada, provision was made for extension of the Canada
Central Railway to Georgian Bay,[2] for construction of a

seconder (*Journals of the Legislative Assembly, ibid.*, p. 9). An appeal
was made to the Imperial authorities in the same year (*ibid.*, p. 13). Lord
Carnarvon gave little satisfaction, except the belief that the road would be
commenced by 1878 (*ibid.*, 1877, p. 13). On August 30, 1878, a motion
for secession was passed by the Legislature (*ibid.*, 1878, p. 106 ff.). Adoption of the Burrard Inlet route and commencement of construction caused
the dissatisfaction to disappear. Contract No. 60, Section A, dated
December 23, 1879, for construction of the road from Emory's Bar to
Boston Bar, twenty-nine miles, was made with Andrew Onderdonk;
Contract No. 61, Section B, dated February 10, 1880, for construction
between Boston Bar and Lytton, twenty-nine miles, with Purcell, Ryan,
Goodwin and Smith; Contract No. 62, Section C, dated December 23,
1879, for construction between Lytton and Junction Flat, 28½ miles;
and Contract No. 63, Section D, dated December 15, 1879, for construction
between Junction Flat and Savonas Ferry, 40½ miles, with A. Onderdonk.
All of the contracts were eventually transferred to this contractor (*Sessional
Paper*, No. 19*m*, 1880, p. 196) and the whole was contracted for completion
on June 30, 1885. The remainder of the line from Emory's Bar to Port
Moody, 85 miles, was let to the same individual in 1882 (*Sessional Papers*,
1882, No. 48).
    [1] Contract No. 1, dated October 17, 1874, was made with Sifton, Glass
and Fleming for construction of a telegraph line between Fort Gary and
Fort Pelly. Contract No. 2, dated October 30, 1874, was made with
Richard Fuller for construction of a line between Fort Pelly and Edmonton.
Contract No. 3, dated November 10, 1874, with F. J. Barnard called for
construction of a line between Fort Edmonton and Cache Creek. Contract
No. 4, dated February 9, 1875, with Oliver, Davidson and Brown, provided
for construction of the remaining line from Prince Arthur's Landing to
Red River (*Canadian Pacific Railway Royal Commission, Conclusions*, vol.
III, p. 111 ff.).
    [2] To connect the Canadian railways with the North-West an Order in
Council of November 4, 1874, advised a subsidy of $12,000 per mile for
an extension of the Canada Central Railway from "Douglas westward to
the eastern end of the branch railway proposed to be built from Georgian
Bay by the government being about one hundred and twenty miles "
(*Journals of the House of Commons*, 1875, p. 219). To this the House of
Commons assented on March 13, 1875 (*ibid.*, p. 221; see also sec. 14, 37
Vic., c. 14). To complete the connexion with Georgian Bay, Contract
No. 12, dated February 27, 1875, was made with Hon. A. B. Foster for
the construction of a road to the mouth of the French River, 85 miles.
The contractor proposed the improvement of the navigability of the French
River to a distance 26 miles from its mouth, making the terminus at
that point. The contract was cancelled (*Sessional Papers*, No. 57, 1877,
p. 12 ff.). An additional survey was made and Contract No. 37, dated
August 22, 1878, with Heney, Charlebois and Flood for construction
between Nipissingen Post and the head of navigation on French River
(50 miles) was agreed upon. This was cancelled on July 25, 1879 (*Sessional
Papers*, No. 19*n*, 1880, p. 2 ff.); Contract No. 16, dated June 10, 1878,
with the Canada Central Railway provided for a change in the earlier
subsidy between Pembroke and Nipissing giving a total subsidy of
$1,440,000 (*Report of the C.P.R. Royal Commission*, vol. III, p. 246 ff.).

railroad from Lake Superior to Red River,[1] and from Red
River to the United States boundary.[2]   With completion
of the latter section transportation of materials to western
Canada was facilitated and sections were built west of Red
River.[3]   Construction was prosecuted under difficulties

[1] Contract No. 13, dated April 3, 1875, was made with Sifton and Ward,
for the construction of a railroad from Fort William to Lake Shebandowan,
45 miles (*Minutes of Evidence taken before the Select Committee of the Senate
appointed to inquire into all matters relating to the Canadian Pacific Railway
and Telegraph west of Lake Superior*, 1879, Addenda No. 5, p. 128).   Lake
Shebandowan as terminus was changed to Sunshine Creek, 32½ miles,
and completed in 1876 (*ibid.*, p. 1 ff.).   Contract No. 14 of the same date
and with the same firm, for the construction of a road from Selkirk to
Cross Lake (77 miles) was not finally completed until 1880 (*Report of the
C. P. R. Royal Commission*, 1882, vol. III, Conclusions, p. 226).   Contract
No. 15, dated January 9, 1877, with Joseph Whitehead, for the grading
of a line from Keewatin to Ross Lake (36½ miles) and for track-laying
from Keewatin to Selkirk (112 miles) was finally given up uncompleted
in 1880, expenditure of $1,875,830 (*ibid.*, p. 246).   Contract No. 25, dated
June 7, 1876, with Purcell and Ryan for grading between Sunshine Creek
and English River (80 miles) and for tracklaying between Fort William
and English River was not completed in 1880 after an expenditure of
$1,346,000 (*ibid.*, p. 317).   Contract No. 42, section A, dated March 7,
1879, with Marks and Conmee, for construction between English River
and Eagle River (118 miles) and section B, dated March 20, 1879, with
Fraser, Grant and Pitblado, for construction between Eagle River and
Keewatin (67 miles) called for completion in 1883 and for the road
to be in running order in 1882 (*Sessional Papers*, No. 19m, 1880, p.
4 ff.).
[2] Contract No. 5, dated August 30, 1874, with Joseph Whitehead, for
the grading of a branch from Emerson to St. Boniface (63 miles) was
completed in 1877 (*ibid.*, p. 153 ; also *Sessional Papers*, No. 82, 1876, p. 3).
Contract No. 5A, dated May, 1877, with the same individual, for construction of an extension of this branch to Selkirk (20 miles) was completed in
1880 (*Sessional Papers*, No. 64, 1878, p. 2).   Contract No. 33, dated June
21, 1878, with Kavanagh, Murphy and Upper, for bridging, track-laying
and ballasting the branch between Emerson and St. Boniface, was undertaken but cancelled (*Report of the Canadian Pacific Railway Royal Commission, ibid.*, pp. 334–6 ; also *Sessional Papers*, No. 5, 1880–1).   The
Canada Pacific Railway Act Amendment Bill, providing for the lease
of the road, was rejected by the Senate on the technical ground that the
assent of the Senate was not provided for in the Bill (*House of Commons
Debates*, 1878, p. 2454), but an agreement was finally made with Mr.
George Stephen on August 3, 1878, permitting a connexion of the branch
with the St. Paul and Pacific Railway.   This was cancelled on March 13,
1879, and contract No. 43, dated March, 1879, was made with Upper, Swift
and Messrs. Folger, for the equipment and operation of the line. This
was cancelled on January 26, 1880 (*Canadian Pacific Railway Royal
Commission, ibid.*, p. 407 ff.).
[3] Contract No. 48, dated August 19, 1879, with Mr. J. Ryan, called
for construction of a section 100 miles west of Red River.   After laying
track 31 miles the contract was cancelled and the work taken over by
the Government (*Sessional Papers*, No. 23k, p. 38 ff.).   Contract No. 66,
dated May 3, 1880, with Bowie and McNaughton, provided for construction
of a section 100 miles farther west.   The contract was cancelled (*ibid.*,
p. 58 ff.).

serious and to some extent recognized [1] as inherent [2] in the later policy. The executive capacity of the then recently organized Federal Government was sorely taxed with the immensity of the task. Since it was obliged to rely on technical skill inadequately developed [3] for a task of that character, mistakes [4] were inevitable.

[1] The MacKenzie administration was not wholeheartedly in favour of Government construction. "There are four great sections and it may be quite advisable, quite possible and altogether it may be the best thing that can be done, that each of these sections should be built by an independent company instead of having one grand company monopolizing the entire system of contracts. We do not expect that any company will make a proposition to build a less portion than one of the sections" (Speech of Alexander MacKenzie, *Globe*, May 13, 1874). "It would undoubtedly be advantageous in many ways to construct the Pacific Railway through the instrumentality of a large company" (Memorandum of Sandford Fleming, September 29, 1874 ; [*Sessional Papers*, No. 48*cc*., p. 30).

[2] "That the construction . . . was carried on as a Public Work at a sacrifice of money, time and efficiency. That numbers of persons were employed . . . who were not efficient . . . having been selected on party grounds. That . . . delays occurred . . . for the necessity of staying operations . . . until the necessary appropriations were made. That the examination of the country over which the line was located was inadequate, failing to give . . . information . . . necessary to enable the Government to estimate . . . the probable cost. That large operations were carried on . . . with much less regard to economy than . . . in a private undertaking. That the practice which permits a Department to originate . . . transactions . . . and . . . to award the contracts . . . is a disadvantage. That the system under which the contracts were let was not calculated to secure the works at the lowest price or the earliest date" (*Report of the C.P.R. Royal Commission, Conclusions,* vol. III, p. 495–6).

[3] "There were not a sufficient number of thoroughly efficient and practical men in the country to aid me in carrying out the work of preliminary operations in what might be deemed the best way" (letter of Sandford Fleming, May 1, 1882 ; *Sessional Papers*, No. 48*cc*., p. 5). "In our judgment this officer (Sandford Fleming) was overtaxed" (*C.P.R. Royal Commission, Conclusions,* vol. III, p. 97).

[4] The Report of the Royal Commission of 1882 presents the results of an investigation into relations of the Government with the Canadian Pacific Railway to that date in three large volumes. No attempt can be made to deal with all the evidence given. From this report, as well as from results of other investigations, general principles can be drawn. The inadequacy of engineering staffs was apparent. The cost of Contract No. 13 was estimated at $270,976. The actual cost was $331,979, an excess of $61,183, despite the fact that a change in location of the line saved $60,000 (*Minutes of Evidence taken before the Select Committee of the Senate appointed to inquire into all matters relating to Canadian Pacific Railway and Telegraph west of Lake Superior*, pp. 2–7). On Contract No. 14, because a careful survey had not been made to link this section with Contract No. 15, it was later found necessary to raise the gradient, which made the original estimate inadequate. Estimate solid rock, 10,000 yds., actual work, 34,442 yds. ; loose rock, est. 3,000 yds., actual 36,720 ; pile driving, est. $1,200, actual $12,586. Total cost, est. $402,950, actual cost $723,134 (*ibid.*, p. 13 ff.). Contract No. 15 in actual cost exceeded the estimated cost $930,915 (*ibid.*, p. 18) because of a change in

Embarrassment to the Government which these mistakes

policy in which trestles were replaced by earth, the gradients lowered and more rock work involved (*ibid.*, p. 20 ff.). Contract No. 25 revealed similar discrepancies : est. cost $1,037,061, actual cost $1,384,645 (*ibid.*, Addenda No. 6, p. 30). Est. solid rock, 260,000 yds., actual 76,800 yds. ; est. loose rock 10,000 yds., actual 110,000 yds. ; est. earth 1,000,000 yds. actual 1,970,000 yds. ; No. of ties est. 210,000, actual 241,000 (*ibid.*, p. 8). Contract No. 5, through less difficult territory, was no more accurately estimated : est. cost $120,000, actual cost to December 31, 1875, $174,800 (*Sessional Papers*, No. 82, 1876, p. 3). Careless surveying on the Georgian Bay branch cost the Government $41,000 (*Sessional Papers*, No. 57, 1877, p. 16). On the same section work on the branch costing $24,807 was abandoned because of a change in policy (*Sessional Papers*, No. 19*n*, 1880, p. 10). The inadequacy of the engineering staffs was evident in other directions. The terminus at Fort William was expensively and inadvantageously located (*Report and Minutes of evidence taken before the Select Committee of the Senate appointed to inquire into and report upon the purchases of lands at Fort William for a terminus to the Canadian Pacific Railway*, p. 4). On the advice of the engineer-in-chief, large quantities of rails were purchased in 1875. Later the prices fell and in addition a great deal of waste was caused by oxidation (*House of Commons Debates*, 1877, vol. III, p. 1688 ff.). The difficulties were enhanced by an almost undue reliance of the Government on expert advice. A change in policy decided upon by the engineers for permanent construction on Contract No. 15 was carried out in spite of the Government's determination " not to do it " (*Minutes of evidence before Committee of the Senate on Canadian Pacific Railway west of Lake Superior, etc.*, p. 59). The Premier against his own judgment accepted the choice of the engineer-in-chief of the terminus at Fort William (*Report and Minutes of evidence taken before the Select Committee of the Senate to inquire into and report upon the purchase of lands at Fort William, etc.*, p. 150). This reliance of the Government on advice of engineers, the inadequacy of this advice and the inexperience of the Government occasioned considerable difficulty with tenders and contracts. On Contract No. 15 the first tenders were received in May, 1876 (*Return to address, Papers connected with awarding of section 15 of C.P.R.*, 1877, p. 4). The lowest was withdrawn (*ibid.*, p. 6), and the next was declined with a forged letter (*ibid.*, p. 12). Later information was gained about the section and the Government advertised for new tenders. The lowest was withdrawn. The next offered security in timber limits or real estate valued at $80,000 but worth only $30,000 (*ibid.*, p. 20). The third proved sound (*ibid.*, p. 30). The security proved inadequate in a similar manner on Contract No. 5 (*Sessional Papers*, No. 58, 1878, p. 5 ff.), on Contract No. 48 (*Sessional Papers*, No. 23*k*, 1880, p. 38 ff.) and on Contract No. 61 (*Sessional Papers*, No. 19*m*, 1880, p. 24). At best construction of the road by sections necessitated an immense amount of supervision to ensure systematic progress. With inaccurate surveys the necessary supervision was impossible. As a result, contractors attempted to combine and further trouble resulted with tenders. Contracts Nos. 13 and 14 were let to the same firm. This was also true of Contracts No. 5, No. 5*a* and No. 15. A low tender on contract No. 15 was obliged to withdraw because of an extension of time on Contract No. 14 (*Return to address, Papers connected with awarding of section 15 of C.P.R.*, 1877, p. 12). Similarly, Contract No. 66 was found difficult for contractors and eventually cancelled because Contract No. 48 had not been completed (*Sess. Papers*, No. 23*k*, 1880, p. 66). Contracts Nos. 60 and 62 were let to one firm and transferred to A. Onderdonk (*Sess. Papers*, No. 19*m*, 1880, p. 116). Contract No. 61, the intervening section, on the advice of the Engineer-in-chief was also transferred to Onderdonk. Contract No. 63

occasioned, aggravated by the persistent efforts [1] of an energetic opposition, led to a search for a plan of construction

was judiciously sold to the same firm (*ibid.*, p. 151). The remaining section, because of a happy mistake of the Bank of Montreal in stamping the cheque of the lowest tender " two days only " was, despite all petitions, also transferred to this firm (*Sess. Papers*, No. 48, 1882). Onderdonk proceeded to form a syndicate, headed by D. O. Mills, and the whole section was constructed under one control (*Sess. Papers*, No. 19*m*, 1880, p. 196). Contract No. 42, section A, was awarded, despite protests of other tenderers (*ibid*,. p. 10), to a firm associated with the holders of Contract No. 25, the preceding section (*ibid.*, p. 6). Contract No. 12 was let to Mr. N. C. Munson, of Boston, but transferred to Mr. A. B. Foster, representative of the Canada Central Railway and the Quebec interests—a device which effectively checked Mr. J. D. Edgar, representative of the Ontario and Pacific Junction Railway and the Ontario interests (*Sess. Papers*, No. 44, 1875, p. 7). Reliance of the Government on advice of the engineers in location of the line was the cause of considerable trouble with settlements and of considerable embarrassment. A petition was presented on April 17, 1873, urging the advantages of Prince Arthur's Landing as a Canadian Pacific junction with Lake Superior (*Sess. Papers*, No. 77, 1877, p. 1 ff.). The choice of Fort William was made the occasion of another petition on February 26, 1875 (*ibid.*, p. 3). Charges were made that the Government was in league with land speculators, and a Committee of the Senate did reveal the fact that extravagant prices had been paid (*Report upon the purchase of lands at Fort William, etc.*, p. 149). The Neebing Hotel, worth $3,000, was sold to the Government for $5,029. Land purchased at $5 per acre was sold at $500 per acre (*ibid.*, p. 5). A valuator of the Government was also a member of a land speculation company (*ibid.*, p. 52-3). The Government took steps to prevent speculation, but after the mischief had been done (*ibid.*, p. 151 ff.). A further protest of Port. Arthur on March 19, 1878 (*Sess. Papers*, No. 186, 1879, p. 22 ff.) led the chief engineer to insist that the shortest route was desirable and that a six-mile extension was unjustifiable (*ibid.*, p. 43). In location of a line through Selkirk, settlers of Winnipeg complained that better land was available along the southern route, that heavy work would be avoided, and that the road would be able to meet its running expenses (*Report and Minutes of Evidence taken before the Select Committee of the Senate to inquire into and report upon the route of the C.P.R. from Keewatin westward*, pp. 15, 25). Mr. Fleming contended that Selkirk was in a direct line to Northcote and available to the trade of Lake Winnipeg and the Saskatchewan River. The located line was twenty-four miles shorter and from the long-run standpoint more central, less costly and had easier gradients (*ibid.*, p. 38 ff.). The Committee recommended an instrumental survey of the southern route (*ibid.*, p. 3 ff.), and this line was later adopted.

The inexperience of the Government was constantly in evidence. Contract No. 5 for the construction of telegraph was broken because the Government had awarded it before a line could be located and at an expense of $18,284 (*Sess. Paper* No. 82, 1876, p. 33). The bonus system applied to the Dawson route made it advantageous for the contractor to discourage people from travelling by that route (*House of Commons Debates*, vol. II, 1876, p. 454).

[1] The House of Commons debates present an array of charge and counter-charge on every possible existing and imagined discrepancy. The Senate was unusually active in the initiation of probes. Eventually charges were made against Sandford Fleming on the floor of the House on March 3, 1880, and he was diplomatically removed from office on May 22, 1880. A Royal Commission was appointed, and the ample report of 1882 presented (See *Sess. Papers*, No. 48*cc*, 1882).

possessing fewer disconcerting features. Though achieved under various difficulties, progress of the work on geographically strategic portions of the route, particularly the completion of the road from the United States boundary to Winnipeg, brought the search of the Government for such a plan nearer success. The economic development of western Canada [1] which made possible the construction of the branch was stimulated with its completion. Increased trade between Manitoba and the United States was a stimulus to [2] increasing demands, incidental to the national and economic growth of Canada,[3] for a more rapid and

---

[1] Population—

	1871		1881
Manitoba	94,021	..	108,891
Winnipeg	241	..	7,985

Trade of Manitoba was geographically directed through the United States. In six months, 1872, the Northern Pacific carried 5,000,000 lb. of freight destined for Fort Gary (Oberholtzer, E. P., *Jay Cooke, Financier of the Civil War*, vol. II, p. 343). The improvement of transportation facilities to the United States furnished striking evidence of the development of Red River Settlement and of the western states, as a phase of western expansion. In 1861 the Hudson's Bay Company placed a small steamer, the *Pioneer*, on the Red River to ply between Fort Abercrombie and Fort Gary. In 1862 a larger boat, the *International*, was added. In 1866 the free traders started trade with Mr. J. J. Hill as agent in St. Paul, and in 1871 placed a steamboat on the river (Pyle, J. G., *The Life of James J. Hill*, vol. I, p. 75). Competition led to an amalgamation in the following year and formation of the Red River Transportation Line in 1872, which later became the Red River Transportation Company. This company absorbed the Merchant's Line with two vessels, the *Manitoba* and the *Minnesota*, in 1875 (*ibid.*, p. 193). In the same year the company had built a line from Crookston to Fisher's Landing on the Red River, securing direct rail communication with St. Paul. After controversial financial manipulation it secured control of the St. Paul and Pacific Railroad on March 13, 1878 (*ibid.*, p. 185 ff.). On December 4 of the same year connexion was made with the Pembina branch of the Canadian Pacific Railroad (*ibid.*, p. 256). The St. Paul and Pacific Company interchanged traffic with the Red River Transportation Company (*ibid.*, p. 282). Satisfactory arrangements were eventually gained in which the American road was given running rights to St. Boniface. With the organization of the St. Paul, Minneapolis and Manitoba Railroad Company, control was secured of the Red River boats from Crookston to Fisher's Landing and from Breckenridge to Barnesville and the whole welded into a complete system (*ibid.*, p. 288).

[2] Jealousy which this increasing trade aroused in Canada had been evident in many directions (see Wilson, W., *Dominion of Canada and the Canadian Pacific Railway*, 1874, and House of Commons Debates for later years.)

[3] The decade was not one of rapid growth but of considerable change. Population :

	1871		1881
Nova Scotia . . .	387,800	..	440,572
New Brunswick . . .	285,594	..	321,233
Quebec	1,191,516	..	1,359,027
Ontario	1,620,851	..	1,926,922

The Canada Year-book, 1915, p. 64.

satisfactory prosecution of construction. The rapidity
desired could alone be accomplished by private enterprise
and central control.   Consequently, the Government ener-

Steam Railway Mileage :

1871	.	.	. 2,695	1877	.	.	. 5,782
1872	.	.	. 2,899	1878	.	.	. 6,226
1873	.	.	. 3,832	1879	.	.	. 6,858
1874	.	.	. 4,331	1880	.	.	. 7,194
1875	.	.	. 4,804	1881	.	.	. 7,331
1876	.	.	. 5,218				

Ibid., p. 466.

The panic of 1873 and the depression which followed had a decided influence
on the trade of Canada.

General Statement of chartered banks :

Calendar Year			Capital paid up		Notes in circulation		Discounts to the people
1871	.	.	$37,095,340	..	$20,914,637	..	$84,799,841
1872	.	.	45,190,085	..	25,296,454	..	106,744,665
1873	.	.	54,690,561	..	27,165,878	..	119,274,317
1874	.	.	60,388,340	..	27,904,963	..	131,680,111
1875	.	.	64,619,513	..	23,035,639	..	136,029,307
1876	.	.	66,804,398	..	21,245,935	..	127,621,577
1877	.	.	65,206,009	..	20,704,338	..	125,681,658
1878	.	.	63,682,863	..	20,475,586	..	119,682,659
1879	.	.	62,737,276	..	19,486,103	..	113,485,108
1880	.	.	60,052,117	..	22,529,623	..	102,166,115
1881	.	.	59,534,977	..	28,516,692	..	116,953,497

Ibid., p. 577.

Exports of Canada to United Kingdom and United States :

Fiscal Year				United Kingdom		United States
1871	.	.	.	$21,733,556	..	$26,715,690
1872	.	.	.	25,223,785	..	29,984,440
1873	.	.	.	31,402,234	..	33,421,725
1874	.	.	.	35,769,190	..	30,380,556
1875	.	.	.	34,199,134	..	25,683,818
1876	.	.	.	34,379,005	..	27,451,150
1877	.	.	.	35,491,671	..	22,160,666
1878	.	.	.	35,861,110	..	22,131,343
1879	.	.	.	29,393,424	..	23,149,909
1880	.	.	.	35,208,031	..	26,762,705
1881	.	.	.	42,637,219	..	31,015,109

Ibid., p. 253.

Imports of Canada from the United Kingdom and the United States :

Fiscal Year				United Kingdom		United States
1871	.	.	.	$48,498,202	..	$27,185,586
1872	.	.	.	62,209,254	..	33,741,995
1873	.	.	.	67,996,945	..	45,189,110
1874	.	.	.	61,424,407	..	51,706,906
1875	.	.	.	60,009,084	..	48,930,358
1876	.	.	.	40,479,253	..	44,099,880
1877	.	.	.	39,331,621	..	49,376,008
1878	.	.	.	37,252,769	..	48,002,875
1879	.	.	.	30,967,778	..	42,170,306
1880	.	.	.	33,764,439	..	28,193,783
1881	.	.	.	42,885,142	..	36,338,701

Ibid., p. 254.

getically [1] sought a group of capitalists to undertake the
task, and as a result of the progress which had been made in

The decline in exports to the United States and the steadiness of those
to the United Kingdom, the general increase in imports from the United
States and the decline in imports from Great Britain and the resulting
unsatisfactory condition of the revenue situation led to the demand for
markets and demand for increased duties. As a result the National
Policy was adopted in 1878 with effects on the trade and revenue situation
shown in the later years. The situation expressed itself in demand for
markets and demand for prosecution of the Canadian Pacific Railway
not only as a result of the discontent throughout the period but also of
the gradual development of Canada.

Fiscal Year

1871	.	$11,807,590	1877	. $12,544,348
1872	.	13,020,684	1878	. 12,791,532
1873	.	12,997,578	1879	. 12,935,269
1874	.	14,407,318	1880	. 14,129,953
1875	.	15,354,139	1881	. 18,492,645
1876	.	12,828,614		

Ibid., p. 257.

Receipts on Consolidated Fund Account :—

Fiscal year					Surplus in year	Deficit in year
1871	.	.	.	.	. $3,712,479	—
1872	.	.	.	.	. 3,125,345	—
1873	.	.	.	.	. 1,638,821	—
1874	.	.	.	.	. 888,776	—
1875	.	.	.	.	. 935,644	—
1876	.	.	.	.	—	$1,900,785
1877	.	.	.	.	—	1,460,028
1878	.	.	.	.	—	1,128,146
1879	.	.	.	.	—	1,938,000
1880	.	.	.	.	—	1,543,228
1881	.	.	.	.	. 4,132,744	

Ibid., p. 532-3.

[1] Following the opinion expressed by Fleming in 1874, the Government
in 1877 asked for tenders for the construction and operation of the whole
line or of sections of the line by companies. Tenders were solicited in
England by Mr. Fleming with the assistance of Sir John Rose. The result
was unsatisfactory, "only one imperfect offer made " (*House of Commons
Debates*, 1879, p. 1899). British investors had learned a lesson from the
Grand Trunk fiasco as shown in the suspicious attitude of the *London
Economist*. The Grand Trunk, hostile to any prospective competitor
for its western traffic and to any competitor for capital, carried on an
energetic campaign. Mr. Potter, President of the Grand Trunk, and
The Times were particularly active in 1875 in thwarting Mr. Hugh Allan's
attempts to secure money for the Montreal Northern Colonization
Railway (later the Montreal, Ottawa and Western Railway), an important
link in the proposed Canadian Pacific Railway. " Let Sir Hugh Allan
build his railway by all means, but with Canadian money " (*The Times and
Its Correspondents on Canadian Railways*, p. 9). The MacDonald administration, in a series of resolutions adopted May 10, 1879 (*House of Commons
Debates*, 1879, p. 1895), recognizing the difficulty of enlisting private
enterprise, proposed to build the line with Imperial support. A board of
Commissioners, including representatives of the Imperial Government,
was to be vested with all the ungranted land for twenty miles along the
railroad and additional land to the extent of 100,000,000 acres. The
Commissioners were given power to sell the land at a price fixed by the

construction of the project, and of the economic development, and the recognized possibilities of the areas involved, success was eventually attained. In June, 1880, it was announced by Sir John A. MacDonald that the necessary co-operation of capitalists had been secured. Conclusive evidence was at hand of the ability of Canada to support a transcontinental railroad and to overcome the barriers which had long held back its development. The economic development of the country became adjusted to the national development, which had made essential the contract of union with British Columbia, and had occasioned the innumerable difficulties of the period. The growing strength of the abutments was sufficient to permit the completion of the bridge. The contract for the construction of the road was signed on October 21, 1880.

Government, but not less than $2 per acre, the proceeds to construct the road. Colonization would proceed with construction. Sir Charles Tupper with several others went to England in accord with the temper of the resolutions to secure Imperial co-operation, but without results. During the Session of 1880 the resolutions were reaffirmed in general, but permission given to sell the land at a price not less than $1 per acre. In the summer, Sir John A. MacDonald, Hon. J. H. Pope, Sir Charles Tupper, Mr. George Stephen and Mr. Duncan McIntyre went to England and consulted various capitalists.

III

Fulfilment of the Contract

The contract for the construction of the road was an index of the growth of civilization in Canada. The details of the contract were evidence of the extent and character of that civilization. Capitalists undertaking the enterprise were significantly representative : Mr. George Stephen, President of the Bank of Montreal; Mr. R. B. Angus, Manager of the same bank ; Hon. J. Cochran, a Quebec cattle breeder, and Mr. Duncan J. McIntyre, Manager of the Canada Central Railway, eloquently represented the interest of Montreal, which had long sought control of a larger share of Western traffic. Mr. R. B. Angus, Mr. George Stephen, Mr. D. A. Smith and Mr. J. J. Hill to a large extent owners of the St. Paul, Minneapolis and Manitoba Railway, prominently bespoke the effect which construction of the Canadian Pacific and the development of traffic in Western Canada would have on the earnings of that line to Winnipeg. The name of Mr. D. A. Smith, though omitted from the contract because of the personal enmity of Sir John A. MacDonald, was of the greatest importance also as representative of land holdings [1] in Western Canada, and was

[1] Smith, early interested in the fur trade, was sent to England in 1870 by the wintering partners of the Hudson Bay Company to present their claims to a share of the proceeds of the sale of the Company's territory to Canada in 1869 (Willson, Beckles, *The Great Company*, p. 299). On his arrival in England he proceeded to take advantage of the rumours that the sale of land to Canada had greatly weakened the Company's position, and bought a majority of the company's stock at a very low price (Preston, W. T. R., *Strathcona and the Making of Canada*, p. 38 ff.). The shareholders were obliged to grant a total of £107,055 to the wintering partners, but nothing was said as to the share of the wintering partners of the land remaining in the hands of the company. The control of the stock by Smith and consequently of the land explained his reticence. " I ought to have pressed it (the question of land) on them. But really

particularly striking testimony to the economic development, prospective and immediate, of that area. Mr. P. Du Pont Grenfell, senior member of Morton, Rose and Company, and the American branch, Morton, Bliss and Company, represented English capital, and the interest of the firm [1] in the construction of the Government sections in British Columbia. The possibilities of colonization and emigration were recognized [2] in the interest of Reinach and Company, of Paris and Frankfort, and of the Société Générale.

The terms of the contract [3] were also significant. The Government agreed to give a subsidy of $25,000,000, of 25,000,000 acres of land, and of completed sections of road from Selkirk to Lake Superior and from Kamloops to Port Moody, which cost with the surveys $37,785,320. The grant of land was given in alternate sections of 640 acres, twenty-four miles deep on each side of the railway from Winnipeg to Jasper House, and sections unfit for settlement and deficiencies were made up by grants of land between parallels 49 and 57 degrees latitude, or by a similar grant of land along the company's branches. To facilitate the company's financial arrangements provision was made for the issue of land grant bonds to the extent of $25,000,000, in which they were deposited with the Government, one-fifth retained as security, and the remainder sold—the proceeds being paid to the company as the work progressed. The aid was given according to the difficulties of construction —the less difficult territory 900 miles west of Selkirk was granted $10,000 and 12,500 acres per mile ; 450 miles west of this line $13,333 and 16,666·66 acres per mile, and from Callander to Lake Superior, $15,384.61 and 9,615·35 acres per mile. Payment was made with the completion of every

---

it seemed such uphill work and I had so much to do " (Willson, Beckles, *Life of Lord Strathcona and Mount Royal*, p. 430). In 1874 he became the land commissioner of the Hudson Bay Company (*ibid.*, p. 543). He was particularly active in the establishment of communication from Red River to the United States Railroads, and in the formation of the St. Paul, Minneapolis and Manitoba Railroad.

[1] M. P. Morton, of Morton, Bliss and Company, was a member of the syndicate formed to construct the sections given out by Government contract in British Columbia (*Sessional Papers*, No. 19m, 1880, p. 196).

[2] *Commercial and Financial Chronicle*, vol. XXXI, p. 344.

[3] App. *B*.

twenty miles, but power was given to requisition an advance of three-fourths of the value of steel rails delivered. Land was granted for road-bed and railway purposes, and power given to locate the main line from Callander to Lake Superior, and from Selkirk to Kamloops by Yellowhead Pass, and to locate branch lines. The material required for construction and operation, and the capital stock, were exempted from taxation for ever, and the land was exempt for twenty years after the grant from the Crown. Favourable to the owners of the St. Paul, Minneapolis and Manitoba Railway, material for the original construction of the road was admitted free of duty, and the construction of any line south or south-west of the Canadian Pacific railway within fifteen miles of latitude 49 within twenty years was prohibited. The contract called for the completion of the road on May 1, 1891. The aid granted by Canada for the construction of the road was ample tribute to the insistence of demands for a rapid prosecution of construction, and to the strength and character of Canadian civilization.

The ratification of the details of the contract by a consistent majority [1] in the Canadian Parliament, in the face of a particularly energetic and hostile campaign, was conclusive proof that the programme of the Government was the programme of Canada. The activity of Ontario and of Toronto against possible lines diverting traffic to Montreal which had been effective in the earlier years was of little avail. A new syndicate, composed chiefly of residents [2] of Ontario offered to construct the road for a subsidy [3] of $22,000,000 and 22,000,000 acres of land. It offered to forgo the privileges, granting exemption from duty on materials and exemption from taxation on lands, and the monopoly implied in the

[1] *House of Commons Debates*, 1880–1, vol. I ; also *Journals House of Commons*, 1880–1.
[2] The leading directors were Sir W. P. Howland, H. H. Cook, A. R. MacMaster of Toronto, Wm. Hendrie, John P. Proctor, John Stuart and A. T. Wood of Hamilton, Allan Gilmour, James McLaren of Ottawa, John Walker, D. MacFie of London, P. S. Stephenson of Montreal, J. Carruthers of Kingston, G. A. Cox of Peterboro', A. W. Ross of Winnipeg, P. Larkin of St. Catherines, K. Chisholm of Brampton, Alexander Gibson of Fredericton, N.B., W. B. Lovitt of Yarmouth, N.S., and Barnet and McKay of Renfrew, Ontario. Of the twenty-one directors, seventeen were from Ontario, of whom eleven were from Western Ontario (*Sessional Papers*, No. 23m, 1882).
[3] *House of Commons Debates*, 1880–1, vol. I, pp. 5, 7–8.

provision prohibiting the construction of a line south of the Canadian Pacific Railway in Manitoba. The Government was given the option, in lieu of accepting construction on the section from Callander to Lake Superior, of accepting the construction of a line to Sault Ste. Marie with a bonus of $12,000 per mile. Construction in British Columbia and the Rocky Mountain section was made the subject of optional postponement. As a further attraction the Government was permitted to take possession of the road at an agreed compensation. Typically, the syndicate implied a charge of American patronage of the original contract, in its personnel of representative Canadian directors. The offer was rejected on January 25, 1881, by 140 to 54.[1]

Failing to thwart the contract as a whole, attempts were made to ensure particular rights. Toronto protested[2] against section 25 which gave the Canadian Pacific Railway Company power to purchase, lease, or otherwise amalgamate with other roads, and especially the Canada Central Railway, giving direct connexion with Montreal. It was claimed that this section violated the neutral character of the terminus and diverted trade from Ontario. It was asked that the Ontario and Pacific Junction Railway which had running rights over the Canada Central projected extension to Sault Ste. Marie, should be granted such powers over sixty-five miles of the Canadian Pacific, without which the running powers over the Canada Central would be useless. Objection was taken to the control of the line to the Sault by the Canada Central Company, and therefore by the Canadian Pacific, as it would be used as a feeder. A memorial of the Toronto Board of Trade suggested as a safeguard that the company " should not be permitted to place any higher mileage rates on the portion of their railway over which Ontario traffic must pass than on the portion over which eastern traffic must pass." As a result of this protest section 24 of the Act adopting the contract provided that the " Company shall afford all reasonable facilities to the Ontario and Pacific Junction Railway Company when their railway shall be completed to a point of junction with the

[1] *House of Commons Debates*, 1880–1, vol. I, p. 812.
[2] *Sessional Paper*, No. 48d, 1882, p. 28.

Canadian Pacific Railway and to the Canada Central Railway for the receiving, forwarding and delivering of traffic upon and from the railways of the said companies," and that it shall "receive and carry all freight and passenger traffic shipped to and from any point on either railway passing over the Canadian Pacific Railway at the same mileage rate and subject to the same charges for similar services."

These changes were not serious departures from the general trend of the act of incorporation, which was in accord with that of the contract. Power was given to construct telegraph or telephone lines, docks, vessels and elevators. Tolls could be reduced by Parliament only after 10 per cent. profit had been made on the capital expended in the construction of the railway, and only after the net income of the company had exceeded 10 per cent on the same amount. To ensure continuity of control a transfer of stock to non-shareholders was subject to the veto of the directors until the completion of the contract. The company was given power to raise capital by the issue of bonds to the extent of $10,000 per mile, and in case no land grant bonds were issued to the extent of $20,000 per mile and guaranteed or preferred stock at $10,000 per mile. The capital stock was fixed at $25,000,000. As soon as $5,000,000 was subscribed, of which 30 per cent. was paid up, and $1,000,000 deposited with the Government, the contract was to be transferred to the company. May 1, 1882, was the date assigned for the payment of 20 per cent. of the $5,000,000 and December 31, 1882, for the remainder. Little restriction was placed on the directors, as only a majority of fifteen and the President were required to be British subjects. This act of incorporation was carried after the failure of twenty-five amendments, and the ratification of the contract was completed on February 1, 1881, by a vote of 128 to 49.

The support of the Canadian Government in the fulfilment of the contract and its energetic execution, were earnests, in addition to the liberality of the terms of the contract and of the act of incorporation and the wholeheartedness of their adoption, of the eagerness of Canada to construct the railroad. The required deposit of $1,000,000 was made with the Finance Minister on February 16, 1881,

and the company was organized on the following day.[1]
Mr. George Stephen was President, Mr. Duncan McIntyre,
Vice-President, a testimony to the strength of Montreal
interests. In addition to these men, Mr. R. B. Angus and
Mr. J. J. Hill formed the executive committee—a tribute
to the importance of the St. Paul, Minneapolis and Manitoba
Railroad. Mr. J. J. C. Abbott was elected as counsel, Mr. C.
Drinkwater, Secretary and Treasurer, and Mr. G. B. Stickney,
General Superintendent of the western division—evidence
that the company had immediately organized as an effective
force. On the same day arrangements were made for
vigorous prosecution of the work. On March 3 stock to
the extent of $6,100,000 had been subscribed and 30 per cent.
paid in. The subscribers [2] of a majority of the stock
reflected the direct influence of the directorate and of the
interests concerned.

Plans [3] were rapidly made for construction. Application
was made and agreed upon that the standard of the Canadian
Pacific should equal the standard of the Union Pacific as at
the time of the Allan contract in 1873 and not as in 1881.
By the end of April 20,000 rails had been purchased in
England for delivery during the summer. To secure a
through line at the earliest possible date, the company
proposed to build a road connecting Sault Ste. Marie with
the Canada Central, and to place steamers on Lake Huron
to Thunder Bay. The Government had contracted for the
completion of the section between Thunder Bay and Selkirk
in 1882, giving the company a through rail and water route
from Selkirk to Montreal. At the same time, plans were
made for construction north of Lake Superior and on other
sections, as well as on a branch line to the Souris coalfields
in Manitoba. To check possible competition from the
Northern Pacific, and to meet the demands of settlers in
the southern area, not only was a shorter route desirable but

[1] *Railway Age*, vol. XIII, p. 116.
[2] Mr. George Stephen, Mr. J. J. Hill and Mr. D. A. Smith each subscribed 5,000 shares. Among other members, Morton, Bliss and Co.
subscribed 7,410 shares ; J. S. Kennedy and Co., 4,500 shares ; D. McIntyre
and Co. 4,750 shares ; H. S. Northcote, 1,860 shares. The remainder was
largely held by foreign parties in smaller sums. *Sessional Paper*, No. 48,
1882, pp. 14–15.
[3] *Railway Age*, vol. XIII, p. 24.

one more southerly than the Government's line located
through the Yellowhead Pass. To secure the best possible
line through the Rocky Mountains surveying parties [1] were
sent from Winnipeg and Victoria on May 2. On the same
date [2] under an order in council of April 9, the road from
Pembina to Selkirk and from Selkirk to Cross Lake, 162
miles, was transferred to the company by the Government.
The Government-located line from Winnipeg by Stonewall
to Portage la Prairie was re-located and shortened seventeen
miles. Location continued, and was completed as far as
Moosejaw Creek in December. Construction followed
rapidly, and in November the road was under operation
from Winnipeg west to Brandon, 145 miles.

The plans for, and prosecution of, rapid construction
made necessary immediate attention to financial arrangements. Funds secured from calls [3] for payment of the subscribed stock were supplemented by arrangements for the
issue of land grant bonds. Encouraged by a sale of 300,000
acres of land at $2.59 per acre in England during the
early spring, the directors announced in July the issue of
$25,000,000 of land grant bonds to be negotiated through
the Bank of Montreal, Morton, Rose and Company, and
Reinach and Company. Accordingly, under the terms of
the contract which permitted the company to locate its
branches and to secure a grant of land along those branches,
the company proceeded to strengthen the basis of the land
grant bonds by locating branches through prospectively
good territory. In August [4] it was planned to continue the
location survey of the Winnipeg and Pembina Mountain
branch, and to provide for its immediate construction,
and for the immediate location and construction of the
Assiniboine branch from a point twenty miles east of
Brandon north-east to Lake Saskatchewan, Fort Ellice and
the Touchwood Hills, and of the Saskatchewan branch
from a point near the Forks of Qu'Appelle in a north-westerly

[1] *Ibid.*, p. 254.
[2] *Sessional Papers* No. 8, 1882, p. 23.
[3] The first call came February 17, 1881, 30 per cent. ; second, April
30, 20 per cent. ; third, June 10, 15 per cent. ; fourth, September 5, 15 per
cent. ; fifth, February 17, 1882, 20 per cent. *Sessional Papers* No. 31,
1884, p. 67.
[4] *Railway Age*, vol. XIII, p. 432.

direction.   On August 16 the company [1] requested that the Government should reserve lands along the probable routes. A mortgage for the land grant bonds followed on August 30,[2] in favour of Sir A. Campbell, the Hon. Alex. MacKenzie, and Mr. S. Thorne of New York as trustees, the bonds being payable October 1, 1931, with interest at 5 per cent. payable semi-annually April 1 and October 1.   The company agreed to accept payment for lands in these bonds at 110.   Provision was made for redemption of the bonds out of the sale of lands at the market price, or by drawing in bonds and paying 10 per cent. premium.   In accordance with the terms of the charter, the proceeds of the sale of the land grant bonds were to be deposited with the Government, and the company was entitled to receive as the work progressed the same number of dollars as the number of acres of the land subsidy which had been earned by it, less one-fifth if the bonds were sold at par, or if sold below par less an amount corresponding to the discount.   Arrangements were made with a New York and a Montreal syndicate to take $10,000,000 at 92½, the Montreal syndicate taking $2,500,000 and the New York syndicate, represented by J. S. Kennedy and Company, the remainder.   The bonds were sold in instalments : $1,000,000 in November ; $1,000,000 in January, 1882 ; $1,000,000 in March; $1,000,000 in May, and $1,000,000 at the first of each month up to November. To facilitate these arrangements a concession of 5,000,000 acres of land and a half interest in each town-site west of Brandon on the main line of the road to the eastern boundary of British Columbia was made by the Canadian Pacific Railway Company to Messrs. E. B. Osler, W. B. Scarth, J. Kennedy Tod and S. H. Northcote.   These individuals, to pay for this concession, secured the right to purchase a sufficient quantity of land grant bonds from the New York syndicate.   Provision was made for the disposal of the remainder of the bonds through the formation of the Canadian North-West Land Company,[3] with head-quarters in London and a capital of $15,000,000.   It had twelve directors.   The

[1] *Railway Age*, vol. XIII, p. 432.
[2] *Sessional Papers*, No. 48, 1882, p. 70.
[3] *Commercial and Financial Chronicle*, vol. XXXIV, p. 662.

Canadian directors were Mr. E. B. Osler, Mr. W. B. Scarth, Mr. D. A. Smith and Mr. Alex. Ramsey. Among the other directors, of whom four were Scotch and four English, were Lord Elphinstone, Sir George Warrender, William John Menzies and the Duke of Manchester. Scotch and Canadian allotments were limited to $10,000,000. Active administration of this company's affairs was placed in the hands of the Canadian directors.

The success of these arrangements depended ultimately on their effectiveness in disposing of the land to settlers. To this end, the company applied, on January 13, 1882, (1) for the location and conveyance of lands already earned in railway belts along the main line, and along the two located branches extending west from Winnipeg, and embracing all odd-numbered lots fairly fit for settlement to a sufficient distance along the two railway belts to complete the quantity earned ; (2) for the preservation by the Government of odd-numbered lots for sale, remaining along branch lines east of the 104th parallel, and for permission to dispose of those lots in anticipation of the Government's action ; and (3) for a grant as part of the deficiency on the main line of a tract of land lying in the north-west territory south of the Pembina Mountain branch and of the Souris branch, and extending from these branches to the boundary line and west to the 104th parallel. On March 14 the Government agreed to grant land in the belt along the main line and along the two located lines named as far west as the 104th parallel, though refusing to permit the disposition of sections before they were earned.

On the basis of these financial arrangements, plans were made for a continuance of rapid location and construction of the line in 1882. On December 20, 1881, a request was made that legislation should be passed during the next session permitting the road to go by a southern route.[1] The required legislation stated that " the Canadian Pacific Railway Company may, subject to the approval of the Governor in Council, lay out and locate their main line of railway from Selkirk to the junction with the western section at Kamloops by way of some pass other than the Yellowhead Pass,

---

[1] *Sessional Papers*, No. 48, 1882, p. 67.

provided that the pass be not less than 100 miles from the boundary." [1] In March, 1882, the company was able to announce [2] the location of 1,650 miles of track, including the Winnipeg and Pembina Mountain branch from Winnipeg to Smuggler's Point, and thence westerly about fifteen miles from and parallel to the International boundary to a point a short distance west of Moose River, 220 miles. In April the Government agreed [3] that a portion of the Sault Ste. Marie branch should become a part of the main line, and the whole was authorized from Callander to Algoma Mills, 191 miles. Location continued throughout the year. Callander was definitely located as the western terminus of the Canada Central, 120 miles from Pembroke.[4] The line from Red Fox Creek to Moosejaw Creek was re-located and extended to Swift Current Creek, 113 miles, and from thence to South Saskatchewan Creek, 148 miles, in November. Location was carried out 195 miles on the Brandon branch,[5] which ran from Brandon south-west near Oak Lake, striking a point about fifteen miles from the International boundary and running parallel to the 49th degree.

Construction rapidly followed location. On February 16, traffic was opened for thirty-one miles west of Brandon, and on October 3 it was opened to Regina, 211 miles farther west. The frequency of application for the subsidy payable on the completion of twenty miles of track is eloquent of the rapidity of construction.[6] On June 8, 1882, a subsidy had

[1] 45 Vic. c. 53.   [2] Railway Age, vol. XIII, p. 432.
[3] Sessional Papers, No. 48, 1882, p. 63.
[4] Ibid., p. 21.
[5] December 31, 1881. Sessional Papers, No. 8, 1882, p. 11.
[6] June 26, 20 miles ; July 26, 20 miles ; July 31, 20 miles ; August 10, 40 miles ; August 22, 20 miles ; August 26, 20 miles ; September 12, 20 miles ; September 19, 20 miles ; September 27, 20 miles ; October 9, 20 miles ; October 17, 40 miles ; October 31, 20 miles ; November 11, 20 miles ; December 2, 20 miles ; December 6, 20 miles (Sessional Papers, No. 27, 1883, p. 52 ff.). For a general description of the rapidity of construction, see Vaughan, W., Life and Work of Sir William Van Horne, p. 76 ff. ; Skelton, O. D., The Railway Builders, p. 159 ff. See also general descriptions of the difficulties involved in construction. As much as $700,000 was spent on one mile, and $500,000 per mile was a common estimate for construction in the Rocky sections. It was found cheaper to build a dynamite factory than to purchase enormous quantities from plants. Muskegs were an additional source of trouble. Litigation with contractors was a characteristic feature—Conmee v. C.P.R. was a suit against contractors for an overpayment of $600,000 due to alleged false measurements.

been paid on 201 miles, and on January 23, 1883, on 581 miles.[1] The Turtle Mountain branch was advanced eighty-nine miles. In a summary report of the secretary of the company in February, 1883,[2] it was stated that track had been laid for forty miles west of Callander, for twenty-five miles east of Algoma, and for several miles east of Prince Arthur's Landing. Despite the late start in 1882 due to heavy snows and April floods 68·89 miles had been laid from March to June and 417·91 miles to the end of the year plus 28·30 miles of side track. Of the total, 30·79 miles had been laid in December. The report pointed out that the company had chosen the shortest possible route between Port Arthur and Callander, and along the whole line, in spite of an increased immediate outlay, the determining factors being the competitive value of the shortest route and the capitalized value of the saving in costs of operation. On the eastern section the grades were not in excess of 52·8 feet per mile and in the central section the maximum was 40 feet per mile. The embankments were solidly built (14 feet at the formation level). In the prairie section the road was built well above the surface of the country to avoid the snow. The ties were of tamarack at 2,640 per mile, and the rails were of steel at 56 lb. per yard.

This progress of construction proved a severe test to the company's financial preparations for 1882 and necessitated energetic measures for a continuance of such rapidity in the following year. In February, 1882, it was announced [3] that the Canadian North-West Land Company had taken $8,500,000 in bonds, the payments to be made monthly from November 1, 1882, to May 1, 1883. On the other hand, the difficulties of settlement and the campaign on the part of hostile interests depreciated the value of the land and rendered it almost unmarketable. Consequently the concession granted by the railroad company was reduced from 5,000,000 acres to 2,200,000 acres, and the syndicate found itself unable to dispose of its land grant bonds at a satisfactory price. The plans proved inadequate to the unusual demands of the situation.

[1] *Sessional Papers*, No. 27, 1883, p. 125.
[2] *Ibid.*, p. 171.   [3] *Ibid.*, p. 153.

With the failure of the land grant bonds to realize expectations, the company was obliged to rely on the sale of its stock, but failure to secure funds from one form of security had its effect on all. Although the first issue of $6,100,000 had been subscribed at par, the sale of the authorized total of $25,000,000 realized only 40c. on the dollar.[1] An evidence of financial difficulty was the company's resort to all possible expediencies. The Government was asked [2] not to deduct the advance on rails to the extent of 75 per cent. of their value from the payment of the subsidy until the financial situation became easier. An advance was asked on rails laid down at Hochelaga on the Quebec, Montreal, Ottawa and Occidental Railway—a road purchased by the Canadian Pacific Railway but according to the terms of the charter not entitled to inclusion.[3] In November permission was requested and given to substitute £339,800 of permanent debenture stock of the Credit Valley Railroad for $1,000,000 cash deposited with the Government as security with an option on the part of the company of resubstituting cash.[4] Constant vigilance characterized the policy of the company in regard to the land grant as an asset offering relief from financial difficulties. Upon the company's insistence an order in council of October 24 [5] reserved for sale 38,000,000 acres—the odd-numbered sections between 52 and 54 degrees latitude and 104 and 116 longitude. In response to further claims an order in council [6] of November 3 gave the odd-numbered sections between the belt of land along the main line and a six-mile belt on the Manitoba and Colonization Railway south of the main line, and between the Province of Manitoba and the Coteau or Dirt Hills, about 2,500,000 acres. Not content with this grant the company asked that it should include all the odd-numbered sections between the railway belt and the international boundary and west from Red River to the Manitoba boundary. Again the Government concurred on January 25, 1883.[7] On November 22, 1882, a grant of 6,204,807 acres earned on 501 miles was asked for on the ground that the

[1] Sessional Papers, No. 31, 1884, p. 106.   [2] Ibid., No. 27, 1883, p. 69.
[3] Ibid., No. 27, 1883, p. 97.
[4] Ibid., No. 27a, 1883, p. 135 ff.   [5] Ibid., No. 27, 1883, p. 187.
[6] Ibid., p. 188.   [7] Ibid., p. 194.

4,963,845 acres already granted had been given after a deduction of one-fifth, which was not according to the terms of the charter. The company insisted [1] that the charter provided that should they not issue land grant bonds secured by mortgage, one-fifth of the lands should be retained by the Government as security for maintenance and working of the road. Land grant bonds had been issued and the Government was therefore not entitled to the deduction. Again the Government finally agreed.

Finally, to meet the situation, in December, 1882, authorized capital stock was increased from $25,000,000 to $100,000,000, and to market this stock under favourable circumstances, a dividend of 3 per cent. was consistently paid. [2] On December 16 a contract was made with the North American Railway Contracting Company, [3] a New Jersey corporation with a capital stock of $3,000,000. Of the 30,000 shares, 21,267 were held in trust for the Canadian Pacific Railway Company [4] in proportion to the holdings of each shareholder. The original holders transferred a proportionate number of shares at cost price to such parties as the company was desirous of obtaining as participators in the enterprises. As a result W. Rockefeller, Winslow, Lanier and Co., Koehn, Loeb and Co., Drexel, Morgan and Co. and other prominent New York interests were represented. The contract stipulated that the road should be constructed from a point forty miles west of Callander to the east end of the Lake Superior section for the sum of $14,099,979 in cash and $20,000,000 in stock, and completed by December 31, 1886, and from a point forty-five miles east of the Saskatchewan river to Kamloops for the sum of $17,880,000 in cash and $25,000,000 in stock and completed by December 31, 1885. The minor provisions of the contract conspicuously protected the railway company. It kept general control with powers to increase the staff if progress was not satisfactory, and to cancel the contract if its orders were not carried out. In payments, 10 per cent. of the stock and cash was retained as security. The con-

---

[1] *Sessional Papers*, No. 27, 1883, p. 183.
[2] *Ibid.*, No. 31, 1884, p. 68. On August 17, February 17 and August 17, 1882 ; and February 17, 1883.
[3] *Ibid.*, p. 52 ff.   [4] *Ibid.*, p. 74.

tractors were given power to sell more stock than was
stipulated in the contract but at a price and in amounts
agreed upon with the railroad company. Provision was
made for the sale of the remainder of the stock in an agreement [1] on December 29 with a syndicate composed of W. L.
Scott, J. S. Kennedy, R. V. Martinsen, J. A. Stewart,
Ed. King and H. F. Spaulding, the issue, comprising
300,000 shares, being taken as follows : 100,000 shares at
50 on February 1, 1883 ; 100,000 shares at 52·50 on June 25,
1883 ; and the remainder at 55 on October 25, 1883. The
stock was disposed of by the syndicate committee without
great difficulty at $60, ensuring the company a supply of
funds from this source.

These attempts to meet the difficult financial situation
and to provide for continuance of the rapid prosecution of
location and construction, in 1883, were temporarily successful. In September, 1882, approval was asked for a line
by Kicking Horse Creek and across Selkirk Range by
Beaver Creek. [2] The early discovery of Moberly led to the
successful location of a line with a maximum grade of 105·6
feet per mile concentrated within twenty miles on each
side of the summit. The line [3] proceeded from the summit
of the Rocky Mountains west down the valley of the Kicking
Horse River forty-four miles, to the valley of the Columbia
River, north-west thirty miles into the valley of the Beaver
River, following it south and west to the summit of the
Selkirks. Descending the Selkirks the route followed the
east fork of the Illecillewaet River twenty miles, to a junction
with the main stream, and from thence continued south-
west twenty-three miles to the west crossing of the Columbia
River. The highest points were the Rocky Mountain
summit, 5,300 feet above sea-level, and the Selkirk summit,
4,316 feet. The maximum grade was 116 feet per mile
descending west from the summit of the Rockies and for
sixteen miles ascending the Selkirk summit and twenty
miles descending the same summit. At the summit of the
Selkirks was a level section three-quarters of a mile long
available for marshalling trains. The line involved a maxi-

[1] *Sessional Papers*, No. 31, 1884, p. 99 ff.
[2] *Ibid.*, No. 27, 1883, p. 25.   [3] *Ibid.*, No. 271, p. 7.

mum curvature of 10 per cent. Contrasted with the location of the Government line located by Yellowhead Pass, including 140 miles with a grade of 52·8 feet per mile, the company's line included sixty-three miles with two heavy grades of twenty miles each. The use of additional engines and wear of track were balanced against the additional operation of seventy-seven miles of line and an increase of two hours for passengers and four hours for freight. Through traffic represented only 10 to 12 per cent. of the whole, and the preponderance of this traffic being westbound the two heavy grades rising eastward were not serious. The operation costs on concentrated maximum grades was less than on several light grades. As a result of the approval of the Kicking Horse Pass line, location proceeded rapidly, and on December 6, 1883, it had been carried out to the summit of the Rocky Mountains.[1] On the eastern section location was prosecuted from both ends of the line between Prince Arthur's Landing and Callander.[2] In 1883 it was located sixty-eight miles east from Prince Arthur's Landing and 130 miles west of Callander. This line had a maximum grade of 53 feet per mile and curves of a minimum radius of 1,433 feet.

Location was rapidly followed by construction, and was accompanied by extension of the company's railway system by acquisition. On June 30, 1883, rails were laid for 960 miles west of Winnipeg,[3] and in September trains were running 881 miles.[4] The section from Selkirk to Port Arthur was under Government contract to be in running order by July 1, 1882, and to be completed by July 1, 1883. In the spring of 1883 the contractors expressed a desire to place the unfurnished portion of the road in the hands of the Canadian Pacific Railway Company. This arrangement[5] placed construction and operation of the section under one control and the contractors were released from the obligation

---

[1] On June 26, the line was located from the Saskatchewan River crossing to Medicine Hat, 123 miles ; on July 24, from Crowfoot Creek to Calgary, 69 miles ; August 25, to Padmore, 55 miles ; September 21, to Forty Mile Creek, 28 miles ; November 9, 35 miles ; December 6, to the Rocky Mt. summit, 5 miles.
[2] *Sessional Papers*, No. 25, 1885, p. 22 ff.
[3] *Ibid.*, No. 10, 1884, p. 13.   [4] *Ibid.*, p. 9.
[5] *Ibid.*, No. 31, 1884, p. 118,

of purchasing heavy equipment necessary to complete the contract. On May 10, the contract was placed in the hands of the company to be completed at contract prices minus a deduction of 15 per cent. for preliminary work done by the contractors,[1] and the opening of navigation in 1883 found the company in control of the whole section. Lake steamers were ready in the same year to carry the traffic from Port Arthur to Algoma Mills. The line from Pembroke to Callander was sufficiently improved to warrant the Government's permission to run trains at thirty miles per hour over the whole route on November 1, 1883.[2] In eastern Canada, with the early control of the Canada Central,[3] over which access was gained to Brockville on the St. Lawrence and to connexions with American railways to New York and Boston, the company proceeded to strengthen its position. The purchase[4] in 1882 of the western division of the Quebec, Montreal, Ottawa and Occidental Railway from Montreal to Ottawa brought an important addition. This included the main line from Montreal to Aylmer, the railway branch and bridge to Ottawa, the branch line to St. Jerome, and a branch from the main line near Mile End station, Montreal, to the Grand Trunk Railway between Dorval station and Montreal. According to the terms of the purchase, through freight and passenger traffic was carried over the Canadian Pacific Railway and the eastern section of the Quebec, Montreal, Ottawa and Occidental Railway to Quebec at rates charged by the Canadian Pacific for all traffic carried past the city of Ottawa in either direction. All rates were apportioned between the Government and the company at a mileage rate calculated *pro rata* according to the distance traversed by traffic on each of the railways. Concessions were made by the Government in regard to the dispatch of emigrant trains from Quebec and to all foreign mails and to the carriage of coal. The Government agreed to use every effort to secure the completion of the Intercolonial Railway

[1] *Sessional Papers*, No. 31, 1884, p. 124. [2] *Ibid.*, No. 27n, p. 15.
[3] The mileage of the Canada Central extended from Ottawa to Carleton Place, 29 miles ; from there to Pembroke, 76½ miles ; from there to Callander station, 120 miles ; and from Carleton Place to Brockville, 45½ miles ; total, 281 miles.
[4] Including Hull to Aylmer branch, 7 miles ; St. Therese to St. Jerome branch, 13 miles ; St. Lin to St. Eustace branch, 8 miles.

to Point Levis, and the installation of a ferry from Point
Levis to Quebec, making provision for the ultimate extension of the road to Halifax.   In addition to this extension
of the main line, branch lines were constructed.   The
branch from Winnipeg to West Selkirk,[1] twenty-two miles,
and the branch from Pembina Mountain Junction to Gretna,
fourteen miles, built in 1882, were supplemented by the
completion [2] of the branch from Pembina Mountain
Junction to Emerson, fifteen miles, which had been encouraged by a Government bonus of $50,000 for a bridge at
the latter point.   In 1883 the Pembina Mountain branch
was in operation for 102 miles.

Again the rapidity of the construction and expansion of
the road exhausted the company's resources and again it
was obliged to resort to all possible expedients.   The policy
of rapid extension necessitated changes in the management
and in the directorate as well as in the financial plans.
Offices had been opened in 1881 in Winnipeg with Mr. A. B.
Stickney as general superintendent and General Rosser as
chief engineer.   In December, 1881, Mr. W. C. Van Horne,
general superintendent of the Chicago, Milwaukee and St.
Paul, was appointed general manager and Mr. T. G. Shaughnessy of the same company became purchasing agent.[3]   In
1882 the directors were Mr. George Stephen, Pres., Mr.
D. McIntyre, Vice-Pres., Mr. D. A. Smith, Montreal; Mr.
J. S. Kennedy, New York; Mr. R. B. Angus, Mr. J. J. Hill,
St. Paul; Mr. H. S. Northcote, Mr. P. du P. Grenfell, Mr.
C. D. Rose, London; and Baron J. de Reinach, Paris.   The
executive committee included Messrs. Stephen, Angus,
McIntyre and Hill.   On May 3, 1883, Mr. J. J. Hill resigned [4]
from the executive committee and the board of directors
because of a policy which involved early construction of
the link north of Lake Superior and the diversion of north-

---

[1] *Sessional Papers*, No. 10, 1884, p. 14.   [2] *Ibid.*, p. 15.
[3] Vaughan, W., *Life and Work of Sir William Van Horne*, pp. 75-6.
[4] " " As regards the Nipissing and Thunder Bay line I have no actual
knowledge . . . it is most unfavourable for the operation of a railroad as a
financial success.   During the summer months it would have to compete
with the Lakes via Thunder Bay and the American lines over our own
road and in the winter I cannot see how it could get enough business to
justify the running of trains."   Letter to R. B. Angus.   July, 1880, Pyle,
J. G. op. cit. p. 314.

west traffic from the St. Paul, Minneapolis and Manitoba over the Canadian route. At the same time the executive committee ceased to exist and another Vice-President, Mr. R. B. Angus, was added. Mr. C. D. Rose and Mr. D. A. Smith made way in the interests of new financial arrangements for Mr. R. V. Martinsen, Amsterdam, and Hon. W. L. Scott, Erie, Pa. The following year, as evidence of the increasing prominence of expert railroad officials in the management, Mr. W. C. Van Horne became Vice-President in the place of Mr. D. McIntyre and Mr. T. G. Shaughnessy became acting general manager. Mr. J. S. Kennedy was replaced by Mr. Turnbull and Messrs. Rose and Smith again appeared on the directorate. In 1885 Mr. Turnbull and Baron de Reinach retired and M̃r. E. B. Osler, of the Ontario and Quebec Railway, Mr. Sandford Fleming and Mr. G. R. Harris, of Boston, were added.

In addition to changes in management some evidence of the financial exigencies of the company—though the weight of the evidence may be seriously lessened if judged according to norms of business astuteness—may be found in the unusually careful surveys made of all the railroad accounts. For instance, complaint was made of overcharging on the part of the Government to the extent of $46,607.65—(1) a contract of wire fencing cancelled by the Government at the time the company took over the road, $18,500 ; (2) fencing on the Pembina branch not executed, $8,000 ; (3) temporary bridge over the Red River not erected directly in connexion with traffic but for traffic purposes, $6,950 ; (4) customs duties which should not have been included in the valuation of engines, $7,599.50 ; (5) freight in store at the time the road was transferred and not worth the charges, $2,158.01 ; (6) overcharge on freight in transit, $3,400.14. To the payment of this the Government agreed [1] on March 27, 1883. On July 11, the company offered to purchase the Government's rolling-stock from Fort William to Rat Portage at certain stipulated prices. It was pointed out depreciatingly that the lack of standard in equipment, the age of the stock, and its rough service were factors seriously affecting its value. The matter was submitted to arbitration

[1] *Sessional Paper*, No. 31, 1884, p. 23.

and the locomotives alone proved to be worth $9,000 more than the company's total estimate.[1] The provision of the charter admitting materials for the construction of the main line free of duty made necessary the payment of drawbacks to Canadian manufacturers supplying these materials. Such drawbacks were a continual source of difficulty especially during periods of financial stress. The company was called upon to return $1,604.00 expended on materials used for the Algoma branch despite a suggestion [2] that an equal amount of materials should be used for the main line. Great care was necessary on the part of the Government to secure affidavits from the company and from contractors. A question was raised as to payment of drawbacks on bridges—steel being admitted free of duty. A ruling [3] favourable to the company held that they should be called iron bridges and entitled to drawbacks.

Late in 1883 the company submitted a definite proposition [4] to continue construction in the following year. Stock to the extent of $55,000,000 had already been issued and the conditions of the market made it impossible to issue more. To meet this situation it was suggested that certain funds should be deposited with the Government to guarantee the payment of dividends for a period of years. A fund of $24,527,145 to pay semi-annual dividends of 1½ per cent. on the entire stock for ten years was to be deposited with the Government, first, $15,000,145 in cash immediately, second, $5,000,000 with interest at 4 per cent. on or before February 1, 1884, and third, $4,527,000 to be paid within seven years. Security for the later payments (2) and (3) was to be furnished (a) by creating a charge on all sums earned by the company as postal subsidy and for transport service— $3,000,000 ; (b) by depositing with the Government $1,781,500 land grant bonds to cover the balance of $4,527,000 with the option of the company to pay such balance at any time in cash—the revenue derivable from these bonds was adjusted at 4 per cent. on $4,527,000 by the payment half-yearly of any deficiency or by the return

[1] Ibid., p. 80 ff.
[2] Ibid., p. 137.   [3] Ibid., p. 140.
[4] George Stephen to the Hon. Minister of Railways and Canals, October 24, 1883 (ibid., p. 1).

to the company of any surplus, and (c) by creating a charge on the $5,000,000 of land grant bonds held by the Government as security for the operation of the road. The Government was to be allowed interest half-yearly on the balance of the fund created, and was to pay from such balance and interest $1,500,000 semi-annually for ten years to the trustees as dividends, the first dividend payable February 17, 1884. Three days later the Government approved [1] the scheme, modifying it to the extent that the company should furnish funds to meet the dividends falling due on February 17, 1884.

On November 5,[2] a happier arrangement was suggested. Since the company did not need to dispose of the whole of its stock at that time, and since it preferred placing the stock on the market as the proceeds were needed for the prosecution of the work, and the extent of the deposit would involve expense and loss of interest, it asked the Government to agree to a reduction of the deposit to an amount sufficient to pay 3 per cent. on $65,000,000 of the stock, the company depositing the remaining $35,000,000 of stock with the Government to be returned as the amount of money required to cover a similar dividend was deposited. Under this arrangement the company would deposit $15,942,645—an amount sufficient to pay dividends at 3 per cent. on $65,000,000 for ten years. Of this the company was to pay first, $8,561,733 immediately and $2,853,912 on February 1, 1884, with interest to be paid semi-annually at 4 per cent., the payment to be secured by land grant bonds deposited—$3,420,000 ; second, within five years the remainder $4,527,000 with interest payable semi-annually at 4 per cent. secured (a) by a charge on all sums earned as postal subsidy and for transport service, $3,000,000 ; (b) by depositing further $1,830,000 of land grant bonds to cover the balance of $1,527,000 with the company's option to pay this balance in cash, the revenue derived from these securities to be adjusted as in the first proposal at 4 per cent. on $4,527,000 ; (c) by a charge on $5,000,000 of the land grant bonds held by the Government. As in the first proposal the Government was to allow interest at 4 per cent. semi-

[1] Ibid., p. 4.　　　　　[2] Ibid., p. 5.

annually on the balance in hand of the fund created and to pay from the fund and the interest $975,000 half-yearly for ten years as dividends to the trustees, the first dividend to be paid on February 17, 1884, and any balance required to be paid by the company. On the $35,000,000 of stock to be deposited, the company had the right to draw to August 17, 1883, as it deposited a sum of money which with interest added would pay a half-yearly dividend to August 17, 1893, on the stock withdrawn, and the Government was to pay to the trustees in addition to $975,000 a further sum equal to $1\frac{1}{2}$ per cent. on the amount of stock withdrawn. Two days later the Government agreed and the Bank of Montreal was appointed trustee.

The attempt to sell stock under favourable circumstances by the payment of dividends met with little success. The questionableness of the policy, the persistent propaganda [1] carried on by hostile interests depreciating the prospects of the road, and the unsatisfactory experiences [2] of financiers with Canadian roads seriously affected the price of Canadian Pacific stock. In December, 1883, it was quoted at 57. In addition to this difficulty as a result of the agreement which gave the Government control of the unissued stock, the contract with the North American Railway Contracting Company [3] was cancelled on November 21, and the company was obliged to carry on construction by other means.

At every turn the company exercised and was obliged to exercise the utmost care in the conservation of its financial resources. An application was made for the release from land grant bonds, to the extent of $10,000,000 in the Bank of Montreal to the order of the Government, of an amount sufficient to pay the company the sum earned in the construction of the line. In the agreement of November 7 a number of these bonds were deposited by the company to secure payments to be made under the agreement, and the Government claimed that these bonds were a first charge on the $10,000,000 of bonds held by the Bank of Montreal, and that

[1] A typical defence against these hostile interests. Mohawk, *The Canadian Pacific Railway and its Assailants.*
[2] *Economic Journal*, vol. XII, p. 409 ; *Economist*, vol. XXXVIII, p. 476 ; vol. XLI, p. 800 ; vol. XLIII, p. 625.
[3] *Sessional Paper*, No. 31, 1884, p. 52 ff.

none of them could be released until the amount required to be deposited under the agreement had been fully earned. It held that bonds pledged under the agreement had been released practically before they were earned. The company replied [1] on January 1, 1884. Construction was complete on 1,121 miles and on this basis according to the charter land was to be granted to the extent of 13,755,763 acres. Since the proceeds of the land grant bonds to be received by the company from the Government were the same number of dollars as acres of land minus one-fifth, $11,004,610 was due to the company. The company asked that this amount minus $10,000,000, or $1,004,610, of the bonds should be released. On January 7 the Government, after carefully reviewing [2] the situation, gave its approval.

On January 15,[3] in a further effort to meet the situation, the company suggested other measures. Its position was as follows:

Subsidy earned.	$12,289,211
Subsidy to be earned	$12,710,789
Land grant earned .	13,755,705 acres
Land grant sold .	3,753,400 ,,
Unsold balance earned .	10,002,305 ,,
Land grant unearned	11,244,295 ,,
Total available .	21,246,600 ,,

The lands sold had realized an average of $2.36 per acre.

Land Grant Bonds.

Bonds sold .	$10,000,000

[1] *Sessional Paper*, No. 25, 1885, p. 181.
[2] The Government's argument was as follows:

Lands earned	13,755,705
,, sold .	3,752,000
Unsold lands	10,003,705

3,752,000 acres sold had redeemed $6,108,500 of land grant bonds. Bonds held by land companies against payments to become due on the lands sold $1,383,000. Balance of purchase money remaining applicable to bonds issued $1,363,500. From 3,752,000 acres sold, $8,854,000 bonds held out of $10,000,000 had been provided for. The balance of bonds in the hands of the public, $1,146,000, had a security of 10,003,705 acres of land unsold. Adding the amount applied for—$1,004,000—made a total of $2,150,000, which was represented by land valued at $1 per acre —$10,003,705. Land was left unpledged—$7,853,000 estimating the value at $1 per acre, an unusually low estimate (*ibid.*, p. 179).
[3] *Sessional Papers* No. 31c, 1884, p. 4.

Bonds redeemed and destroyed . . . $6,667,000
Bonds held by land companies against payments
    for lands sold and not yet due . . . 846,000
Balances payable by individuals or lands sold not
    yet due 1,363,500

Total $8,876,500
Balance of bonds to be provided for out of unsold
    lands. 1,123,500
Balance of bonds in Government hands . . 15,000,000

Bonds existing $16,123,500
Lands earned and unsold, 10,002,305 acres at $2.36 23,605,440
Surplus from earned lands after paying bonds . $7,481,940
The liability of the company on bonds—in hands
    of public $1,123,500
Bonds charged with lien for payment of balance
    required to secure guarantee dividend. . 5,258,000

Total liability $6,381,500
Total lands available (earned and unsold) plus
    unearned, 21,246,600 acres at $2.36 . . $43,361,420
Stock :
    In hands of Government subject to $8,575,000
        for payment of dividends . . . $35,000,000
    On hand, from which it had obtained an
        advance of $5,000,000 . . . . $10,000,000

Expenditure to December 31, 1883 :
    1,121 miles main line · $23,563,564
    269 miles branch line. 3,827,092
    Improving railway received from Government 353,601
    Equipped lines and branches . . . 8,638,306
    Equipped extensions, Brockville and Mon-
        treal from Callander 3,203,050
    Materials on hand 4,028,604
    Paid in advance of dividend . . . 8,710,240
    Paid interest on capital stock . . . 2,128,000
    Interest on land grant and expenses . . 372,880
    Advances toward acquiring line to seaboard 3,482,251
    Acquired real estate for termini . . . 390,789

                         $58,695,377
Received cash and land subsidy . . . 21,318,222

Balance $37,377,155

It was estimated that about $27,000,000 was required for the completion of the road. Speedy construction was urged to develop the country and to secure a return on the capital already expended. The company asked, in the first place, for the release of $1,000,000 which had been deposited in 1881 and substituted by Credit Valley securities in 1882 as a guarantee for the completion of the road. It had expended $37,377,155 and during the last nine months had earned a net revenue of $978,660. The retention of the securities not only impaired the company's resources, but was an imputation on the value of the railway and the good faith of the company, and was no longer necessary. In the second place it asked that the subsidy should be paid on progress estimates as the payment on the mileage basis was inequitable, some miles being more difficult than others. Its third request was that the date of payment by the company of $2,853,912 in February, 1884, should be extended until it was needed for the payment of secured dividends on November 7, 1888, when the balance of the fund was payable. Lastly it requested a loan of $22,500,000 with the unpledged land grants as per statement—the proceeds of the lands to be appropriated (a) in payment of interest on the loan, (b) to establish a sinking fund to extinguish the principal. Further security was offered in a first charge on the company's main line and property including the Pembina branch and lines east of Callander. The advance was to be paid as the work proceeded. Four days later the Government engineer, Mr. Schreiber, recommended [1] that the suggestions should be adopted. The proposals [2] were approved by the Government on January 31.

The Act [3] embodying the terms of this agreement, after the usual bitter protests of the opposition, was sanctioned by Parliament. The security definitely provided was (1) a first lien on all the company's plant from Callander to Port Moody ; (2) a first lien on the section of main line between Callander, Brockville and Montreal, subject to a mortgage of $5,333,333 ; (3) a first lien and charge on all the land of the company earned and to be earned subject to the bonds

[1] *Sessional Paper*, No. 31c, 1884, p. 11.   [2] *Ibid.*, p. 16.
[3] 47 Vic. c. I.

outstanding. The land grant was placed in the hands of trustees to pay the proceeds of bonds held by the public, to pay the amount due in November, 1888, to the Government and to pay the advance. No bonds could be issued on the Government's security. No portion of the $35,000,000 stock could be issued without the Government's consent, and the proceeds of any issue were to be used to pay the Government advances. Six months' default in payment of the interest on principal created a statutory foreclosure. Provision was made for extinguishment of a current debt of $7,500,000, and the company agreed to complete the central and eastern sections of the road in May, 1886.

Following these financial arrangements and preparations, location and construction were again rapidly pushed forward in 1884. On the Rocky Mountain section the company was obliged to apply [1] for authority to construct a temporary line for about thirteen miles, dropping into the Kicking Horse Valley with a grade of about 232 feet per mile for four miles, and joining the original line at a point west of the most troublesome portion. It was estimated that the rapid construction of the permanent line to complete it in the time required by the contract would increase the cost of construction to an extent sufficient to build a temporary line. To this the Government agreed [2] on May 30. Location was carried forward ninety-two miles during the year and completed in March, 1885.[3] On the eastern section also location was rapidly carried to completion.[4]

Construction on the mountain section proceeded slowly but steadily and the company was able to predict completion in the fall of 1885. In the eastern section in October, 1884, 185 miles of track had been laid west of Callander, and sixty-seven miles east of Port Arthur.[5] In December there remained 254 miles.[6] The branch from Algoma Mills to

[1] W. C. Van Horne to the Hon. Minister of Railways and Canals, May 19, 1884, *Sessional Paper*, No. 25, 1885, pp. 10–11.   [2] *Ibid.*, p. 13.

[3] On June 21, 1884, 35 miles west of the Rocky Mt. summit ; July 25, 10 miles ; September 13, 15 miles ; September 21, 18 miles ; November 2, 14 miles ; January, 1885, 74 miles ; March, 82 miles. *Ibid.*, No. 25, 1885, p. 10 ff.

[4] In May, 1884, 261 miles east of Nepigon River ; July, 39 miles to Lake Nipissing ; in August, 40 miles. From Callander west in May, 60 miles ; August, 27 miles ; September, 35 miles. *Ibid.*, p. 22 ff.

[5] *Ibid.*, p. 34.   [6] *Ibid.*, p. 39.

Sudbury Junction, ninety-five miles, the link which gave the company a through rail and water route from Winnipeg to Montreal, was completed.[1]

Extension of the system through acquisition continued in 1884 as in the previous year. On January 4 an important step in the control of traffic in eastern Canada was made in the lease of the Ontario and Quebec Railway.[2] This included the Toronto, Grey and Bruce Railway leased on July 26, 1883, for 999 years; the London Junction Railway leased on November 19, 1883; the Credit Valley Railway system acquired by amalgamation on November 30, and the Atlantic and North-West Railway acquired by purchase on December 3. The lease gave the company better terminal facilities and secured access to important ports and connexions. The line to Owen Sound gave the company a larger share of the traffic shipped from the west to western Ontario and strengthened its hold on western trade. The St. Lawrence bridge gave additional facilities in Montreal. Connexions were made at St. Thomas with the Canada Southern branch of the Michigan Central, permitting the Canadian Pacific to share in the trunk-line seaboard traffic.

These acquisitions constituted a serious invasion on the territory of the Grand Trunk. The severity of the competition which followed led to a tentative agreement in which the Grand Trunk recognized the right of the Canadian Pacific to traffic going north-west and the latter road agreed to leave the Grand Trunk in possession of its district, but effective control by the Canadian Pacific of the Ontario and Quebec Railway made the agreement impossible[3] and competition was renewed. The Grand Trunk attempted to prevent the Canadian Pacific from gaining access to the seaboard. Running rights of the Canadian Pacific over the North Shore Railway to Quebec were rendered valueless

[1] *Sessional Paper*, No. 11, 1885, p. 12.
[2] Branches included : Fraxa Junction to Teeswater, 67 miles ; Streetsville Junction to Melville Junction, 32 miles ; Cataract Junction to Elora, 27 miles ; Western Junction to St. Lin Junction, 2 miles. The Atlantic and North-West Railway included a line from Mile End to the south end of the St. Lawrence bridge, the bridge itself, the section from Windsor Street, Montreal to Western Junction and the line from Smith Falls to Perth.
[3] *Railway Age*, vol. XV, p. 289.

by the transfer of control over the North Shore Railway to the Grand Trunk. With the acquisition of this control, it proceeded to construct the Jacques Cartier Union Railway from Sault au Recollet, a point on the Canadian Pacific Railway, to a point on its own road, $6\frac{1}{2}$ miles,[1] for the purpose of connecting the North Shore Railway with the Grand Trunk system. In the face of an ominous silence on the part of the Canadian Pacific the road was approved by the Government on October 10, 1883, and completed on December 8.[2] The North Shore Railway in the sale of its western division to the Canadian Pacific was given equal rights with the Canadian Pacific over the portion of the line between St. Martin's Junction and Montreal. The Grand Trunk attempted within these rights to put up and take in traffic with its own engines and staff at the junction with the Jacques Cartier Railway, using in this way 4 miles of Canadian Pacific track. The Canadian Pacific objected and insisted on certain rates for all cars going over its lines.[3] The Grand Trunk retaliated with a refusal to grant running rights of the Canadian Pacific over the North Shore line to Quebec and constructed an extension of the Jacques Cartier Union Railway to St. Vincent de Paul, making a direct connexion with the North Shore Railway.[4] The Dominion Government at this juncture offered to secure an outlet to Quebec for the Canadian Pacific by a subsidy to a line parallel to the North Shore Railway, which prospect of competition brought the Grand Trunk to terms.

An Act [5] was passed by the Canadian Parliament authorizing the setting aside of $15,000,000 to be used for the purpose of securing access to Quebec for the Canadian Pacific Company. Following this step on September 19, 1885, an agreement [6] was made with the Grand Trunk in which that company transferred all the shares, all the railroad property,[7] and $180,000 of unissued bonds of the North Shore Railway to the Government, and agreed to secure the

---

[1] *Ibid.*, No. 31, 1884, p. 87.
[2] *Ibid.*, p. 90.   [3] *Ibid.*, p. 92.   [4] *Ibid.*, p. 96.
[5] 48–49 Vic., c. 59.
[6] *Sessional Paper*, No. 35d, 1886, p. 1 ff.
[7] Including branches from Piles Junction to Grandes Piles, 27 miles ; Berthier Junction to Berthier, 2 miles ; Joliette Junction to St. Felix, 17 miles.

resignation of the directors of the North Shore Railway, to pay all the accounts of that railway between March 4, 1882, and September 20, 1885, and all other obligations incurred between April 20, 1883, and September 20, 1885, and to cancel all agreements with the Jacques Cartier Union Railway and the North Shore Railway. The Government agreed to pay $525,000 and in addition the cost of extra fuel laid in store for the winter and to assume obligations on property in Quebec and Hochelaga valued at $82,500. On the same date another agreement [1] was made with the Canadian Pacific Railway, transferring the shares of the North Shore Railway to Mr. George Stephen and the Hon. D. A. Smith, and the obligations assumed by the Government to this company. Interest secured at the rate of 4 per cent. on the $970,000 remaining after $525,000 had been paid out of the $15,000,000 set aside in the Act, was used to make up any deficiency of the operating receipts for the payment of bond charges. The remaining $5,000 was paid to the Grand Trunk in compensation for the cancellation of contracts made by the North Shore Railway with the Canadian Express Company, the Shedden Cartage Company and the Richelieu and Ottawa Navigation Company. With these measures the North Shore road became the property of the Canadian Pacific.

Again the rapid expansion of the system through construction during 1884 depleted the company's financial resources despite every effort to conserve them. On April 21 the company claimed [2] that certain accounts had been wrongly included in the floating debt and deducted from the loan of $7,500,000 : (1) advances on Duluth rails $280,736.09 should have been spread over the estimates and not deducted in a lump sum ; (2) deductions for rolling-stock on the Thunder Bay Section $185,890 should have been included in the Canadian Pacific Railway contract to complete that section, as also for rails between Port Arthur and Rat Portage $100,223.07 and timber and ties $9,538 45. The Government approved [3] the payment of $249,043.87, and agreed that the materials used on the Thunder Bay

[1] Sessional Paper, No. 35d, 1886, p. 6.
[2] Ibid., No. 25, 1885, p. 186.   [3] Ibid., p. 189.

Section should be spread over the estimates as the work was completed. On July 5, the Government returned [1] $1,004,000 of land grant bonds which the company had given in the belief that the Loan Act of 1884 called for a deposit of $10,000,000 with the Government which possessed at that time $8,996,000. On November 22 a question was raised [2] as to whether the $8,996,000 of land grant bonds held by the Government were to be treated as issued by the company in advance of their being earned, and whether the trustees of the land grant mortgage should pay interest on them as it came due, or whether they were to be treated as issued only after they had been earned. A Government ruling on January 7, 1885,[3] safeguarded the position of the company. It stated that the money received in payment of the $8,996,000 was to pay, first, the interest on the loan and on $7,380,912, the amount provided to secure the dividends ; second, on the capital of the $7,380,912 ; third, on the capital of the loan. Since the holders of land grant bonds were not desirous of having a charge on the proceeds of the land increased beyond what was clearly authorized, and since the security of the issued bonds would be lessened by charging the lands earned with the total issue, therefore the bonds earned by the company should be treated as issued and interest collected on them while unearned bonds should not be treated as issued.

In April, 1885,[4] the company had $7,000,000 of notes outstanding and due in two months. The blanket mortgage on the road given under the Act of 1884 and the deposit of $35,000,000 of stock with the Government made it impossible to secure funds either from the sale of stock or bonds. The company proposed[5] accordingly that its total debt to the Government, $29,880,912, consisting of the loan of $22,500,000 plus $7,380,913, the amount due according to the agreement of November 10, should be met by the delivery to the Government of $35,000,000 of first mortgage bonds with interest at 5 per cent. secured by a mortgage on the entire property, except the Algoma branch and other portions of the road

[1] *Ibid.*, No. 25a, 1885, p. 4.
[2] *Ibid.*, p. 6.   [3] *Ibid.*, pp. 7–8.
[4] See *Canada and Its Provinces*, vol. X, p. 439.
[5] 48–49 Vic. c. 57.

already mortgaged. The $35,000,000 of unissued stock in the hands of the Government was to be cancelled. The total debt was to be repaid with interest at 4 per cent. on May 1, 1891. As security the company offered for $20,000,000 of the debt the same amount of first mortgage bonds. The remainder of the debt—$9,880,912—was to be secured by a lien on the unsold and unpledged lands of the company. The remaining first mortgage bonds—$15,000,000—were divided into two portions, first, $8,000,000 as security for a temporary loan of $5,000,000, and the remaining $7,000,000 to be paid by the Government to the company as it was demanded. To this the Government finally consented.[1]

To a slight extent the Act of 1885 weakened the security provided in the loan Act of 1884. In the first Act a lien was given on the postal subsidy and in the second Act a lien was given on all the property as well as the subsidy. A ruling[2] was made that the Government was no longer entitled to money from the postal subsidy and transport service except in the case of amounts collected for these services on the Algoma branch and the company's leased lines. Such amounts were to be retained by the Government except in the case of leased lines in which the revenues were pledged. Difficulties[3] were also occasioned in the payment of the company's floating debt. On July 25, 1885, the company reported a floating debt on May 31 of $9,782,804.67 and asked for $4,782,804.67 to be paid out of the proceeds of the $7,000,000 portion of the bonds provided for in the Act, in addition to the temporary loan of $5,000,000. The company failed to show, however, that the debt had not been reduced at the later date and on July 31 the Government recommended the payment of only $1,104,538 plus $1,895,462, making a total of $3,000,000 which had been shown to be still due on the floating debt after the payment of $5,000,000.

Meanwhile, steps were taken for the issue of bonds. In conformity[4] with the Act the Government appointed the Rt. Hon. G. G. Glyn, Baron Wolverton ; the Rt. Hon. A. C. Baring, Baron Revelstoke ; and Hon. Sir Charles Tupper,

---

[1] For a dramatic description see Skelton, O. D., *Life and Times of Sir Wilfrid Laurier*, I, pp. 281–2 ; also Vaughan, W., op cit., p. 124 ff.
[2] *Sessional Paper*, No. 35, 1886, p. 16.
[3] *Ibid.*, p. 202 ff.   [4] *Ibid.*, p. 207.

as trustees of the mortgage. The bonds were dated July
1, 1885, and ran for thirty years at 5 per cent. There were
2,600 of £1,000 bonds, 5,800 of £500 and 6,900 of £100.
Interest on $20,000,000 to be paid to the Government was
4 per cent. and the whole sum was to be repaid before May 1,
1891. Elaborate provision was made for the default of
payment of interest or principal. On July 29 the mortgage [1]
was changed in the interests of negotiability, and the provision, that there should be a certificate upon it signed by the
trustees and the place for keeping the London register should
be at Messrs. Baring & Co., where the bonds and interest
were payable, was omitted. The company secured permission [2] from the Government to accept the proceeds in
lieu of the bonds to be held as security and steps were taken
for the final sale. Sir John Rose offered to purchase at 75,
but $15,000,000 were sold [3] to Baring Bros. at 90 and an
option given for the remainder at 91. They were offered
to the public at 95. The favourable reception of the bonds
was the result partly of missionary work [4] carried out by
Sir Charles Tupper, High Commissioner for Canada, partly
of the recovery following the depression of 1883 and 1884,
partly of the consistent support of the Canadian Government
to the railway and of the construction activities and railway
operations of the company. The favourable sale enabled
the company to repay [5] the loan on August 27, 1885, and
to secure the release of the $8,000,000 of bonds held by the
Government as security. On October 19, the $3,000,000
loan from the Government was repaid [6] and $4,800,000 of
bonds released.

The strenuous efforts to secure financial support from
the Government were stimulated by prospects of completing
the main line in 1885. The British Columbia section under
Government contract was completed on July 29, 1885.[7]
On the eastern section the road was of sufficient importance

---

[1] *Ibid.*
[2] *Ibid.*, No. 35, 1886, pp. 3–5.
[3] Saunders, E. M., *Life and Letters of Sir Charles Tupper*, vol. II, p. 59.
[4] *Ibid.*
[5] *Sessional Paper, Ibid.*, p. 10.
[6] *Ibid.*, p. 12 ; see also Skelton, O. D., op cit., p. 282.
[7] This line was handed over to the C.P.R. authorities on June 30, 1886.
Sessional Paper, No. 34b, 1887, p. 125.

to aid in the conveyance of troops to suppress the North-West Rebellion in 1885.[1] The section was finally opened for traffic from Callander to Port Arthur, 651 miles, on November 2.[2] On the mountain section the Government engineer reported that on October 10, 1885, 36 miles of track remained to be laid.[3] On November 7 Mr. Donald A. Smith drove the last spike at Craigellachie.[4] The Canadian Pacific Railway, with the completion of these links, extended from Montreal to Vancouver.

The fulfilment of the contract in the completion of the main line of the road was a significant landmark in the spread of civilization throughout Canada. It was significant of the strength and character of the growth of civilization within the boundaries of three distinct areas which served as buttresses for this transcontinental bridge. With this addition to technological equipment, the civilization of these areas changed in its character, and its extent, and became more closely a part of a civilization narrowly described as Canadian, and typically, western. These changes are recorded to some extent in the history of the Canadian Pacific Railroad and the history of Canada.

[1] The aid of the company in the transport of troops has generally been regarded as of considerable moment in persuading Parliament to accede to the financial arrangements in 1885. Van Horne even suggested that the Canadian Pacific ought to erect a monument to Louis Riel. Skelton, O. D., op cit., p. 278.

[2] Sessional Paper, No. 13, 1886, p. 11.

[3] Ibid., No. 35a, 1886, p. 11.

[4] Willson, Beckles, Lord Strathcona : The Story of his Life, p. 208.

IV

Expansion of the Road and the Development of Freight Traffic

AN index of the effectiveness of the road as an addition to the technological equipment of Canadian civilization was the amount of traffic carried. The extension of this equipment in the physical property of the road prior to the completion of the main line was accompanied by, and to a slight extent dependent on, an immediate development of traffic, especially of freight. Extension after the completion of the main line became increasingly the result, and continued as a cause, of this development of freight traffic. The importance of freight with reference to the particular characteristics of the road made necessary a marked increase in passenger traffic essential to settlement of western Canada, but such increase was subsidiary to the increase in freight. Built through a long stretch of unproductive territory, the road required a large outlay of fixed capital, which in turn necessitated the most rapid possible prosecution of construction of the main line and of branch lines, and the use of every possible device calculated to develop traffic. Immigration was encouraged by the efforts of the Canadian Pacific[1] on its own initiative and in co-operation with the Canadian Government.[2] Settlement was encouraged in every possible

---

[1] See Carnarvon, *Speeches on Canadian Affairs*, pp. 315–32 ; also description of colonies largely encouraged by C.P.R. *Sessional Paper*, No. 15a, 1889. For reference to the importation of immigrants as labour for the construction of the road see *Sessional Paper*, No. 54a, 1885 ; No. 54, 1900 ; No. 36b, 1905 ; also *Report of Royal Commission to Inquire into methods by which Oriental Labourers have been induced to come to Canada*, 1908.

[2] See reports of the High Commissioner on Emigration from United States and Europe. *Sessional Papers*, No. 5d, 1889 ; No. 6, 1890 ; No. 6e, 1891 ; No. 7b, 1892.

way. An energetic advertising campaign [1] and developmental rates were directed to that end. To direct traffic over the main line eastbound from Winnipeg, traffic south through the United States was discouraged, and the monopoly clause was rigidly enforced. Upon the increase in population [2] in western Canada largely depended the freight traffic of the road and to the development of freight energies were largely directed.

A. FREIGHT TRAFFIC AND EQUIPMENT PRIOR TO THE COMPLETION OF THE MAIN LINE

Under Government operation the first train left St. Boniface on February 10, 1880, and despite very difficult weather and lack of equipment, service was continued from that date.[3] The principal items of freight for the first five months ending June 30, 1880, were steel and provisions.

FREIGHT CARRIED TO JUNE 30, 1880 [4]

Iron and steel (largely steel rails)	15,779,719 lb.
Hides and skins	25,360 lb.
Oats	34,660 bus.
Wheat	31,841 bus.
Potatoes	3,775 bus.
Butter and cheese	9,528 lb.
Meat	1,290,263 lb.
Groceries	19,600,668 lb.
Total	30,467 tons.[5]

The commodities were typically those of an expanding agricultural settlement, exporting the raw products—grain (wheat and oats in about equal proportions) and hides and skins, and importing settlers' necessities such as groceries

[1] See Vaughan, W., op cit., p. 136 ff. Ham, George, *Reminiscences of a Raconteur*, p. 273 ff. Skelton, O. D., *The Railway Builders*, p. 178. Mavor, James, *Report to the Board of Trade on the North-West of Canada*, p. 12 ff.

[2] Population—

	1901	Increase per cent.	1891	Increase per cent.	1881
British Columbia	178,657	81·98	98,173	98·49	36,247
Manitoba	255,211	67·16	152,506	144·95	62,266
The Territories	211,649	113·86	98,967	75·33	56,446

Canada Year-book, 1903, p. 85.

[3] *Sessional Papers*, 1880–1, No. 5, p. 24.
[4] *Ibid.*   [5] *Ibid.*, p. 77.

and railroad supplies. In the following ten months the
monthly average of freight carried increased from 6,093 to
11,699 tons,[1] and although the number of miles in operation
increased from 280 to 367, the monthly average of tons of
freight carried per mile increased from 21·8 to 31·9. The
transfer of this section of road to the Canadian Pacific Railway Company on May 2, 1881 [2] materially increased the
amount of the mileage under operation and changed the
amount and character of the traffic. The number of miles
increased to 609 and included roads acquired in Ontario,
especially the Canada Central. The monthly average of
tons of freight carried per mile increased from 31·9 to 74·5.[3]
The individual items of traffic and their relative importance
are shown in the following table :

FREIGHT CARRIED DURING YEAR ENDING JUNE 30, 1882

Grain	3,937,166 bus.
Flour	40,006 bls.
Live stock	49,137 head.
Lumber	136,164,645 feet.
Firewood	12,532 cords.
Manufactured articles . .	104,236 tons.
Other articles . . .	313,568 tons.

Settlers' necessities and farm products still remained
important items, although the importance of the Ontario
roads was reflected in manufactured goods and lumber.
In the remaining years before the completion of the main
line, the rapid expansion of the road as shown in the increased
mileage from 609 to 4,338 [4] brought an increase in the
amount [5] of freight carried from 634,153 to 1,655,969 tons,
and a decrease in the amount of freight carried per mile.
The increase in traffic before the completion of the main

[1] *Sessional Papers*, 1882, No. 8, p. 23.
[2] *Ibid.*, p. 18.
[3] *Ibid.*, 1883, No. 8, p. 23.
[4] *C.P.R. Report*, 1885.
[5] Freight carried:

1882 . . . . 634,153 tons.	1884 . . . . 1,244,476 tons.
1883 . . . . 1,065,272 ,,	1885 . . . . 1,653,969 ,,

Compiled from *Sessional Papers*, 1883–6.

Note.—Because of the incomplete character of statistics presented in
early company reports, it has been found necessary for purposes of comparison in the first years of operation to use material furnished in reports
of the company to the Government.

line and the trend of particular items [1] was significant. The amount of grain carried declined in 1883, increased in 1884 and almost doubled in the following year. The amount of flour carried, reflecting in part the demands of increasing settlement, increased five times in 1883, tripled in 1884 and made a substantial increase in the last year. Live stock proved to be more under the influence of the grain trade and of the depression of those years, and fluctuated accordingly, practically doubling in 1883, declining almost to its lowest level in the next year and tripling in 1885. Lumber, influenced by the increasing demands of the new country, steadily increased to 1884 and declined slightly in 1885. Firewood, dominated by similar circumstances, as well as by climatic variations, increased five times in 1883, declined in 1884 and reached its highest level the following year. Manufactured articles, continuing to reflect the influence of the Ontario section of the road, steadily increased, more than tripling during the period. Flour, manufactured articles and lumber were significant items, and grain was of decided importance.

The expansion in mileage and the increase in traffic during the period were directly reflected in freight train mileage.[2] The total train mileage during the first five months of operation was 69,164, making an average of 13,832 train miles per month. In the next ten months the total increased to 214,607, a monthly average of 21,460. In the first year

[1] Traffic carried 1882 to 1885 (year ending June 30):

	1882	1883	1884	1885
Grain, bus.	3,937,166	3,213,085	4,727,671	7,842,343
Flour, bls.	40,006	213,528	713,662	915,219
Live stock, head	49,137	79,295	51,491	162,396
Lumber, feet	136,164,645	266,744,097	285,938,029	263,812,396
Firewood, cord	12,532	61,736	42,577	73,577
Manufactured articles, tons	104,236	229,491	267,657	393,219
Other articles, tons	313,568	260,916	287,454	443,290

Compiled from *Sessional Papers*, 1882-6.

[2] Train mileage, 1882-5:

	Freight Train Miles	Mixed Train Miles	Total Mileage
1882	544,929	—	937,243
1883	3,384,575	54,473	4,321,296
1884	2,683,590	1,534,231	5,278,542
1885	2,639,368	943,528	5,343,261

Compiled from *Sessional Papers*, 1883-6.

of the company's operation this was almost quadrupled to 937,243, a monthly average of 66,946. Of that year's total train miles, 544,929, or more than half, were freight train miles. As a reflection of the addition of roads in eastern Canada the number increased six times in 1883 and declined slightly in the two remaining years. Mixed train mileage, to some extent influenced by freight traffic and by construction activities, reached its highest point in 1884 and declined markedly in 1885.

The amount of freight train mileage directly influenced the amount and character of equipment. In the first five months of operation, the road was seriously handicapped by a lack of locomotives, a difficulty increased by the severity of the winter.[1] At the end of this period, relief had been obtained and the road possessed seven locomotives, two first-class passenger cars, one baggage-car, six box-cars, and forty platform-cars. In the next ten months equipment was increased to ten locomotives, six first-class cars, two smoking-cars, twenty-one box-cars, and one hundred and forty-eight platform-cars.[2] At the end of the company's first year of operation [3] the road had 118 engines, and this number was steadily increased and almost tripled by 1885. Cattle and freight cars were tripled in 1883, increased slightly in 1884 and almost doubled in 1885. As a result of construction activities, platform-cars steadily increased and more than doubled throughout the period. From the same activities, tool-cars increased from ten in 1883 to 241 in 1885.

The expansion of the road and the increase in traffic which directly determined the increase in train mileage and consequently in equipment, were responsible for the development of other facilities. In 1882 the road had 181 miles of telegraph of one wire and 714½ miles of two wires. In 1885 the line was opened for commercial service between

[1] *Sessional Papers*, 1881, No. 5, p. 23.   [2] *Ibid.*, 1882, No. 8, p. 86.
[3] Equipment, 1882–5 :

	Engines	Platform Cars	Cattle and Freight	Tool
1882	118	2,063	580	—
1883	186	3,579	1,602	10
1884	245	4,386	1,876	153
1885	315	4,400	3,072	241

Compiled from *Sessional Papers*, 1882–6.

Lake Superior and the Rocky Mountains.[1] With the acquisition of the Canada Central Railway and a terminus at Brockville,[2] the first elevator was acquired at that point in 1883. Completion of the section from Winnipeg to Port Arthur [3] led to the construction a year later of an elevator of 300,000 bushels capacity at the latter point. In 1885 elevator facilities in this locality were increased by the construction of an elevator with 1,350,000 bushels capacity at Fort William,[4] and an addition in the capacity of Port Arthur elevators of 350,000 bushels. The establishment of lake service necessary for a connexion between Port Arthur and Algoma led to the purchase of the *Athabaska* and the *Alberta*. The use of this lake service in connexion with the acquisition of the Ontario and Quebec Railway, and terminal facilities at Owen Sound, necessitated the construction of an elevator of 250,000 bushels capacity at that point in 1885. Acquisition of terminal facilities in Montreal,[5] led to the construction of two elevators of 1,200,000 bushels capacity at that point in the same year. The rapid increase in equipment necessitated the building of car-shops. Extensive shops at Hochelaga near Montreal for the manufacture of locomotives and passenger-cars were completed in the spring of 1883 [6] and in the same year general repair shops were constructed at Carleton and Winnipeg.

B. EXPANSION OF THE ROAD FROM THE COMPLETION OF THE MAIN LINE TO 1900

The increase in freight traffic which followed and stimulated the expansion of the road prior to the completion of the main line, continued to stimulate and follow its expansion after that time. In 1885 the company was in possession of a main line from Port Moody to Montreal and Quebec, of a line tapping the Great Lakes traffic at Owen Sound and Toronto and running eastward to Ottawa by Smith Falls, of a line extending from Toronto to St. Thomas and tapping the trunk line traffic, of a line to Brockville and American

[1] *C.P.R. Report*, 1885.   [2] *Dept. of Railways Report*, 1883.
[3] *Ibid.*, 1884.   [4] *C.P.R. Report*, 1885.   [5] *Ibid.*, 1886.
[6] *Ibid.*, 1884.

connexions, and of several branch lines which increased the traffic on these through routes. The enormous overhead charges occasioned by the length of the main line stimulated the energies of the company toward the development of traffic chiefly by extending and improving the connexions of the through routes and by developing branch lines.

To increase the control of through traffic to the Atlantic coast plans were made to secure access to ports which were free from the navigation difficulties incident to Montreal and Quebec. On October 6, 1883, the company foreclosed the bonds of the South-Eastern Railway.[1] A road was built from the south end of the St. Lawrence bridge to Farnham, 35·74 miles, to connect with this system in 1886–7.[2] In this way access was gained to the ports of Boston and Portland through arrangements with the Boston, Lowell Railway at Newport. To secure more direct access a line was also projected from Montreal to St. John or Halifax. From 1872 to 1875 the International Railway Company of Canada had constructed a line from Lennoxville to Megantic, 65 miles, and in 1879 this was extended from Megantic to the boundary, 15 miles. On November 2, 1886, the Atlantic and North-West Company purchased the International Railway Company and on December 6, leased the entire system in perpetuity to the Canadian Pacific Railway. The Waterloo and Magog Railway from Waterloo to Sherbrooke, 35 miles, built in 1874–5, was purchased by the Atlantic and North-West Company on June 10, 1888. The International Railway Company of Maine, under the control of the Atlantic and North-West Company and the Canadian Pacific Railway Company, and organized for the purpose of constructing a railway from the boundary to Mattawamkeag, 144·84 miles, completed its work in the same

[1] This system included the Lake Champlain and St. Lawrence Junction Railway from Stanbridge to St. Guillaume, 60 miles, acquired by a 29-year lease ; the Richelieu, Drummond and Arthabaska Counties Railway from Sorel to Drummondville, 37 miles ; from Drummondville to L'Avenir, 5 miles (later abandoned) ; and from Drummondville to Drummondville Junction, 59 miles, acquired by amalgamation ; and the Newport and Richford Railway from Abercorn to East Richford and from North Troy to Newport, 21 miles, acquired by 99-year lease.

[2] C.P.R. Report, 1887. Details as to the acquisition of roads were obtained directly from the company through the courtesy of Mr. W. H. Curle, K.C., General Solicitor.

year. This line from Montreal to Mattawamkeag, constructed and acquired in sections by the Canadian Pacific Railway, was provisionally extended farther eastward by an agreement with the Canadian Government on April 8, 1889.[1] This agreement was superseded by a more fortunate arrangement in the acquisition on July 1, 1890, by a 990-year lease, of the New Brunswick system which gave the company a direct line to St. John. In September an agreement was made with the Intercolonial for an exchange of traffic at St. John for Halifax. The company had finally secured an outlet to the Atlantic seaboard over a line 279 miles shorter between St. John and Montreal, and 101 miles shorter between Halifax and Montreal, than the Intercolonial route.

The energies directed to the prosecution of a through line from Montreal to the seaboard were stimulated and accompanied by an increase in traffic with the improvement and construction of through connexions west of Montreal. In competition with the Grand Trunk for trunk line traffic the Canadian Pacific was obliged to carry traffic to Montreal

---

[1] The Government agreed to build a road from a point of junction with the New Brunswick Railway near Harvey to a point of junction with the Intercolonial Railway near Salisbury and to lease this road as well as running rights over the Intercolonial from Salisbury to Moncton in perpetuity to the company. The agreement further provided for the carrying of freight between points west of Maine and Intercolonial points east of Moncton either way. The Intercolonial was entitled to the Halifax division of rates. These divisions were based on a constructive distance equal to the distance from Halifax to Moncton plus 15 per cent. On this constructive distance and the actual distance carried by the lessees the through rate was prorated. But it was not entitled to a proportion of the through rate exceeding its local tariff rate for the portion of the line over which the freight was carried. On freight between points on lines operated by the Canadian Pacific east of the west boundary of the state of Maine and Intercolonial points east of Moncton either way, the through rate was prorated on the actual mileage, provided that on intermediate local points on the Intercolonial, that road was entitled to its proportion for the next junction or terminal points eastward, and that on freight to and from local points on any line operated by the company east of Fredericton, from and to Intercolonial points east of Moncton either way, each party was entitled to its local tariff rates. Further arrangements were made as to passenger traffic and the establishment of a through route from Montreal to Halifax. For these rights the Canadian Pacific Company agreed to pay $1 per year for the first twenty years and thereafter $73,400 per year payable half-yearly and to pay the taxes and charges as though it was the owner of the road. Repairs and maintenance between Salisbury and Moncton were paid on wheelage basis. The bridge at Fredericton was leased in perpetuity, the rent consisting of maintenance and repairs. *Sessional Paper*, No. 36a, 1889, p. 285.

through Smith Falls and Ottawa. To improve its competitive position a direct line was built from Smith Falls to connect with the lines of the Atlantic and North-West Company at Montreal and completed [1] in 1887. To strengthen control of this traffic and of the Toronto-Montreal traffic, the company constructed a branch from Leaside Junction to Bay St., Toronto, and improved facilities [2] at the latter point. Difficulties [3] with the connexions at St. Thomas led to the extension of the road from Woodstock to London in 1887 [4] and to Windsor in 1888-9.[5] A steel ferry was constructed on the Detroit River and final agreements with American roads placed the Canadian Pacific on an effective competitive basis with the Grand Trunk for the seaboard traffic of the middle western states. To secure a larger share of traffic from the north-western states, control was secured of the Minneapolis, St. Paul and Sault Ste. Marie Railway Company and of the Duluth, South Shore and Atlantic Railway Company. The Canadian Pacific line was extended from Algoma to Sault Ste. Marie and connexions were made at that point with the Minneapolis Railway in 1888 [6] and with the Duluth Railway in 1889. As a result of increased traffic from these connexions, various improvements were necessitated on the line between Montreal and Chalk River. The alignments were improved and grades reduced to a maximum of 40 feet per mile going west and to a maximum of 35 feet per mile going east.[8] For the same reason the Montreal and Ottawa railway was leased on November 15, 1892, and a line from Ottawa to Montreal, 87 miles, was completed in 1898. This improvement of through connexions was continued on the western portion of the line. With the approaching pressure of traffic from western Canada, the section between Lake Nipissing and Winnipeg was improved by the replacement of wooden bridges with permanent embankments in 1888 [9] and following years. The indirect route of the Canadian Pacific by Smith Falls to Toronto became increasingly disadvantageous and an agreement was made in 1888 with

[1] C.P.R. Report, 1889.   [2] Ibid., 1888.   [3] Ibid., 1886.
[4] Ibid., 1887.   [5] Ibid., 1889.   [6] Ibid., 1887.
[7] Ibid., 1889.   [8] Ibid., 1888.   [9] Ibid., 1890.

the Grand Trunk permitting the Canadian Pacific to use its direct line from North Bay to Toronto.[1]

The importance of through traffic for a line of the Canadian Pacific's length and character led to efforts to secure control of Oriental and Pacific coast traffic. An extension of the road was constructed from Port Moody to the entrance of Burrard Inlet, 9 miles, in 1885–6 [2] for the purpose of acquiring better harbour and terminal facilities. In the mountains extensive snow-sheds were built and completed in 1887.[3]   In 1889 and 1890 a branch was built from Mission to American connexions with Seattle and points on American railways along the Pacific coast.[4] Connexions with the Orient were sought and acquired. In response to an advertisement of the Imperial Government of October, 1885, the Canadian Pacific [5] offered to furnish fortnightly service between Vancouver and Hong Kong for £100,000 per year for ten years. This offer was rejected since the payment by the Imperial authorities to the Peninsular and Oriental Steam Navigation Company for the conveyance of China mails would not be reduced by the diversion of only a part of the mails to another route. Emphasizing the importance of the Canadian Pacific route for the conveyance of mail and for military and naval purposes, a modification of the offer was made in July, 1887. In this tender the company agreed to a monthly service proposing to bring Shanghai within the main route of mail steamers and to include the land carriage within the time contract. The Canadian Parliament authorized a payment of £15,000 for a monthly service between Vancouver and Hong Kong and £25,000 for a fortnightly service. The advantages of this line in giving direct communication through British territory and affording an alternative route to the east, saving several days over the Suez route, finally led the Imperial authorities to accept this proposition. On July 15, 1889, a contract was signed in which the Imperial authorities gave

[1] *Ibid.*, 1888.
[2] *Ibid.*, 1885.   [3] *Ibid.*, 1887.   [4] *Ibid.*, 1891.
[5] *Copy of Treasury Minute dated July* 18, 1889, *and of contract with C.P.R. dated July* 15, 1889, *for conveyance of Her Majesty's mails, troops and stores between Halifax or Quebec and Hong Kong and for hire and purchase of vessels as cruisers and transports.*

a subsidy of £45,000 and the Canadian Government £15,000 annually for ten years. The agreement [1] called for one complete monthly service, 684 hours from April to November, and 732 hours from December to March, between Halifax or Quebec and Hong Kong. Vessels were to call at Yokohama and Shanghai. Provision was made for the transport of troops and the vessels were built under Admiralty supervision. The Admiralty was given power to purchase the boats under stipulated conditions. This arrangement gave the Canadian Pacific a through route from Halifax to Hong Kong. The *Empress of India* was the first steamship completed, and the *Empress of China* and the *Empress of Japan* were added in time to permit a full working schedule by the midsummer of 1891. [2]

The efforts to acquire control of the traffic of the Orient and of the Pacific coast increased competition with American lines and particularly with the Great Northern. [3] To strengthen its position the company constructed a branch from Pasqua, near Moosejaw, [4] on the main line to the boundary to connect with a branch of the Minneapolis, St. Paul and Sault Ste. Marie from Hankinson, North Dakota, in 1893. This branch shortened the distance between the Pacific coast and St. Paul and Chicago and gave the company a greater competitive advantage for this traffic. For the same competitive reasons and to prevent the extension of American roads into British Columbia, a line from Dunmore to Lethbridge, 107 miles, was acquired by lease in 1893 and by purchase [5] in 1897 from the Alberta Railway and Coal Company, and extended by construction to Crow's Nest Pass, and from that point by the lease of the British Columbia Southern Railway in 1898 [6] to Kootenay Landing on the lakes of British Columbia, 182 miles. Two years later under the charter of the latter railway, a line was built extending the route from Nelson to Proctor, 20 miles, [7] and connecting with the Columbia and Kootenay Railway to

[1] *Ibid.*   [2] *C.P.R. Report*, 1891.
[3] See Vaughan, W., op cit., p. 220 ff.
[4] *Railroad Gazette*, vol. XV, p. 645.
[5] *C.P.R. Report*, 1897.
[6] *Ibid.*, 1898.   [7] *Ibid.*, 1898.

Robson, 27 miles, leased in 1890.[1] In the following year the road was completed to Columbia River bridge and in 1901–2 to West Robson, connecting with the Columbia and Western Railway from West Robson to Midway, 100 miles, acquired in 1898.

The improvement and establishment of through connexions stimulated and were stimulated by the construction and acquisition of branch lines. The pressure of overhead charges occasioned by the increasing length of the main line, and the competitive and less remunerative character of through traffic, intensified the necessity for the development of local main line and branch line traffic. The development of this traffic in turn necessitated through connections. The barren character of the country from Winnipeg to eastern Canada, and the consequent heavy overhead charges on this section of the road, continued to be decided stimuli to the early extension of branches and the development of traffic in western Canada. Branches constructed in this area prior to the completion of the main line became the basis for a rapidly extended system. With the completion of the main line the company possessed parallel lines running on each side of the Red River south of Winnipeg to the United States boundary, one of which extended north to West Selkirk, and a line running from one of these branches parallel to and fifteen miles from the United States boundary to Manitou. On May 26, 1884, the Manitoba and South-West Colonization Railway was leased in perpetuity from June 1 of that year. This line ran westward midway between the main line and the southern Manitou branch and was extended to Holland in 1885[2] and to Glenboro in 1886.[3] The Manitou branch was extended under the same charter to Deloraine[4] in 1884–5. The ends of these parallel lines were joined to the main line by the construction of a branch running south-west from Brandon. With the Souris coal-fields in view, 17 miles on this line were laid in 1889[5] to Souris, 16 miles in 1890 to Hartney, 82 miles in 1891 and 47 miles in the next year to Estevan.[6] The southern Manitou branch was extended to meet this Souris

[1] *Ibid.*, 1890.   [2] *Ibid.*, 1885.   [3] *Ibid.*, 1886.
[4] *Ibid.*, 1886.   [5] *Ibid.*, 1889.   [6] *Ibid.*, 1890–2.

branch at Napinka, 18 miles. The branch midway between this line and the main line was extended 21 miles from Glenboro in 1890, 6 miles to Nesbitt in 1891, and 18 miles to Souris on the Souris line in the following year.[1] Another line was added with the construction of a branch from Elm Creek to Carman in 1889-90.[2] Westward expansion of the system continued in the following decade. Provision was made for the occupation of the entire western and northern area. On October 10, 1890, a road was completed from Regina to Prince Albert, 150 miles, which had been leased to the Canadian Pacific Railway by the Qu'Appelle, Long Lake and Saskatchewan Railroad and Steamship Company on August 7, 1889.[3] In 1890 and 1891 a road was built from Calgary north to Strathcona, 190 miles, and in 1892 south to West MacLeod, 103 miles, and leased to the Canadian Pacific by the Calgary and Edmonton Railway.[4] Generally the company included in these lines an area defined by the sector of a circle, with Winnipeg as centre, with the main line to Calgary as a radius and with the arc extending from West MacLeod to Strathcona. Within this area, a line was constructed west of the Souris branch from Menteith to Pipestone,[5] and in 1898, 17 miles beyond. The Deloraine branch was extended to Waskada in 1892, 18 miles, and to Lyleton, 37 miles, in 1902-3.

In British Columbia similar efforts in the construction and acquisition of branch lines for the development of traffic were made. On August 22, 1890,[6] control had been secured of the Columbia and Kootenay River Navigation Company by 999-year lease. The construction of the road from Nelson to Robson, 26 miles, connecting the Columbia and Kootenay Lakes, made available for over 250 miles a line of steamboat and railway communication to such important sources of traffic as the Kootenay mining district. The Shuswap and Okanagan Railway was leased for twenty-five years on August 4, 1892, and construction of a road from Sicamous on the main line to Okanagan Landing, 51 miles, gave access to agricultural and mining districts for over 100 miles.[7] In 1893 the lease of the Nakusp and

[1] *Ibid.*   [2] *Ibid.*, 1890.   [3] *Ibid.*, 1889.   [4] *Ibid.*, 1891.
[5] *Ibid.*   [6] *Ibid.*, 1889.   [7] *Ibid.*

Slocan Railway connected the Upper Arrow Lake at Nakusp
with the Slocan mining district, 36 miles, and with Sandon,
4 miles. This connexion was greatly improved by the
construction of a branch from Arrowhead to Revelstoke,
28 miles, in 1893–6. A branch from Slocan City to Slocan
Junction, 31 miles, built in 1897, and the addition of several
short branches by construction [1] and acquisition,[2] served
the mining areas effectively.

East of Winnipeg similar measures were taken for the
development of traffic, particularly contributing to the
support of the through line seaboard connexions. In 1885
a branch was built from Buckingham Junction to Buckingham, 4 miles, to the phosphate mines,[3] in 1887 a branch
from Glenannan to Wingham, 5 miles, to the salt district,[4]
and two branches from Sudbury to the copper mines, in
1899–1901 a branch from Molson to Lac du Bonnet, 22
miles, to a timber district, and in 1901 a branch from Dyment
to Ottamine, 7 miles, to a mining district. On January 1,
1891, the Guelph Junction Railway [5] was leased for 99 years
from September 18, 1888, including a line running from
Guelph to Guelph Junction, 15 miles. In the same year
control was acquired over the Lake Temiskaming Colonization Railway. In 1893 a branch from Mattawa to Temiskaming, 32 miles, was completed and in 1896 a branch from
Kipawa Junction to Kipawa, 9 miles. Under the charter of
the Atlantic and North-West Railway a branch was built
from Eganville Junction to Eganville, 20 miles, in 1898, to
tap an important timber area. The lease of the Montreal
and Ottawa Railway included a branch from Rigaud to
Point Fortune, 7 miles. The Montreal and Western Railway, leased in 1892, consisted of a branch from St. Jerome to
Labelle, 67 miles. The New Brunswick Railway system,
leased in 1890, included important branches—from Watt
Junction on the main line to Edmunston, 178 miles, passing

[1] Spur to Slocan mines, 4 miles ; Lardeau to Gerrard on the Trout
Lake Mining district, 33 miles, 1902.
[2] Columbia and Western Railway leased in perpetuity, July 12, 1898.
Trail to Rossland, 12 miles ; Smelter Junction to Castlegar Junction, 19
miles ; Eholt Junction to Phœnix, 9 miles ; Greenwood to Mother Lode,
7 miles ; Kootenay and Arrowhead Railway, leased August 15, 1901,
North Star Junction to Kimberley, 19 miles.
[3] *C.P.R. Report*, 1885.   [4] *Ibid.*, 1887.   [5] *Ibid.*, 1887.

through the important town of Woodstock and including two short lines to the Maine boundary, the Houlton branch, 3 miles, and the Presque Isle branch from Aroostook Junction to Presque Isle, 33 miles ; from Watt Junction south to the seaboard at St. Andrews, and the Maine boundary at St. Stephen ; and from Fredericton Junction to Newburg Junction, passing through Fredericton, 80 miles. The Tobique Valley Railroad, leased in 1897, included a branch from Perth Junction to Plaster Rock, 28 miles, and the St. Stephen and Milltown Railway leased in the same year, a branch from Milltown Junction to Milltown, 5 miles. In addition to the construction and acquisition of branches for the development of traffic, agreements were made to the same end. With the New York Central, the Michigan Central and the Canada Southern, a contract [1] was made for the completion and joint control of the Toronto, Hamilton and Buffalo Railway giving access to the Hamilton, Brantford and Niagara districts. In 1897 this contract became more effective with an agreement securing running rights over the Grand Trunk line from Toronto to Hamilton.

C. Freight Traffic and Equipment, 1885–1900

The expansion of the system in its completion of through connexions and its development of branches was largely the cause, and in part the effect, of the growth of traffic. Mileage [2] had increased during the period from the completion of the main line to the end of the century from 4,338 to 7,000, and during the same period the number of

---

[1] *Ibid.*, 1895.

[2] Mileage, 1885–99 :

1885	4,338	1893	6,327
1886	4,464	1894	6,344
1887	4,960	1895	6,444
1888	5,074	1896	6,476
1889	5,186	1897	6,568
1890	5,564	1898	6,681
1891	5,766	1899	7,000
1892	6,015		

Compiled from *C.P.R. Reports* and *Sessional Papers*.

tons of freight [1] carried increased from 1,655,969 to 6,620,903. This general increase in freight was steady, with the exception of a slight falling off in 1888, a decrease in the years of depression of 1893–4, and a rapid increase toward the end of the period. It was especially the result of the rapid increase in the number of bushels of grain carried, and reflected the importance of the road's expansion in western Canada. With considerable fluctuations, largely occasioned by climatic conditions, the amount of grain carried [2] increased from 7,842,343 bushels in 1885 to 42,763,253 in 1899. The frost and the rebellion of 1885–6 reduced the rate of increase in 1887, and the exceptional harvest of 1887 was recorded in the increase of 1888. Another early frost brought a decline in 1889. Except for a bad harvest in 1893, a slight decline in 1898, and a rapid recovery in the following year, the increase in the later years was consistent.

The expansion of the road, particularly in western Canada, and the rapid increase in the amount of grain carried during the period, were directly related to the increase of other commodities carried. Wheat was of dominant importance in grain traffic, and the increase in the amount of

[1] Freight carried, 1885–99, tons :

1886	2,046,195	1893	4,226,959
1887	2,144,327	1894	3,891,884
1888	2,496,557	1895	4,274,667
1889	2,638,690	1896	4,420,550
1890	3,378,564	1897	5,174,484
1891	3,846,710	1898	5,582,038
1892	4,230,670	1899	6,620,903

Compiled from *C.P.R. Reports*.

[2] Grain carried, 1886–99, bushels :

1886	10,960,582	1893	23,636,715
1887	15,013,957	1894	25,314,827
1888	15,965,682	1895	27,628,593
1889	13,803,224	1896	32,528,256
1890	20,167,888	1897	37,756,201
1891	24,894,141	1898	35,443,084
1892	29,309,887	1899	42,763,253

Compiled from *C.P.R. Reports*.

flour [1] carried roughly paralleled the increase in the amount of grain carried. The number of barrels of flour carried increased from 1,000,044 in 1886 to 4,005,226 in 1899. With the exception of a decline in 1894 and in 1897, and a rapid increase in 1899, this increase was remarkably steady, fluctuating less than grain. This fact strongly points to the pressure of wheat on milling capacity. An increase in 1889, with a decline in grain carried in that year, is explained, in part, by the rapid increase in grain in the previous years, which left the millers with grain on hand. Similarly the steady increase in 1893 is explained by the heavy crop of 1892. The crop failure of 1893 was reflected in the decline of flour in 1894. During later years, with the importance of increasing mileage in eastern Canada, and the importance of other grain than wheat, fluctuations in flour carried became less the result of fluctuations in grain carried. In 1897 flour declined but grain increased, and in 1898 flour increased but grain declined.

The number of tons of manufactured articles [2] carried was influenced directly by the expansion of the road, and was also sensitive to the agricultural situation. It increased from 476,698 in 1886 to 1,793,663 in 1899. With the exception of a slight decline in 1887, occasioned by the unsettled western conditions in 1885–6, and a marked decline in 1894 due to the depression of the middle 'nineties, the increase

---

[1] Flour carried, 1886–99, barrels :

1886	. . . . .	1,000,044	1893	. . . . .	2,514,163
1887	. . . . .	1,010,157	1894	. . . . .	2,439,418
1888	. . . . .	1,667,584	1895	. . . . .	2,832,304
1889	. . . . .	2,024,007	1896	. . . . .	3,291,299
1890	. . . . .	2,216,914	1897	. . . . .	2,911,072
1891	. . . . .	2,318,999	1898	. . . . .	3,292,450
1892	. . . . .	2,480,563	1899	. . . . .	4,005,226

Compiled from *C.P.R. Reports.*

[2] Manufactured articles, 1886–99, tons :

1886	. . . . .	476,698	1893	. . . . .	1,114,195
1887	. . . . .	470,699	1894	. . . . .	968,352
1888	. . . . .	600,521	1895	. . . . .	1,050,014
1889	. . . . .	762,238	1896	. . . . .	1,070,675
1890	. . . . .	927,787	1897	. . . . .	1,310,827
1891	. . . . .	985,090	1898	. . . . .	1,529,044
1892	. . . . .	1,055,533	1899	. . . . .	1,793,663

Compiled from *C.P.R. Reports.*

was again steady and consistent. This was largely the result of expansion in western Canada, though the foothold which the road had secured in eastern Canada and in the manufacturing cities of the United States was of considerable importance. The effect of the depression was eloquent of the influence of eastern connexions. Climatic conditions, though transient and becoming less serious to agriculture because of improved farming, were much less consequential to the manufacturing industries. The number of tons of other articles [1] carried were influenced by conditions similar to those affecting manufactures, and increased during the period from 498,940 to 1,461,144.

Lumber was dependent on the demands of the growth of western Canada, on the control of the road in Eastern Canada and the United States, and on the development of traffic in timber areas. The total number of board feet [2] carried increased from 327,760,432 in 1886 to 957,702,349 in 1899. As in the case of manufactures, and in response to the close relationship between building operations and depressions, the number declined in 1887, in the years of depression of 1893–4, and slightly in 1896, although the decline during the years of depression was more serious because of the bad harvest of 1893–4. The number of

[1] Other articles, 1886–99, tons :

1886	498,940	1893	978,193
1887	534,976	1894	864,615
1888	586,396	1895	930,101
1889	632,518	1896	878,261
1890	726,014	1897	994,813
1891	860,789	1898	1,119,097
1892	898,501	1899	1,461,144

Compiled from *C.P.R. Reports.*

[2] Lumber, 1886–99, feet :

1886	327,760,432	1893	668,176,926
1887	310,180,542	1894	545,488,960
1888	351,446,992	1895	638,806,374
1889	473,462,550	1896	636,128,418
1890	574,560,194	1897	831,895,383
1891	630,690,093	1898	840,145,338
1892	700,209,056	1899	957,702,349

Compiled from *C.P.R. Reports.*

cords [1] of firewood carried increased during the period from 75,625 to 202,461. It was dominated largely by the demands of settlers in western Canada for such necessities as fuel, and by the demands of the railroad. With the exception of a decline in 1889, brought about by difficulties incident to the bad harvest of that year, a decline in 1896 conforming with other commodities at that time, and a slight decline in 1899, the increase was persistent.

The movement of livestock [2] was largely significant of the influence, on traffic of the road, of the eastern agricultural situation characterized by mixed farming, and of the growth of ranching in western Canada. The number of head of livestock carried increased during the period from 244,257 to 810,559. The exceptional harvest of 1887 was followed by a decrease in the amount of livestock carried, and the poor harvest of the following year brought an increase in that number. In 1893 and in 1897, years of bad harvest, the number of livestock carried decreased—a change which points to the growing importance of mixed farming, the livestock industry depending more directly on grain, and a bad harvest restricting the marketing of the finished product. It was further a possible indication of the increasing prosperity of farmers, a bad harvest not necessarily leading to the sale of livestock.

The expansion of the road and this growth of traffic occasioned a rapid increase in train mileage. This was particularly significant with an increase in weight of the

---

[1] Firewood, 1886–99, cords :

1886 75,625	1893 170,294
1887 97,541	1894 174,020
1888 107,654	1895 177,032
1889 100,288	1896 166,831
1890 109,478	1897 185,208
1891 121,010	1898 203,336
1892 145,280	1899 202,461

Compiled from *C.P.R. Reports.*

[2] Livestock carried, 1886–99, head :

1886 244,257	1893 332,589
1887 205,572	1894 468,218
1888 251,297	1895 562,135
1889 276,514	1896 766,219
1890 288,853	1897 663,773
1891 309,639	1898 715,018
1892 375,292	1899 810,559

Compiled from *C.P.R. Reports.*

average freight train-load. The average freight train-load [1] increased from 162·2 tons in 1889 to 231 2 tons in 1899. The number fluctuated with a slight decline in 1890 and in 1897, a marked decline in 1893 due to the depression and the bad harvest of that year, and a very rapid increase in 1899. The marked increase in weight of the average train-load and the increase in the total train mileage from 5,024,148 in the fiscal year of 1886 to 18,424,701 in the calendar year of 1899, were important indices of the growth of traffic and of the expansion of the road. Total train mileage [2] increased consistently with the exception of a decline in 1893 and 1894. The increasing importance of freight was evident in the increase of freight train mileage [3] from 2,525,572 in the fiscal year of 1886 to 10,982,873 in the calendar year of 1899, and in the persistency of the

[1] Average freight train-load, 1889–99.

$$\text{Tons} = \frac{\text{Number of tons of freight carried one mile}}{\text{Number of freight ton miles :}}$$

1889	162·2	1895	195·4
1890	160·0	1896	199·5
1891	161·7	1897	199·0
1892	182·0	1898	204·1
1893	173·3	1899	231·2
1894	185·5		

Compiled from *C.P.R. Reports.*

Note.—No basis for compilation from 1882 to 1888 is available. Company reports omit statistics as to train mileage, and Government reports omit freight carried one mile.

[2] Total train mileage, 1886–99 :

1886	5,024,148	1893	14,522,612
1887	6,880,700	1894	12,943,703
1888	10,077,416*	1895	13,344,580
1889	10,956,316	1896	14,712,595
1890	13,023,312	1897	16,100,733
1891	14,322,370	1898	17,656,893
1892	14,525,677	1899	18,424,701

Compiled from *C.P.R. Reports* and *Government Reports.*

* First three years from *Government Reports.*

[3] Freight train mileage, 1886–99 :

1886	2,525,572	1893	8,385,880
1887	3,238,103	1894	7,082,645
1888	5,702,948*	1895	7,625,462
1889	5,964,585	1896	8,870,134
1890	7,547,058	1897	9,826,734
1891	8,605,829	1898	10,496,129
1892	8,691,132	1899	10,982,873

Compiled from *C.P.R. Reports* and *Government Reports.*

* First three years from *Government Reports.*

increase, which began in 1892, and though followed by a decline to 1895, continued to 1899.

The growth of traffic and the increase in train mileage, accompanied by an increase in the weight of the train-load, were directly the causes and the effects of improved gradients and alignments and improved standards of equipment. The total number of freight and cattle cars [1] increased from 7,838 to 19,005 during the period. This increase was persistent though it slackened in 1889 in accordance with the grain situation of that year, and in the middle 'nineties, and gained rapidly during the latter part of the period, especially in the last year. Locomotives,[2] influenced by the passenger situation, and by improved standards evident in the increased average train-load, increased less rapidly. From 1886 to 1899 the number rose from 372 to 690, increasing steadily during the early part of the period, remaining stationary from 1894 to 1896, and increasing rapidly in the remainder of the period. The number of conductors' vans [3] dependent upon the freight train mileage, the average train-load, the size of the locomotives and the proportion of through to local traffic increased during the period from 178

[1] Freight and cattle cars, 1886–99 :

1886	8,253	1893	14,505
1887	9,296	1894	14,555
1888	11,020	1895	14,890
1889	11,318	1896	15,162
1890	13,071	1897	15,544
1891	14,077	1898	16,942
1892	14,304	1899	19,005

Compiled from *C.P.R. Reports.*

[2] Locomotives, 1886–99 :

1886	372	1893	578
1887	374	1894	584
1888	408	1895	584
1889	413	1896	584
1890	484	1897	598
1891	530	1898	644
1892	569	1899	690

Compiled from *C.P.R. Reports.*

[3] Conductors' vans, 1886–99 :

1886	178	1893	297
1887	185	1894	297
1888	202	1895	297
1889	202	1896	297
1890	230	1897	312
1891	253	1898	348
1892	291	1899	362

Compiled from *C.P.R. Reports.*

to 362, increasing steadily to 1888, remaining stationary through 1889, increasing rapidly to 1893, remaining stationary again through 1896, and increasing rapidly during the remainder of the period.   Boarding, tool and auxiliary cars [1] indicating the increase in construction activities, rose in number from 71 in 1886 to 682 in 1899, the increase being steady and rapid, except for the year 1887, and the years of depression, and a decrease in 1895.

This increase in traffic which led to an increase in train mileage and in equipment was again the cause and the effect of the improvement of physical property of the road and of the development of other services.   In 1890 72-lb. rails [2] were laid on 171 miles of main line and on 68 miles of the Ontario division, displacing lighter rails of 56 and 60 lb. which were used in sidings and branches.   In the following year [3] 200 miles of heavy rails were laid.   Alignments were improved, grades were reduced, and permanent embankments constructed.   In 1890 over 200 wooden bridges were replaced by permanent structures of masonry, iron or solid embankments, and an equal number [4] in 1891. For the accommodation of grain traffic from western Canada the elevator capacity of Owen Sound and Montreal had been increased in 1885 and 1886.   At Fort William an elevator of 1,500,000 [5] bushels capacity was constructed in 1888 and one of 1,250,000 [6] in 1891.   The *Aberdeen*[7] was added to the lake steamship fleet in 1894 to accommodate the same traffic. Freight terminals [8] in Toronto and Montreal were improved in 1888.   Increasing traffic on the Pacific coast made necessary the additions of the *Athenian* and the *Tartar* to the Pacific steamship service in 1898.   Twelve [9] river steamers were acquired in British Columbia in the same

---

[1] Boarding, tool and auxiliary cars, 1886–99 :

1886 71	1893 522
1887 86	1894 543
1888 86	1895 533
1889 136	1896 554
1890 308	1897 575
1891 398	1898 627
1892 412	1899 682

Compiled from *C.P.R. Reports.*

[2] *C.P.R. Report,* 1890.   [3] *Ibid.,* 1891.   [4] *Ibid.,* 1890–1.
[5] *Ibid.,* 1888.   [6] *Ibid.,* 1891.   [7] *Ibid.,* 1894.   [8] *Ibid.,* 1888.
[9] *Ibid.,* 1898.

year, and seven more added in the following year. In
September, 1886, telegraph connexions were opened between the important towns of Ontario and Quebec,[1] and
a connexion established with the Postal Telegraph Company
and the Baltimore and Ohio Company to all points in the
United States.[2] Under the joint construction of the
Canadian Pacific and the Postal Telegraph Co. a line was
built between Vancouver and San Francisco. The whole
service was rendered more complete by connexions with
the Commercial and French Atlantic Cables.[3] In addition
the Company continued its policy of erecting equipment
plants. Plants were established at Perth, and in 1887 Vancouver was equipped with workshops as well as yards,
wharves and terminal requirements.[3]

D. Expansion of the Road, 1900—

The expansion of the road in the completion of through
connexions, the development of branch lines, and the growth
of traffic, characteristic of the period prior to the completion
of the main line, and of the later period ending with the
century, continued in the following years. The projection
of the system in western Canada, which resulted in the
increase in traffic and particularly in grain traffic, conspicu-
ous in the closing years of the century, was rapidly extended.
Branch lines were continually being added in other sections of
Canada. The consequent rapid increase in traffic gave a
decided impetus to the further improvement and construction
of through connexions. In the picturesque language of
Sir William Van Horne, enlargement of the hopper necessitated a widening of the spout.

In 1900 a step toward the extension of the road in western
Canada to the north of the main line was made with a lease,
on April 6, of the Great North-west Central[4] from Chater
on the main line to Hamiota, 51 miles, and later to Mineota,
20 miles. Control of this area for the development of
traffic and for protection from other lines became more
effective with the construction of a connexion from Varcoe
to McGregor, 55 miles, and with the lease, on May 1, of the

[1] *Ibid.*, 1886. [2] *Ibid.* [3] *Ibid.*, 1887.
[4] *Ibid.*, 1901.

Manitoba and North-western Railway [1] from Portage la Prairie to Yorkton, 223 miles, and from Minnedosa to Gauthier Junction on the Great North-west Central Railway, 18 miles. The leases included two branches from Binscarth to Russell, 12 miles, and from Forrest to Lenore, 41 miles, the latter constructed in 1901–2. South of the main line the Pipestone branch was extended, and in 1903–4 completed, from Arcola to Regina, 113 miles. This extension not only tapped new territory, but gave an additional line from Regina to Winnipeg. A branch was completed from this line at Stoughton to the St. Paul-Moosejaw line at Weyburn, 37 miles, in 1908. The system was extended westward from Yorkton to Lanigan from 1902 to 1909, and the area more effectively served by a line north-west from Kirkella on the main line to Lanigan, in the latter year. To this line was added a short connexion from Virden to McAuley, 36 miles, built in 1908. An extension westward from Lanigan to Wetaskiwin on the Calgary and Edmonton line, 100 miles, was completed in 1910. In the following year connexions from this line to the main line were completed from Colonsay to Regina, 132 miles, and the Lanigan-Kirkella connexion joined to this branch by a line from Bulyea to Valeport, 18 miles. Still another connexion with the main line was made from Moosejaw to Macklin, 267 miles, in 1912. With this extension of the system, the company had a direct line from Northern Alberta to Portage la Prairie and Winnipeg, and to Moosejaw and St. Paul, and through connexions in alternate routes with the main line, by branches from Macklin, Colonsay and Lanigan. The road had been extended to occupy the territory of which the limits were set in the previous period. Numerous branches and connexions had been made to complete the system. A line from Reston to Wolseley on the main line, 122 miles, built in 1908, lightened the increasing burden on the main line to Winnipeg by affording further connexion with the alternate southern route. From 1909 to 1911 connexion between Calgary and Lethbridge was improved by a road from Kipp to Aldersyde, 85 miles. In 1914 lines from Bassano to Swift Current, 230 miles, and from Gleichen to Shepard, 40

[1] *Ibid.*

miles, were completed, giving practically an alternate and more direct route from Calgary to Swift Current than the main line. A line from Lacombe to Kerrobert, on the Macklin-Moosejaw connexion, 221 miles, completed in the same year, gave access to valuable territory and improved the connexions of Northern Alberta to the main line, particularly in the Kerrobert to Wilkie branch joining with the Wetaskiwin-Winnipeg line, completed the preceding year. Branches more immediately concerned with the development of traffic, though to a large extent with ultimate through connexions, were continually added. The Stonewall branch to Foxton, 19 miles, constructed in 1898, was extended to Teulon, 19 miles, in 1901; to Kamarno, 8 miles, in 1905, and to Icelandic River, 29 miles, in 1910. The West Selkirk branch was constructed from Selkirk to Winnipeg Beach, 25 miles, in 1903; to Gimli, 10 miles, in 1905, and to Riverton, 26 miles, in 1913–14. The Snowflake to La Riviere branch, 16 miles, completed in 1903, was extended by a line from Wood Bay to Mowbray, 26 miles, in the same year, and to Windy Gates in 1908–9. The Rudyard-Kaleida branch, 6 miles, was constructed in 1905. A line from Lauder was extended to Alida, 55 miles, from 1902 to 1912. In 1910–13 a line was built from Estevan to Neptune, 55 miles, and in 1911–12 one from Swift Current to Vanguard, 45 miles. Construction was continued westward from Weyburn to Stirling, and with the completion of a few miles of road practically two direct lines will be available from Vancouver to Winnipeg. Connexion between these lines was improved by construction of a branch from Moosejaw to Expanse, 35 miles, in 1912, and its extension to Assiniboia, 29 miles, in 1917. In 1910 a branch was built from Langden to Acme, 40 miles. This branch was improved in 1912 by the construction of a line from Bassano to Irricana Junction, 72 miles. The system was improved in Southern Manitoba by a connexion from Lauder to Boissevain, 36 miles. Various short branches were commenced on different parts of the system. In 1907 the Asquith branch, 7 miles, was built; in 1910 the Calgary-Strathcona branch extension to Edmonton, 2 miles; in 1911 a branch from Wilkie to Cutknife, 28 miles, and in

1912 from Reford to Kelfield ; in 1914 from Coronation to
Lorraine, 19 miles, and in the same year from Suffield
to Lomond, 84 miles. Under the charter of the Alberta
Central Railway a line from Red Deer to Loch Earn, 64
miles, was acquired in 1912. In the same year the Alberta
Railway and Irrigation Company, leased on January 1, gave
the company control over a connexion with the American
roads with a line from Lethbridge to Coutts, and over branches
from Stirling to Cardston, 67 miles, and from Raley to Kim-
ball, 8 miles. The leases of the Edmonton, Dunvegan and
British Columbia from Edmonton to Grand Prairie, 407
miles, and of the Central Canada Railway from McLennan
to Peace River Crossing, 48 miles, in 1920, and to Berwyn,
25 miles, in 1921, gave the company access to the Peace River
district. With these branches and connexions the company possessed a network of roads which ensured its position
in western Canada.

The expansion of the system and the consequent development of traffic in western Canada influenced construction
in British Columbia and in Ontario. Partly as a result of
this traffic, but particularly as a result of the continued
development of traffic in British Columbia, lines were constructed in that area to connect with the main line. On
August 31, 1901,[1] the Vancouver and Lulu Island Railway,
consisting of a line from Steveston to English Bay, 14 miles,
was leased. In 1905 the company purchased [2] the Esquimault and Nanaimo Railway on Vancouver Island. This
purchase included a line from Victoria to Wellington, 77
miles, which was extended to McBride's Junction, 18 miles,
in 1909–10 and to Alberni, 40 miles, in 1911. In the following year, a line was built from Dunraven to Cowichan Lake,
19 miles, in 1913 to Osborne Bay, 3 miles, and in 1914
from McBride's Junction to Comox, 45 miles. In 1905–6
connexions were made with Spokane by a branch to Kings-
gate, 10 miles, and to Grand Forks, 4 miles. A line was
built from Ehaine Junction to New Westminster, 10 miles,
in 1909, and short branches from Port Moody to North
Vancouver in 1910, from Three Forks to Whitewater, and
from Waldo to Caithness, 11 miles, in 1912. The Kootenay

Central [1] was acquired in 1910, and in 1914 a line had been built from Golden to Colvalli, 166 miles, connecting the main line with the Crow's Nest Pass line, and giving an alternative rail route through the mountains. In 1909 the "Big Hill" Grade between Hector and Field was reduced by the construction of spiral tunnels. Further connexion with the main line was afforded in the lease [2] of the Kettle Valley Railroad in 1913 from Midway to Carmi and its extension to Hope on the main line, 277 miles, in 1915. This line was improved by the construction of a branch from Merritt to Otter Summit, 30 miles. With the acquisition of the Kaslo and Slocan Railway, in 1918,[3] from Retallack to Kaslo, 18 miles, the company had effectively consolidated the traffic area of British Columbia and provided for connexions with the main line which gave practically a through route other than the main line from Vancouver to Winnipeg.

The development of traffic in the west by the construction of branch lines and of through connexions and the pressure of this traffic on the main line and especially the portion of the main line leading to the Atlantic seaboard was of dominant importance to construction in eastern Canada. The gradual development of alternate routes in the extension of branches in western Canada and British Columbia was an indication of the effect of increased traffic. In the eastern area the effects were more pronounced. To accommodate the traffic of western Canada a double track was completed from Winnipeg to Fort William [4] in 1907, and westward to Portage La Prairie, Brandon and Regina in 1910 and the following years, and in the same year a short cut was built from Molson to Whittier Junction. Largely under pressure of the same traffic, the Wisconsin Central Railway was leased [5] in 1909 to the Minneapolis, St. Paul and Sault Ste. Marie Company, giving a direct line to Chicago and an alternate route from western Canada by Chicago and Detroit to Montreal. To shorten the line to the seaboard by the Great Lakes, the terminal was changed from Owen Sound to Port McNicoll, and, under the charter [6] of the Georgian Bay and Seaboard Railway, a road was built from this point

[1] *Ibid.*, 1910.   [2] *Ibid.*, 1913.   [3] *Ibid.*, 1918.
[4] *Ibid.*, 1907.   [5] *Ibid.*, 1909.   [6] *Ibid.*, 1912.

to Bethany Junction, 88 miles, in 1910. The consequent pressure from this branch of traffic from the north-west on the Toronto to Montreal line led to the construction, under the charter [1] of the Campbellford, Lake Ontario and Western Railway leased on April 16, 1913, of a line from Glen Tay to Agincourt, 184 miles, giving, with the construction of a double track from Glen Tay to Montreal, practically two routes from Toronto. West of Montreal a double track had been built to Brookport, at which point traffic was divided between the ports of New York, Boston and Halifax. In Nova Scotia the lease [2] of the Dominion Atlantic Railway from Truro to Windsor, and from Windsor to Halifax, gave the company an independent connexion with the latter port, although no such connexion between St. John and Truro had been obtained.

The improvement of lines to the seaboard was accompanied by the construction of branch lines and a constant increase of connexions. The project of the Grand Trunk Pacific and the resulting traffic over the North Bay to Toronto Grand Trunk line, as well as the constant difficulties of the Canadian Pacific incidental to the possession of running rights over this line, led to the construction of an independent road. A line from Bolton Junction to Romford Junction, 126 miles, completed in 1908, gave a direct independent connexion from Sudbury to Toronto. Branches as feeders to the main line were continually acquired, constructed and extended. On November 1, 1902, the company acquired a line from Hull Junction to Maniwaki, 81 miles, and from Hull to Aylmer, from Hull to Ottawa, and from Aylmer to Waltham, 70 miles, in the lease of the Ottawa Northern and Western Railway. In 1903 a through connexion was secured from Renfrew on the main line to Kingston on Lake Ontario, 103 miles, with the control [3] of the Kingston and Pembroke Railway. This included the short branch from Godfrey to Zaneville, 4 miles. In 1904, with the lease of the Tilsonburg, Lake Erie and Pacific Railroad,[4] connexion was established with Lake Erie at Port Burwell from Ingersoll Junction. This line was extended from Ingersoll Junction to Embro, 6 miles, in 1908, to Ingersoll, 5 miles,

[1] *Ibid.*   [2] *Ibid.*   [3] *Ibid,* 1903.   [4] *Ibid.,* 1904.

in 1910, and, with the lease [1] of the St. Marys and Western Ontario Railway, in 1909, to St. Marys, 15 miles. Under the charter of the Guelph and Goderich Railway, leased [2] in 1906, connexion was made with Lake Ontario by the construction of a line from Guelph to Goderich, 81 miles, in 1907. Under this charter a branch was built from Linwood to Listowel, 16 miles, in 1908. In the same year the lease [3] of the Berlin, Waterloo, Wellesley and Lake Huron Railway gave the company a line from Galt to Hespeler, 7 miles, and from Preston to Waterloo, 13 miles. In 1915 the lease [4] of the Lake Erie and Northern Railway extended this line from Galt to Port Dover on Lake Erie, 51 miles. Direct connexion was secured from Guelph Junction to Hamilton, 16 miles, in 1912, under the lease [5] of the South Ontario Pacific Company in 1911. The Lindsay, Bobcaygeon and Pontypool Railway, leased [6] in 1903, consisted of a road, completed in 1904, from Burketon Junction to Bobcaygeon, 39 miles. In 1906 the lease [7] of the Walkerton and Lucknow Railway gave a line from Saugeen Junction to Walkerton, 38 miles, completed in 1908. The Joliette and Brandon Railway, leased [8] in 1906, was a line from St.Felix to St. Gabriel, 12 miles. The Northern Colonization Railroad, leased in 1904, included a line from Labelle to Nominingue, 24 miles, and an extension to Mont Laurier, 35 miles, built in 1909. The lease [9] of the Orford Mountain Railway in 1909 gave the company a connexion with the Montreal-St. John line to the Newport or Boston line at Troy Junction, and included a branch from Eastray to Windsor Mills. The St. Maurice Valley Railway, leased in 1910, was a branch from Three Rivers to Grandmere, 27 miles. The Cap de la Madeleine Railway, leased in 1912, was a short branch from Piles Junction to Cap de la Madeleine and to pulp mills on Bellevue Islands, 4 miles. In the same year the lease [10] of the Quebec Central Railway afforded a connexion by two lines from Levis, on the St. Lawrence, to Sherbrooke and Megantic on the Montreal-St. John line, and included a branch from Valleyfield Junc-

[1] *Ibid.*, 1912.   [2] *Ibid.*, 1906.   [3] *Ibid.*
[4] *Ibid.*, 1914.   [5] *Ibid.*, 1911.   [6] *Ibid.*, 1903.
[7] *Ibid.*, 1906.   [8] *Ibid.*   [9] *Ibid.*, 1909.   [10] *Ibid.*, 1912.

tion to St. Sabine and English Lake, constructed in 1915. The lease of the Glengarry and Stormont Railway in the latter year gave more direct connexion with the St. Lawrence in the line from St. Polycarpe's Junction, on the Toronto-Montreal line, to Cornwall, 28 miles. In New Brunswick the company improved its position in 1904 by securing running rights over the Fredericton and St. Marys bridge, and in 1905 by purchasing the St. John bridge and railway extension line from Fairville to the junction with the Intercolonial Railway in St. John, 2 miles. In 1910 an important connexion with American roads was acquired in the lease [1] from the New Brunswick Southern Railway of a line from West St. John to St. Stephen, 82 miles. In the same year a line was leased [2] from the New Brunswick Coal and Railway Company from Minto to St. Martins, on the Bay of Fundy, 98 miles. The latter line was extended to Gibson, 31 miles, in the lease [3] of the Fredericton and Grand Lake Coal Company, and connected with the Canadian-Pacific system in the acquisition of a line from Marysville Junction to Marysville, 3 miles. The lease of the Southampton Railway in 1914 included a line from Southampton Junction to Otis, 13 miles. In Nova Scotia the lease of the Dominion Atlantic Railway in 1912 included a line throughout the length of the province from Windsor to Yarmouth, 228 miles, a connexion from Kentville to the Bay of Fundy at Kingsport, 14 miles, and short branches, completed in 1914, from Wilmot to Torbrook, 5 miles, and from Centerville to Weston, 15 miles. During the war and afterwards additions in eastern Canada have been few. In 1921 provision was made for construction, by the Interprovincial and James Bay Railway Company, of a line from Kipawa to Des Quinze River, and of a branch to Ville Marie, making a total of 76 miles.

E.   FREIGHT TRAFFIC AND EQUIPMENT, 1900—

The continued rapid expansion of the road, especially in western Canada, brought a phenomenal increase in traffic, particularly, as was to be expected, in grain. The upward trend of traffic in the closing years of the century

---

[1] *Ibid.*, 1910.   [2] *Ibid.*, 1912.   [3] *Ibid.*, 1914.

proved significant. The number of tons of freight carried [1] increased from 7,155,813 in 1901 to the highest point, 31,198,685, in 1917. Except for a slight decline in 1908, occasioned largely by the depression of that year, the increase to 1913 was steady and persistent. Largely due to the war, a slight decline followed in 1914, and a marked decline in 1915, but owing to the exceptional grain harvest, a rapid and temporary recovery was made in 1916 and in 1917. A decline set in to 1919, and despite another recovery in the following year, continued in 1921. The importance of grain in the general freight movement was apparent. The number of bushels of grain carried [2] increased from 32,927,468 in 1901 to the highest point, 276,788,209, in 1916—an increase which, largely influenced by climate conditions and the development of the Canadian west, was not consistent. A

[1] Freight carried 1901–21, tons :

1901*	 7,155,813	1912	 25,940,238
1902	 8,769,934	1913	 29,471,814
1903	 10,180,847	1914	 27,801,217
1904	 11,135,896	1915	 21,490,596
1905	 11,892,204	1916	 29,276,872
1906	 13,933,798	1916 (six months) .	16,200,453
1907	 15,733,306	1917†	 31,198,685
1908	 15,040,325	1918	 29,856,694
1909	 16,549,616	1919	 25,102,821
1910	 20,551,368	1920	 30,160,134
1911	 22,536,214	1921	 23,710,606

Compiled from C.P.R. Reports.
* Fiscal year. † Calendar year.

Note.—Statistics to 1899 are given for the calendar year. Statistics beginning with 1901 are for the fiscal year to 1916. In some cases statistics are given in the C.P.R. *Reports* for the half year, *i.e.* from Jan. 1, 1900, to June 30, 1900, in others from Jan. 1, 1900, to June 30, 1901, and in still others omitted for the half year. Statistics are given for the half year June 30 to Dec. 30, 1916, and in some cases are omitted. For the year 1917, and thereafter statistics, are for the fiscal year.

[2] Grain carried, 1901–21, bushels :

1901*	 32,927,468	1912	 151,731,691
1902	 52,719,706	1913	 171,952,738
1903	 63,822,710	1914	 184,954,241
1904	 52,990,151	1915	 126,909,828
1905	 59,739,180	1916	 276,788,209
1906	 82,196,648	1916 (six months).	146,332,583
1907	 93,207,009	1917†	 213,340,507
1908	 88,345,234	1918	 137,070,428
1909	 97,236,150	1919	 121,059,921
1910	 112,795,345	1920	 172,536,485
1911	 111,169,982	1921	 175,506,119

Compiled from *C.P.R. Reports.*
* Fiscal year. † Calendar year.

bad harvest in 1904 led to a decline in that year. This was followed by a rapid and steady increase to 1907 and a decline in 1908, a further increase to 1910, a slight decline in 1911, much the most rapid increase to 1914, a rapid decline in the following year and a remarkable increase in 1916. These fluctuations were followed by a marked decline to 1919. The remaining years to 1921 gave evidence of recovery. Although grain was dominant, the importance of other commodities was evident. The bad harvest of 1904 had little effect on the total amount of freight carried, and although the decrease in the amount of grain carried in 1908 brought a decrease in the total amount of freight carried, this decrease was accentuated by the depression of 1907. In 1910 the amount of grain carried remained stationary and the total traffic increased rapidly. The total amount of freight carried before the war reached a climax in 1913, a year earlier than the climax for the amount of grain carried. On the other hand, in the war period, the total traffic decreased slightly in 1914 and grain increased, but the decrease was much greater in 1915 because of a marked decrease of grain in that year. The bumper crop of 1916 brought a marked increase in total traffic, and, during the remainder of the period, with the exception of 1921, fluctuations in grain carried paralleled fluctuations in total freight carried.

The grain situation exercised a significant influence on the movement of other commodities. The number of barrels of flour increased [1] from 3,735,873 in 1901 to the highest point, 13,727,970, in 1917. Although wheat was the dominant grain carried, other grains continued to

---

[1] Flour carried, 1901–21, barrels :

1901*	3,735,873	1912	8,459,850
1902	4,921,993	1913	8,093,936
1903	5,110,757	1914	8,802,250
1904	5,270,432	1915	8,538,600
1905	5,010,868	1916	10,499,620
1906	5,994,535	1916 (six months)	5,710,800
1907	6,256,702	1917†	13,727,970
1908	5,843,988	1918	13,301,740
1909	6,683,354	1919	12,787,020
1910	7,489,812	1920	9,644,410
1911	8,469,744	1921	11,718,510

Compiled from *C.P.R. Reports.*
* Fiscal year.   † Calendar year.

increase in importance as a result of the expansion of the road in eastern Canada and of the tendency toward mixed farming. The rapid increase in grain to 1903 was followed more gradually by flour, the latter commodity reaching its climax in 1904, the year in which grain decreased. This decrease in grain was followed by a decrease in flour in 1905. From 1905 to 1907 the increase in grain again surpassed the increase in flour. From the steady increase in flour and consequently of milling capacity during these years, a slight decrease in grain in 1908 brought a decrease in flour in the same year. Both commodities increased to 1910 in a more uniform manner. Grain declined slightly in 1911 and flour increased. In 1912 a marked increase in grain was accompanied by a slight decline in flour. In the following year flour continued to decline, but recovered in 1914. Grain continued to increase after 1911. The increasing importance of other grains was evident. The steady increase in the total amount of grain to 1914 brought the recovery of flour in that year. The decrease in grain in 1915 led to a decrease in flour, and during the remainder of the period, with the exception of 1920, the two commodities moved concurrently. The effect of rapid fluctuations in grain on the milling capacity occasioned varied reactions. Flour mills, unable to adapt themselves to a rapid increase in grain, in the effort to keep pace with expansion, found themselves without grain in some years, and in other years unable to handle the supply until the year following.

The importance of other grains was partly indicated in the livestock industry, both of which were to some extent indices of the progress of mixed farming. The number of head of livestock carried [1] increased from 945,386 in 1901

[1] Livestock carried, 1901–21, head :

1901* 945,386	1912 1,663,315
1902 963,742	1913 1,782,986
1903 1,103,686	1914 2,481,360
1904 1,314,814	1915 2,833,726
1905 1,360,560	1916 2,190,389
1906 1,428,320	1916 (six months) . 1,262,617
1907 1,537,467	1917† 2,190,596
1908 1,349,771	1918 2,364,870
1909 1,371,873	1919 2,603,571
1910 1,381,183	1920 1,947,976
1911 1,567,665	1921 1,612,049

Compiled from *C.P.R. Reports.*
* Fiscal year.   † Calendar year.

to the maximum of 2,833,726 in 1915. The number was marked by a steady increase to 1907, a decrease in 1908, coinciding with the decrease in grain in that year, a gradual recovery to 1910, a rapid increase to 1915, a marked decline in 1916, a gradual recovery to 1919, and a decline to 1921. To 1914 the number of head of livestock fluctuated closely with the amount of grain carried. In 1915 the decrease in grain and the abnormal war situation led to an increase in livestock. The rapid increase in 1916 brought a rapid decrease in the following year. Generally, the decided increase in livestock paralleled the increase in grain, and particularly of grain other than wheat. The whole situation was directly an evidence of the increase in mixed farming. The war period brought an increase in the number of livestock marketed—a fact explanatory of the decline in later years. The general influence of livestock on the freight situation was slight. In 1915 the total freight carried had its most marked decrease.

The agricultural situation had a direct influence on manufacturing. The number of tons of manufactured articles carried increased from 1,954,386 in 1901 [1] to a maximum of 10,148,568 in 1917. This increase paralleled closely that of the total amount of freight carried, increasing gradually to 1907, declining in 1908, increasing rapidly to 1913, declining rapidly to 1915, increasing rapidly to 1917, declining to 1919, increasing in 1920, and declining again in 1921. The concurrent fluctuations were directly illustrative of the growing importance of manufactures and of the dominant importance of agriculture. The steady increase

[1] Manufactured articles, 1901–21, tons :

1901*	1,954,386		1912	7,196,225
1902	2,288,234		1913	9,519,346
1903	2,665,260		1914	8,148,012
1904	3,119,659		1915	6,024,590
1905	3,250,067		1916	7,960,723
1906	3,818,625		1916 (six months)	4,643,384
1907	4,385,854		1917†	10,148,568
1908	3,981,888		1918	9,718,373
1909	4,425,241		1919	7,854,163
1910	5,468,548		1920	9,330,111
1911	5,759,344		1921	6,853,857

Compiled from *C.P.R. Reports.*

* Fiscal year.   † Calendar year.

to 1904 slackened in 1905 largely because of the depression and the bad harvest of 1904. The decline in grain in 1908 and the depression of that year were accompanied by a decline in manufactures. With these minor exceptions, including the slight decline of grain in 1911, the rapid increase of grain to 1913 was followed by a rapid increase of manufactures. In the year ending June 30, 1914, grain increased, but manufactures rapidly decreased. In part this increase in grain resulted in low prices [1] in 1913–14. At the same time the price [2] of steel and other metals increased. Partly as a result, the number of tons of manufactured articles carried declined. The decline in grain carried in 1915 accentuated this decline in that year. The war demand and the exceptional crops led to a rapid increase in 1916, and the readjustment situation brought a decline to 1919. Recovery came in 1920, only to be followed by the decline of 1921. The trend of manufactured articles was followed closely by that of " other articles." The number [3] of tons increased from 2,206,079 in 1901 to the maximum of 9,798,523 in 1918. Without definite information as to the character of the various articles concerned, it is apparent that these commodities were influenced by conditions similar to those dominating the manufacturing situation. Both classifications were affected by the agricultural situation, and bore witness to the expansion of the road to the manufacturing centres of eastern Canada and the United States.

[1] *Wholesale Prices in Canada*, 1916, p. 37.
[2] *Ibid.*, p. 66.
[3] Other articles, 1901–21, tons :

1901*	2,206,970	1912	9,092,821
1902	2,571,136	1913	9,625,665
1903	2,942,736	1914	9,159,112
1904	3,620,515	1915	7,423,163
1905	3,894,259	1916	8,228,156
1906	4,098,819	1916 (six months)	4,659,294
1907	4,794,295	1917†	8,788,423
1908	5,102,116	1918	9,798,523
1909	5,916,248	1919	7,589,275
1910	7,567,052	1920	9,625,065
1911	8,971,037	1921	7,018,876

Compiled from *C.P.R. Reports*.

* Fiscal year.   † Calendar year.

The number of feet of lumber carried [1] followed closely the number of tons of manufactured articles. It increased from 899,214,646 in 1901 to a maximum of 3,241,312,802 in 1918. The increase to 1904 was consistent and gradual. The number of feet carried increased more rapidly to 1907, but, influenced by depression and agricultural conditions, declined to 1909. Recovery was rapid to 1913. As in the case of manufactures, a rapid decline followed to 1915, and a rapid increase to 1917. In 1918 the hectic prosperity of an abnormal war situation caused a further increase, and a cessation of that prosperity a decrease in 1919. The following year brought a slight recovery which proved temporary with the decline to 1921. Again lumber was dominated by the agricultural situation and reflected the expansion of the road to timber areas.

The number of cords of firewood carried [2] increased from 204,818 in 1901 to a maximum of 339,631 in 1918. It increased rapidly in 1903, gradually in 1904, declined in 1905, recovered in 1906-7, declined rapidly in 1908-9, increased to 1912, declined to 1915, increased rapidly to 1918 except for a slight decline in 1917, and declined in

[1] Lumber, 1901-21, feet :

1901*. . . .	899,214,646	1912 2,806,735,006
1902	1,033,569,377	1913 3,210,306,090
1903	1,190,378,217	1914 2,953,125,699
1904	1,267,804,321	1915 2,180,735,600
1905	1,435,758,930	1916 2,696,804,934
1906	1,804,648,962	1916 (six months) 1,499,916,534
1907	1,989,444,728	1917†. . . . 3,178,554,667
1908	1,764,445,495	1918 3,241,312,802
1909	1,726,944,584	1919 3,143,431,200
1910	2,292,821,963	1920 3,565,175,867
1911	2,441,007,107	1921 2,382,570,398

Compiled from *C.P.R. Reports.*

[2] Firewood, 1901-21, cords :

1901*	204,818	1912 305,079
1902	204,963	1913 293,536
1903	268,401	1914 287,910
1904	270,803	1915 254,428
1905	261,794	1916 298,426
1906	264,456	1916 (six months) . 124,206
1907	274,629	1917† 295,277
1908	249,605	1918 339,631
1909	249,628	1919 279,925
1910	280,878	1920 272,546
1911	298,345	1921 204,836

Compiled from *C.P.R. Reports.*

* Fiscal year.   † Calendar year.

1919 to 1921. Generally the amount of firewood carried depended on the availability of coal. In the depression of 1903–4 cordwood increased and the prosperity of the following years brought a decline. Again, in 1907–8 it increased. The rapid expansion of traffic to 1912 brought an increase in the use of firewood, but the decline started in 1913 and continued to 1915. The scarcity of coal and the war situation brought a rapid increase to 1918, and with the readjustment came a decline in 1919, continuing in 1921.

The expansion of the road, especially in western Canada, and the growth of traffic, were reflected in the rapid increase in train mileage, an increase which was significant again in view of a marked rise in the average train-load. The latter increased from 221·1 tons in 1901 to a maximum of 582·8 in 1917, an increase which was persistent and steady, with the exception of a decline in the years of 1904, 1911, 1918, and 1919. Gradual recovery was evident in 1920, but a decline followed in 1921. The importance of the grain traffic was apparent in the close correlation between the average train-load [1] and the number of bushels of grain carried. The total train mileage [2] increased from 18,181,415

[1] Average train-load, 1901–21, tons :

1901*	. . . . . .	221·1		1912	. . . . . .	405·3
1902	. . . . . .	275·4		1913	. . . . . .	415·3
1903	. . . . . .	289·2		1914	. . . . . .	447·8
1904	. . . . . .	275·9		1915	. . . . . .	469·9
1905	. . . . . .	287·9		1916	. . . . . .	554·4
1906	. . . . . .	310·8		1917†	. . . . . .	582·8
1907	. . . . . .	326·9		1918	. . . . . .	577·1
1908	. . . . . .	329·7		1919	. . . . . .	556·2
1909	. . . . . .	338·5		1920	. . . . . .	577·0
1910	. . . . . .	377·7		1921	. . . . . .	574·1
1911	. . . . . .	371·4				

Compiled from *C.P.R. Reports*.

[2] Total train mileage, 1901–21 :

1901*	. . .	18,181,415		1912	. . . .	46,957,511
1902	. . .	21,128,299		1913	. . . .	51,832,790
1903	. . .	23,053,079		1914	. . . .	47,578,236
1904	. . .	24,185,527		1915	. . . .	36,812,879
1905	. . .	25,765,138		1916	. . . .	45,614,367
1906	. . .	29,686,664		1916 (six months) .		24,347,109
1907	. . .	32,012,771		1917†	. . . .	45,332,831
1908	. . .	32,783,415		1918	. . . .	40,958,405
1909	. . .	34,920,198		1919	. . . .	42,349,387
1910	. . .	38,367,112		1920	. . . .	46,719,665
1911	. . .	40,775,846		1921	. . . .	39,407,334

Compiled from *C.P.R. Reports*.

* Fiscal year.   † Calendar year.

in 1901 to a maximum of 51,832,790 in 1913. This increase was rapid and consistent, but was followed by a decline to 1915. The recovery in 1917 proved temporary. There followed a decline to 1918, an increase to 1920, and a decline in 1921. Freight train mileage [1] adheres to these fluctuations, with the exception of a slight decline in 1908 and in 1919, the number increasing from 10,415,831 in 1901 to a maximum of 27,611,103, in 1913. These fluctuations correlated closely with the amount of freight carried, except in the year 1917, in which there was an increase in freight carried, and a decline in train mileage—a situation explained largely by the decline in grain and the abnormal war situation in that year. Mixed train mileage [2] was of relatively slight importance, depending largely on the construction activities of the road and the strain on the company's resources incidental to the war. From 1902 to 1916 it increased from 1,390,876 to 2,098,825. As portions of the system were constructed and developed, mixed trains were superseded by regular service, and the stationary character of mixed train mileage was an indication of the steady expan-

[1] Freight train mileage, 1901–21 :

1901*	10,415,831	1912	25,638,692
1902	11,792,221	1913	27,611,103
1903	13,353,188	1914	24,164,242
1904	13,810,180	1915	16,896,368
1905	14,429,739	1916	25,355,997
1906	17,186,263	1916 (six months)	13,315,730
1907	18,187,263	1917†	25,182,863
1908	17,788,649	1918	22,326,115
1909	18,816,900	1919	19,994,867
1910	20,574,576	1920	24,335,581
1911	21,701,893	1921	18,828,421

Compiled from *C.P.R. Reports*.

[2] Mixed train mileage, 1902–21 :

1902*	1,390,876	1913	1,888,015
1903	1,553,902	1914	1,890,364
1904	1,564,348	1915	1,939,478
1905	1,537,781	1916	2,098,825
1906	1,413,152	1916 (six months)	1,061,048
1907	1,411,870	1917†	2,056,414
1908	1,798,673	1918	1,966,362
1909	1,932,776	1919	1,943,410
1910	1,672,993	1920	1,846,046
1911	1,680,421	1921	1,647,291
1912	1,727,792		

Compiled from *C.P.R. Reports*.
* Fiscal year.   † Calendar year.

sion of the road throughout the period. During the war and other periods of strain, there was evident an attempt to substitute a mixed service when the situation warranted.

Increased freight, and increased freight train mileage, necessitated increased equipment. The number [1] of freight and cattle cars increased from 20,083 in 1901 to 88,090 in 1914. The policy involved in the increase of this form of equipment was the resultant of difficult conditions. The heavy overhead costs entailed by an oversupply of equipment made necessary a policy involving few additions. At the same time the large car shops incidental to an expanding system obliged the company to spread the increase in equipment evenly over a number of years. The importance of grain as an item of traffic, and its marked fluctuations as a result of climatic variations, caused an additional complication. The company had to meet the peak load situation within the year, because of the importance of grain and the strong seaboard movement of traffic. The peak load over a series of years, occasioned by business cycles and business growth was a further difficulty. The consequent policy was one of steady increase, though to some extent influenced by particular conditions. As a result, during exceptionally good harvest years, considerable complaint was made by shippers because of a lack of cars. During the abnormal war situation the company possessed an oversupply of equipment. The number declined to 1916, and afterward increased slowly.

---

[1] Freight and cattle cars, 1901–21 :

1901*.	.	.	.	.	.	20,083	1912	.	.	.	.	.	61,446
1902	.	.	.	.	.	21,159	1913	.	.	.	.	.	79,085
1903	.	.	.	.	.	26,170	1914	.	.	.	.	.	88,090
1904	.	.	.	.	.	28,066	1915	.	.	.	.	.	87,108
1905	.	.	.	.	.	30,101	1916 (ending June 30th)	87,108
1906	.	.	.	.	.	34,152	1916 (ending Dec. 31st)	87,074
1907	.	.	.	.	.	40,405	1917†.	.	.	.	.	.	87,301
1908	.	.	.	.	.	44,692	1918	.	.	.	.	.	87,513
1909	.	.	.	.	.	47,748	1919	.	.	.	.	.	87,681
1910	.	.	.	.	.	48,850	1920	.	.	.	.	.	88,057
1911	.	.	.	.	.	52,602	1921	.	.	.	.	.	90,648

Compiled from *C.P.R. Reports*.

* Fiscal year.   † Calendar year.

The number [1] of conductors' vans was subject to similar considerations. Important factors were the number of freight train miles, the size of the freight trains, the size of locomotives and the proportion of through to local traffic. The number increased from 363 in 1901 to 1,427 in 1914, and declined to 1,324 in 1919. In 1920 a slow recovery had begun, but in 1921 the number remained stationary.

The increase in the number [2] of locomotives was dependent to a very large extent on the train mileage, the amount of traffic, and the capacity of the locomotives. From 1901 to 1915 the number increased from 708 to 2,255, and remained stationary to 1921. Locomotives proved more difficult than freight cars or conductors' vans to adjust to the demand situation.

Boarding, tool and auxiliary cars [3] were largely dominated

[1] Conductors' vans, 1901–21 :

1901*	363	1912	1,065
1902	448	1913	1,274
1903	492	1914	1,427
1904	511	1915	1,424
1905	602	1916	1,420
1906	658	1917†	1,359
1907	722	1918	1,340
1908	777	1919	1,324
1909	797	1920	1,337
1910	867	1921	1,337
1911	923		

Compiled from *C.P.R. Reports.*

[2] Locomotives, 1901–21 :

1901*	708	1912	1,820
1902	745	1913	2,052
1903	840	1914	2,248
1904	963	1915	2,255
1905	1,016	1916	2,255
1906	1,109	1917†	2,255
1907	1,296	1918	2,255
1908	1,399	1919	2,255
1909	1,478	1920	2,255
1910	1,534	1921	2,255
1911	1,637		

Compiled from *C.P.R. Reports.*

[3] Boarding, tool and auxiliary cars, 1901–21 :

1901*	886	1912	4,254
1902	928	1913	5,414
1903	984	1914	5,850
1904	993	1915	6,467
1905	1,189	1916 (ending June 30th)	6,867
1906	1,745	1916 (ending Dec. 31st).	6,901
1907	2,108	1917†	6,735
1908	2,726	1918	6,542
1909	3,013	1919	6,390
1910	3,437	1920	6,629
1911	3,896	1921	6,762

Compiled from *C.P.R. Reports.*

* Fiscal year.   † Calendar year.

by the construction activities of the company, by increased mileage, and by increased traffic, which necessitated additional facilities. The number increased from 886 in 1901 to 6,901 in 1916, declined to 1919, and recovered slightly in 1920 and in 1921. The possibility of using these cars for other purposes made them much more susceptible to the company's control. In so far as they were capable of being changed to freight cars the number was to some extent dependent upon the supply of this form of equipment.

In general, equipment increased gradually and steadily during the early years of the period and rapidly during the years from 1909 to 1913, in which the increase in freight reached its climax. The depression which followed proved disastrous under these circumstances, and made it necessary for the company to resort to every possible expedient in adjusting equipment to the changed conditions. The success with which this was accomplished depended largely upon the character of the equipment.

Increase in equipment was accompanied by an increase of other services necessary to handle the rapid growth of traffic. These services were partly the result of an increase in passenger traffic, but the dominance of freight traffic was evident. With the development of traffic in the interior of British Columbia in the access to the various lakes and rivers, additional boats were acquired. A Pacific coast service was established in 1903 with the acquisition of twelve boats, and with the development of traffic on Vancouver Island and on other parts of the coast, additional boats were brought into the service each year. On the Atlantic coast two steamers were enlisted for the Bay of Fundy service in 1912 as a necessary supplement to the company's acquisition of roads in that area. The increase in through traffic stimulated, and was stimulated, by the improvements of ocean services. On the Pacific the *Monteagle* was added in 1906 and the *Empress of Russia* and the *Empress of Asia* in 1913. The pressure of traffic to the Atlantic seaboard made necessary provisions for an Atlantic ocean service. In 1903 the Beaver Line, consisting of fourteen steamships, was purchased from the Elder Dempster Company. The *Empress of Britain* and the *Empress of*

Ireland were added in 1906, the *Cruizer* in 1907, and the *Medora*, the *Metagama*, the *Missanabie* in 1915. In the same year the Canadian Pacific Ocean Steamship Services Company was organized, and the Allan Line of steamships, including eighteen boats, was acquired. During the war, several boats were purchased or requisitioned by the Admiralty, and others were lost. Provision for the replacement of these losses was made in the purchase of boats after the war. In 1921 several German boats were purchased and other new boats constructed, the total tonnage in that year being 438,604. Improvement of service accompanied the addition of boats. In 1903 a bi-weekly service from Montreal to London, and a weekly service from Montreal to Bristol and Liverpool were established. In 1912 a four-weekly service with the *Ruthenia* and the *Tyrolia* was organized between Trieste and Canada. This service conformed to an agreement with the Austrian Government permitting the Canadian Pacific to attach observation cars on State-owned railways through the Alps. On the Pacific, a Canadian-Australian service was added in 1903.

The elevator service at Fort William was improved, and with the change of terminus to Port McNicoll, new elevators were built at that point. In 1904 in connexion with the company's land holdings, and for the development of traffic, an important irrigation scheme was launched in Southern Alberta. The pressure of western traffic made it advisable for the company to control its own coal mines, and the competition in British Columbia made the development of other mines desirable. Important mines were early acquired in British Columbia, and in 1907 the company entered on an elaborate coal-mining policy. Integration of necessity accompanied the rapid increase in the traffic of the road.

F. Conclusion

The spread of western civilization, especially in the region roughly included in the Hudson Bay drainage basin, long delayed by the inhospitable barrier north of Lake Superior, led to the construction of technological equipment represented by the physical property of the road, and with its construction, was greatly hastened. Additions to this equipment in the matter of branch lines and other forms of physical property were causes and effects of this rapid growth. This marked increase in the growth of civilization in the Hudson Bay drainage basin was accompanied by a continued growth in other areas in the Pacific Coast drainage basin and in the St. Lawrence drainage basin. This growth was again the cause and the effect of additions to technological equipment in those areas. Constant additions to equipment in the Hudson Bay drainage basin necessitated improvements and changes in equipment in the matter of double tracks, new roads and other forms of physical property in the drainage basins of the continent and particularly in the St. Lawrence drainage basin. The growth and character of the freight traffic carried during the forty years of the company's history from 1881 to 1921 were to a large extent indices of the effectiveness of the physical property of the road as a part of the technological equipment of western civilization in North America.

V

The Freight Rate Situation

THE growth of civilization attendant upon the expansion of the physical property of the road, and the development of traffic throughout the history of the road, largely determined, and were largely determined by, the freight rate policy of the company. Upon freight rate policy principally depended the earnings of the road and its possibilities of physical growth. This interdependence was particularly important with the large degree of freedom from regulation which the charter guaranteed. Article 20 of the Act of Incorporation declared : " The limit to the reduction of tolls by the Parliament of Canada provided for by the eleventh sub-section of the seventeenth section of ' The Consolidated Railway Act, 1879,' respecting tolls is hereby extended, so that such reduction may be to such an extent that such tolls when reduced shall not produce less than 10 per cent. per annum profit in the capital actually expended in the construction of the railway, instead of not less than 15 per cent per annum profit, as provided by the said sub-section ; and so also that such reduction shall not be made unless the net income of the company, ascertained as described in said sub-section, shall have exceeded 10 per cent per annum instead of 15 per cent per annum as provided by the said sub-section. And the exercise by the Governor in Council of the power of reducing the tolls of the company as provided by the tenth sub-section of said section seventeen is hereby limited to the same extent with relation to the profit of the company, and to its net revenue, as that to which the power of Parliament to reduce tolls is limited by said sub-section eleven as hereby amended." [1]

[1] Appendix B.

This article was strengthened by article 15, which eliminated possible competition in an important section of western Canada. It declared : " For twenty years from the date hereof, no line of railway shall be authorized by the Dominion Parliament to be constructed south of the Canadian Pacific Railway, from any point at or near the Canadian Pacific Railway, except such line as shall run south-west or to the westward of south-west ; nor to within fifteen miles of latitude 49. And in the establishment of any new Province in the North-West Territories, provision shall be made for continuing such prohibition after such establishment until the expiration of the same period." These guarantees of freedom from regulation were scarcely limited by article 24,[1] which ensured non-preferential treatment to Toronto and Montreal.

These provisions gave the company effective control of its rate policy, but such control was limited by various incidental circumstances, and was largely confined to areas which were not subject to competition. Rates in eastern Canada were regulated by competition from waterways and from other railroads, and the area in which the company could exercise its control was consequently limited to western Canada. Geographic features made inevitable the competition in eastern territory and the competition with American roads for transcontinental traffic. Lower rates, and the large overhead charges incidental to the long stretch of unproductive territory north of Lake Superior, necessitated strenuous efforts to direct traffic over this long stretch of

---

[1] " The said Company shall afford all reasonable facilities to the Ontario and Pacific Junction Railway Company, when their railway shall be completed to a point of junction with the Canadian Pacific Railway, and to the Canada Central Railway, . . . and the said Canadian Pacific Railway Company shall receive and carry all freight and passenger traffic shipped to and from any point on the railway of either of the said above-named railway companies passing over the Canadian Pacific Railway or any part thereof, at the same mileage rate and subject to the same charges for similar services, without granting or allowing any preference or advantage to the traffic coming from or going upon one of such railways over such traffic coming from or going upon the other of them, reserving, however, to the said Canadian Pacific Railway Company the right of making special rates for purchasers of land, or for immigrants or intending immigrants, which special rates shall not govern or affect the rates of passenger traffic as between the said company and the said two abovenamed Companies or either of them " (Appendix B).

line, and to make the non-competitive area of western Canada as productive as possible. These efforts of the company to direct traffic over the line east of Winnipeg for obvious reasons received the support of eastern Canada. An application for a charter for the Emerson and Turtle Mountain Railway [1] was earlier refused on the ground that it would divert traffic through the United States. An order in council of April 18, 1879, expressed the opinion of the Government that it was " very desirable that all railway legislation should originate here, and that no charter for a line exclusively within the province of Manitoba should be granted by its legislature without the Dominion Government assenting thereto." The monopoly clause of the Canadian Pacific Railway Company charter was a result of the same opinion.

The people of Manitoba naturally protested against the operation of this policy. On December 22, 1880, while the act of incorporation was under discussion, the Manitoba legislature formally objected [2] to the power given to the company to build lines or branches other than the main line, without obtaining permission from the Canadian Parliament, and to other features of the act. The Canadian Government replied through the statements of Sir John A. McDonald and Hon. Thomas White on the floor of the House of Commons that the Dominion Parliament possessed no power over Manitoba, and that nothing prevented that province from granting a charter for a railway from Winnipeg to the boundary. It was explained that the contract only prevented [3] American roads from tapping the line in the prairie section west of the Manitoba boundary. Accordingly the Manitoba legislature incorporated three railways : the Winnipeg South-Eastern Railway, with power to construct a road running south-east to the boundary and to amalgamate with other companies ; the Manitoba Tramway Company, with power to build tramways along all public highways and across any land ; the Emerson and North-Western Railway Company, with powers to construct a line from Emerson to Mountain City and thence to any point on the western boundary of the province, and to lease

---

[1] *Sessional Paper*, No. 58b, 1888.   [2] *Ibid.*   [3] *Ibid.*

other roads. The Canadian Pacific Company [1] protested to the Dominion Government that these charters were in violation of its rights, and pleaded the interests of the Dominion in sustaining traffic to support the long unprofitable line along the north shore of Lake Superior. Consequently the Government disallowed,[2] first, the charter of the South-Eastern Railway, and later the charters of the other two companies. Manitoba temporarily accepted this verdict, recognizing the inadvisability of interfering with the company when all its energies were directed to the construction of the main line.

The question was a source of continual trouble. The rates first charged by the company in western Canada were those used by the Government before the transfer of the road. This tariff was a straight distance tariff, with four classes of rates for merchandise and seven special classes. The local mileage rate was a direct mileage rate, with an even spread and little discrimination. With an increase in distance the rates increased less rapidly and the spread between the classes of rates more rapidly. In general, the special classes [3] were designed to promote settlement.

[1] *Sessional Papers*, No. 48h, 1882, p. 40. [2] *Ibid.*, p. 45.

[3] First special class :
  Grain.
  Potatoes.
  Mill stuffs.

Second special class :
  Flour.
  Meal.
  Lime.

Third special class :
  Salt.
  Cement lime.
  Stucco.
  Land plaster.

Fourth special class :
  Lumber.
  Shingles.
  Laths.
  Rails.
  Timber.
  Sawlogs.
  Telegraph poles.

Fifth special class :
  Livestock.

Sixth special class :
  Agricultural implements.
  Furniture.
  Household goods.
  Machinery.
  Farm wagons.
  Doors.
  Sash.
  Tile.
  Nails.
  Unfinished wood pumps.
  Pork.

Seventh special class :
  Coal.
  Coke.
  Brick.
  Sand.
  Iron ore.
  Stone.
  Pig iron.
  Shingle and stave bolts.
  Tanners backs.
  Hoops.
  Hay.
  Railroad iron.
  Sawdust.
  Ice.

Still lower rates [1] were given on settlers' effects. Immigrants movables C.L. (car load) were given one-half the special rates of the sixth class, and L.C.L. (less than car load) were given one-half first-class rates. In continuance of this policy of adjusting rates for the development of traffic, immigrants were given through tickets at one and a half cents per mile. On March 23, 1883, the company with the Government's approval introduced [2] a new and higher tariff constructed along the same lines. It was adjusted with low rates on immigrant's effects, on coal, cordwood, lumber and grain, as was the earlier tariff. It was considerably higher than the tariff in eastern Canada, but ostensibly justified on the grounds of increased costs of operation— in the west fuel was cited as 110 per cent. higher than in eastern Canada, labour 45 per cent., and general supplies 60 per cent.—and of the heavy overhead charges occasioned by the fact that the country was very sparsely settled. [3]

To this new schedule the Winnipeg Board of Trade objected. It was held that rates should not be made to cover the cost of operating the railroad, and in a letter to the company of March 20, 1883, [4] it was claimed that liberal terms had been given the company by the Government because it was expected that the road would be run at a loss. High rates meant high prices on commodities, and consequently were injurious to the trade and growth of the country, and therefore reacted to the company's own detriment. The old rates were regarded as sufficiently high, and an additional average increase of 59 per cent. [5] was

[1] *Sessional Paper*, No. 48g, 1882, p. 35.
[2] *Ibid.*, No. 27j, 1883, p. 3.   [3] *Ibid.*   [4] *Ibid.*, No. 31, 1884, p. 44.

[5] Per 100 lb.	1st Cents.	2nd Cents.	3rd Cents.	4th Cents.
(1) New St. Vincent to Winnipeg . .	43	36	29	22
Old ,, ,, ,, . .	25	21	18	13
Increase	18	15	11	9
Percentage of increase . . .	72	71	61	61
(2) New Winnipeg to Portage la Prairie.	38	32	26	19
Old ,, ,, ,, .	26	21	16	13
Increase	12	11	10	6
Percentage of increase . . .	46	52	62	46
(3) New Winnipeg to Brandon . .	65	54	43	32
Old ,, ,, ,, . .	41	33	27	21
Increase	24	21	16	11
Percentage of increase . . .	39	64	59	52

—*Ibid.*, p. 45.

predicted to be disastrous. Turning to the particular, Winnipeg had its own grievances. It complained that the company had led its merchants to expect low rates from Winnipeg to Thunder Bay during the navigation season, so that they could lay in large stores at a moderate cost, and so that Winnipeg could become a distributing centre. This was expected to redound to the advantage of the company, as a large distributing point would provide the railroad with labour and materials at a reasonable price and give it a constantly increasing traffic. The new tariff, on the other hand, was practically a discrimination against Winnipeg as a distributing point. Goods bought by Winnipeg merchants were increased in price an average of nearly 20 cents per 100 lb.[1] and this, plus 4 cents per 100 lb. for transportation each way between the distributing house and the station, made a total increase of 28 cents per 100 lb. above the cost of direct shipments to such points as Brandon, Portage la Prairie and Regina. It was shown

[1] Per 100 lb.	1st Cents.	2nd Cents.	3rd Cents.	4th Cents.
(1) Winnipeg and Portage la Prairie. Through rate St. Vincent to Portage la Prairie	62	52	41	31
St. Vincent to Winnipeg	43	36	29	22
Winnipeg to Portage la Prairie	38	32	26	19
	81	68	55	41
Extra charge against Winnipeg	19	16	14	10
(2) St. Vincent to Brandon	80	67	54	40
St. Vincent to Winnipeg	43	36	29	22
Winnipeg to Brandon	65	54	43	32
	1·08	90	72	54
Extra charge against Winnipeg	28	23	18	14
(3) St. Vincent to Broadview	1·09	91	73	55
St. Vincent to Winnipeg	43	36	29	22
Winnipeg to Broadview	95	79	63	48
	1·38	1·15	92	70
Extra charge against Winnipeg	29	24	19	15
(4) St. Vincent to Regina	1·28	1·07	86	64
St. Vincent to Winnipeg	43	36	27	22
Winnipeg to Regina	1·15	96	76	58
	1·58	1·32	1·05	80
Extra charge against Winnipeg	30	25	19	16

Ibid., No. 31, 1884, p. 46.

that the new Canadian Pacific tariff was 65 per cent. higher than the winter rate on the Grand Trunk (the lowest rate on that line) for an equal distance, and that the Grand Trunk special tariff for manufacturers and wholesale merchants was lower than the ordinary fourth-class rate of the Canadian Pacific. The remedy proposed was a special tariff for goods shipped to local points from Winnipeg.

These complaints, though producing no immediate results, were significant protests against the exercise of the company's power to adjust rates in a non-competitive area. The exercise of this power was evident in other directions and with similar results. A special east-bound grain rate, adopted January 5, 1884,[1] was designed for the purpose of drawing traffic over the line from Winnipeg to Port Arthur and of preventing its diversion to St. Vincent on the American boundary and over American roads. The rate to Port Arthur on a mileage basis was much lower than the rate to St. Vincent, and consequently had a tendency to draw traffic by the Port Arthur route. On March 16, 1886, the Manitoba and North-west Farmers' Alliance and People's Rights Association, in a meeting at Brandon, accused the Canadian Pacific of a pooling arrangement with the St. Paul, Minneapolis and Manitoba Railway, which gave the latter 12 per cent of the east-bound traffic receipts of the Canadian Pacific Railway to induce [2] it to refrain from taking produce to the market at lower rates. It was alleged that the charge was 4 cents per bushel on wheat exported. This accusation was denied by the company in a statement which explained that the lack of competition was due to the fact that no

[1]

To Port Arthur		From	To St. Vincent	
Rates cents per 100 lbs.	Distances Miles		Rates cents per 100 lbs.	Distances Miles
28	435	Winnipeg	14	68
34	501	Emerson	5	2
30	491	Portage la Prairie	18	124
33	568	Brandon	23	201
37½	699	Broadview	27	332
40	792	Regina	32	425
41½	834	Moosejaw	33	467
47	946	Swift Current	35½	579
54½	1,095	Medicine Hat	38½	728
63	1,275	Calgary	45	908

Sessional Paper, No. 31, 1884, p. 62.

[2] Ibid., No. 34b, 1887, p. 134.

road could carry wheat at Canadian Pacific rates without loss. The Canadian Pacific in comparing its traffic with that of American roads, published a statement showing the relative earnings for 1884, 1885 and 1886.

	1884 cents.	1885 cents.	1886 cents.
Freight per ton per mile	1·45	1·20	1·10

Omitting the through traffic, the earnings in 1886 were 1·14 cents per ton per mile, which was much lower than those of American roads.

These difficulties were a part of a growing agitation against the monopoly clause which was carried on with more vigour after the completion of the main line.   In 1883, in connexion with the charter of the Emerson and North-Western Railway, it had been held that a road could be incorporated for the people within the province, but not beyond its boundaries,[1] a connexion with foreign lines being contrary to the spirit of the B.N.A. Act, which protected the interests of the Dominion,[2] and in 1886 it was held that the Federal Government had the power to disallow roads connecting with lines outside the province.[3] The issue was definitely stated, and the people of Manitoba insisted that the policy of disallowance should be abandoned.   In 1884 Sir Charles Tupper had stated [4] that it would be abandoned with the completion of the road.   Several months had passed after its completion with no result.   On March 4, 1887, Hon. Thomas White intimated [5] that it had been abandoned.   Nevertheless, bills incorporating the Manitoba Central Railway and the Winnipeg and Southern Railway, passed April 19, 1887, were neglected [6] by the governor in council until August 9 and then disallowed.   The Red River Valley Company was chartered, on June 1, 1887, to run from Winnipeg to West Lynne, and a contract was made on June 29 to build the road for $782,340.   The work was started, but on July 6 the act was disallowed.[7]   On June 9 a definite protest [8] had been adopted in a resolution of the legislature against the continuance of the policy.   It stated that the province

---

[1] *Ibid.*, No. 58b, 1888.   [2] *Ibid.*   [3] *Ibid.*   [4] *Ibid.*
     [5] *Ibid.*   [6] *Ibid.*   [7] *Ibid.*   [8] *Ibid.*

had been prevented access to world markets, that excessive rates had crippled its energies, and that immigration had been deterred. The policy was characterized as an arbitrary exercise of the veto power and a violation of the spirit of the B.N.A. Act.

On September 12 the Canadian Pacific Railway declared [1] its position. It claimed protection from the encroachment of American lines on the usual ground that the enormous expense involved in the construction of the road from Lake Nipissing to Red River, nearly 1,100 miles of unproductive territory, entitled it to an advantage. It was urged that the interests of the older provinces should be protected in view of the expenditure made by them. The interests of 10,000 people of Manitoba were not to be allowed to prevail against those of 5,000,000 people of the Dominion. A plea was made that the company, recognizing a moral obligation, had expended over $5,700,000 on branch lines south and south-west of Winnipeg. The action of the Government of Manitoba in attempting to divert traffic by the construction of a road to the boundary was therefore characterized as unfair, unjust, and a breach of faith.[2] The company threatened, in a telegram to Premier Norquay, moreover, to move its principal western shops to Fort William, leaving nothing at Winnipeg but its ordinary division shops.

The Winnipeg and Brandon Boards of Trade, on October 1, replied in an open letter [3] to the shareholders of the Canadian Pacific Railway. They insisted that the B.N.A. Act did not impair the right of self-government, and that the Federal authorities had no right to disallow Manitoba railroad legislation. The president of the company had quoted the words of the contract " that the Dominion Government should not authorize a line running south." The actual words were " Dominion Parliament." Parliament could not give a pledge that the power of disallowance would be

[1] C.P.R. Co. *Letter of President Stephen to the shareholders.*
[2] " It would be absurd to urge that the completion of 66 miles of railway, undertaken by the Government of Manitoba, would ruin the vast Canadian Pacific system, but its construction would be a violation of the contract with this company, and the directors feel it to be their duty to maintain the rights of the company in this matter " (*Ibid.*, p. 7).
[3] *Open letter to the shareholders of the C.P.R.*

exercised, since that power was a prerogative of the Crown over which Parliament had no control. The decision of the European and North American Railroad case was to the effect that it was within the power of a province to construct a railway to the boundary as a local road. The company was reminded of the fact that Winnipeg had given it a bonus of $200,000, a free right of way worth $20,000, exemption of all its property within the city from taxation for ever, and the Louise bridge, costing $250,000. Further, the expenditures on branch lines undertaken, because of a " moral obligation," had been met by the proceeds of land grants and by assistance from the Provincial Government, and in any event the branches were remunerative. On October 12 the Executive Council of Manitoba [1] issued a formal protest in a memorial covering much the same ground.

To this the Canadian Government replied on January 4, 1888.[2] Its argument was related entirely to the interests of Canada. According to its interpretation the B.N.A. Act gave the Dominion exclusive jurisdiction over trade and commerce, and consequently over the powers of the province to build a road beyond its boundaries. The monopoly clause was essential to the construction of the road, and without the road the western provinces would be dependent on American lines for six months of the year. The company had built the road before the allotted time at an increased expenditure, and a fortiori was entitled to protection. The Government of Manitoba had moreover agreed to the rights of the Dominion to disallowance at different periods, as in the extension of the boundaries of the province it had acquiesced in the policy by allowing the new territory to be subject to all provisions enacted respecting the Canadian Pacific. It was inconceivable that the great interest of the Canadian Pacific in the development of the country should permit it to sanction any step which would retard prosperity. It was charged that the Northern Pacific was behind the whole movement to strike the Canadian Pacific in the centre with a line to Winnipeg, and to control, through competition, transcontinental traffic.

[1] *Sessional Paper*, No. 58b, 1888.   [2] *Ibid.*

Manitoba was insistent. The company refused to yield. Finally the Canadian Government gave way.

On April 18, 1888, an agreement [1] was made between the Government and the Canadian Pacific providing for the cancellation of the monopoly clause. In consideration, the Government agreed to guarantee the payment of interest on a new issue of bonds by the company up to $15,000,000, the principal to be payable not later than 50 years and the interest payable half-yearly at $3\frac{1}{2}$ per cent per year, the bonds to be secured by the unsold lands of the company. The proceeds from the sale of lands and the interest on these proceeds were used to constitute a fund to satisfy the principal of the bonds and to pay the interest on them. The land grant bonds of the former issue held by the company, $4,000,000, were to be destroyed, and the mortgage, created under this agreement, to become subject to the land grant bonds in the hands of the public, $3,463,000, although the sums due for lands already sold, $1,200,000, were to be applied toward the payment of bonds outstanding. The proceeds from the sale of the bonds were to be spent according to a definite schedule: first, for capital expenditure on the main line between Quebec and Vancouver in buildings, snow sheds, sidings, permanent bridges, filling trestles, reducing grades and curves and other improvements, and on vouchers and pay rolls, $5,498,000 ; second, for required rolling stock, locomotives, box cars, passenger cars, flat cars, tool cars, etc., $5,250,000 ; third, for required improvements on the main line, elevators, bridges, locomotive shops, sidings, docks, lake and coast steamers, the remainder, $4,252,000. Provision was made for an increase in the expenditure for the third class, and a corresponding decrease in the other classes. The company was given authority to lease its line from St. Boniface to the American boundary, and in the event of the construction of a line between the same points with the sanction of the Dominion Government, to cease operating either one of its two lines between those points.

Cancellation of the monopoly clause did not fulfil expectations, as was evident in renewed and later complaints. On

[1] 51 Vic. C32.

November 15, 1894, a Railway Rates Commission was appointed to investigate the situation. In its report [1] of May 7, 1895, the position of the Canadian Pacific was largely supported. It agreed " that density of population, with volume of tonnage carried, with a fairly even balance of loaded trains hauled in both directions, are the most important factors in determining what are reasonable rates." Conclusions were supported on the basis of comparisons made with American roads operating under similar conditions with similar commodities and between points of similar characteristics. It found that the Canadian Pacific gave lower grain rates than such roads. This was also true of livestock. Rates on coal were lower even than those given by roads operating in a coal area. Lumber rates were of the same favourable character, and although lumber was carried from British Columbia to Ontario at a lower mileage rate than to Manitoba, the western farmer had no ground for complaint. Agricultural implements were carried at a lower mileage rate. Merchandise carried over an all-rail route by the Canadian Pacific was considerably higher than that carried by American roads, but the Commission explained that about 80 per cent of this business was carried by a lake and rail route on which a lower rate was given. The high price of clothing was attributed to the large profits of merchants rather than to high freight rates. Dairy products were carried at higher rates, but a blanket rate was given west of Winnipeg to Vancouver of $1.75 per 100 lb. The rate on cordwood was higher than that of the Northern Pacific, but equal to that of the Grand Trunk. Local rates, " it must be admitted," were higher than in eastern provinces, but the commission held they were necessary to pay the cost of transportation. On the same basis the high rates on branch lines were regarded as inevitable. The Commission referred all matters to the cost of transportation. Finally, it concluded with a statement made by the company to the effect that it held 18,000,000 acres of land and upwards of 3,000 miles of railway in the north-west, that its interests were identical with the interests of its patrons, and for this reason it could not subscribe to

[1] *Sessional Paper*, No. 39, 1885.

any policy unfavourable to the settlers.   A lengthy statement made by Vice-President Shaughnessy, stated that the company's prosperity was the result of its rigid economy, that the development of the west depended upon its financial standing, and that expenses of operation were higher in the west and consequently justified higher rates.   In any case, the averages per passenger per mile and per ton per mile were much lower on the Canadian Pacific west of Lake Superior than on American roads in the same territory.

Obviously the report was of such a character as to give little satisfaction.   It was not until 1897 that an act [1] was passed designed to meet the situation.   In this act a subsidy was granted to the Canadian Pacific Railway for the line from Lethbridge through the Crow's Nest Pass to Nelson at $11,000 per mile to be paid on the completion of sections of ten miles of track.   This was granted under several conditions : (1) the road was to be built through the town of Macleod ; (2) when it was opened for traffic to Kootenay Lake the local rates and tolls on the railway and on " any other railway used in connexion therewith and now or hereafter owned or leased by or operated on account of the company south of the company's main line in British Columbia, as well as the rates and tolls between any point on any such line or lines of railway and any point on the main line of the company throughout Canada or any other railway owned or leased by or operated on account of the company, including its line of steamers in British Columbia, shall be first approved by the Governor in Council or by a Railway Commission, if, and when, such commission is established by law, and shall at all times thereafter and from time to time be subject to revision and control " ; (3) a reduction to be made in the general rates or tolls of the company or its freight tariff (whichever was the lowest) on classes of merchandise west bound from and including Fort William and all points east of Fort William on the company's railway to all points west of Fort William on the main line or on any line throughout Canada owned, leased or operated by the company, whether the shipment was by all rail or lake and rail, the reductions being on all green and fresh fruits,

[1] 60–61 Vic. C5, 1897.

33⅓ per cent., coal oil, 20 per cent., cordage and binder twine, agricultural implements, iron, wire, window glass, paper for building purposes, roofing felt, paints, livestock, wooden ware and household furniture, each 10 per cent. A reduction was also stipulated for rates on grain and flour from all points on its main line, branches and connexions west of Fort William to Fort William and Port Arthur, and all points east, of 3 cents per 100 lb.

These restrictions and provisions for further regulation were followed by the appointment of a commission to investigate the whole problem. On February 10, 1899, Prof. S. J. McLean submitted a report on Railway Commissions, railway rate grievances and regulative legislation which was of an illuminating and convincing character. It was stated that communities in the north-west which had non-competitive rates found it advantageous to transport their produce by wagon to some point where competitive rates prevailed. " The development of the traffic of the distant manufacturer has been given an advantage over the home manufacturer." Rates to intermediate points in the north-west were fixed at the same figure or even higher than rates to the coast. " There is no doubt that the population and business of this section have not been allowed to move and develop in accordance with natural principles." The effect of competition could not be questioned. On May 1, 1887, the rates [1] from Winnipeg, Portage la Prairie and Brandon to Fort William on first-class freight were $1.33, $1.41 and $1.58 respectively. On October 28, 1888, after the opening of the Northern Pacific from Winnipeg to Duluth, rates between the above points were reduced to $1.16, $1.25 and $1.42 respectively. The rate to Regina, a non-competitive point, remained the same.

The whole situation was finally discussed in another report [2] of January 17, 1902, by the same author. " It is impossible to bring a car-load of oats on local rates from Portage la Prairie to Winnipeg." The Canadian Pacific had not always been influenced as was supposed by the best interests of the country. Distributive rates were

[1] 45 C.S.C.R. 322 (1912).
[2] Both reports are found in *Sessional Paper*, No. 20a, 1902.

granted when the volume of business warranted, but withholding the rates checked development and increased the
prosperity of the distributive point.   Brandon and Winnipeg had struggled for distributive rates, and in the struggle
the interests of the country had been sacrificed to the
interests of the railroad.   No regulation existed which
ensured uniform development.   A wide discrepancy was
found between C.L. and L.C.L. from Winnipeg to points
west and between other points—a discrepancy which
favoured the wholesale distributing points.   Disproportions
were found in rates in the country west of Winnipeg, especially in the grain rates on branch lines.   On some articles the
freight charges were more than twice the cost of the article.
Complaints as to minimum weights of car lots were sustained
by facts.   Through rates to the north-west were found to
be ill-adjusted to the development of Canadian industry,
and to interfere with the expansion of the trade of eastern
Canada.   Winnipeg complained of discrimination at Fort
William, in which the Canadian Pacific gave lower rates to
favoured lake carriers.   As a result, and on the advice of the
report, an act [1] was passed in 1903 establishing the Board of
Railway Commissioners.

The establishment of a regulative body, and the control
of this body, over the rates of the Canadian Pacific acquired
in the Crows Nest Pass agreement seriously curtailed the
freedom of the company in the determination of its rate
policy.   On the other hand, the regulation of rates by the
Board of Railway Commissioners was destined not to prove
a panacea [2] for the difficulties involved.   The competitive
character of rates in eastern Canada and on transcontinental
traffic and the stretch of unproductive territory north of
Lake Superior continued to necessitate the imposition of
higher rates in non-competitive territory.   As was stated
in the Eastern Rates decision, " I am aware that an absolute
parity is impracticable, but as conditions become similar
reasonable parity ought to be obtained." [3]   The rapidity
with which conditions in western Canada were to become

[1] 3 Edw. VII, c. 58.
[2] For an excellent treatment of the rate situation, see MacGibbon, D. A.,
Railway Rates and the Canadian Railway Commission.
[3] VI, J.O.R.R. 154.

similar to conditions in eastern Canada depended on a number of circumstances.

Competition in western Canada and consequently lower rates followed the construction of other roads, but the effectiveness of this competition was seriously lessened by the financial conditions of these roads. The Canadian Northern was started in Manitoba in 1896. In 1906 a system of more than 2,400 miles had been completed in the prairie provinces, and in 1916 this had been extended to over 5,000 miles. After the construction of its western system, and its connexions to Vancouver, this company made extensions eastward to secure control of eastern traffic and to secure an outlet to the Atlantic seaboard.[1] In 1916 it had a total mileage of 9,648, extending east to Quebec, and touching the important centres of Duluth, Toronto, Ottawa and Montreal. This achievement had been accomplished with a comparatively small land grant, $38,874,000 in subsidies, and the guarantee of vast sums of money by the Dominion Government. On June 30, 1916, the Canadian Northern passed the payment of interest on $25,000,000 of income debenture stock, and after charging interest against capital to the amount of $5,445,389, was $248,000 short of meeting its bonded indebtedness.[2] The Grand Trunk Pacific was provided for in two acts of parliament dated October 24, 1903.[3] A main line was to be built from Moncton to Prince Rupert, the section east of Winnipeg, by the Government, and leased to the Grand Trunk with Government assistance. The road was built and operated by the Grand Trunk Pacific from Winnipeg to Prince Rupert, 2,228 miles. The very high cost of the eastern section built by the Government and on which the company agreed to pay a rental, provided an excuse for its refusal to take over the line. For the year ending December, 1916, the Grand Trunk Pacific had a net income of $826,653 with which to meet interest charges of $8,846,544.

The weak condition of these transcontinental roads, largely occasioned by undeveloped western territory and

---

[1] *Report of the Royal Commission to inquire into Railways and Transportation in Canada*, 1917, p. 21.
[2] *Ibid.*, p. 39.   [3] *Ibid.*, p. 20.

by the long unproductive lines north of Lake Superior, were
of decided influence in limiting the powers of the Board
with reference to the reduction of western rates. In the
Western Rates case,[1] which was an attack on the general
freight level of western Canada, the Board stated " that
rates based upon the Canadian Pacific's power to stand
reductions would inevitably bankrupt not only the Canadian
Northern and the Grand Trunk Pacific, but for the future
preserve the western provinces to that company in so far
as any new companies or new lines were concerned."[2] "A
railway is entitled to a reasonable surplus," and " rates
should be considered, having regard to the traffic necessities
of western Canada and a fair return to the carrier—apart
entirely from any question of reserves of the company on
the one hand, or the liabilities on the other."[3] In the
decision of the 15 per cent. case [4] it was stated that " the
Board's duty—is to control and adjust rates, having regard
to the systems of railways that Parliament had authorized.
The Board must take the railway ownership just as it finds
it." In this case, having regard to the increased expenses,
especially increased wages, the Board ruled that " subject
to the limitation worked by the Crows Nest Agreement as
extended by this judgment and to the specific conditions
herein contained, the companies are permitted to raise their
general rates 15 per cent., and make the specific advances
herein allowed."

The Drayton-Acworth Report and its adoption in the
amalgamation of the Canadian Northern and the Grand
Trunk Pacific in the Canadian National Railways did not
materially change the situation. Provision was made
through an order in council,[5] following a continued increase
in expenses and wages, for suspension of the Crows Nest
agreement, and on August 1, 1918, increases were granted
in railway freight rates in Canada similar to the increases
granted in American territory under the McAdoo award.
Nor is it probable that the co-ordination of all Government
railways under one Board as proposed by the King adminis-

[1] *Board of Railway Commissioners of Canada, File No.* 18755, *Judgment.*
[2] *Ibid.,* p. 34 ff.   [3] *Ibid.,* p. 92.
[4] *Report of Board of Railway Commissioners,* 1918, pp. 104–5.
[5] *Ibid.,* 1919, p. 48.

tration will seriously affect the general problem.[1] Deficits
have been met by the Dominion Parliament, but it is ques-
tionable whether Parliament will encourage increased
deficits to permit the reduction of rates in western Canada,
The gradual reduction of deficits through the development
of traffic on the national railways, through the realization
of various economies secured in the proposed co-ordination,
and through the increase in traffic taken from the Canadian
Pacific, may warrant a reduction of rates in western Canada,
but prediction is dangerous. It is even more dangerous
with the existence of the Canadian [2] and the American
tariffs, which render competition from American roads in
western Canada ineffective, and consequently strengthen
the monopoly of Canadian roads in that area, and with the
rise of the Progressive party, which this situation has largely
provoked.

Although the Board has been limited in questions relating
to the general rate situation in the north-west, it has exercised effective control over rates of a local character.
Various decisions in rate difficulties of the east as of the west
illustrate the extent of this control and the general policy of
the Board. In the Almonte Knitting Company case a ruling [3]
was given that higher rates were warranted on branch lines
than on the main line, because of the increased cost of
operation. Similarly in the Vancouver Eastbound v. Winnipeg Westbound rate case [4] it was held that the Company
was justified in charging a higher rate on the mountain section than on the prairie section. In the case [5] of The Attorney-General of British Columbia v. The Canadian Pacific, it
was requested that the province of British Columbia should
be placed on the same favourable basis in respect to tolls

[1] *Globe*, April 12, 1922.
[2] The words of Van Horne during the Reciprocity Campaign are very
much in point : " Shall we be permitted to recede from reciprocity when
Mr. Hill has extended his seven or eight lines of railway into the Canadian
North-West—lines which have for some years been resting their noses on
the boundary line, waiting for reciprocity or something of the kind to
warrant them in crossing—and when other American channels of trade
have been established affecting our territory, and when the American
millers have tasted our wheat and the American manufacturers have got
hold of our markets ? Shall we be permitted to recede ? Not a bit of
it ! We are making a bed to lie in—and die in." " I am out to do all
I can do to bust the damned thing." Vaughan, W., op. cit., p. 347.
[3] 3 C.R.C. 441.   [4] 7 C.R.C. 125.   [5] 5 C.R.C. 202.

over the Canadian Pacific in that province as in other portions
of the Dominion of Canada over the main line of that railway.
The Board held, in reply to the argument that the national
character of the road and the subsidies granted entitled
British Columbia to this consideration, that it did not matter
as to the land and money grants to the company, as nothing
appeared in the contract requiring the company to establish
and maintain over the whole line of railway when completed
the same or similar tolls under different circumstances.
The company was bound to charge the same or similar tolls
at the same time and under the same circumstances only.
The position of the Board, amplified in these decisions, was
of significance in the leeway afforded the company in its
determination of rates on branch lines and on sections of the
main line. Similar freedom was given to the company in
the establishment of developmental rates.[1] Again the
Board placed the company under no obligation to meet
competition from water routes.[2] It solved with commend-
able success, questions of discrimination in car-load rates,[3]
in classification,[4] and in rates,[5] and every effort [6] was made
to acquire facts essential to sound decisions.

Rulings and decisions of the Board of Railway Commissioners have to a large extent adjusted rate difficulties permitting the uniform economic development of western
Canada, but the general rate question has been beyond control. Primarily, the rate situation in that area has been a
monopoly situation. Competition has increased with the
construction of new roads, but the difficult financial conditions of these roads, chiefly the result of the long stretch
of unproductive territory separating eastern from western
Canada, seriously lessen its effectiveness in the reduction of
rates.

[1] Brampton Communication Rates Case, 8 C.R.C. 42.
[2] Blind River Board of Trade v. The Grand Trunk, Canadian Pacific
Railways, Northern Navigation and Dominion Transportation Companies.
15 C.R.C. 147.
[3] 17 C.R.C. 279.   [4] 4 C.R.C. 148.
[5] Regina Rates Case, 11 C.R.C. 380.
[6] In the Cardston Board of Trade v. The Alberta Railway and Irrigation
Company, the Railway Company operated a railway and collieries and
owned large areas of irrigated land and town lots. It was claimed that
tolls should not be reduced since the railway and irrigation works were
run at a loss and the land and coal areas covered the deficit. The Board

The pressure of freight rates in western Canada as a non-competitive area has depended to some extent on freight rates on the lines of the company in competitive territory. Competitive transcontinental traffic became increasingly serious with the opening of the through line to Vancouver and the continual development of new connexions. The opening of the transcontinental line was followed by active competition with American roads for through business in both directions, between all Pacific coast points and all points of the United States on or east of the Missouri River. The Canadian Pacific definitely attempted to compel American roads to grant differentials. Contending that the natural disadvantages of the road should be compensated by the privilege of offering to the public a lower rate, it engaged a steamer line from San Francisco to take shipments of freight on through rates to various points in eastern states. American rates, as a result, were lowered on April 27, 1887, and again on May 25. In January, 1888, an arrangement was finally made in which the Canadian Pacific became a member of the Transcontinental Association, and agreed with the other lines upon through rates considerably higher than those which previously prevailed,[1] although that road was given certain differentials on San Francisco traffic only—a differential of 15 cents per 100 lb. on first-class traffic, and of 5 cents on the lowest commodity class—from San Francisco to

regarded the control acquired over this railway company as a " very material factor in the case." The chief commissioner adopted the recommendation of the chief traffic officer that the territory in which the A.R. & I. operated was in all respects similar to that of the Canadian Pacific in Southern Alberta, and that the A.R. & I. freight rates should not exceed those in effect for similar distances and on similar commodities on the line of the Canadian Pacific (5 C.R.C. 236). In Wylie Milling Company v. Canadian Pacific, the company owned 51 per cent. of the stock of the Kingston and Pembroke Railway. It was claimed by the railroad that the companies were separate corporations, and should be treated separately, each being entitled to its own rates. The Board, with the precedent of the Interstate Commerce Commission, stated " that the purchase by the Canadian Pacific Railway Company of a majority interest in the stock of the Kingston and Pembroke road was not made with a view to a directly remunerative investment, but to secure certain advantages which it was thought would accrue from control of the rates and operations of that road, and the company enjoying the advantages should discharge the obligations growing out of such control. Therefore we are logically forced to conclude that the Kingston and Pembroke Railway should be considered a part, and treated as a part, of the Canadian Pacific Railway "(14 C.R.C. 5).
[1] I.C.C.R., 1888, p. 114.

St. Paul, Minneapolis and common points.   From San Francisco to points further east the concessions were progressively larger—at Chicago, Cincinnati, Pittsburg and New York— reaching at New York, Boston and Philadelphia, 28 cents first class and 5 cents lowest commodity class.[1]

With the exception [2] of limitations enforced by the Interstate Commerce Commission, this agreement persisted to 1897.   The investigation of the committee, under the chairmanship of Senator Cullom, found that the differential given by the American roads to the Canadian Pacific on business to and from San Francisco remained in force except for the year from January 1, 1891, to January 2, 1892, when it was alleged that it had been dropped in consideration of a payment of a lump sum by American roads.   With the constant improvement of through connexions on the part of American roads, the equilibrium was destroyed, and freight difficulties complicated with passenger difficulties led to a situation which made necessary the abolition of the agreement.   Transcontinental traffic has remained of a competitive character, though disturbances occasioned by rate wars have practically disappeared with the increasing influence of regulative bodies in both the United States and Canada.   The improvement of transcontinental facilities in the United States and Canada in the construction of railways and the opening of the Panama Canal has made the effects of competition even more serious.

Competition of through transcontinental traffic has on the other hand been much less serious than competition in eastern Canada and in trunk line territory.   In 1889 the number of

---

[1] I.C.C.R., 1889, pp. 59–60.

[2] In 1890 a suit was brought by the City of New York against the Canadian Pacific and other roads.   The Canadian Pacific had been forced by steamship companies to bear a part of the reduction of through rates, and to surrender a larger portion of the earnings as well as greater control of the rates.   Consequently rates from Yokohama to Chicago were the same as rates from Yokohama to New York.   In the decision it was ruled that the Canadian Pacific and other roads were to " desist from carrying traffic shipped from any foreign port through any port of entry of the United States or any port of entry in a foreign country adjacent to the United States upon through bills of lading destined to any place within the United States at any other than upon the inland tariff covering other freight from such port of entry to such place of destination."   The Canadian roads evaded the force of the decision by selecting a few articles which were typically imports and placing them in a commodity class with greatly reduced rates (4 I.C.C.R., p. 447).

car-loads going via the Canadian Pacific averaged twenty-nine per month, or one car per day, which was roughly the amount of traffic diverted from American lines.[1] In 1891 less than 1 per cent. of the competitive traffic was carried by the Canadian Pacific, and the gross earnings of the east-bound shipments of this road were 1·36 per cent. of the gross earnings of all roads on this traffic. Of the traffic originating in California, Oregon and Washington, the Canadian Pacific carried ·23 per cent. of the gross revenue. Of the traffic between British Columbia and Canada it carried 83·21 per cent. West-bound traffic to California, Oregon and Washington was slight. The proportion carried by the Canadian Pacific was ·81 per cent. The proportion carried between Canada and British Columbia was 86·28 per cent. The total east- and west-bound earnings of transcontinental traffic from Vancouver in 1891 were 12·7 per cent of the total transcontinental traffic, the remainder being earnings on domestic traffic between Eastern Canada and British Columbia. In its share of traffic from China and Japan, the Canadian Pacific carried an average of 42 per cent. of the tea and 16 per cent. of the silk from 1887 to 1892, but this increase in tea shipments was more largely at the expense of the Suez Canal route than of the American routes. Since that time transcontinental traffic has greatly increased, but it still remains relatively unimportant.

Competition in eastern Canada and on trunk line traffic was more serious. On April 1, 1885,[2] the schedule of the Canadian Joint Freight Association was adopted by the Canadian Pacific and other Canadian roads in eastern Canada. According to expectations, the rates involved were considerably lower[3] on a strictly mileage basis than the

---

[1] Raymond, A. C., *The Canadian Railway Question*, p. 38.
[2] *Sessional Paper*, No. 35, 1886, p. 159 ff.
[3]

	RATES	
	Western Division First Class	Eastern Division First Class
Miles	Cents per lb.	Cents per lb.
10	15	10
15	18	12
25	24	16
50	35	24
100	54	36
300	1.02	60
500	1.43	80
1,000	2.28	1.50

rates charged in western Canada. Frequent rate wars made stability impossible, and between competitive points rates fluctuated persistently and sank to lower levels. The American roads, in an attack on the Canadian Pacific, as a Government-subsidized road, first asked, by a resolution in Congress, for the abolition of the transit in bond system, but this was defeated by commercial organizations of various important American cities who registered their protests in no uncertain manner. An attempt in the 50th Congress to prohibit the importation of merchandise in bond through American seaports for Canadian markets was defeated by the same forces.[1] Propaganda was conducted in pamphlets, in the press, and on the floor of Congress. Mr. A. N. Towne, general manager of the Southern Pacific Railway, was a prominent figure in this hostility. The agitation was even reflected in the antagonistic attitude of President Harrison,[2] and a Senate committee on interstate commerce, under the chairmanship of Senator Cullom, was appointed to take evidence. Careful investigation revealed important facts.[3]

It was found that on several occasions rates of the Canadian Pacific between Minneapolis and St. Paul and New York and Boston were lower than rates agreed upon with the other roads. In January, 1891, the rate from New York to St. Paul was 15 cents below the agreed basis, and in April, 13 cents, and 23 cents lower than the all-rail trunk lines. Nor were these rates raised with the closing of navigation. The Canadian Pacific was undoubtedly the aggressor, but it was finally pointed out that the rates were not persistently under differentials claimed by Canadian roads, and in traffic from Boston and New York, American roads were in all cases a part of the through route. The routes viâ the Sault and viâ Chicago were competitive routes, and rates fluctuated at various intervals. Diversion of traffic from the Chicago route was unquestioned. Of flour shipped from Minneapolis, the percentage carried by the Chicago, Milwaukee and St. Paul decreased from 38·47 per cent. in 1884 to 12·53 per cent. in 1891. The percentage carried by the Soo

---

[1] See a history of the case : Raymond, A. C., op. cit.
[2] Messages and Papers of the Presidents, vol. IX, p. 346.
[3] 6 I.C.C.R., p. 280 ff.

line increased from the date of opening in 1888 to 17 per cent.
in 1892. The percentage of corn carried over the latter
route varied from 70 to 85 per cent., of oats, rye and barley
from 30 to 53 per cent., and of wool from 76 per cent. upward,
although this increase was not entirely a diversion to the
Canadian Pacific, since a large portion was hauled to Glad-
stone and shipped by the lakes to Buffalo. On through
rates from Missouri River points to the seaboard the
Canadian Pacific had frequently departed from the normal
basis, but the southern American routes had been even more
flagrant violators.

Competition for seaboard traffic was not confined to
Canadian and American roads. It was also serious between
Canadian roads. With the arrangements by which the
C.P.R. received traffic from the Wabash at Detroit, it carried
the inconsequential portion of about 3·4 per cent. of the
total eastward dead-freight traffic from Chicago to the
Atlantic seaboard. In 1892 the Wabash carried 10·9 per
cent. of the total Chicago dressed beef, of which the greater
portion found its way over the Canadian Pacific. As a result
the Grand Trunk suffered a loss of 25 per cent. of its
former share in this traffic. This investigation effectively
answered the argument of Canadian domination in trunk
line traffic and conclusively precluded the charges of American roads, proving as it did their inevitable complicity in
Canadian criminality. Charges against the Canadian Pacific
implied proof of innocence on the part of American roads
in complying with the Interstate Commerce Law by main-
taining their public through rates. The advantage of the
Canadian Pacific lay in its ability to quote through rates
without consulting other roads.

As with transcontinental traffic, competition has continued in Eastern Canada and on trunk line traffic, though rate
wars have practically disappeared through the influence of
American and Canadian regulative bodies. The effects of
canal improvements and increased Great Lakes traffic, of
the addition of railway facilities, and of the improvement of
railway systems through the centralization of railway
managements have been evident. The difficulties attending
this competition were especially prominent during the war

196 HISTORY OF THE CANADIAN PACIFIC RAILWAY

and led to the decision [1] on June 9, 1916, of the Board of Railway Commissioners in the Eastern Rates Case, permitting an increase in rates in territory east of Fort William. Rates in this territory have been inevitably of a competitive character.

The essentially competitive character of Canadian Pacific transcontinental and trunk line traffic, which found expression in rate wars and which was later regulated by the Board of Railway Commissioners and by the Interstate Commerce Commission, was therefore of dominant importance in the determination of the company's rate policy. Low earnings or losses incidental to competition in this traffic made it necessary that higher rates should be charged in western Canada as a more or less non-competitive area. Conditions in eastern Canada and in western Canada were not such as to give a parity in rates. A change of conditions making possible this parity depends on a multitude of uncertain factors, but a reduction of rates in the immediate future is scarcely probable.

[1] *Board of Railway Commissioners' Report,* 1917, pp. 7–8.

VI

Passenger Traffic

THE general expansion of the physical property of the road, especially in western Canada, dominated, and was largely dominated by, the freight situation. The importance of western Canada made inevitable an unusually marked interrelationship between the freight situation and the passenger situation. The movement of population to that area preceded and followed the development of freight traffic. And in general the development of freight traffic stimulated, and was stimulated by, the development of passenger traffic.

A. PASSENGERS CARRIED

The opening of the railroad to western Canada was followed immediately by immigration. During the first five months of Government operation of the road from the United States boundary to Winnipeg, 17,640 passengers [1] were carried. The next ten months, which included the summer months of 1880, brought an increase in the monthly average of passengers [2] carried from 3,520 to 7,560, and, despite an increase in mileage from 280 to 367, an increase in the monthly average of passengers carried per mile from 12·5 to 20·8. The first year of company operation which included the mileage in Eastern Canada and increased total mileage to 609, brought an increase [3] to 45·6 in the monthly average of passengers carried per mile. Rapid

---

[1] *Sessional Paper*, 1880–1, No. 5, p. 77.
[2] *Ibid.*, No. 8, 1882, p. 23.
[3] *Ibid.*, No. 8, 1883, p. 23.

increase, partly the result of the expansion of the road in eastern Canada, but largely dominated by expansion in the west, continued to 1890. The number of passengers carried [1] increased from 388,785 in 1882 to 26,685,730 in 1890—an increase which, with the exception of the years prior to the completion of the main line, was, if not steady, persistent. The number increased in 1899 to 3,818,857 [2] and in 1920 to a maximum of 16,925,049. The increase was steady and rapid from 1890 to 1893 and was followed by a decline to 1895, a gradual recovery to 1897, and a rapid gain to 1900. Fluctuations were largely occasioned by the period of depression, by the grain situation, and by the Klondike rush in 1898. In 1887 an exceptional harvest had little effect on the passenger situation until two years later when there was a marked increase. Effects of the large harvest in 1892 were lost in the depression of the following years. The bountiful harvest of 1897 contributed to the increase of 1898 though the rate wars and the gold rush were of particular importance. The general upward trend which dominated the fluctuations continued as the result of the

---

[1] Passengers carried, 1882–1890 :

1882 388,785	1887 1,949,215
1883 800,419	1888 2,135,735
1884 919,263	1889 2,457,306
1885 1,427,367	1890 2,685,730
1886 1,791,034	

Compiled from *Sessional Papers*, 1883–91.

[2] Passengers carried, 1890–1921 :

1890* 2,792,805	1907 8,779,620
1891 3,165,507	1908 9,463,179
1892 3,258,289	1909 9,784,450
1893 3,311,247	1910 11,172,891
1894 3,009,015	1911 12,080,150
1895 2,983,793	1912 13,751,516
1896 3,029,887	1913 15,480,934
1897 3,179,589	1914 15,638,312
1898 3,674,502	1915 13,202,603
1899 3,818,857	1916 13,833,978
1901† 4,337,799	1916 (six months) . 9,184,295
1902 4,796,746	1917* 15,462,276
1903 5,524,198	1918 14,396,753
1904 6,251,471	1919 15,815,982
1905 6,891,511	1920 16,925,049
1906 7,753,323	1921 15,318,358

Compiled from *C.P.R. Reports*.

* Calendar year.　　　　　† Fiscal year (six months omitted).

opening of the west, and expansion in more thickly populated territory in eastern Canada and the United States. The increase to 1909, with the exception of a slight falling off in the last year due to the depression and the bad harvest, was steady and rapid. In 1910 it gained momentum and was unusually rapid in 1913. The beginning of the war brought a marked decline. A partial recovery was evident in 1917 as a result of the favourable agricultural situation in that year, but the increasing rates during the war and the transportation restrictions led to another decline in the following year. In 1920 recovery was in evidence, but the following year brought a decline. In general the passenger situation was dependent on the freight situation and particularly on the agricultural situation. The rapid increase from 1900 to 1913 was, to no small extent, dominated by the expansion of western Canada.

B. TRAIN MILEAGE

Increase in the number of tons of freight carried was largely reflected in the freight train mileage. Passenger train mileage was not as dependent upon the number of passengers carried. Passenger train mileage was related to the development of the system, to the adoption of passenger schedules, and to the essentially large element of fixed charges characteristic of passenger equipment, and was less elastic to the demands of traffic than freight train mileage. As a result of the nature of the relationship between passenger miles and the extension of the system the number of passenger train miles [1] increased rapidly from 317,841 in 1882 to 4,566,758 in 1890. The acquisition of lines in the east and the construction of lines in the west occasioned persistent fluctuations throughout the period. In 1899 the

---

[1] Passenger train miles, 1882–90 :

1882	.	.	.	317,841	1887	.	.	.	2,738,184
1883	.	.	.	936,721	1888	.	.	.	3,633,789
1884	.	.	.	1,060,721	1889	.	.	.	4,191,477
1885	.	.	.	1,260,365	1890	.	.	.	4,566,758
1886	.	.	.	1,665,960					

Compiled from *Government Reports.*

number increased [1] to 7,441,828 and in 1921 to 18,931,622. The years from 1890 to 1893 were characterized by a gradual but steady increase, to 1895 by a decline, and to 1900 by a rapid recovery. Decreased traffic during the depression was accompanied by a decline in train mileage, and increased traffic with increased railway mileage during the end of the decade was accompanied by an increase in the number of train miles. From 1900 to 1913 increase in passenger train mileage was rapid and steady with no fluctuations such as characterized freight train mileage in the same period. Increased traffic and increased mileage necessitated a constant increase in the number of passenger schedules. On the other hand the element of fixed charges peculiar to passenger equipment operated as a constant check to a rapid increase. Constant pressure was exercised to prevent an undue expansion of equipment and of train mileage. Partly as a result of these efforts an increase in traffic in 1914 was accompanied by a decrease in train mileage, but passenger mileage decreased less rapidly than traffic following 1914. The rapid increase in 1916 and 1917 in traffic was accompanied by a relatively slight increase in train mileage, though undoubtedly the situation was complicated by war-time restrictions. Passenger train mileage was dominated by several factors, of which traffic, mileage, inelastic schedules, and overhead charges were most important.

[1] Passenger train miles, 1891-1921 :

1891*	. . . .	5,716,541	1908	. . . .	13,196,093
1892	. . . .	5,834,545	1909	. . . .	14,170,522
1893	. . . .	6,136,732	1910	. . . .	16,119,453
1894	. . . .	5,861,058	1911	. . . .	17,393,532
1895	. . . .	5,719,118	1912	. . . .	19,591,027
1896	. . . .	5,842,461	1913	. . . .	22,333,592
1897	. . . .	6,273,999	1914	. . . .	21,523,630
1898	. . . .	7,160,764	1915	. . . .	17,977,033
1899	. . . .	7,441,828	1916	. . . .	18,159,545
1901 †	. . . .	7,765,584	1916 (six months)	.	13,315,730
1902	. . . .	8,300,140	1917*	. . . .	18,093,554
1903	. . . .	8,309,015	1918	. . . .	16,665,928
1904	. . . .	8,810,180	1919	. . . .	20,411,110
1905	. . . .	9,797,618	1920	. . . .	20,538,038
1906	. . . .	11,086,929	1921	. . . .	18,931,622
1907	. . . .	12,413,638			

Compiled from *C.P.R. Reports*.

* Calendar year.   † Fiscal year (six months omitted).

C. Passenger Equipment and Services

The importance of overhead charges can be more adequately appreciated in a discussion of equipment. At the end of the first five months of Government operation the road possessed two first-class passenger cars and one baggage car. In the next ten months this number was increased by an addition of four first-class cars and two smoking-cars.[1] From 1882 to 1890 under company operation [2] the first-class cars increased from 46 to 125, the second-class cars from 18 to 146 and the baggage, mail and express cars from 25 to 135. Second-class cars increased much more rapidly than first-class cars, surpassing them in number in 1888. This situation was evidently a result of the company's immigration policy and of the policy of converting older first-class cars to second-class cars, to reduce overhead charges. Baggage, mail and express cars were dependent upon increase in passenger schedules. The relatively rapid increase of this form of equipment was significant of the development of local service. First- and second-class cars increased [3]

[1] *Sessional Paper*, No. 8, 1882, p. 86.

[2] Equipment, 1882–90 :

	1st Class Cars		2nd Class Cars		Baggage, Mail, and Express Cars
1882 . . .	46	..	18	..	25
1883 . . .	90	..	28 •	..	44
1884 . . .	78	..	33	..	48
1885 . . .	100	..	86	..	61
1886 . . .	110	..	99	..	93
1887 . . .	120	..	109	..	100
1888 . . .	120	..	134	..	100
1889 . . .	116	..	133	..	124
1890 . . .	125	..	146	..	135

Compiled from *Government Reports*.

[3] First- and second-class passenger cars, 1891–21 :

1891*	517	1908	1,382
1892	546	1909	1,461
1893	575	1910	1,515
1894	575	1911	1,689
1895	576	1912	1,841
1896	580	1913	2,063
1897	588	1914	2,174
1898	622	1915	2,182
1899	627	1916	2,183
1901 †	662	1916	2,189
1902	678	1917*	2,191
1903	725	1918	2,179
1904	814	1919	2,183
1905	881	1920	2,174
1906	997	1921	2,191
1907	1,191		

Compiled from *C.P.R. Reports*.

* Calendar year.   † Fiscal year (six months omitted).

from 461 in 1890 to 627 in 1899 and to 2,191 in 1921. From 1891 to 1893 increase in passenger traffic and in mileage was accompanied by an increase in equipment. In the depression of the following years, with a slight increase in mileage, a decline in traffic and financial difficulties, equipment remained practically stationary. The rapid increase in traffic in 1898 brought a rapid increase in equipment in that year, and occasioned a very slight increase in the following year. The decade, with the exception of fluctuations due to the depression, was characterized by a general increase in equipment, in traffic and in mileage. The strong upward movement evident toward the end of the century continued to 1913. A rapid increase in mileage and in traffic led to a rapid increase in equipment. Traffic and mileage were determining factors. Years characterized by a slight falling off in traffic were characterized by the addition of a smaller number of cars. In 1904, in 1905, and in 1909 a slight falling off in traffic was accompanied by a slight decline in the rate of increase in equipment. The effect of the inelasticity of passenger schedules and of the difficulties of overhead cost were shown particularly in the war period. Following a rapid and steady increase of traffic, of mileage and of equipment to 1913, a slight falling off in traffic in 1914 and a decline in 1915 were accompanied in both years by an increase in equipment. During the remainder of the period, traffic with some fluctuations recovered, but in 1920 the number of first- and second-class passenger cars was the same as in 1914. In 1921 the number of these cars recovered to the high level of 1917. Inelasticity in passenger schedules made it impossible for the company to adjust the number of cars to actual traffic demands. It was evident that during the period ending with 1913 the company was under equipped—a situation partly the result of the rapidity of the expansion and partly the result of the desirability of reducing overhead charges. The wisdom of the course was justified during the war period when slight increases could be made despite a decrease in traffic. A decline to 1920 with an increase in traffic and an increase in 1921 with a decline in traffic illustrate the difficulties of adjustment.

The problem of adjusting supply of equipment to demand was even more acute with first-class sleeping- and dining-cars and equipment more generally necessary for the conduct of tourist traffic, although the peculiar character of the road's territory, to some extent, rendered these forms of equipment as essential as passenger cars.   From 1889 to 1899 the number of first-class sleeping- and dining-cars increased from 56 [1] to 113 and in 1921 to 539.   Passenger cars were more directly influenced by an expansion of mileage, and establishment of service on branch lines.   Sleeping- and dining-cars were confined more generally to through traffic and consequently were not as dependent on mileage as on through connexions.   During periods of expansion which were coincident with periods of prosperity, the number increased most rapidly as from 1889 to 1892, 1898 to 1903, and from 1906 to 1913.   During periods of depression the number remained stationary as from 1894 to 1897, in 1904 and 1905, and in 1914 and 1915.   In the later years of the war the number actually decreased.   Tourist traffic, dependent on periods of prosperity, was liable to considerable fluctuation. Consequently it was unusually difficult to adjust the supply of equipment to the demand.   On the other hand the schedules were more elastic than the regular passenger schedules. The decline during the war period suggests the possibility of adjusting this equipment to other purposes.   On the other hand, the increase in 1921 with a decline in traffic suggests conclusions of a different character.

Parlour cars, official and paymasters' cars are unfortunately classified together, but parlour cars were undoubtedly also largely subject to the demands of the tourist traffic.   From

---

[1] First-class sleeping- and dining-cars, 1889–1921 :

1889*	.	.	.	56	1901†	.	.	.	115	1912	.	.	.	369
1890	.	.	.	61	1902	.	.	.	124	1913	.	.	.	436
1891	.	.	.	73	1903	.	.	.	139	1914	.	.	.	502
1892	.	.	.	86	1904	.	.	.	141	1915	.	.	.	502
1893	.	.	.	86	1905	.	.	.	141	1916	.	.	.	498
1894	.	.	.	99	1906	.	.	.	160	1916	.	.	.	486
1895	.	.	.	99	1907	.	.	.	224	1917*	.	.	.	468
1896	.	.	.	99	1908	.	.	.	245	1918	.	.	.	480
1897	.	.	.	99	1909	.	.	.	275	1919	.	.	.	475
1898	.	.	.	111	1910	.	.	.	294	1920	.	.	.	483
1899	.	.	.	113	1911	.	.	.	318	1921	.	.	.	539

Compiled from *C.P.R. Reports.*
    * Calendar year.   † Fiscal year.

1889 to 1899 the total number [1] of all cars classified under this head increased from 22 to 33 and in 1921 to 124. The number of official and paymasters' cars was directly related to the company's policy of administration and to the expansion of mileage. During periods of depression the number remained stationary, as from 1893 to 1897. The unusual demands of passenger traffic in 1898 for increased cars led to a decrease. The general increase in traffic and in mileage from 1901 to 1913 and especially in 1912 and 1913 led to a marked increase in the number of these cars as of other equipment. During the war period the number rapidly increased in 1917 but remained practically stationary to 1921. The difficulty of adjusting this type of equipment to the demand was very much lessened by the possibility of converting it to the use of other passenger traffic.

The increase in passenger traffic and the consequent increase in passenger train mileage and in passenger equipment made necessary an increase in other facilities essential to the handling of this traffic. Many of these facilities, as in the case of steamship services, were developed largely in response to the demands of freight traffic, but passenger traffic was of considerable importance. Facilities necessary for passenger traffic were constantly extended. In 1888 in connexion with tourist traffic, hotels were built at Banff and Vancouver.[2] Later hotels were erected and improved at Victoria, Winnipeg, Caledonia Springs and other points strategic for the handling of this traffic. The construction and improvement of stations throughout the whole history

---

[1] Parlour cars, official and paymasters' cars, 1889–1921 :

1889*	. . .	22	1901†	. . .	33	1912	. . .	75
1890	. . .	25	1902	. . .	40	1913	. . .	84
1891	. . .	28	1903	. . .	45	1914	. . .	96
1892	. . .	28	1904	. . .	48	1915	. . .	97
1893	. . .	30	1905	. . .	47	1916	. . .	100
1894	. . .	30	1906	. . .	50	1916	. . .	106
1895	. . .	30	1907	. . .	51	1917*	. . .	122
1896	. . .	30	1908	. . .	57	1918	. . .	122
1897	. . .	30	1909	. . .	60	1919	. . .	123
1898	. . .	26	1910	. . .	61	1920	. . .	124
1899	. . .	33	1911	. . .	67	1921	. . .	124

Compiled from *C.P.R. Reports*.

* Calendar year.   † Fiscal year.

[2] *C.P.R. Report*, 1888.

of the road was generally a result of the demands of passenger traffic.

D. PASSENGER RATE POLICY

Growth of passenger traffic, and expansion of physical property, essential to the conduct of this traffic during the history of the road, as with freight traffic, largely determined, and was largely determined by, the passenger rate policy. The factors which determined the freight rate policy were largely determinants of the passenger rate policy. The rapid development of western Canada which occasioned a developmental freight rate policy during the early years of the company's history occasioned a developmental passenger rate policy. Immigration was essential to expansion. The Government passenger rate in western Canada adopted by the company in these first stages of the history of the road was three cents per mile, but immigrants were given through tickets at one and a half cents per mile.[1] In the tariff adopted by the company on March 23, 1883,[2] consistently with a general increase, the rate was raised, on branch lines, and on the line from Brandon to the crossing of the Saskatchewan River, on which traffic was light, to four cents per mile. · On other portions of the western lines it remained at three cents. Immigration rates continued to be much lower and in a resolution [3] of June 9, 1885, the company was given permission to grant special rates for the promotion of emigration from the United States to the North-West, even to the point of carrying passengers free from Emerson or Gretna, to points on the railway, in order to counteract fully the adverse efforts of American railways. These tariffs were testimonials to the necessity of the development of the west from the standpoint of passenger traffic and of freight traffic, but they were also testimonials, in the high local rates, to the fact that western Canada was a non-competitive area. As with the freight situation, competition on transcontinental passenger traffic and on eastern passenger traffic was inevitable. With these competitive areas and

[1] Sessional Paper, No. 48g, 1882, p. 36.
[2] Ibid., No. 27j, 1883, p. 3.
[3] Ibid., No. 35, 1886, p. 201.

the consequent reduction of rates came the necessity for increased rates in non-competitive areas.

The inelastic character of passenger traffic and its particular difficulties with reference to overhead charges, tended to make competition more severe than that characteristic of freight traffic. The Canadian Pacific in its negotiations in 1887 with American transcontinental roads successfully claimed a differential of $10 and $5 on first- and second-class tickets respectively between the Pacific coast and Chicago and points east. It was an intermediate carrier receiving an unduly low share of the total receipts and it was alleged, considering the commission paid by the railroads to ticket agents, that this road actually carried second-class passengers at a loss. The number of transcontinental passsengers carried was small, though its percentage of California traffic, as a result of the rate situation, increased from 1·24 per cent. in 1889 to 3·06 per cent. in 1892. The Pacific steamers started in 1891 greatly strengthened the road's control of Oriental trade. Canadian immigration restrictions gave the company an increased share of the Chinese passenger traffic. Moreover, a transcontinental British route was favoured by British travellers. This gradual change [1] in the situation made the compromise agreed upon by the transcontinental association in the granting of differentials impossible. In 1893 the Great Northern Railway was opened for business between St. Paul and Seattle. In the completion of this road, the Canadian Pacific lost its connexion viâ Winnipeg with St. Paul, since the St. Paul, Minneapolis and Manitoba Railway was a part of the Great Northern, and with it the differential through the St. Paul and Port Arthur gateways. The hurried extension of the Minneapolis, St. Paul and Sault Ste. Marie from St. Paul to a point on the main line of the Canadian Pacific near Moose Jaw served as a substitute, but competition was unavoidable. The Great Northern reduced its fares from St. Paul to Puget Sound points from the regular tariff rates of $60 first class and $40 second class to $25 and $18 respectively. This cut-throat competition was terminated by an agreement dated February 1, 1894, stipulating that the Canadian Pacific should

[1] 7 I.C.C.R. 71.

be given train service into Seattle, Tacoma, and Portland,
in return for waiving its claim to a differential over the
Great Northern from St. Paul, and for certain facilities in
the way of train service to Vancouver. In 1895 a transcontinental association was formed in which this agreement
between the Canadian Pacific and the Great Northern was
recognized and the amount of the differential through the
Port Arthur gateway reduced from $10 to $7.50 first class,
and continued at $5 second class. The decision of the
Trans-Missouri rate case led to the dissolution of the association and with its dissolution the Northern Pacific and the
Great Northern claimed the differentials were no longer
valid. Unable to persuade other roads through the fear of
rate disturbances, lower rates were not published but tickets
were sold for less than the published rate by increasing the
commission given to ticket agents in the expectation that
the commission would be divided with the purchaser of the
ticket. As a result the Canadian Pacific did not receive
its share of the traffic in the Klondike rush of 1898 and on
inquiry discovered the cause of the trouble. A rate war
was the result. The Canadian Pacific asked that the
question be settled by arbitration, but the Great Northern
refused. The subject came before the Interstate Commerce
Commission as a result of a request of American roads for aid
in the continued suspension of the long and short haul
clause. In the discussion of the right of the Canadian
Pacific to a differential, which was the heart of the question,
it was found that the distance from Boston to Vancouver
was fifteen hours and from Boston to Seattle twenty-nine
hours shorter by the American lines than by the Canadian
Pacific. The actual distance did not warrant this discrepancy, the distance from Boston to Seattle being 3,240
miles by the American lines and 3,323 miles by Canadian
Pacific, and from Boston to Vancouver 3,346 miles by
American lines and 2,935 miles by Canadian Pacific. The
claim of the Canadian Pacific was weakened further since the
time from Boston to Vancouver by the " Soo " line was
127 hours and by the main line 140 hours, and the time from
Boston to Seattle by the " Soo " line was 131 hours and by
the main line 144 hours. Finally the Canadian Pacific

agreed to accept the ruling of the commission, and abandoned
its claim to a differential.

Transcontinental competition was complicated with, and
additional to, competitive difficulties on the eastern section
of the road. In the investigation [1] of Senator Cullom's
committee it was alleged that by lower rates and by the
payment of commissions to agents the Canadian Pacific
had received an undue share of the traffic from points in the
eastern states to St. Paul and Minneapolis. For five months
ending July 15, 1892, the Canadian Pacific had carried over
75 per cent. of the European immigrants destined for the
western states, American roads connecting with the Canadian
Pacific having received their full local rate and the loss being
borne by that company. On east-bound traffic it was
found that the differentials offered by the " Soo " line were
such as to compel lines west of Chicago to leave that line
in absolute control of the field. This competitive situation
became more serious with the transcontinental controversy.
The Grand Trunk had been particularly active in securing
working connexions with American roads and consequently
became involved. As a competitive measure, it cancelled [2]
the agreement permitting the Canadian Pacific cars to be
run over the Toronto and North Bay route, making it necessary for these cars to follow the circuitous route over the
Canadian Pacific line by Smith Falls—refusing to carry
Canadian Pacific traffic at the rate of $14 per 12-ton car for
206 miles and demanding $21. Toronto traffic for the Pacific
coast was forced, in this way, to travel an additional 150
miles. As a counter-measure, the Canadian Pacific proceeded
to deny the right of the Grand Trunk to sell tickets on even
terms between Toronto and Winnipeg although the Canadian
Pacific had the shorter route. Further, rates were cut one-
half on all competitive points between Montreal and Toronto.
Considerable loss to both roads was the result. Eventually
an agreement was signed restoring rates to their old basis
and permitting the Canadian Pacific to run cars over the
Grand Trunk line from Toronto to North Bay.[3]

In general, therefore, with the exception of greater com-

[1] 6 I.C.C.R., p. 288 ff.   [2] *The Economist*, 1898, vol. 20, p. 1520.
[3] *Ibid.*, p. 1693.

petition occasioned by the importance of fixed charges, the passenger rate situation was dominated by factors similar to those which dominated the freight rate situation. Inevitable competition on international traffic, and on Atlantic seaboard traffic, and consequently increased pressure toward higher rates in western Canada as a non-competitive area, influenced the passenger rate situation as it did the freight rate situation. The organization of the Board of Railway Commissioners due to these circumstances and the effects of consequent regulation discussed in relation to freight rates pertained generally to passenger rates.

VII

Earnings from Operations

A. FREIGHT EARNINGS

THE amount of freight carried and the freight rate policy of
the company were factors directly reflected in freight earnings.   This item was of dominant and increasing importance as a constituent of gross earnings.   The percentage
of freight to gross earnings increased from 57·5 per cent.
in 1882, to 60·6 per cent. in 1890, to 64·1 per cent. in 1899
and to 66·7 per cent. in 1921.   Gross earnings during the
first five months of Government operation totalled $104,976,[1]
an average of $20,995 per month, and in the next ten
months, increased to $291,498,[2] a monthly average of
$29,149.   Under Canadian Pacific management on June
30, 1882, it had increased to $1,546,214, or a monthly aver-
age of $110,443.   In 1890 this had increased tenfold to
$15,572,986,[3] in 1899 to $29,230,038 and in 1920 to the
maximum of $216,641,349.   Gross earnings per mile
increased with considerable fluctuation from $2,529 in
1882 to $3,062 in 1890, the fluctuations varying with fluc-
tuations in mileage and in earnings.   The expansion in
mileage more than offset the increase in earnings to 1884.
A more rapid increase in earnings brought an increase in
gross earnings per mile to 1888, and a more rapid increase in mileage, a decrease to 1890.   Gross earnings per

---

[1] *Sessional Papers*, No. 5, 1881, p. 77.
[2] *Ibid.*, No. 8, 1882, p. 79.
[3] See footnote 1 on opposite page.

mile [1] increased from \$2,989 in 1889, to \$4,176 in 1899 and to \$14,357 in 1921. With the rapid increase in mileage this increase was an excellent index to the growth of traffic and to the intensive development of the road. Fluctuations were occasioned generally by earnings rather than mileage. To 1896 the depression acted as a decided check, but following that year the increase was steady and rapid. In the following period the expansion of earnings and of mileage was singularly rapid, but of earnings more than mileage. The highest point was reached in 1913 and was followed by a decrease in 1914 accentuated by increased mileage. The serious decrease in 1915 was the result of a decline in earnings, and the recovery in the remainder of the period was largely due to stationary mileage. [2] In conclusion, fluctuations in

[1] 1882–1921 :

	Gross Earnings	Gross Earnings per Mile		Gross Earnings	Gross Earnings per Mile
1882*	\$1,546,213·93	2,539	1904	\$46,469,132·24	5,577
1883	4,490,351·78	2,522	1905	50,481,882·25	5,812
1884	5,177,016·12	1,688	1906	61,669,758·16	7,018
1885	6,928,869·29	2,069	1907	72,217,527·64	7,889
1886	8,874,950·22	2,354	1908	71,384,173·22	7,573
1887	10,650,254·08	2,491	1909	76,313,320·96	7,725
1888	12,711,010·01	2,726	1910	94,989,490·33	9,425
1889	13,016,611·81	2,616	1911	104,167,808·21	10,072
1890	15,572,985·62	2,306	1912	123,319,541·23	11,453
1891†	20,241,095·98	3,510	1913	139,395,699·98	12,264
1892	21,409,351·77	3,559	1914	129,814,823·83	10,978
1893	20,962,317·44	3,313	1915	99,865,209·78	7,994
1894	18,752,167·71	2,956	1916	129,481,885·74	10,024
1895	18,941,036·87	2,939	1916	76,717,965·36	Six
1896	20,681,596·84	3,194		months ending Dec. 31, 1916.	
1897	24,049,785·07	3,662	1917§	152,389,335·00	11,731
1898	26,138,977·13	3,912	1918	157,532,698·00	12,125
1899	29,230,038·26	4,176	1919	176,929,060·00	13,214
1900‡	14,167,797·89	Six months ending June 30, 1900.			
1901	30,855,206·55	4,080	1920	216,641,349·30	16,165
1902	37,503,053·78	4,945	1921	193,021,854·40	14,357
1903	43,957,373·04	5,673			

* 1882–90 from *Government Reports*.   † 1891–1921 from *C.P.R. Reports*.
‡ Change to fiscal year.   § Calendar year.

[2] Mileage, 1901–21 :

1901*	7,563	1909	9,878	1916	12,917
1902	7,587	1910	10,078	1916	12,955
1903	7,748	1911	10,342	1917†	12,990
1904	8,332	1912	10,767	1918	12,993
1905	8,568	1913	11,366	1919	13,389
1906	8,777	1914	11,825	1920	13,402
1907	9,154	1915	12,368	1921	13,444
1908	9,420				

Compiled from *C.P.R. Reports*.

* Fiscal year.   † Calendar year.

gross earnings followed closely fluctuations in freight traffic. The steady increase to 1891, the stationary period to 1893, the decline in 1894–5, and the strong recovery toward the end of that period were movements characteristic of the amount of freight carried and of gross earnings. In the later period the rapid increase to 1907, the decline in 1908, the strong rapid movement culminating in 1913, the rapid decline in 1915 and the recovery to 1917 were similarly movements characteristic of both items. The increase in rates during the war brought an increase in gross earnings but a decline in freight carried in 1918 and 1919. To 1921 fluctuations in freight carried were concurrent with fluctuations in gross earnings.

Without exception fluctuations in gross earnings were closely paralleled by fluctuations in freight earnings. During the first five months of Government operation earnings from freight totalled $64,272,[1] a monthly average of $12,854, and in the next ten months $164,252,[2] a monthly average of $16,425. At the end of the first year under company operation, the monthly average was $63,598. In 1890 [3] freight earnings had increased more than tenfold—an increase which was steady, except for the troublesome years from

[1] *Sessional Paper*, No. 5, 1881, p. 77.
[2] *Ibid.*, No. 8, 1882, p. 79.
[3] Freight earnings, 1883–1921 :

1883*. . . . $3,755,915·00	1904 . . . . $29,235,821·04
1884 . . . . 3,410,365·39	1905 . . . . 31,725,290·10
1885 . . . . 4,881,865·58	1906 . . . . 39,512,973·18
1886 . . . . 6,112,379·89	1907 . . . . 45,885,968·16
1887 . . . . 6,924,130·47	1908 . . . . 44,037,597·97
1888 . . . . 8,017,313·66	1909 . . . . 48,182,520·11
1889 . . . . 8,852,702·39	1910 . . . . 60,158,887·03
1890 . . . . 10,106,644·02	1911 . . . . 65,645,227·59
1891 . . . . 12,665,540·26	1912 . . . . 79,833,734·03
1892 . . . . 13,330,540·19	1913 . . . . 89,655,223·33
1893 . . . . 12,673,075·38	1914 . . . . 81,135,295·12
1894 . . . . 11,445,377·78	1915 . . . . 60,737,737·25
1895 . . . . 11,877,851·95	1916 . . . . 89,654,405·19
1896 . . . . 13,187,560·31	1916 (six months) 51,945,291·60
1897 . . . . 15,257,896·94	1917*. . . . 103,635,795·00
1898 . . . . 16,231,444·93	1918 . . . . 110,187,728·10
1899 . . . . 18,738,884·96	1919 . . . . 111,064,441·68
1901†. . . . 18,983,185·51	1920 . . . . 145,303,399·70
1902 . . . . 24,199,428·14	1921 . . . . 128,849,445·63
1903 . . . . 28,502,081·76	

Compiled from *C.P.R. Reports*.

* Calendar year.   † Fiscal year (six months omitted).

1883 to 1885 and the slight falling off in 1888–89. These earnings increased from $8,852,702 in 1889, to $18,738,885 in 1899, and to $128,849,446 in 1921.

Fluctuations in freight earnings paralleled closely the number of tons of freight carried and the number of tons of freight carried one mile. The number of tons of freight carried one mile [1] increased from 406,822,166 in 1885, to 1,208,014,731 in 1890, to 2,539,171,900 in 1899, and to 10,087,106,000 in 1921. The relation of the increase in the amount of freight carried to the increase in the amount of freight carried one mile is significant as evidence of the development of through traffic. To 1890 freight carried one mile increased rapidly with a relatively slight increase of the number of tons carried, affording direct evidence of the development of through traffic following the completion of connexions with the west and with through lines. With the establishment of these connexions and as a result of the depression of the nineties, the last decade of the century was characterized by a less rapid increase in the number of tons carried one mile. Local traffic became of more importance. The importance of this traffic increased after the beginning of the century. The number of tons carried one mile decreased more rapidly than the number of tons carried in 1904–5, and in 1909 the total number of tons

---

[1] Freight carried one mile, tons, 1885–1921 :

1885*	406,822,166	1905	4,155,256,309
1886	555,438,159	1906	5,342,248,625
1887	687,786,049	1907	5,946,779,961
1888	784,972,511	1908	5,865,089,008
1889	967,508,450	1909	6,372,269,174
1890	1,208,014,731	1910	7,772,012,635
1891	1,391,705,486	1911	8,062,102,013
1892	1,582,554,352	1912	10,391,650,965
1893	1,453,367,263	1913	11,470,001,871
1894	1,313,948,410	1914	10,821,748,859
1895	1,490,639,847	1915	7,940,151,342
1896	1,769,958,865	1916 (six months)	14,057,685,773
1897	1,955,911,006	1916 (six months)	7,872,405,297
1898	2,142,319,887	1917*	14,677,957,266
1899	2,539,171,900	1918	12,885,684,625
1901†	2,383,633,945	1919	11,121,322,012
1902	3,247,922,167	1920	13,094,508,975
1903	3,862,242,993	1921	10,087,106,000
1904	3,809,801,952		

Compiled from *C.P.R. Reports.*

* Calendar year.   † Fiscal year (six months omitted).

carried one mile increased much less rapidly than the total number of tons carried. On the other hand the importance of through traffic continued and increased. In 1907 the total amount of traffic carried decreased more rapidly than the number of tons carried one mile. The importance of grain was reflected in the amount of freight carried one mile and through traffic was largely influenced by the grain situation in western Canada, as was especially evident in the later period. In 1911 the falling off in the increase of freight carried one mile was due directly to the falling off in grain carried. In 1916 the rapid increase in the amount of grain carried was reflected in a more rapid increase of freight carried one mile than of the total freight carried. The importance of grain therefore introduced an elastic element in the number of tons carried one mile as compared to the number of tons carried. The general relatively greater increase in traffic carried than in traffic carried one mile was a striking tribute to the development of local traffic, resulting from the intensive development of the west and the expansion of the road in the east.

The growing importance of local traffic was more striking in the movement of traffic density [1]—a variable of mileage and of traffic carried one mile. Freight density increased from 93,781 tons in 1885 to 217,112 in 1890, to 362,738 in 1899, and to 750,305 in 1921, a particularly bad year. To 1890 the rapid increase in traffic density, despite a rapid increase in mileage, was evidence that important areas of traffic were being tapped with new lines, and being developed

[1] Traffic density, 1885–1921, tons :

1885*.	.	93,781	1897	.	.	297,794	1910	.	.	771,186
1886	.	. 124,426	1898	.	.	320,658	1911	.	.	779,549
1887	.	. 138,666	1899	.	.	362,738	1912	.	.	965,139
1888	.	. 158,324	1901†	.	.	315,170	1913	.	. 1,009,150
1889	.	. 192 385	1902	.	.	428,090	1914	.	.	915,158
1890	.	. 217,112	1903	.	.	498,482	1915	.	.	641,991
1891	.	. 241,364	1904	.	.	457,249	1916*	.	. 1,088,308
1892	.	. 261,455	1905	.	.	484,973	1917	.	. 1,129,942
1893	.	. 229,708	1906	.	.	608,664	1918	.	.	991,740
1894	.	. 207,116	1907	.	.	649,637	1919	.	.	830,631
1895	.	. 231,322	1908	.	.	622,224	1920	.	. 1,044,210
1896	.	. 273,310	1909	.	.	645,097	1921	.	.	750,305

Compiled from *C.P.R. Reports.*

* Calendar year.   † Fiscal year.

with the old lines. For this the expansion of the road in eastern Canada and the connexions in the United States were responsible. The increase continued to 1892 with an increase in mileage. Adverse conditions of the period brought a decline to 1894, but more stationary mileage in the following year produced a favourable change. Local development of traffic to the end of the decade was evident in a marked increase of traffic density with an increase in mileage. The movement gained headway with the turning of the century and increased to 1903, but a decrease in traffic and an increase in mileage in the following year brought a decline. The succeeding years to 1913 with the exception of slight fluctuations were characterized by a strong upward movement of traffic density which was significant of intensive development. From 1913 to 1915 a decrease in traffic and an increase in mileage brought a rapid decrease in traffic density. The rapid increase in traffic in 1916 brought recovery. During the remainder of the period, the mileage being comparatively stationary, fluctuations were occasioned almost entirely by traffic. The later history of the road was characterized generally by a steady and marked increase in traffic density and by marked intensive development.

Lower rates were an additional partial index of the development of through traffic which accompanied this increase in local traffic. Earnings per freight ton mile [1] decreased from ·9 cents in 1889 to ·8 in the following year and to ·7 in 1896. This was partly the result of the increase in through traffic which accompanied the expansion of the road in the west. Grain, the most significant item of

[1] Earnings per freight ton mile, in cents, 1889–1921 :

1889	· · · ·9	1901	· · · ·7	1912 · · · ·7
1890	· · · ·8	1902	· · · ·7	1913 · · · ·7
1891	· · · ·8	1903	· · · ·7	1914 · · · ·7
1892	· · · ·8	1904	· · · ·7	1915 · · · ·7
1893	· · · ·8	1905	· · · ·7	1916 · · · ·6
1894	· · · ·8	1906	· · · ·7	1917 · · · ·7
1895	· · · ·8	1907	· · · ·7	1918 · · · ·8
1896	· · · ·7	1908	· · · ·7	1919 · · · 1·0
1897	· · · ·7	1909	· · · ·7	1920 · · · 1·04
1898	· · · ·7	1910	· · · ·7	1921 · · · 1·19
1899	· · · ·7	1911	· · · ·8	

Compiled from *C.P.R. Reports*.

traffic, steadily increased. From 1896 to 1910 the rate remained stationary, partial evidence of the growing importance of other commodities than grain, of the intensive development of the road and of the relative minor importance of through traffic. In 1910 grain and manufactures remained practically stationary and with the consequent decrease of through traffic, earnings per freight ton mile increased to ·8 cents. In 1916 the large harvest increased the amount of through traffic and the freight rate per ton mile decreased to ·6 cents. In 1918 grain and manufactures decreased, and the average freight charge per ton mile increased, the increase in this year and in the following years being complicated with changes in the rate situation incidental to the difficulties of the period. The general stationary character of freight earnings per ton mile throughout the whole period was the result of a close relationship between freight earnings and the amount of freight carried one mile. Fluctuations were due largely to the nature of the traffic, the development of the road, and the proportion of through to local traffic.

Freight earnings and gross earnings were largely influenced in the general increase and in the fluctuations by the agricultural situation in western Canada. The intensive development of the road was principally the result of the growth of the west, and the importance of through traffic depended largely on grain. The relation of freight earnings to grain and the western agricultural situation has been particularly important because of a rate policy which necessitated higher rates in western Canada. The growing importance of the west has stimulated, and been accompanied by, a marked development of the east, and an expansion of the road in that area which in turn has had its influence on earnings, and contributed to the intensive development of the road, characteristic of later years.

B. Passenger Earnings

The character and amount of passenger traffic carried and the passenger rate policy were factors directly reflected in passenger earnings. The character of the traffic as related to passenger earnings was largely the result of the importance of local in comparison with through traffic, as shown in the relation of the number of passengers carried one mile to the number of passengers carried.   The number of passengers carried one mile [1] increased from 116,702,980 in 1885 to 253,905,182 in 1889, to 397,417,473 in 1899 and to 1,373,928,588 in 1921.   The importance of through traffic as a factor influencing the number of passengers carried one mile was evident particularly in relation to tourist traffic.   Fluctuations were dominated largely by periods of prosperity and of depression which directly affected tourist traffic.   Of more general importance was the expansion of the road, especially the development of through connexions and the opening of the west.   With the completion of the main line, the establishment of connexions and the competitive advantages for transcontinental traffic, the number of passengers carried one mile to 1890 increased more rapidly than the number of passengers carried.   The depression of the following decade brought a more rapid decline in the number of passengers carried one mile than in the number of passengers carried, and the recovery, a more rapid increase.   The effects of the Klondike rush of 1898 in an increase of through traffic and of the number of passengers carried one mile were evident the following year in a rapid decline in the number of passengers carried one mile, but in an increase in the number of passengers

[1] Passengers carried one mile, 1885-1921 :

1885*	116,702,980	1905	736,774,844
1886	150,466,149	1906	870,339,686
1887	174,687,802	1907	1,064,564,999
1888	212,766,866	1908	1,052,010,356
1889	253,905,182	1909	1,071,149,528
1890	274,940,328	1910	1,355,266,088
1891	320,659,837	1911	1,457,332,937
1892	328,838,647	1912	1,626,577,067
1893	334,307,590	1913	1,784,683,370
1894	260,804,129	1914	1,587,368,110
1895	260,317,256	1915	1,164,488,630
1896	263,607,453	1916	1,255,561,198
1897	317,997,951	1916 (six months)	850,190,050
1898	430,493,139	1917*	1,480,023,872
1899	397,417,743	1918	1,280,533,734
1901†	419,353,393	1919	1,776,740,850
1902	534,777,153	1920	1,732,050,259
1903	635,855,533	1921	1,373,928,588
1904	677,940,496		

* Calendar year.   † Fiscal year (six months omitted).

Compiled from *C.P.R. Reports*.

carried. This elasticity characteristic of the number of passengers carried one mile and largely the result of tourist traffic was illustrated in the depression of 1907–8. Passengers carried increased in 1908 but passengers carried one mile declined. Again, the beginning of depression in 1914 brought a decline in passengers carried one mile but an increase in passengers carried. The difficulties of 1920 produced similar results. Fluctuations, on the other hand, dependent on periods of prosperity and depression were not of dominant importance. The development and expansion of the road from 1901 to 1913 was accompanied by a rapid increase in the number of passengers carried one mile. Generally the development of through traffic was characteristic of the expansion of the road, of the completion of through connexions, and of the opening of the west.

The general increase of through traffic incidental to expansion and the intensive development of the road were reflected in passenger density, a function of mileage and passengers carried one mile. Passenger density increased from 26,902 in 1885 to 50,488 in 1889, to 56,787 in 1899 and to 102,196 in 1921.[1] The rapid increase in the number of passengers carried one mile and the slight increase in mileage to 1889 were reflected in the increase in passenger density and the rapid increase in mileage in 1890 brought a decline. Passengers carried one mile was responsible for the rapid increase in the next year, and increase in mileage for the decline in the two following years. Mileage remained stationary during the

[1] Passenger density (No.), 1885–1921 :

1885*.	.	26,902	1897	. .	48,416	1910	. .	134,470
1886	. .	33,706	1898	. .	64,435	1911	. .	140,914
1887	. .	35,219	1899	. .	56,787	1912	. .	151,070
1888	. .	42,913	1901†.	.	55,448	1913	. .	157,019
1889	. .	50,488	1902	. .	70,485	1914	. .	134,238
1890	. .	49,414	1903	. .	82,067	1915	. .	94,153
1891	. .	55,612	1904	. .	81,365	1916	. .	97,202
1892	. .	54,669	1905	. .	85,991	1917*.	.	113,935
1893	. .	52,838	1906	. .	99,161	1918	. .	98,555
1894	. .	41,110	1907	. .	116,295	1919	. .	132,701
1895	. .	40,396	1908	. .	111,607	1920	. .	129,230
1896	. .	40,705	1909	. .	108,437	1921	. .	102,196

* Calendar year.　　　　　　† Fiscal year.

period of depression and passenger density declined. The period of recovery and particularly the gold rush of 1898 brought a marked increase. From 1899 to 1901 density declined, in the first year as a result of passengers carried one mile and later as a result of mileage. During the following period of rapid expansion terminating in 1913, passenger density, with the exception of the years of depression 1904 and 1908–9, increased steadily and rapidly and despite a rapid increase in mileage. During the war a decline in passengers carried one mile and a relatively stationary mileage brought a decline in density. The number of passengers carried one mile explained the increase in 1919 and the decline in 1920 and in 1921. Passenger density throughout the history of the road generally had shown a marked increase and though subject to wide fluctuations due to the elastic character of a portion of the number of passengers carried one mile it was a significant index of the intensive development of the road. It was especially significant of the extent to which the inhospitable area north of Lake Superior had ceased to be a barrier to communication, and of the expansion of the west.

The importance of through traffic was also evident in earnings per passenger per mile.[1] From 1885 to 1890 earnings per passenger per mile declined from 2·4 to 1·7 and after considerable fluctuation reached the latter point again in 1899, but increased to the highest point, 2·9, in 1921. The development of through connexions, the influence of developmental rates, and the expansion of the road in

---

[1] Earnings per passenger per mile, in cents, 1885–1921 :

1885*	.	.	.	2·4	1897	. . . 1·8		1910	. . . 1·8		
1886	.	.	.	2·1	1898	. . . 1·5		1911	. . . 1·9		
1887	.	.	.	1·9	1899	. . . 1·7		1912	. . . 1·9		
1888	.	.	.	1·7	1901†	. . . 1·9		1913	. . . 1·9		
1889	.	.	.	1·7	1902	. . . 1·7		1914	. . . 2·0		
1890	.	.	.	1·7	1903	. . . 1·7		1915	. . . 2·0		
1891	.	.	.	1·7	1904	. . . 1·8		1916	. . . 1·9		
1892	.	.	.	1·6	1905	. . . 1·8		1917*	. . . 2·0		
1893	.	.	.	1·6	1906	. . . 1·8		1918	. . . 2·4		
1894	.	.	.	1·8	1907	. . . 1·8		1919	. . . 2·6		
1895	.	.	.	1·6	1908	. . . 1·8		1920	. . . 2·8		
1896	.	.	.	1·8	1909	. . . 1·8		1921	. . . 2·9		

Compiled from *C.P.R. Reports*.

* Calendar year.   † Fiscal year.

competitive areas brought a steady reduction from the date of the completion of the main line to 1893. The depression and consequent decline in through traffic brought an increase in 1894, but rate wars were disturbing factors. The Klondike rush brought a rapid decline in 1898, and the falling off in through traffic in the following year an increase. The decade was characterized by rate wars, depression, and declines in through traffic. Fluctuations were the result. The first year of the century brought an increase, and the two following years a decrease. In 1904 the rate increased to 1·8 and at this point remained until 1910, increasing in 1911 to 1·9 and remaining at that point until 1913. The rapid increase in through traffic was exceeded by the increase in local traffic. During the war years, with the exception of a decline in 1916, occasioned by the increased passenger traffic incidental to the large harvest of that year, rates increased steadily. The period beginning with the century was characterized by a general steadiness, as contrasted with the uncertainties of the previous decade, and reflected the influence of the Board of Railway Commissioners. The increase during the war period was partly the result of orders from this body, and partly the result of the decline of through traffic in proportion to local traffic.

The intensive development of the road, evident in the increasing prominence of local traffic, bespoke a marked and steady increase in earnings, through traffic being related more closely to fluctuations. During the first five months of Government operation of the line to Winnipeg, passenger earnings totalled $32,530, or $6,506 per month, and in the remaining period of Government operation, increased to $101,749 or $10,174 per month. The first year of company operation ending on June 30, 1882, and including the mileage of the road in eastern Canada, brought an increase to $596,825 or $42,630 per month. In 1890 passenger earnings [1]

---

[1] Passenger earnings, 1882–90 :

1882	. . . .	$596,824·78	1887	. . . .	$3,367,800·58
1883	. . . .	1,229,904·27	1888	. . . .	3,536,796·15
1884	. . . .	1,562,213·98	1889	. . . .	4,127,319·41
1885	. . . .	2,479,894·21	1890	. . . .	4,526,292·20
1886	. . . .	2,768,841·17			

Compiled from *Government Reports.*

had increased to $4,526,292. This increase followed the
expansion of the road in eastern Canada, the opening of the
west, and the constant development of through connexions.
In 1899 passenger earnings [1] increased to $7,098,097 and
in 1920 to the maximum of $49,125,739. The decade
ending in 1900 was characterized by fluctuations as the
result of rate wars and especially of the depression. Beginning with recovery after this depression and ending in 1913,
with the exception of slight falling off in 1904 and 1907–8,
passenger earnings increased rapidly and steadily. Decline
followed in 1914 and in the war years to 1916. With higher
rates, increase and recovery were evident to 1920. Decline
in passenger traffic brought the decline in earnings in 1921.
Necessarily passenger earnings were the result of passenger
traffic and passenger rates. The essentially competitive
character of passenger business, the intensive development
of the road resulting from expansion in the west and in the
east, and the consequently greater proportionate increase in
local traffic than in through traffic, and the passenger rates
responsible for, and resulting from, this development, were
reflected in passenger earnings. Through traffic essentially
important as evident in the fluctuations was not dominant
and declines were partly offset by the steadying influence of
the Board of Railway Commissioners.

Through traffic was a determining factor in parlour-car

[1] Passenger earnings, 1891–1921 :

1891*.	$5,459,789·46	1908 . . . . $19,900,432·01
1892 .	5,556,316·40	1909 . . . . 20,153,000·83
1893 .	5,656,204·90	1910 . . . . 24,812,020·86
1894 .	4,840,412·33	1911 . . . . 28,165,556·41
1895 .	4,683,137·74	1912 . . . . 31,812,207·82
1896 .	4,820,143·30	1913 . . . . 35,545,061·63
1897 .	5,796,115·12	1914 . . . . 32,478,146·58
1898 .	6,538,589·58	1915 . . . . 24,044,282·83
1899 .	7,098,096·70	1916 . . . . 24,690,652·19
1901†.	8,083,369·60	1916 (six months) 15,988,424·21
1902 .	9,359,522·00	1917*. . . . 30,238,986·00
1903 .	11,001,973·71	1918 . . . . 30,837,253·89
1904 .	12,418,419·33	1919 . . . . 46,182,151·12
1905 .	13,583,052·11	1920 . . . . 49,125,738·88
1906 .	16,041,615·52	1921 . . . . 41,565,884·99
1907 .	19,528,878·09	

Compiled from *C.P.R. Reports.*

* Calendar year.   † Fiscal year (six months omitted).

and sleeping-car earnings. These earnings [1] increased from
$24,071 in 1883 to $268,097 in 1890 and to $721,006 in
1904. After 1904 statistics as to this item were included
in miscellaneous earnings. The opening of the main line
and the improvement of through connexions were responsible
for the steady increase to 1890 as they were responsible for
the development of through traffic. The importance of
the situation in western Canada, and of immigration to that
area, was evident in the slight increase in 1888 in consonance
with the bad harvest of that year and in the rapid increase
of 1893, following the heavy crop of 1892. The decline
during the years of depression accompanied the decline in
through traffic. A general increase in through traffic followed with recovery, and with the rapid increase in 1898
occasioned by the rush to the Klondike. A slight relapse
from this hectic year led to a gradual and steady increase to
1904.

C. MISCELLANEOUS EARNINGS

Other earnings, partly influenced by the passenger situation
and partly by the freight situation, fluctuated accordingly.
Express earnings [2] were presented from 1889 to 1904,

[1] Parlour- and sleeping-car earnings, 1883–1904 :

1883*	. . . $24,071·00	1894	. . . $331,719·69
1884	. . . 43,492·60	1895	. . . 302,637·63
1885	. . . 73,523·55	1896	. . . 303,688·48
1886	. . . 118,658·99	1897	. . . 361,777·38
1887	. . . 176,826·39	1898	. . . 455,345·07
1888	. . . 187,694·13	1899	. . . 441,647·54
1889	. . . 239,103·14	1901†	. . . 472,181·91
1890	. . . 268,096·76	1902	. . . 530,764·89
1891	. . . 303,545·09	1903	. . . 637,642·05
1892	. . . 331,202·73	1904	. . . 721,006·14
1893	. . . 380,470·10		

Compiled from *C.P.R. Reports*.

[2] Express earnings, 1889–1904 :

1889*	. . . $242,806·70	1897	. . . $530,749·65
1890	. . . 260,268·43	1898	. . . 615,631·43
1891	. . . 288,633·25	1899	. . . 663,960·52
1892	. . . 302,259·34	1901†	. . . 691,208·56
1893	. . . 333,975·39	1902	. . . 737,107·82
1894	. . . 342,472·29	1903	. . . 909,098·02
1895	. . . 387,605·93	1904	. . . 1,062,339·84
1896	. . . 460,201·90		

Compiled from *C.P.R. Reports*.
* Calendar year.   † Fiscal year (six months omitted).

increasing during the period from $242,807 to $1,062,340.
Without exception the increase persisted throughout the
period, though it was less rapid during the years of depression
and more rapid during years of recovery. This increase
was eloquent of the inelastic character of the express business
and of the continued expansion of the road. Miscellaneous
earnings, including earnings from telegraph, grain elevators,
the steamship service and other sundry sources, are difficult
to analyse because of changes in accounting practice.
From 1882 to 1890 this item [1] increased from $19,731 to
$1,090,217, and in 1904 [2] to $2,350,282. In 1905, with the
inclusion of express earnings and parlour- and sleeping-car
earnings, it increased to $4,469,544 and in 1921 reached the
maximum of $20,713,980. Fluctuations were rapid and
explainable largely on the basis of changes such as those
incidental to accounting. The marked increase in 1885
was due to the addition of the boat service on the lakes and
the decline in the following year to the completion of the
main line and the transportation of traffic by rail. Changes
of a similar character doubtless explain the marked decline
in 1889 and the marked increase in 1890. Government

[1] Miscellaneous earnings, 1882-90 :

1882 . . . . $19,730·82	1887 . . . . $540,220·89
1883 . . . . 53,502·95	1888 . . . . 1,067,870·35
1884 . . . . 86,851·70	1889 . . . . 243,846·94
1885 . . . . 295,787·46	1890 . . . . 1,090,217·22
1886 . . . . 288,301·64	

Compiled from *Government Reports.*

[2] Miscellaneous earnings, 1891-1921 :

1891*. . . . $1,007,489·47	1908 . . . . $6,706,388·09
1892 . . . . 1,405,110·53	1909 . . . . 7,198,977·67
1893 . . . . 1,422,475·18	1910 . . . . 9,226,836·99
1894 . . . . 1,294,056·46	1911 . . . . 9,524,290·24
1895 . . . . 1,149,687·44	1912 . . . . 10,814,041·84
1896 . . . . 1,302,458·87	1913 . . . . 13,273,732·06
1897 . . . . 1,499,785·07	1914 . . . . 15,068,667·22
1898 . . . . 1,687,991·55	1915 . . . . 12,693,856·14
1899 . . . . 1,669,063·35	1916 . . . . 13,752,260·93
1901†. . . . 1,973,452·62	1916 (six months) 8,030,861·20
1902 . . . . 2,020,832·46	1917*. . . . 18,514,554·00
1903 . . . . 2,248,672·24	1918 . . . . 16,513,156·00
1904 . . . . 2,350,281·77	1919 . . . . 18,199,134·14
1905 . . . . 4,469,543·56	1920 . . . . 20,713,979·58
1906 . . . . 5,408,161·49	1921 . . . . 19,667,265·22
1907 . . . . 6,079,744·37	

Compiled from *C.P.R. Reports.*

* Calendar year.   † Fiscal year (six months omitted).

reports which reveal these wide fluctuations differ from the company reports which point to a steady increase with the exception of the decline in 1890. Specific causes of fluctuations are difficult to discover. Steamship earnings [1] were dominated by considerations similar to those which dominate freight and passenger earnings and with the expansion of steamship lines became increasingly important. Earnings from grain elevators were closely related to the harvest situation. Hotel earnings were subject to general conditions influencing through traffic and tourist traffic. With the depression, miscellaneous earnings declined rapidly. The importance of through passenger traffic was evident in the rapid increase in 1898 and in the slight decline in the following year. With the beginning of the century a rapid increase followed. The inclusion of express and parlour- and sleeping-car earnings in miscellaneous earnings after 1904 renders the explanation of fluctuations more difficult. To 1913 the increase was rapid and steady, which was generally the case with freight and passenger earnings, but in 1914 the increase continued and freight and passenger earnings declined. During the war years, with the exception of 1918 in which miscellaneous earnings declined, fluctuations were parallel. Though factors influencing the movements of freight and passenger earnings generally influenced miscellaneous earnings, other less elastic factors were in evidence.

D. MAIL EARNINGS

Earnings from mails were significant of the place of the Canadian Pacific in the development of Canada. Mail and sundry earnings increased from $8,174 during the first five months of Government operation to $25,497 in the next ten months. Mail and express earnings during the first year of company operation totalled $39,274 and increased [2] to

[1] The Canadian Pacific Ocean Steamship Company was organized as a separate company in 1915 and net earnings were transferred to special income account.

[2] Mail and express earnings, 1882–90 :

1882	. . . .	$39,273·73	1887	. . . .	$457,580·98
1883	. . . .	95,012·59	1888	. . . .	486,585·40
1884	. . . .	137,241·57	1889	. . . .	550,330·90
1885	. . . .	254,462·26	1890	. . . .	601,995·73
1886	. . . .	251,492·38			

Compiled from *Government Reports*.

$601,996 in 1890. Mail earnings increased to $618,385 in 1899 and to $2,939,259 in 1921.[1] To 1890 the increase was steady and consistent with the expansion of the road. The elections brought a rapid increase in 1891 and were followed by a decline in the next year. During the period of depression the increase was persistent though slow, receiving considerable stimulus in the election of 1896. The year following the election brought a decline. From that year to 1915 mail earnings constantly increased —slowly, at first, but with acceleration in the later years. During the war, 1915 brought a marked increase, 1916 a slight decline, 1917 another marked increase and 1918 a heavy decline. The overseas situation, elections and Government regulations involving taxation and other restrictions were largely responsible. The increase of the last two years is significant of general recovery. The general expansion had been occasioned largely by the expansion of the road and by the expansion of Canada, as well as by postal regulations which have made this expansion more directly contributory to mail earnings.

[1] Mail earnings, 1891–1921 :

1891* . . . . $516,098·45	1908 . . . . $739,575·59
1892 . . . . 483,922·58	1909 . . . . 778,822·35
1893 . . . . 496,134·49	1910 . . . . 791,245·45
1894 . . . . 498,129·16	1911 . . . . 832,733·97
1895 . . . . 540,116·18	1912 . . . . 859,557·54
1896 . . . . 607,543·98	1913 . . . . 921,682·92
1897 . . . . 603,210·49	1914 . . . . 1,132,714·91
1898 . . . . 609,974·57	1915 . . . . 1,389,333·56
1899 . . . . 618,385·19	1916 . . . . 1,384,567·43
1901† . . . . 651,805·35	1916 (six months) 753,388·55
1902 . . . . 655,407·47	1917* . . . . 1,429,404·61
1903 . . . . 657,905·26	1918 . . . . 1,354,570·91
1904 . . . . 681,224·12	1919 . . . . 1,483,332·26
1905 . . . . 703,896·48	1920 . . . . 1,498,231·14
1906 . . . . 707,007·97	1921 . . . . 2,939,258·56
1907 . . . . 722,937·02	

Compiled from *C.P.R. Reports.*

* Calendar year.   † Fiscal year (six months omitted).

VIII

Expenses

A. INDICES OF EFFICIENCY

GROSS earnings, including earnings from freight and passenger traffic and from other sources of less importance, were largely the result of the expansion of traffic and of the rate situation. These factors depended upon in part, and determined in part, the efficiency of the road. Efficient operation was to a large extent responsible for the expansion of the road, and the expansion of the road made possible efficient operation. Rates were dependent upon efficiency of operation, and efficiency of operation was dependent upon rates. A partial index of efficiency was given in train mile earnings. Earnings per train mile [1] to 1890 were subject to unusual fluctuations, decreasing from 1·649 in 1882 to 1·391 in 1890. These earnings [2] increased to 1·58

[1] Earnings per train mile, 1882–90 :

	Cents		Cents		Cents
1882	1·649	1885	1·296	1888	1·191
1883	1·038	1886	1·766	1889	1·224
1884	·980	1887	1·548	1890	1·391

[2] Earnings per train mile, 1891–1921 :

	Cents		Cents		Cents
1891*	1·41	1902	1·77	1912	2·62
1892	1·47	1903	1·90	1913	2·68
1893	1·44	1904	1·81	1914	2·72
1894	1·44	1905	1·95	1915	2·68
1895	1·41	1906	2·07	1916	2·83
1896	1·45	1907	2·25	1917*	3·36
1897	1·49	1908	2·17	1918	3·84
1898	1·48	1909	2·18	1919	4·17
1899	1·58	1910	2·47	1920	4·63
1901†	1·69	1911	2·55	1921	4·89

* Calendar year.   † Fiscal year.

cents in 1899 and to 4·89 in 1921. As a function of total train mileage and of gross earnings, train mile earnings fluctuated in accordance with fluctuations in these items. The rapid increase in total mileage from 1882 to 1884, proportionate to the increase in gross earnings, brought a decline in train mile earnings, and the rapid increase in gross earnings during the next two years, proportionate to the increase in train mileage, brought an increase. From 1886 to 1888 the increase in train mileage brought a decline, and to 1890 the increase in earnings brought an advance. In the following decade a further increase in earnings to 1892 brought a further increase in train mile earnings. During the years of depression to 1894 the movement of earnings and of train mileage was parallel, train mile earnings remaining the same. A decline in earnings in 1895 caused a movement downwards. Throughout the remainder of the decade, with the exception of 1898, in which year a greater proportionate increase in train mileage brought a decline, train mile earnings recovered rapidly. The advance continued to 1921, with the exception of declines in the depressing years of 1904, 1908 and 1915. The increase during the war period, with the exception of 1915, was largely the result of increased earnings the result of increased rates. Changes in the rate situation in the period following the depression of the nineties was to some extent, at least, the result of more efficient operation.

The adequacy of train mile earnings as an index of efficiency may be better understood from an analysis of freight train mile earnings and passenger train mile earnings. Freight train [1] mile earnings, as a function of freight train mileage and freight earnings, in the period ending in 1890, declined with considerable fluctuation from 1·633 in 1882

---

[1] Freight train mile earnings, 1882–90 :

		Cents			Cents			Cents
1882	. .	1·633	1885	. .	1·401	1888	. .	1·336
1883	. .	·919	1886	. .	2·164	1889	. .	1·408
1884	. .	1·263	1887	. .	1·940	1890	. .	1·624

Compiled from *Government Reports.*

to 1·624 in 1890. They increased [1] from 1·33 in 1890 (Company reports) to 1·76 in 1899, and to 6·84 in 1921. Freight train mile earnings declined in 1883, advanced to 1886, declined again to 1888, and increased in the last two years. The rapid expansion of the road in 1883 in eastern Canada and in the west brought a rapid increase in train mileage and a consequent reduction of freight train mile earnings. In 1884 the increase in mixed train mileage offset a decline in freight train mileage, and contributed to an increase in freight train mile earnings, which continued to 1886. Though train mileage was adjusted in part to traffic—an evidence of efficient operation—the increase had a less favourable aspect because of the increase in mixed train mileage. The expansion of mileage in the following years and the bad harvest of 1888 brought a decline which culminated in the latter year. In the years to 1894 (with the exception of 1893 when earnings declined) traffic and earnings surpassed mileage—evidence that freight was handled more efficiently during a period of expansion. Inability to adjust train mileage to traffic was characteristic of the years of depression with the decline in train mile earnings from 1894 to 1896. The recovery during the remainder of the decade, which continued throughout the history of the road, with the exception of 1898, in which year through traffic increased, of 1904, of 1908 and of 1915, was followed by a rapid increase in train mile earnings. Over the whole period freight earnings increased more rapidly than freight train mileage, and only during years of depression was it found difficult to adjust freight train mile-

[1] Freight train mile earnings, 1890–1921 :

	Cents			Cents			Cents
1890*	1·33	1902		2·05	1912		3·11
1891	1·41	1903		2·13	1913		3·24
1892	1·53	1904		2·11	1914		3·35
1893	1·51	1905		2·19	1915		3·59
1894	1·61	1906		2·29	1916		3·57
1895	1·58	1907		2·52	1917*		4·09
1896	1·48	1908		2·47	1918		4·93
1897	1·55	1909		2·56	1919		5·00
1898	1·54	1910		2·92	1920		5·50
1899	1·76	1911		3·02	1921		6·84
1901†	1·82						

Compiled from *C.P.R. Reports.*

* Calendar year.   † Fiscal year.

age to freight demands represented in earnings. Imperfect as freight train mile earnings were as an index of efficient operation because of changes in the rate situation and because of increased freight rates during the war, the general increase warrants the conclusion that efficiency had rapidly improved, and that the company within reasonable limits was successful in adjusting train mileage to the traffic demands. The difficulties of adjustment were alleviated in part by the intensive development of the road which made it less dependent upon grain as the chief source of revenue. Bad harvests became less serious. Through traffic being less remunerative was less dangerous in its fluctuations. Depressions and their more serious effects on through traffic became less disastrous, and rendered train mileage more amenable to the company's control. Moreover, a period of rapid expansion was of decided advantage in this adjustment. Freight train mile earnings were to a large extent an index of the constantly improving efficiency of the road and of changing conditions which made greater efficiency possible.

Passenger train mile earnings, because of the more inelastic character of the passenger business, were less amenable to control. Earnings [1] per passenger train mile decreased from 1·877 in 1882 to ·992 in 1890 and to ·95 [2] in 1899, and increased to the maximum of 2·81 in 1920. The earlier period was characterized by unusual fluctuations. The rapid increase in train mileage in 1883, as a result of expansion in competitive territory in eastern Canada, was not accompanied by an equally rapid increase in earnings. Improved

[1] Passenger train mile earnings, 1882–90 :

	Cents		Cents		Cents
1882 . .	1·877	1885 . .	1·408	1888 . .	·973
1883 . .	1·312	1886 . .	1·722	1889 . .	·984
1884 . .	1·472	1887 . .	1·229	1890 . .	·992

[2] Passenger train mile earnings, 1891–1921 :

	Cents		Cents		Cents
1891* . .	·95	1902 . . .	1·13	1912 . . .	1·62
1892 . .	·95	1903 . . .	1·32	1913 . . .	1·59
1893 . .	·92	1904 . . .	1·40	1914 . . .	1·50
1894 . .	·82	1905 . . .	1·38	1915 . . .	1·33
1895 . .	·82	1906 . . .	1·44	1916 . . .	1·35
1896 . .	·82	1907 . . .	1·57	1917* . .	1·66
1897 . .	·92	1908 . . .	1·58	1918 . . .	1·85
1898 . .	·91	1909 . . .	1·42	1919 . . .	2·59
1899 . .	·95	1910 . . .	1·53	1920 . . .	2·81
1901† . .	1·04	1911 . . .	1·61	1921 . . .	2·19

* Calendar year.   † Fiscal year.

connexions in the following year brought a more rapid increase in earnings, and rapid expansion in 1885 a more rapid increase in train mileage. Bad harvest conditions due to the early frost of 1885 and the increase in mixed train mileage led to a decline in passenger train mileage in 1886 which, with a slight increase in earnings, brought an increase in train mile earnings. The rapid increase in passenger train mileage in the two following years occasioned by the opening of the main line and the decrease in mixed train mileage brought a decline. From 1888 to 1890 expansion of mileage was less rapid, and train mile earnings increased. The uncertain character of the period incidental to rapid expansion rendered adjustment of train mileage to traffic difficult. The movement characteristic of the last two years of the period continued in 1891. In 1892 increase in passenger earnings paralleled increase in train mileage, and train mile earnings remained stationary. During the depression traffic declined, and the inability to adjust passenger train schedules to the situation brought a decline in mileage earnings—much more marked than in freight train mile earnings in the same period. Recovery began in 1896, and with the exception of 1898 and of the years of depression, 1905 and 1908, continued until 1912. The years of depression and the decline in traffic, especially in through traffic, and the inelasticity of passenger service, rendered the decline of passenger train mile earnings more serious than in the case of freight train mile earnings. The difficulty of adjusting passenger schedules to the demand, enhanced by the more serious character of overhead charges, was particularly evident in the war years. The decline beginning in 1913 continued to 1915. Higher rates were responsible for the rapid increase in the later years. The period from 1896 to 1913 was generally characterized by increased efficiency, though the increase in train mile earnings was partly the result of a proportionate increase in local traffic, the disappearance of rate wars, and the influence of the Board of Railway Commissioners. Passenger train mile earnings gave less evidence of efficiency than freight train mile earnings. Regulations were more stringent, overhead charges were more serious, and competition of more consequence. Passenger service was more dependent on densely populated areas, in which competition was more severe. The inelasticity of passenger schedules incidental to competition, and to public demands for convenience and service was a handicap making adjustment of passenger train mileage to passenger traffic unusually difficult.

B. TOTAL EXPENSES.

Increased efficiency reflected in the increase in freight train mile earnings, and, to a less extent, in passenger train mile earnings was immediately reflected in expenses. During the first five months of operation on the part of the Government, working expenses [1] totalled $78,892, a monthly average of $15,778. In the next ten months these expenses [2] increased to $236,945, a monthly average of $23,694. The difficulties of operation incidental to the opening of the line were evident in the number of accidents. In the first five months [3] on 161 miles of road out of a total of eighteen accidents, fifteen were due to bad track. Under company [4] operation expenses increased from $1,148,299 in 1882 to $9,424,166 in 1890, to $16,999,873 in 1899,[5] and to the maximum of $183,488,305 in 1920.

[1] *Sessional Paper*, No. 5, 1881, p. 77.
[2] *Ibid.*, No. 8, 1882, p. 79.   [3] *Ibid.*, No. 5, 1881, p. 84.
[4] Total expenses, 1882–90 :

1882	. . .	$1,148,299·34	1887	. . . .	$7,299,045·16
1883	. . .	3,953,468·61	1888	. . . .	9,034,360·27
1884	. . .	4,747,777·42	1889	. . . .	8,997,312·05
1885	. . .	4,557,519·73	1890	. . . .	9,424,166·45
1886	. . .	5,633,251·32			

Compiled from *Government Reports*.

[5] Total expenses, 1891–1921 :

1891*.	. . .	$12,231,436·11	1907	. . . .	46,914,218·83
1892	. . .	12,989,004·21	1908	. . . .	$49,591,807·70
1893	. . .	13,220,901·39	1909	. . . .	53,357,748·06
1894	. . .	12,328,838·63	1910	. . . .	61,149,534·46
1895	. . .	11,460,085·88	1911	. . . .	67,467,977·64
1896	. . .	12,574,015·10	1912	. . . .	80,021,298·40
1897	. . .	13,745,758·76	1913	. . . .	93,149,825·83
1898	. . .	15,663,605·51	1914	. . . .	87,388,896·15
1899	. . .	16,999,872·77	1915	. . . .	65,290,502·49
1900†	. . .	8,889,851·06	1916	. . . .	80,255,965·50
(Six months ending June 30, 1900)			1916 (six months)		45,843,199·90
1901	. . .	17,849,520·41	1917*	. . . .	105,843,316·00
1902	. . .	23,417,141·37	1918	. . . .	123,035,310·00
1903	. . .	28,120,527·26	1919	. . . .	143,996,523·58
1904	. . .	32,256,027·21	1920	. . . .	183,488,304·00
1905	. . .	35,006,793·29	1921	. . . .	158,820,114·09
1906	. . .	38,696,445·53			

Compiled from *C.P.R. Reports*.
* Calendar year.   † Fiscal year.

The general trend and the fluctuations of total expenses depended upon the changes in constituent items. Though difficulties incidental to obtaining early statistics and to reclassification of accounts are a decided handicap to thorough analysis, general conclusions may be suggested. In direct relation to the amount of traffic carried were expenses incurred in conducting transportation. In the period preceding 1890,[1] according to Government reports, " engine repairs " increased from $378,116 in 1882 to $3,314,817 in 1890. The item " motive power," according to company reports, increased to $8,989,111 in 1903.[2] In the following years this item was included in " conducting transportation." In the earlier period fluctuations were due to several causes. The general increase was largely the result of expansion and increased train mileage. The increase in " engine repairs " expenses in 1883 and 1884 followed the increase in total train mileage. The decline of these expenses in 1885 was due largely to the slight increase in train mileage, to the rapid increase in the number of locomotives, and to the improvement of types. In 1886, on the other hand, a slight decline in train mileage, but a continued increase in locomotives, brought an increase in expenses, and an increase in train mileage in the following two years was accompanied by a continued increase in expense. A marked increase in locomotives in 1889 again brought a decline. From 1890 to 1892 increased train

---

[1] Engine repairs, 1882–90:

1882	. . . .	$378,116·09	1887	$2,724,196·22
1883	. . . .	1,693,745·20	1888	3,265,139·83
1884	. . . .	2,111,017·20	1889	2,997,740·27
1885	. . . .	1,761,784·30	1890	3,314,817·50
1886	. . . .	2,180,709·82		

Compiled from *Government Reports*.

[2] Motive power, 1885–1903:

1885*	. . . .	$1,915,250·49	1894	$3,682,487·33
1886	. . . .	2,488,787·84	1895	3,614,109·16
1887	. . . .	2,969,716·91	1896	3,914,148·08
1888	. . . .	3,224,922·69	1897	4,211,586·61
1889	. . . .	3,065,441·11	1898	4,866,253·15
1890	. . . .	3,655,244·22	1899	5,286,871·50
1891	. . . .	4,217,975·09	1901†	5,745,730·55
1892	. . . .	4,298,589·12	1902	7,387,065·81
1893	. . . .	4,361,489·02	1903	8,989,111·77

Compiled from *C.P.R. Reports*.

 * Calendar year.   † Fiscal year (six months omitted).

mileage brought an increase in " motive power " expense. A decline in freight train mileage in 1893 failed to offset the effects of an increase in passenger train mileage, and expenses increased despite a decrease in total train mileage. In the following year a marked decline of total train mileage brought a decline in expenses. In 1895 the influence of passenger train mileage, which declined with an increase in freight train mileage and in total train mileage, brought a decline in expenses. With the exception of 1901, in which again an increase in passenger train mileage and a decline in freight train mileage and in total train mileage was accompanied by an increase in expense, an increase in total train mileage brought an increase in expense to 1903. Throughout the whole period to 1903 the general increase in train mileage occasioned an increase in " engine repairs " or in " motive power " expense. Fluctuations followed passenger train mileage rather than freight train mileage. The inelasticity of passenger service was apparently a determining factor in the fluctuations of this item of expense, though the trend throughout the period was dominated by the general traffic situation and consequently by freight train mileage and by the general increase in the average train load.

Expenses headed " conducting transportation " appear only under the company's classification, and include, after 1904, expenses classified as " motive power." From 1885 to 1890 this item [1] of expense increased from $1,225,803

[1] Conducting transportation expense, 1885–1921 :

1885*.	. . .	$1,225,802·71
1886 .	. . .	1,543,166·54
1887 .	. . .	1,831,211·21
1888 .	. . .	2,154,684·26
1889 .	. . .	2,192,165·37
1890 .	. . .	2,576,725·72
1891 .	. . .	3,032,475·80
1892 .	. . .	3,324,577·85
1893 .	. . .	3,427,511·72
1894 .	. . .	3,016,505·22
1895 .	. . .	2,884,191·18
1896 .	. . .	3,200,516·30
1897 .	. . .	3,434,755·39
1898 .	. . .	4,014,178·20
1899 .	. . .	4,256,097·31
1901†.	. . .	4,476,123·74
1902 .	. . .	5,361,067·27
1903 .	. . .	6,434,321·57
1904 .	. . .	14,045,459·79
1905 .	. . .	$16,905,848·92
1906 .	. . .	18,785,695·80
1907 .	. . .	23,765,138 08
1908 .	. . .	24,112,713·82
1909 .	. . .	25,568,989·65
1910 .	. . .	27,425,237·61
1911 .	. . .	31,537,518·82
1912 .	. . .	38,923,050·02
1913 .	. . .	46,074,299·26
1914 .	. . .	42,250,286·37
1915 .	. . .	32,083,169·65
1916 .	. . .	38,915,381·50
1916 (six months)		21,943,020·86
1917*.	. . .	53,029,260·00
1918 .	. . .	61,047,812·79
1919 .	. . .	68,054,174·76
1920 .	. . .	86,086,611·54
1921 .	. . .	73,557,749·11

Compiled from *C.P.R. Reports.*

* Calendar year.　　　　† Fiscal year (six months omitted).

to $2,576,726. In 1899 it had increased to $4,256,097 and in 1920 to a maximum of $86,608,611. To 1892 the increase in the amount of freight carried one mile and in the number of passengers carried one mile was accompanied by an increase in " conducting transportation " expenses. In 1893 a decline in the amount of freight carried one mile and an increase in the number of passengers carried one mile, and the decline in freight train mileage and the increase in passenger train mileage already noted, brought an increase in " conducting transportation " expense as in " motive power " expense. In the following year a general decline in traffic brought a general decline in expense, but in 1895, as with " motive power " expense, " conducting transportation " expense again declined with a decline in passenger train mileage and in the number of passengers carried one mile and with an increase in freight train mileage, total train mileage and the amount of freight carried one mile. With the exception of 1914 and 1915 the increase beginning in 1896 continued to 1920. In 1901 with " conducting transportation " expense as with " motive power " expense, the increase in passenger train mileage and in the number of passengers carried one mile offset the decrease in freight train mileage, total train mileage and the amount of freight carried one mile, and brought an increase. With the exception of this year, fluctuations of " conducting transportation " expense paralleled the fluctuations of total train mileage to 1916. In the later war years [1] as a result of rising prices a decline in the total train mileage in 1918 was accompanied by an increase in " conducting transportation " expenses, and the increase in train mileage to 1920 by a more rapid increase in these expenses. A decline in train mileage and in wages in 1921 brought a decline in expenses. Generally " conducting transportation " expenses followed the increase of traffic incidental to the expansion of the road. Transportation expenses increased less rapidly, and fluctuations upward were less marked than in train mileage, increased efficiency being largely responsible. Expanding

---

[1] For a description of the effects of increased prices due to the war, see a letter from the Canadian Pacific to the Board of Railway Commissioners, *Report of the Board of Railway Commissioners*, 1918, p. 81 ff.

traffic was handled more efficiently, and with a greater reduction of overhead charges. On the other hand, because of overhead charges, a decline in traffic was not accompanied by a proportionate decline of expenses, as was evident in 1914 and 1915. In 1904 and in 1908 expenses increased more rapidly than total train mileage. Freight train mileage actually declined in the latter year. The decline in through traffic during years of depression occasioned a greater decline in train mileage than in expenses, though more particularly in relation to freight train mileage than to passenger train mileage. The general movement of " conducting transportation " expenses and " motive power " expenses as the result of the expansion of the road was characteristic of " traffic " expense. This classification has been made since 1908. It increased [1] from $1,734,086 in that year to $6,289,622 in 1921, and was not relatively important. Comprising chiefly wages and salaries of passenger and freight agents and expenses of advertising agencies the increase to 1913 paralleled closely the increase in mileage and in traffic to that year. The increase in 1914, despite a decline in traffic, and the marked decrease in the two following years despite an increase of traffic in 1916 made it apparent that though in the long run these expenses were largely determined by the demands of traffic during short periods, fluctuations were the result of a variety of factors, including the rise in prices, the rise in wages, and the control and policy of the company. Fluctuations in later years corresponded with fluctuations in train mileage and in traffic, but in 1921 these expenses increased with a decline in traffic.

Parlour and sleeping-car expenses were related to the movement, especially of through passenger traffic. These

[1] Traffic expense, 1908–21 :

1908* . . . . $1,734,086·57	1915 . . . . $2,990,163·97
1909 . . . . 2,123,860·02	1916 . . . . 2,798,699·40
1910 . . . . 2,436,651·26	1917† . . . . 3,084,944·00
1911 . . . . 2,623,280·98	1918 . . . . 3,011,578·67
1912 . . . . 2,880,800·32	1919 . . . . 3,829,686·56
1913 . . . . 3,376,980·85	1920 . . . . 4,999,345·21
1914 . . . . 3,626,612·08	1921 . . . . 6,289,621·86

Compiled from *C.P.R. Reports.*

* Fiscal year.   † Calendar year (six months omitted).

expenses increased,[1] from $24,099 in 1885 to $64,096 in 1890, to $85,582 in 1899, and to a maximum of $2,492,641 in 1920. In the years immediately following the completion of the main line, the opening of the west occasioned a rapid increase in immigration, in through traffic and in parlour and sleeping-car expenses. The dependence of these expenses on this movement brought a rapid increase to 1893, with the exception of a decline in 1889 due to the bad harvest of the previous year. The relation of parlour and sleeping-car expenses to through traffic and the decline of this traffic during a period of depression occasioned a decrease in 1894 and 1895. The recovery and the stimulus of the Klondike rush in 1898 led to a rapid increase in that year, and was followed by a decline in 1899. Following the expansion of the road these expenses increased to 1914 —the rate of increase falling off in 1904. Consistently with the decline of tourist and through traffic due to the war situation they declined rapidly to 1916 and gained only slightly in 1917. The rise in prices as with other expenses and the recovery after the war brought about the rapid increase from 1918 to 1920. A decline in traffic and prices led to the decline in these expenses in 1921. Generally this item of expense was dependent on the expansion of the road and the establishment of through connexions,

---

[1] Parlour and sleeping-car expenses, 1885–1921 :

1885*	$24,098·99	1905	$172,123·61
1886	38,533·25	1906	231,688·62
1887	52,468·57	1907	318,823·80
1888	59,451·74	1908	395,628·72
1889	50,794·18	1909	461,433·37
1890	64,096·14	1910	600,796·11
1891	68,698·38	1911	731,738·62
1892	69,463·04	1912	944,594·34
1893	85,138·10	1913	1,241,700·07
1894	80,854·57	1914	1,348,979·47
1895	68,015·68	1915	1,111,253·29
1896	71,311·49	1916	990,410·87
1897	78,673·90	1916 (six months)	530,118·23
1898	86,197·99	1917*	1,006,038·00
1899	85,582·18	1918	1,214,389·52
1901†	99,348·26	1919	1,861,428·05
1902	115,770·33	1920	2,492,640·78
1903	144,349·83	1921	2,271,391·04
1904	161,026·09		

Compiled from *C.P.R. Reports.*

* Calendar year.　　　　　† Fiscal year.

and particularly it was closely related to through traffic characteristic of periods of prosperity.

Expenses incidental to lake and river steamship traffic increased [1] from $50,794 in 1889 to $417,045 in 1899 and to a maximum of $1,492,991 in 1920. These expenses were determined largely by the number of vessels owned by the company, and by the increasing traffic which made possible expansion in that direction. With the acquisition of new boats these expenses increased very rapidly to 1891. This was followed by a slight decline to 1894, and the general increase in steamship business brought an increase to 1896. The acquisition of steamers in British Columbia territory caused the rapid jump of over 100 per cent. in 1897. Increased traffic and extension of the service brought a continuous increase to 1904. The depression occasioned a slight decline to 1906. Further extension of service stimulated the recovery beginning in 1907, and in 1914 expenses had more than doubled in seven years. A decline in 1915, accompanying the general decline of traffic in that year, was followed by a continued increase from 1917 to 1920, partly the result of recovery from the war period but largely the result of characteristic rising prices. To some extent these expenses were influenced by the varying navigation seasons and by periods of depression, but generally the expansion of the company and the improvement of its through connex-

[1] Lake and river expense, 1889–1921 :

1889*	$50,794·18		1906		$511,390·47
1890	108,335·92		1907		564,552·11
1891	165,092·67		1908		750,197·84
1892	149,489·78		1909		758,988·88
1893	134,549·63		1910		858,834·34
1894	114,111·60		1911		989,768·74
1895	133,877·06		1912		1,064,011·53
1896	147,332·12		1913		1,113,808·10
1897	333,381·68		1914		1,183,397·69
1898	413,195·02		1915		1,051,781·69
1899	417,045·72		1916		829,811·73
1901†	447,249·10		1917*		1,054,683·00
1902	468,943·88		1918		1,181,589·41
1903	470,773·06		1919		1,335,003·19
1904	519,994·12		1920		1,492,991·54
1905	515,397·02		1921		1,455,213·13

Compiled from *C.P.R. Reports.*

* Calendar year (six months omitted 1916).

† Fiscal year (six months omitted 1901).

ions on the extension of steamship service were dominant factors.

General expenses increased,[1] according to Government reports, from $436,360 in 1882 to $3,581,282 in 1890, and, according to company reports,[2] from $950,754 in 1890 to $1,680,933 in 1899, and to $9,460,681 in 1921. The rapid increase of 1887 and 1888 in other items of expense was characteristic of this item. This increase continued to 1893, and was followed by a decline to 1895, the years of depression, and by rapid recovery to 1899. In 1901 the decreased freight train mileage and total train mileage were accompanied by a decline in general expense. Passenger mileage, which dominated " motive power " expense and " conducting transportation " expense in that year and occasioned an increase in those items, was not dominant in general expense. On the other hand, the decline in 1904 of general expense was accompanied by an increase in freight carried, in freight train mileage and in total train mileage. The decline in the amount of freight carried one mile was significant but not dominant, and the marked decline of general expense in that year suggests improved efficiency and reduction on

[1] General expense, 1882–90 :

1882	. . . .	$436,359·89	1887	. . . .	$2,369,522·62
1883	. . . .	1,410,476·08	1888	. . . .	3,134,574·19
1884	. . . .	1,553,876·86	1889	. . . .	3,370,259·13
1885	. . . .	1,654,846·57	1890	. . . .	3,581,281·86
1886	. . . .	1,894,894·18			

Compiled from *Government Reports.*

[2] General expense, 1890–1921 :

1890*	. . . .	$950,754·06	1907	. . . .	$2,188,857·87
1891	. . . .	1,194,214·86	1908	. . . .	1,942,756·25
1892	. . . .	1,272,474·75	1909	. . . .	2,356,402·99
1893	. . . .	1,281,603·28	1910	. . . .	2,548,799·89
1894	. . . .	1,252,060·52	1911	. . . .	2,771,425·00
1895	. . . .	1,086,900·45	1912	. . . .	3,444,395·51
1896	. . . .	1,216,122·25	1913	. . . .	3,953,769·74
1897	. . . .	1,336,022·47	1914	. . . .	4,322,103·93
1898	. . . .	1,589,777·06	1915	. . . .	3,963,202·80
1899	. . . .	1,680,932·66	1916	. . . .	4,014,753·69
1901†	. . . .	1,670,904·35	1916 (six months)		2,318,687·20
1902	. . . .	2,088,848·86	1917*	. . . .	5,023,609·00
1903	. . . .	2,323,315·02	1918	. . . .	5,421,601·38
1904	. . . .	1,589,134·79	1919	. . . .	6,105,783·08
1905	. . . .	1,634,698·91	1920 (incl. taxes)		8,969,995·75
1906	. . . .	1,964,093·00	1921 (incl. taxes)		9,460,681·07

Compiled from *C.P.R. Reports.*

* Calendar year.   † Fiscal year (six months omitted).

the part of the company of constituent items of general
expense, as salaries of officers and clerks, cost of general
supplies, insurance and general administration.   A decline
in freight train mileage, in freight carried and in freight
carried one mile in 1908 occasioned a decline in general
expense.   In 1914 general expense increased with traffic
expense, despite a decrease in freight train mileage, in
passenger train mileage and in freight and passenger traffic
—a result of the difficulty of adjusting these expenses to
the rapid increase in traffic culminating in the preceding
year.   In the remaining years of the period general expenses
fluctuated with other items of expense, rising rapidly toward
the end with the rise in prices and with the inclusion and increase of taxes.[1]   General expenses were dependent in the
long run on the expansion of the road.   Fluctuations were the
result of increasing efficiency, of minor traffic fluctuations
and of the company's control.

As in other items of expense, " car repairs " was dependent
generally on the traffic situation.   This expense increased,
according to Government reports [2] from $56,883 in 1882

[1] The burden of taxation on the earnings of the company has been
slight because of charter provisions exempting the capital stock and property of the company. The Saskatchewan legislature in the Railway
Taxation Act of 1908 holding that only the real and personal property
were exempt, levied a tax on the gross earnings. This claim has been
disputed by the company, but the tax has been paid under an agreement
with the Saskatchewan Government. In the fiscal year of 1918 the company
paid $85,000. The exemption did not apply to the property of subsidiary
companies, and this has been subject to taxation. Dominion taxation
has been limited to a regulation adopted during the war and becoming
effective through an Order in Council on January 1, 1918. From that
date until one year after the declaration of peace the Canadian Pacific
was called upon to bear additional and special taxation on the basis of
one-half its net earnings from railway operation in excess of 7 per cent.
on its common stock up to $7,000,000, and an income-tax on all earnings
except those from railway operation not exceeding the net earnings due
to increase in rates. These taxes were not exacted after 1919. Taxes
were earlier included under general expense and also from 1920. During
the war a special fund was set apart for war taxes, and all taxes were not
included in that item. In any case the changes made in the accounts
concerned have been relatively unimportant, and on the whole taxation
has been unusually light. See Clark, A. B., op. cit.; also *Report of Ontario
Commission on Taxation*, 1905.
[2] Car repairs, 1882–90 :

1882	. . . .	$56,882·67	1887	. . . .	$586,805·14
1883	. . . .	258,309·58	1888	. . . .	653,721·76
1884	. . . .	321,044·40	1889	. . . .	456,960·88
1885	. . . .	347,655·05	1890	. . . .	521,823·77
1886	. . . .	455,948·47			

Compiled from *Government Reports*.

to $521,824 in 1890, and, according to company reports,[1] under the classification " maintenance of cars " to $1,295,282 in 1899 and under the classification " maintenance of equipment " after 1904 to a maximum of $46,350,793 in 1920. In the first period, as a result of the expansion of the road, " car repairs " increased consistently to 1888. In 1889 the rapid increase in equipment and the slight increase in train mileage brought a decline. An increase beginning in 1890 continued to 1892, and was followed by a rapid decline in 1893 as a result of a decrease in traffic. With slight additions to the number of cars and a continued decline in traffic, " maintenance of cars " increased slightly in 1894. The general difficulties of the period culminating in 1895 and the consequent economies practised brought a marked decrease in that year, despite a slight increase in traffic. An increase began in 1896, and with the general expansion of the road continued rapidly to 1904. The increase of over 100 per cent. in that year was the result of the change of classification to " maintenance of equipment." This item increased to 1911, in which year consistent additions of equipment and a slight falling off in traffic brought a decline. During the remainder of the period, fluctuations paralleled fluctuations in traffic, and with other items of expense increased rapidly from 1917 to 1920 and declined in 1921. The general movement of maintenance

[1] Maintenance of cars, 1891–1903 :

1891*	$704,446·52	1897	955,013·12
1892	956,988·47	1898	962,263·83
1893	831,195·50	1899	1,295,282·03
1894	868,402·98	1901†	1,661,225·04
1895	710,997·12	1902	1,868,045·17
1896	881,402·52	1903	2,487,976·69

Compiled from *C.P.R. Reports.*

    * Calendar year.   † Fiscal year (six months omitted).

Maintenance of equipment, 1904–21 :

1904	$5,873,162·91	1913	$17,198,573·38
1905	6,616,257·17	1914	16,617,247·21
1906	7,369,565·84	1915	11,307,965·04
1907	9,083,248·61	1916	16,695,955·87
1908	9,358,138·48	1917*	23,404,263·50
1909	11,080,886·50	1918	28,226,991·04
1910	12,567,493·86	1919	33,897,727·64
1911	12,056,160·11	1920	46,350,792·61
1912	13,608,708·19	1921	36,746,816·45

Compiled from *C.P.R. Reports.*

    * Calendar year (six months omitted).

of equipment expense followed closely the movement of traffic.

" Maintenance of way and structures " was more generally related to the policy of the company and more generally subject to the company's control.   " Maintenance expense," according to Government reports, increased from $276,941 in 1882 to $2,006,237 in 1890,[1] and " maintenance of way and structures," according to the company's reports,[2] to $3,488,254 in 1899, and to a maximum of $32,573,927 in 1920.   In the earlier period, with the expansion of the road, maintenance expenses increased steadily to 1889. The decline in 1890, in spite of an increase in traffic, was partly the result of the anxiety of the company to secure a favourable reserve against the exhaustion in 1893 of the funds deposited with the Government as a guarantee of dividends, and the decline in 1895 was partly the result of the difficult financial situation of the company during the period of depression, though warranted in part by the decline in traffic of the preceding year.   With recovery, maintenance expenses increased steadily from 1896 to 1908.   The depression in 1907 and the consequent decline in gross earnings

[1] Maintenance expense, 1882-90 :

1882	$276,940·69	1887	1,618,511·18
1883	399,377·86	1888	1,980,924·49
1884	755,838·96	1889	2,172,350·77
1885	793,233·81	1890	2,006,237·38
1886	1,101,698·85		

Compiled from *Government Reports.*

[2] Maintenance of way and structures, 1891-1921 :

1891*. . . .	$2,519,825·13	1908	$10,410,751·61
1892	2,570,254·81	1909	10,074,049·04
1893	2,808,677·34	1910	13,653,938·04
1894	2,972,024·83	1911	15,561,086·29
1895	2,659,733·89	1912	17,719,795·21
1896	2,807,151·63	1913	18,498,741·05
1897	3,018,748·90	1914	16,426,582·05
1898	3,274,642·90	1915	11,400,538·89
1899	3,488,253·73	1916	14,671,291·20
1901†. . . .	4,196,188·47	1916 (six months)	8,245,741·01
1902	5,634,497·17	1917*. . . .	17,470,069·00
1903	6,723,241·17	1918	22,646,105·94
1904	7,372,408·26	1919	28,912,220·30
1905	8,527,035·07	1920	32,573,927·27
1906	9,105,249·56	1921	29,038,641·43
1907	10,110,957·49		

Compiled from *C.P.R. Reports.*

* Calendar year.   † Fiscal year (6 months omitted).

occasioned a slight decline in 1909. The importance of
traffic was reflected in the parallel fluctuations of maintenance expenses and other items of expense more generally
dominated by traffic. Maintenance of way per mile—the
resultant of mileage and maintenance of way and structures
—illustrated the general movement of maintenance expenses
more strikingly. Maintenance of way per mile, according
to Government reports, declined [1] from $455 in 1882 to
$394 in 1890, and, according to company reports,[2] increased
to $498 in 1899 and to a maximum of $2,430 in 1920. As
a result of the rapid increase in mileage, maintenance expenses
per mile decreased rapidly in 1883 and slightly in 1885, and
in the remaining years to 1889 increased. In 1890 the
decline in maintenance expenses and the increase in mileage
brought a marked decrease in maintenance expenses per
mile. In 1892 increasing mileage brought a decrease. In
1895 a decrease in maintenance expenses was largely
responsible for decline. In 1908 increasing mileage brought
a decline in maintenance expense per mile. In 1909 the
same factor with a decline in maintenance expenses occasioned a rapid decrease. Again, increasing mileage brought
a decline in maintenance expenses per mile in 1913. The

[1] Maintenance per mile, 1882-90 :

1882 . . . . . . $454·74	1887 . . . . . . $378·68
1883 . . . . . . 224·36	1888 . . . . . . 424·90
1884 . . . . . . 246·52	1889 . . . . . . 436·78
1885 . . . . . . 236·92	1890 . . . . . . 394·54
1886 . . . . . . 292·30	

Compiled from *Government Reports*.

[2] Maintenance of way per mile, 1891-1921 :

1891* . . . . . $437·01	1907 . . . . . $1,104·49
1892 . . . . . 427·30	1908 . . . . . 1,104·47
1893 . . . . . 443·91	1909 . . . . . 1,019·84
1894 . . . . . 468·67	1910 . . . . . 1,354·82
1895 . . . . . 412·74	1911 . . . . . 1,504·64
1896 . . . . . 433·47	1912 . . . . . 1,645·75
1897 . . . . . 459·61	1913 . . . . . 1,627·55
1898 . . . . . 490·14	1914 . . . . . 1,389·14
1899 . . . . . 498·32	1915 . . . . . 921·77
1901† . . . . . 554·83	1916 . . . . . 1,138·85
1902 . . . . . 742·65	1917* . . . . . 1,134·88
1903 . . . . . 867·73	1918 . . . . . 1,742·96
1904 . . . . . 884·83	1919 . . . . . 2,159·40
1905 . . . . . 995·21	1920 . . . . . 2,430·52
1906 . . . . . 1,037·39	1921 . . . . . 2,159·97

* Calendar year.   † Fiscal year.

rapid decline of maintenance expenses to 1915 resulted in a more rapid decline of expenses per mile. Maintenance expenses occasioned the increase in maintenance expenses per mile during the remainder of the period with the exception of 1917, in which increased mileage brought a decline. Maintenance of way and structure, in the general increase, was the result of the expansion of the road, and in fluctuations was to some extent dominated by the financial policy of the company.

Commercial telegraph increased [1] from $50,619 in 1886 to $241,758 in 1890, to $489,808 in 1899, and to $2,852,416 in 1918. The rapid increase of the telegraph system and the increase in traffic occasioned the steady increase of the early years to 1892. A decline followed to 1895 with the exception of a slight increase in 1894. An increase began in 1896 and continued steadily to 1913 as a result of the general expansion characteristic of the period. Decline beginning in 1914 continued in the war years to 1916. With rising prices these expenses increased to 1918. Though relatively unimportant these expenses were largely dominated by the general movement of traffic.

[1] Commercial telegraph, 1886–1918 :

1886* . . . . $50,619·28	1904 . . . . $590,722·89
1887 . . . . 180,794·89	1905 . . . . 635,432·50
1888 . . . . 207,952·76	1906 . . . . 728,762·24
1889 . . . . 241,757·76	1907 . . . . 882,640·87
1890 . . . . 288,697·36	1908 . . . . 887,534·41
1891 . . . . 328,707·60	1909 . . . . 933,137·61
1892 . . . . 345,986·39	1910 . . . . 1,057,783·35
1893 . . . . 335,736·80	1911 . . . . 1,196,899·08
1894 . . . . 342,411·52	1912 . . . . 1,435,944·28
1895 . . . . 302,261·34	1913 . . . . 1,691,953·38
1896 . . . . 336,030·71	1914 . . . . 1,613,687·64
1897 . . . . 377,576·69	1915 . . . . 1,382,507·16
1898 . . . . 457,097·36	1916 . . . . 1,339,161·02
1899 . . . . 489,807·64	1916 (six months). 853,353·89
1901† . . . . 449,058·69	1917* . . . . 1,770,450·00
1902 . . . . 492,902·88	1918 . . . . 2,852,416·30
1903 . . . . 547,438·15	

Compiled from *C.P.R. Reports*.

* Calendar year.   † Fiscal year (six months omitted).

In the remaining years, this item is not included in expenses, but net earnings from commercial telegraph are classified under other income.

IX

Total Receipts

A. NET EARNINGS

THE relation of total expenses to gross earnings was reflected in operating ratio. Operating ratio during the first period [1] fluctuated widely, rising rapidly from 74·2 in 1882 to 91·7 in 1884, declining to 63·4 in 1886, rising to 71·0 in 1888, and declining to 60·5 in 1890. The rapid rise of 1883 and 1884 was the result of the rapid increase in expenses in these years occasioned by the rapid expansion of the road, especially in territory not productive of traffic. The completion of the rail and water route in 1885 and the beginning of operation over the main line in 1886 brought a decline in those years, the situation being reflected in the actual decline of expenses in 1885 and the relatively slight increase in 1886, largely a result of the decline in engine repairs, and in the increase in earnings, largely the result of increase in freight earnings and in grain. The rapid rise in 1887 and 1888 of operating ratio was the result of a marked increase in every item of expense occasioned by the expansion of those years and a relatively smaller increase in earnings shown in every item of earnings. The decline in expenses, the result of a decrease in car repairs and engine repairs in 1889, and the slight increase in 1890, the result of a decrease in maintenance expenses, and the increase in earnings especially the result of increased earnings from " other sources " in 1890, brought a slight decline of operating ratio in 1889 and a marked decline in 1890. The operating ratio of the years of the period to 1890 was obviously the result of uncertainties incidental to early years of the road's expansion.

[1] Operating ratio, 1882–90 :

1882	. . .	74·2	1885	. . .	65·7	1888	. . .	71·0
1883	. . .	88·0	1886	. . .	63·4	1889	. . .	69·1
1884	. . .	91·7	1887	. . .	68·5	1890	. . .	60·5

The importance of grain and the control exercised by the company in the later years of the decade were significant factors, but underlying the changes of the period were difficulties of early growth. From 1890 to 1894 operating ratio [1] changed slightly, rising in the latter year to 65·75. To 1892 increased expenses paralleled closely earnings, with consequent slight change in operating ratio. A decline in earnings, largely the result of a decline in freight earnings incidental to a decline in traffic due to grain, but more especially to manufactured articles, and an increase in expenses in 1893, which the decline in maintenance expenses failed to offset, and a relatively slight decrease in expenses in 1894, brought an increase in operating ratio. In 1895 the slight recovery of earnings, occasioned by increased traffic largely the result of the agricultural situation, and the general decline of expenses, led to a marked decline of operating ratio. To the end of the century earnings and expenses generally increased, though at varying rates, with the result that the operating ratio fluctuated accordingly, but, with the greater relative increase of earnings as a result of increasing traffic especially of grain, and also of manufactured articles, generally declined. In the decade from 1890 to 1900 the expansion of the road in the earlier years and the consequent increase in fixed capital and overhead charges resulted in a rapid increase in operating ratio during the depression. In the later years the relatively slight growth of fixed capital during the depression and the recovery of traffic toward the end of the century occasioned a decline of operating ratio.

From 1901 to 1904 operating ratio increased gradually

---

[1] Operating ratio, 1891–1921 :

1891*	. . 60·43	1902	. . 62·44	1912	. . 64·89
1892	. . 60·43	1903	. . 63·97	1913	. . 66·82
1893	. . 63·07	1904	. . 69·42	1914	. . 67·32
1894	. . 65·75	1905	. . 69·35	1915	. . 66·04
1895	. . 60·50	1906	. . 62·75	1916	. . 59·75
1896	. . 60·80	1907	. . 64·96	1917*	. . 69·46
1897	. . 57·16	1908	. . 69·47	1918	. . 78·10
1898	. . 59·92	1909	. . 69·92	1919	. . 81·39
1899	. . 58·16	1910	. . 64·38	1920	. . 84·70
1901†	. . 60·75	1911	. . 64·77	1921	. . 82·28

* Calendar year.   † Fiscal year.

to 1903 and rapidly in 1904. In the earlier years expenses increased more rapidly than earnings, and operating ratio increased accordingly. In 1904 a slight increase in earnings with a decline in grain and in other articles, and a general increase in expenses brought a rapid rise. A year later the operating ratio remained practically stationary, but in 1906, the result of a rapid increase in earnings due largely to the grain situation and to a steady increase in expenses, declined rapidly. In the years to 1909, following an increase in earnings in 1907, a decline in 1908 and a slight increase in 1909, generally the result of similar fluctuations in freight earnings and again of similar fluctuations in grain and manufactured articles, partly the effects of the depression and the continued steady increase in expenses, operating ratio increased slightly in 1907, rapidly in 1908 and remained stationary in 1909. In 1910 a rapid increase in earnings, again largely the result of the grain situation, occasioned a decline. To 1913 the relatively greater increase in expenses brought a steady increase, and in 1914 a relatively greater decline in earnings produced the same result. In 1915 a marked decline in earnings and a more rapid decline in expenses brought a decline in operating ratio, and in the following year a rapid increase in earnings, occasioned by the exceptional harvest reduced the operating ratio to a much more marked extent. In the remaining years of the period the rapid increase in expenses due to rising prices brought the operating ratio to the highest point of the period in 1920. A decline in expenses led to a slight decline in the following year.

Generally from 1900 to 1913 operating ratio increased. The heavy overhead charges incidental to the rapid expansion of the road brought during a period of depression a decided increase in operating ratio. Increasing importance of fixed capital incidental to constant expansion of the road made inevitable during the period a steady though gradual rise. That this persistent increase was due to the increase in the company's fixed capital was evident in 1915, in a year in which greatly increased traffic brought a marked decline in the ratio. This general tendency towards increase of operating ratio was accentuated by the rising costs of the war period. The expansion of the road in mileage, equipment and services, the effects of the vast stretch of unprofitable territory separating eastern and Western Canada, and of the difficult east-bound grades,[1] the dependence of the road on grain which necessitated a situation subject to uncertain climatic conditions, to a decided peak load in expenses, and to a long back haul, and the importance of passenger traffic with its inelastic characteristics, were factors in the increase in operating ratio. Large overhead charges were involved which made adjustment to traffic conditions unusually difficult.

The expansion of the road and the success of the company in meeting the situation were registered in net earnings. During the first period of Government operation net earnings totalled $26,084,[2] or $5,216 per month. In the next ten months [3] they increased to $54,553, or $5,455 per month, and in the first year of the company's operation to $397,914, a monthly average of $28,422. In 1890, according to Government reports,[4] they had increased to $6,148,819; in 1899, according to company reports,[5] to $12,230,165 and in 1921

[1] Particularly the grade from Winnipeg to the height of land between Lake Superior and Hudson Bay. See White, James, *Altitudes in Canada*, p. 1 ff.

[2] *Sessional Papers*, No. 5, 1882, p. 77.   [3] *Ibid.*, No. 8, 1882, p. 79.

[4] Net earnings, 1882–90 :

1882	.	.	.	$397,914·59	1887	. . . .	$3,351,208·92
1883	.	.	.	537,883·77	1888	. . . .	3,676,649·74
1884	.	.	.	429,238·70	1889	. . . .	4,019,299·76
1885	.	.	.	2,371,349·56	1890	. . . .	6,148,819·17
1886	.	.	.	3,241,698·90			

Compiled from *Government Reports*.

[5] Net earnings, 1891–1921 :

1891*	.	.	.	$8,009,659·87	1907	. . . .	25,303,308·81
1892	.	.	.	8,420,347·56	1908	. . . .	$21,792,366·02
1893	.	.	.	7,741,416·05	1909	. . . .	22,955,572·90
1894	.	.	.	6,423,309·08	1910	. . . .	33,839,955·87
1895	.	.	.	7,480,950·99	1911	. . . .	36,699,830·57
1896	.	.	.	8,107,581·74	1912	. . . .	43,298,242·83
1897	.	.	.	10,303,775·89	1913	. . . .	46,245,874·15
1898	.	.	.	10,475,371·62	1914	. . . .	42,425,927·68
1899	.	.	.	12,230,165·49	1915	. . . .	33,574,627·29
1900†	.	.	.	5,277,946·83	1916	. . . .	49,225,920·46
(Six months ending June 30, 1900.)					1916 (six months)		30,874,765·86
1901	.	.	.	12,109,375·35	1917*	. . . .	46,546,019·00
1902	.	.	.	14,085,912·41	1918	. . . .	34,502,388·00
1903	.	.	.	15,836,845·78	1919	. . . .	32,933,036·42
1904	.	.	.	14,213,105·03	1920	. . . .	33,153,044·60
1905	.	.	.	15,475,088·46	1921	. . . .	34,201,740·31
1906	.	.	.	22,973,312·63			

Compiled from *Company Reports*.

     * Calendar year.   † Fiscal year.

to $34,201,740. In the earlier period following gross earnings and the operating ratio, and the result of factors dominating these items, net earnings increased in 1883, declined in 1884, and increased steadily to 1892. The depression brought a decline to 1894. With recovery net earnings increased to 1899, and with the exception of a slight decline in 1901, in 1904 and in 1908, this increase continued to 1913. A decline followed in 1914 and 1915, but the highest point was reached in 1916. In the later years they declined to 1919, rising slightly in 1920 and in 1921. Net earnings per mile varied with mileage and net earnings.[1]

B. OTHER INCOME

Fluctuations in other income largely followed fluctuations in net earnings from operation, and were largely the result of the same movements. Interest on loans and deposits as an item of this classification fluctuated to some extent with net earnings and was predetermined by net earnings, which made possible a financial policy on the part of the company permitting the direction of resources to liquid investments. The expansion of the road which occasioned the growth of net earnings was characterized by integration and the acquisition of other roads. This expansion was principally accomplished through the purchase of securities which in interest and dividends contri-

---

[1] Net earnings per mile, 1882–90 :

1882	. . $653·39	1885	. . $708·28	1888 . . $795·07
1883	. . 302·18	1886	. . 860·09	1889 . . 808·06
1884	. . 139·99	1887	. . 784·09	1890 . . 1,209·20

Net earnings per mile, 1891–1921 :

1891*	. $1,389·11	1902 . . 1,856·58	1912 . . 4,021·38
1892 .	. 1,399·88	1903 . . $2,043·99	1913 . . $4,068·79
1893 .	. 1,223·55	1904 . . 1,705·84	1914 . . 3,587·81
1894 .	. 1,012·50	1905 . . 1,816·14	1915 . . 2,714·63
1895 .	. 1,160·91	1906 . . 2,617·44	1916 . . 3,810·96
1896 .	. 1,251·94	1907 . . 2,764·18	1917* . 3,583·21
1897 .	. 1,568·78	1908 . . 2,311·96	1918 . . 2,655·45
1898 .	. 1,567·93	1909 . . 2,323·90	1919 . . 2,459·70
1899 .	. 1,747·16	1910 . . 3,357·86	1920 . . 2,473·73
1901†	. 1,601·13	1911 . . 3,548·62	1921 . . 2,544·01

* Calendar year.   † Fiscal year.

buted to " other income." [1] The dependence of " other income " on the ownership of securities of subsidiary companies, on " loans and deposits," and on the reclassification of accounts with reference to the inclusion in later years of net earnings from ocean and coastal steamship lines, and from commercial telegraph and news department, and of interest from land sales, occasioned marked changes in the total. In the period ending with the century the subsidiary companies the Duluth, South Shore and Atlantic Railway, and the Minneapolis, St. Paul and Sault Ste. Marie Railway were important contributors, income from these companies increasing from $203,603 in 1892 to $1,150,199 in 1899, being two-thirds of total " other income " in the latter year. Fluctuations during this decade followed the difficulties of these roads during the period of depression and their repayment of aid. After 1900 the acquisition of other securities, the addition of new accounts, and the rapid expansion of the road with the consequent increase in net earnings and in surplus available in liquid forms, brought a steady though fluctuating rise. In 1921 " other income " totalled $10,987,189, of which $2,307,332 came from investments and other resources (Exhibit C), $1,840,866 from deposits and dividends on other securities, $2,785,615 net earnings from ocean and coastal steamship lines and $4,053,386 from the commercial telegraph and news department, hotels, rentals and miscellaneous. Par value of

[1] Other Income, 1892–1921 :

1892*	$203,602·72	1908 . . . . $1,541,874·03
1893	209,862·87	1909 . . . . 1,906,578·40
1894	333,825·91	1910 . . . . 2,426,477·29
1895	552,912·96	1911 . . . . 5,046,856·40
1896	511,165·10	1912 . . . . 5,158,585·40
1897	340,706·48	1913 . . . . 6,598,151·33
1898	423,366·86	1914 . . . . 8,587,870·53
1899	1,150,198·57	1915 . . . . 10,969,331·69
1900†	1,011,358·67	Six months.
1901	933,425·25	1916 . . . . 9,940,954·94
1902	958,826·64	1916 (six months) 6,415,352·45
1903	1,286,812·41	1917* . . . . 10,713,299·32
1904	1,691,268·51	1918 . . . . 8,128,751·51
1905	1,584,663·47	1919 . . . . 9,049,341·70
1906	1,316,870·47	1920 . . . . 10,966,447·81
1907	1,640,831·70	1921 . . . . 10,987,199·12

Compiled from *C.P.R. Reports.*
* Calendar year.   † Fiscal year.

acquired securities (Exhibit C) in that year was $63,966,727 and the cost of these securities $38,356,460. Par value of acquired securities of leased and controlled lines (Exhibit B) totalled $16,507,005 and cost $128,109,814. The company held also Imperial and Dominion Government Securities, $27,310,675 and Provincial and Municipal Securities, $2,016,721. Fundamentally, the items concerned were largely influenced by considerations dominant over net earnings.

C. PROCEEDS FROM LAND SALES

Net earnings and " other income " reflected directly the expansion of the railroad, and were determined by influences largely coincident with influences affecting receipts from land sales. The settlement of western Canada and the importance of grain were significant factors in the growth of earnings, and were directly related to the sale of land. The dependence of earnings on settlement, and the control of the company over lands in western Canada, occasioned by the terms of the charter, and the efforts of the company during the period of the construction of the main line, incidental to strengthening the position of its land grant as a basis for land grant bonds, for settlement, for purposes of strategy in railway competition, and for immediate and ultimate returns from sales, rendered the land situation important.

After the completion of the main line, adjustments [1] were made for the final transfer of the land grant. An agreement in 1886 [2] permitted the deduction of 6,793,014

[1] Of considerable importance was the fixing of a western limit to the land grant. The charter had placed the limit at Jasper House, but in the Act of 1882, changing the route from Yellowhead Pass to Kicking Horse Pass, no provision was made for the necessary rearrangements. Early in February, 1884, the Government suggested that the land grant should terminate about the same number of miles from the summit of the mountains as Jasper House had been by the route contemplated in the Act of [incorporation. The company asked that the limit should be set at the same distance on the new line as Jasper House on the old line or to the summit of the Rocky Mountains. This plan gave the company access to sections supplying timber and coal. With the same object in view it asked that a base line should be run along the valley of the Bow River. The agreement dated March 3, 1886, placed the limit at a point on the Canadian Pacific Railway where it was intersected by the boundary line between ranges ten and eleven. *Sessional Paper*, No. 34, 1887, p. 12.
[2] 49 Vic. c. 9, p. 66.

acres, valued at $1·50 per acre, from the original land grant for the purpose of cancelling the remaining debt of $10,189,521 (increased with interest from $9,880,912). The Act provided that the Government should retain lands of equal average value and quality with the lands constituting the portion of the company's land grant not "heretofore" disposed of by the company. In the passage of the Act through the House of Commons it was stated on behalf of the Government that out of lands to be conveyed to the company, there would be taken a proportion of the area so conveyed, which would be equal to the ratio which the whole area to be retained by the Government would bear to the balance of the company's grant of 25,000,000 acres remaining undisposed of by the company at the time of the passing of the Act. Consequently the Government refused to accept a suggestion of the company that the land grant should simply be reduced to 18,206,986 acres, and asked the company to furnish a statement [1] showing the amount of land disposed of at the time of the passing of the Act, to define the lands it proposed to accept in the railway belt, and to define the locality in which it proposed to accept the remainder of the grant. In the same spirit the Government refused to grant land requested to the extent of 9,000,000 acres along six "projected" branch lines. A month later the company proposed that the "projected" lines be regarded as common front lines and on each side 24 miles deep the lands in odd-numbered sections be applied to the land grant. It agreed to specify within six weeks the lands within these belts which would be accepted as part of the land grant— being not less than 7,000,000 acres, to be granted on demand, and the acreage to be ascertained after all the deductions were made. The lands were to be selected so that a minimum of railways would open a maximum of territory. The company being in possession of large tracts of land would construct its own lines or encourage other lines through the territory because of the benefits to be derived. The negotiations finally terminated with a suggestion made on May 20, 1890.[2] At that time the company had selected

[1] *Sessional Paper*, No. 34, 1892, p. 4.
[2] *Ibid.*, No. 34, 1892, p. 7.

8,347,440 acres from the railway belt and the territory in southern Manitoba. There remained about 800,000 acres to be selected. The order in council of October 24, 1882, had reserved the area between the 52nd and 54th parallels of latitude and the 104th and 116th degrees of longitude which contained about 19,000,000 acres of farming land. The Government proposed to retain the eastern half of this territory and, for ample allowance, to add another piece of land bounded on the north by the 52nd parallel, on the east by the 104th degree, on the west by the 110th degree, and on the south by the South Saskatchewan River from the 110th degree to its intersection with the northern boundary of the 48-mile belt of the main line, and the 104th degree. From the section comprised in the eastern half of the territory set aside in the October, 1882, order in council, a belt of land 24 miles wide extending north-west from the southern boundary of the reservation to the 110th degree was to be excepted for the purpose of securing the construction of a road from Saskatoon north-west to the North Saskatchewan. This road was to be built by the company and finished by April 1, 1892. Since the company proposed building a line from the point at which the branch touched the North Saskatchewan to the 110th meridian it was assumed it would extend this proposed line through Battleford to Edmonton. For the selection of the remainder of the grant, therefore, a common front line was laid down—a right line from the south-west angle of Township 35, Range 4, west of 3rd meridian to Battleford and a right line thence to the 110th degree— the depth of a belt of land on each side to be 12 miles. It was estimated this area would yield 1,000,000 acres of land, giving the company a reasonable margin from which to select. The western half of the reservation of the October, 1882, order in council with the exception of lands accepted by the company was to be released for settlement after January 1, 1891. The company suggested that the land grant should be released on January 1, 1892, instead of January 1, 1891, and that the date of completion for the road between Saskatoon and the North Saskatchewan River should be changed to October 1, 1892. With the adoption of these suggestions an agreement embodying the propositions was signed on January 7, 1891.[1]

The expiration of the reservation and the provision for the construction of branch lines for the promotion of settlement were evidences of an increasing demand for settlement of the country. This increasing demand and the resulting policy of the Government directed to the opening of the country were particularly advantageous to the company. Not only was traffic developed with settlement, but to encourage the construction of branches essential to settlement the Government acceded more willingly to requests for additional grants of land. On May 16, 1889, an application [2] was made for a land grant on a line from Brandon to or near Township 3, Range 27, and west 100 miles, and on a line from Township 3, Range 27, east to Deloraine, 25 miles. These lines were an extension of the Manitoba South-West Colonization Railway, but under the charter of that company the time for completion had elapsed. On May 18 [3] the Government approved of construction by the Canadian Pacific Railway Company and agreed to a land grant of 6,400 acres per mile or 800,000 acres. Conditional [4] to the grant the branches were to be built before the end of 1890, and the location was to be approved by the Government, but such conditions were not of a serious character. On June 4 another application [5] was made for a land grant of 6,400 acres per mile on the line from Souris to Glenboro, about sixty miles, and to this, with conditions similar to the grant of May 18,[6] the Government agreed. To facilitate financial arrangements it was further provided that the line should be divided into three sections of 20 miles each and the grant transferred with the completion of each section. On June 18 this provision was extended to the earlier branches. The date for completion,[7] December 31, 1890,

[1] *Ibid.*, No. 34, 1892, p. 21.
[2] *Ibid.*, No. 31a, 1890, p. 20. [3] *Ibid.*
[4] The agreement stipulated further—the lands to be fit for settlement, the company to reimburse the Government 10 cents per acre for the cost of surveying, each *bona fide* settler on the land granted to the company at the time the grant was earned had the right to retain land occupied by him to an extent not over 320 acres on paying the company a rate not over $2.50 per acre payable one-quarter in cash and one-quarter in each of three succeeding years with interest at 6 per cent.
[5] *Ibid.*, p. 21.
[6] *Ibid.*, p. 23. [7] *Ibid.*, No. 34, 1892, p. 64.

was changed to November 1, 1891, and again because of difficulties in securing rails to November 1, 1892.[1] Again under similar terms [2] a grant of 6,400 acres per mile was approved on February 7, 1891, for an extension of the Souris branch to the lignite coal-fields, 60 miles, to be completed December 31, 1891. The total land grant to these branches was 1,568,000 acres. To provide [3] for this the belt of land 24 miles wide from near Saskatoon through Battleford, north-west to the 4th meridian, set aside in the agreement of January 7, 1891, was widened by an addition of two strips on each side of the belt of 12 miles each, and in addition, a triangular piece of land bounded by the combined belts, by the line between Townships 34 and 35 from its intersection by the south-west limit of the combined belts to the 4th meridian, and on the west by the 4th meridian, was reserved, making a total of 1,900,000 acres.

Final adjustments of the land grant were made throughout the decade. Difficulties continued as to delay in selection. Early in 1892 a dispute [4] arose over the grant of land to the Great North-west Central Company made from the belt of the Canadian Pacific. The Canadian Pacific refused to adopt the suggestions of the Government and submit the matter to arbitration, but insisted that the Government had no power to grant lands within its belt, and eventually gained its point. Land granted to the Qu'Appelle, Long Lake and Saskatchewan Railway from the Canadian Pacific belt before the surveys had been made was returned on their completion.[5] The northern boundary of the belt was also adjusted to meet the grant of the Manitoba and North-West Railway.[6] If it was to the interest of the Government to secure an early selection of land, it was to the interest of the company to delay selection. Several sections of the land grant within the railway belt were declared to be arid or semi-arid and not acceptable to the company. Finally, to settle the question, the Government agreed to

[1] Sessional Paper, No. 34, 1892, p. 73.
[2] Ibid., No. 25, 1891, p. 109.
[3] Ibid., p. 108.
[4] Ibid., No. 34, 1892, p. 96.
[5] Ibid., p. 55.
[6] Ibid., No. 34, 1887, p. 93.

grant a solid block of land of 3,000,000 acres in southern Alberta.[1]

The land grant given directly by the Dominion Government in accordance with the act of incorporation and in accordance with the policy of opening new territory to settlement was supplemented by land acquired through the lease of other roads and the acquisition of charter privileges belonging to other railroad companies. Expansion of the road in British Columbia carried out largely through the acquisition of other companies brought additional grants. In 1892 the Columbia and Kootenay Central gave 190,000 acres and later the Columbia and Western 1,347,905 acres and the British Columbia Southern 3,600,000 acres. In western Canada the lease of the Manitoba South-West Colonization Railway brought 1,349,424 acres and in 1902 the Great North-West Central 320,004 acres. The latest acquisition relates to a grant of 4,000 acres per mile to the Interprovincial and James Bay Railway Company for the construction of a road from Kipawa to Des Quinze River, and to Ville Marie, altogether 76 miles.

The land grant, acquired by the act of incorporation, and increased by special grants for the construction of branch lines, and by the lease of other companies, enhanced in value by the policy of the company in delaying selection,[2] was not the only form of real estate of which the company became owner through the terms of the charter, through business astuteness, and through the desire of the Government to encourage the construction of transportation facilities. On January 12, 1882, for instance, the Government,[3] unable to transfer property necessary to facilitate operations which belonged to the Ontario Government, went as

[1] Irrigation works were begun by the company on this section in 1904. For the western portion of the block, water was diverted from the Bow River about 2 miles east of Calgary and carried in a main canal 17 miles to a larger reservoir for distribution. This system was completed in 1912. For the central and eastern portions a huge dam was built at Bassano and the water distributed through a canal system.
[2] Lands were first examined in the more immediate neighbourhood of principal settlements, and though at first rejected, with increased settlement and enhanced value were at length selected. Typical transactions are those stating acceptance of lands formerly rejected. *Sessional Paper*, No. 35, 1886, p. 242.
[3] *Ibid.*, No. 27, 1883, p. 32.

far as possible, and gave the company all the rights and privileges which it enjoyed. Under similar circumstances at Port Arthur a grant of land 200 feet wide and 2 miles long was requested for terminal facilities. Although this was a larger stretch of land than permitted by the Consolidated Railway Act of 1879 the Dominion Government recommended [1] to the Ontario Government that the application should be granted as far as possible [2] and expropriated the amount given under the Act of 1879. Again authority was given to expropriate 200 feet [3] along the road from Current River to River Nepigon, 64 miles, and from Moosejaw to Calgary [4] on the ground that this was necessary to secure protection from snow. At English Bay [5] despite the protest of the Superintendent-General of Indian Affairs 80 acres were expropriated for terminal facilities. In other localities the company was equally favoured.[6] On the other hand an application of January 29, 1883, for lands on the eastern section from Callander west, in addition to those granted by the Consolidated Railway Act, was refused.[7]

In questions relating to the right of way the company was generally fortunate. The contention that the extension of the main line from Port Moody to Vancouver did not entitle the company to the necessary right of way was settled favourably to the company on the ground that such an extension was a branch.[8] On the basis of this decision the contention of the Government in January, 1891, that the company was not entitled to a free right of way for a spur at Revelstoke was also defeated.[9] In a dispute in which the Government declared its intention of including the right of way within the total land grant of 25,000,000 acres, the company again protested successfully.[10] Questions [11] arose in June, 1886, as to whether the right of way through

---

[1] *Sessional Paper*, No. 27, 1883, p. 35.
[2] Lots to be reserved to access facing Thunder Bay and reasonable access to the waters of the bay to be given inhabitants.
[3] The Consolidated Railway Act grants 99 ft.
[4] *Sessional Paper*, No. 35, 1886, p. 23.   [5] *Ibid.*, No. 34b, 1887, p. 93.
[6] *Ibid.*, No. 25, 1885, p. 48.   [7] *Ibid.*, No. 27, 1883, p. 37.
[8] Major *v.* C.P.R. 13, C.S.C.R. 233.
[9] *Sessional Paper*, No. 34, 1892, pp. 58–9.
[10] *Ibid.*, No. 36, 1889, p. 239.   [11] *Ibid.*, No. 34, 1887, p. 103.

homestead lands for which the entry was not granted at the date of the passing of the Act, was vested in the company without a patent issuing from the Crown, and if the entry for the homestead was granted before the passage of the Act, whether the company was entitled to the right of way through the homestead free of charge, and whether the Government had the right to exclude the right of way from the patent to the homesteader ; all of these were decided in the company's favour and provision was made for the settlement by the Government of cases where the patent had been granted without reservation of the right of way.[1] In the construction of branches the Government generally made reservations of sections of land for right-of-way purposes.[2] On the other hand in the case of school sections a different verdict was reached. On June 26, 1889, consent [3] was asked to appropriate land in so far as it was within townships surveyed on or before October 21, 1880, and therefore vested in the Crown for school purposes. It was claimed that the land had greatly increased in value because of the railway and therefore should be sold to the company at a nominal price. To this the Government [4] replied that the company was entitled to a free grant of land required for railway purposes on the school sections in those townships which were not surveyed until after the location of the railway through such townships, but where the survey had preceded the location, the company was required to pay for its right of way. If the lands were disposed of before the location of the line the company had no claim on them. A charge of $5·20 per acre was levied for the right of way acquired under these rulings.

Station grounds and other lands for railway purposes were generally secured under favourable arrangements. Land necessary for sidings was usually granted upon the approval of the Government engineer. Ballast pits were granted where occasion demanded. On the line from Winnipeg to Calgary 2,832 acres were claimed for ballast pits [5] of which 2,077 acres were chosen from Government lands and

---

[1] Ibid., No. 34, 1887, p. 100.
[2] See the case of the Selkirk branch, 1887, Ibid., p. 94.
[3] Ibid., No. 25, 1891, p. 89.
[4] Ibid., p. 93 ff.   [5] Ibid., No. 35, 1886, p. 20.

597 from company lands. On the same stretch of line nearly one hundred station grounds from 300 ft. x 2,650 ft. (nearly 20 acres) upwards [1] were claimed. The company was also permitted to make arrangements leading to the abandonment by a settler of his claim to any portions of an even-numbered section needed for railway station grounds. From the western limits of the land grant to the eastern boundary of British Columbia the company was permitted by virtue of an agreement [2] of March 3, 1886, to select from vacant Dominion lands a tract of land not exceeding 160 acres adjoining each station. The land granted in this way was subtracted from the total land grant, but since it comprised chiefly the town sites, the arrangement was distinctly favourable to the company. At Donald, [3] British Columbia, a grant of 88 acres was given to the company, and a section of 502 acres sold at $2·50 per acre. At Griffin Lake and at Glacier, [4] lands were given for the purpose of ejecting squatters who were erecting buildings which interfered with the tourist trade, though on a similar plea, the Government refused to sell the town site at Golden [5] at $2·50 per acre, or to sell 500 acres at Revelstoke. For land situated in Government parks, leases were granted at favourable rates. For a lease [6] of 38 acres to be used for hotel purposes a charge of $20 per acre per year was made on five acres for 42 years and of $5 per acre per year on the remainder for 21 years. The regular rates were $30 per acre per year. There were, on the other hand, several evidences of resistance on the part of the Government. On October 6, 1886, the company [7] claimed a grant of 101 acres in Winnipeg as necessary for railway purposes. The Department of Railways recommended [8] the grant although the Government engineer had pointed out that it would only be necessary if the whole was to be used as stockyards. On July 29, 1890, an offer was made [9] subject to the condition that the company reserved the right to obtain it as a free grant. Upon the Government's refusal to accept these terms the

[1] *Ibid.*, p. 15.
[2] *Ibid.*, No. 34, 1887, p. 13.
[4] *Ibid.*, No. 36, 1889, p. 3.
[6] *Ibid.*, No. 25a, 1888, p. 53.
[8] *Ibid.*, No. 34b, 1887, p. 119.
[3] *Ibid.*, No. 25a, 1888, p. 6.
[5] *Ibid.*, No. 25, 1891, p. 38.
[7] *Ibid.*, No. 34, 1887, p. 98.
[9] *Ibid.*, No. 25, 1891, p. 16.

company purchased [1] the land on September 22 at $100 per acre—the Government deducting 8 acres given as right of way. At Glacier, British Columbia, in a similar fashion, the company refused to purchase [2] 40 acres, reserving the right to obtain the grant free of charge. With the Government's offer to place the matter in the hands of the Exchequer Court, the company returned a cheque for the purchase price of the land. At Griffin's Lake [3] the Government refused to grant 3½ acres of extra land and the company was obliged to purchase. At Tappen siding [4] even cheese-paring was evident—a grant of 14·97 acres was asked but only 13·42 acres given, and the remainder, 1·55 acres, purchased at $5 per acre. The Government engineer was continually on the alert in his approval of the number of acres granted. At Illicilliwaet on July 19, 1887, the company asked [5] for 56 acres and was granted 30 acres. At Moberly [6] on February 23, 1889, a grant of 45 acres was asked for—14 acres were given. At Field [7] on December 2 46 acres were applied for and 26 acres granted. At Beaver [8] on January 16, 1890, an application for 51 acres succeeded in securing 17 acres. At Sicamous [9] on February 10, 1891, an application for 5½ acres declared not to be excessive for the use of the C.P.R. and the Shuswap and Okanagan Railway was refused on the ground that the latter railway was a leased line.

The company was fortunate with respect to the location of town sites, as it had been generally with other forms of real estate. Early in 1883 an agreement[10] was made placing all town sites, (1) sections belonging jointly to the Government and to the country, (2) those belonging to the company, in the hands of trustees. These trustees, Messrs. R. B. Angus, E. B. Osler, D. A. Smith and W. B. Scarth, were accountable to the Government for the proceeds of the sales of land belonging to it. Letters patent were issued directly to the company for its lands. Under this agreement, four sections were laid out at Regina, two at Moosejaw, four at

[1] *Ibid.*, p. 17.
[2] *Ibid.*, p. 50.
[3] *Ibid.*, No. 25, 1891, p. 10.
[4] *Ibid.*, No. 34, 1896, p. 36.
[5] *Ibid.*, No. 25a, 1888, p. 16.
[6] *Ibid.*, No. 31a, 1890, p. 7.
[7] *Ibid.*, p. 5.
[8] *Ibid.*, p. 16.
[9] *Ibid.*, No. 25, 1891, p. 48.
[10] *Ibid.*, No. 34c, 1887, p. 146.

Qu'Appelle and one at Virden, and transferred to the trustees —the proceeds being divided equally between the Government and the company. The arrangement proved generally advantageous in the control given to the company in the location of town sites.

To some extent, a similar form of control was given over the agricultural policy of districts in which the land grant was reserved. On April 12, 1886, an agreement [1] was made with the Government in which all odd sections were regarded as railway lands although not yet accepted by the company. Rent of these lands was paid to the Government and the account adjusted with final acceptance. The company secured the advantage of rent [2] from the lands before they were accepted and at the same time exercised practical control of the agricultural policy of the districts concerned. The Government leased large tracts of land to ranchers on condition that the lease should terminate upon the application of the company for the land. The company exercised [3] its prerogative much to the chagrin of ranching communities.

The general business capacity of the company was amply shown in transactions involving the transfer of lands and the necessary issue of patents. Promptness in the issue of these instruments was essential in the sale of lands, and in securing power to evict squatters. To avoid unusual delays, the company compiled a list of lands most speedily required and patents were registered in the shortest possible time. Difficulties occasioned by the refusal of registrars to register the instruments were overcome through measures suggested by the company. In 1887 on application of the company,[4] delays and expense were reduced through the issuance of patents direct to purchasers of company lands. Attempts were made to eliminate the governmental red tape involving unusual delays in cases of mistake in the name of the patentee, of filing acts of incorporation and letters of attorney, of incomplete descriptions, of the death

[1] *Sessional Paper*, No. 34, 1887, p. 31.
[2] To March 31, 1887, rent received on the company's account totalled $7,711.
[3] *Sessional Paper*, No. 31a, 1890, p. 18.
[4] *Ibid.*, No. 34, 1887, p. 106.

of the patentee, and of changes in the form of patents, but with little success. Many sections were asked for in error, were already sold or squatted upon. There were errors in plans and surveys, and lands were sold by the company outside its belt by mistake. Inaccurate descriptions in patents for the right of way largely disappeared and some improvement was made by excepting the right of way from patents to settlers and granting the patents direct to the company. In the form of patents the company insisted that no reservations [1] should be made to the Crown for gold, silver, copper or other mines, and a patent reserving fisheries was immediately returned for correction. In this the Government did not concur but promised to omit such reservations in later patents. [2]

Questions regarding timber limits were of a particularly difficult character. [3] The company was careful to protect its own interests but careless in regard to interests of the Government. In September, 1885, protests [4] were made by the company against the cutting of timber on sections within the reserve of the Manitoba and South-Western Railway. The Government recognized the validity of the protests, and parties owning timber mills on the sections involved were notified that their licences would not be renewed. On the other hand charges were made that the company was unusually wasteful [5] in the cutting of lumber on Government lands. It was stated that lumbermen [6] were selling lumber cut for the company to other parties. Complaints were made that on the Bow River [7] the company was cutting timber belonging to others. It was held [8] that the timber in question, namely that on the berths of the Eau Clair and Bow River Timber Company, had been cut before the grants were made, but the Government proved this untrue. Charges [9] that timber of more than 5 in. at the butt was used, were denied. The company [10] persistently refused to give any statement as to the amount

[1] *Ibid.*, No. 25, 1885, p. 230.
[2] *Ibid.*, No. 36, 1889, p. 281.
[3] For a statement of the general privileges granted, see Clause 10, Article 6 and Clause 19 of the Act of Incorporation, Appendix B.
[4] *Sessional Paper*, No. 35, 1886, p. 261.
[5] *Ibid.*, p. 259. [6] *Ibid.*, p. 257. [7] *Ibid.*, p. 262.
[8] *Ibid.*, p. 266. [9] *Ibid.* [10] *Ibid.*, p. 264.

of lumber cut. To check the abuses which these protests implied the Government adopted various measures but with varying success. As to the cutting of timber without a permit it was decided [1] to hold the company liable for timber cut by trespassers until it proved itself guiltless. Moreover, permits were restricted [2] to timber used for construction purposes on the main line. It was even held that the company was not entitled [3] to take timber free for the construction of the extension of the main line to Vancouver. Restrictions [4] were placed on the right of the company to cut timber for sale because of the disadvantages to other lumber dealers of competition. In an attempt of the Government to supply timber necessary for construction purposes, five timber berths [5] of ten square miles each were reserved in convenient localities one on each side of Boulder Creek, and one on the Columbia River, the Kicking Horse River and Otter Tail Creek. Timber [6] licences could be obtained for an area not exceeding 1,000 acres and for not more than four years at $10 per year and a charge of 15 c. per tree and 20 c. per 1,000 feet in logs. In the construction of snowsheds, the company held that timber used for this purpose was timber used in the construction of the main line and therefore should be free under the terms of the contract. For this purpose [7] it was claimed that cedar was necessary and could not be found within the reservations, and that the reservations were too far distant. It was also claimed that the reservations had been made to prevent a combination of mill owners from obtaining a monopoly on timber. For these reasons the company proceeded to cut timber outside of the limits. Against this the Government protested, stating that there was no danger of monopoly since the company controlled the freight rates, and that the object of the reservations was to prevent the slashing of trees. Finally it threatened to sell the reservations if the company persisted in cutting timber on Crown lands.

In the collection of timber dues the Government finally

---

[1] *Sessional Paper*, No. 34, 1887, p. 39.   [2] *Ibid.*
[3] *Ibid.*, p. 42.   [4] *Ibid.*, p. 46.   [5] *Ibid.*, p. 56.   [6] *Ibid.*, p. 51.
[7] *Ibid.*, No. 25a, 1888, p. 27.

secured the promise from the company that it would make deductions in the case of all parties contracting with it who had not a clearance from the Government. In the case of good trees cut by contractors, the company [1] was charged the price of lumber. For cordwood a charge of 25 c. per cord was made, for ties 3 c. each, for piles ½ c. per foot, and for fence posts \$2·50 per thousand. From December, 1885, to May 31, 1887, \$4,744·75 was paid [2] for cordwood, and the Government sanctioned [3] the deduction of 26,919 cords claimed to have been used on construction engines although the amount was recognized as exorbitant. To a contention [4] of the company on February 3, 1890, that it was entitled to patents with the construction of every ten miles of line and therefore was not required to pay timber dues, a ruling was given that the company had no right to timber farther than 50 feet from the centre of the track. To an application[5] for limits 14 and 15 on the Columbia River, the Government answered in offering them by tender.

The more immediate results of the charter privileges pertaining to land grants [6] and other forms of real estate, enhanced in value largely through the business astuteness of the company, were revealed in the amount of proceeds from these sources. The most significant item of these

---

[1] *Ibid.*, No. 34, 1887, p. 49.
[2] *Ibid.*, No. 25a, 1888, p. 29.
[3] *Ibid.*, p. 42.
[4] *Ibid.*, No. 25, 1891, p. 78.
[5] *Ibid.*, p. 80.
[6] According to the charter "lands of the company in the North-West Territories until they are either sold or occupied shall also be free from such taxation for twenty years after the grant thereof from the crown." Attempts of the prairie provinces to tax these lands for school and municipal purposes have been unsuccessful, 35 C.S.C.R. 551. The Privy Council, as the result of an appeal, held, in a judgment of February 3, 1911 (1911 *Appeal Cases*, p. 328), that unoccupied lands were not taxable until twenty years after the actual grant of letters patent to the settler and that lands sold on the instalment plan were not taxable until all the instalments were paid. This situation has been an important factor in the natural resources question. Martin, Chester, *Natural Resources Question, Report of the Ontario Commission on Railway Taxation,* 1905, p. 190 ff.; Clark, A. B., *An Outline of Provincial and Municipal Taxation in British Columbia, Alberta and Saskatchewan;* Vineberg, S., *Provincial and Local Taxation in Canada.* Land acquired through subsidiary companies and in other ways on the other hand is liable to taxation except in cases of special provision. These taxes vary in different provinces and are relatively unimportant. *Ibid.*

returns was that from land sales.[1] In 1890 the company had sold 3,601,428 acres of the grant secured from the Manitoba South-West Colonization Railway and had realized $11,462,165 or an average of 3·09 c. per acre—the average price of land sold in that year being 3·834 cts. Deducting 6,793,014 acres surrendered by agreement to the Government and adding 640,000 acres earned on the Souris branch, the company held in that year 16,488,959 acres. During the next decade the land situation reflected the general period of depression. In 1893 scarcely any land was sold and it was not until ten years later that the price reached the level of 1890. In the later years to 1914 the average rapidly increased—the price in that year being $16·57. The war period generally brought a decline. Land in Alberta brought under cultivation by irrigation works sold at a much higher price. The average price in 1909 was $24·71 per acre, in 1918 $42·94 and in 1921 $53·13. The receipts from the land grant varied widely as a result of the susceptibility of the land situation, of the policy of the company in opening up settlements, of climatic conditions, of periods of boom peculiar to the north-west, and of periods of depression influencing the trade of Canada

---

[1] Land receipts, 1889–1921 :

1889*	$31,183·52	1907	$8,316,335·43
1890	33,541·85	1908	5,701,854·20
1891	14,018·18	1909	4,193,129·62
1892	105,788·80	1910	6,106,488·15
1893	65,064·88	1911	877,616·73
1894	68,860·40	1912	927,136·11
1895	20,317·18	1913	5,795,977·60
1896	216,941·62	1914	1,129,177·08
1897	217,081·29	1915	374.550·16
1898	233,598·11	1916	3,106,382·51
1899	400,608·25	1916 (six months)	1,547,080·19
1901†	667,128·11	(18 months).	
1902	1,569,901·48	1917*	6,588,740·40
1903	2,908,028·55	1918	5,834,054·65
1904	2,703,053·21	1919	4,654,512·43
1905	3,302,758·98	1920	3,852,376·77
1906	5,168,501·63	1921	1,979,480·89

These statistics are compiled from company reports from sections described as Receipts and Expenditure, sub-heading Land Department, Deferred Payments. Sales expenses and other items are deducted from the proceeds of sales as per account.

Compiled from *C.P.R. Reports.*

* Calendar year.   † Fiscal year.

generally. From $105,789 in 1892, they declined to $20,317 in three years as a result of the depression. In 1902 proceeds from land sales had increased to $1,569,901 and in 1913 to $5,795,978. A general decline was evident in the war years and to 1921. The largest returns—$8,316,335—from land sales were received in 1907. These proceeds were supplemented by receipts from the sale of town sites. In 1890 the sale of town sites had brought $2,056,291. From nine acres of land given by the Government of British Columbia at Vancouver Island in consideration of the extension of the main line to Port Moody, 9 miles, the company secured sufficient revenue to pay for the extension and to build a branch to Westminster in addition. To 1916 the proceeds from land and town sites [1] totalled $123,810,124.

In 1921 the company held 5,606,351 acres valued at approximately $91,962,630. Of this 3,446,416 acres were agricultural lands in the western provinces valued at from $10 to $13 per acre, 352,714 acres were irrigated lands valued at from $30 to $40 per acre, 563,732 acres were timber lands valued at from $1·50 to $3 per acre, 1,073,651 acres in British Columbia valued at from $2 to $5 per acre and 94,584 acres in town sites in the prairie provinces. Total town sites were valued at $20,157,900. In addition coal lands, petroleum rights and natural-gas rights were held at nominal figures. It is scarcely possible that the number of acres held will increase appreciably through later land grants, but that there will be an increase in value is probable. At best the land grant is an asset which will continue to decrease in importance, though such a decrease is not of vital significance to the prosperity of the company. The total proceeds [2] secured from the land grant and town sites to 1916 were less than the net revenue from operation for three years ending June 30, 1916, and about equal to the gross revenue from operation in the year 1912. The importance of land sales as an item in the gross receipts of the

[1] *Railway Inquiry Commission Report*, 1917, p. xvii.
[2] $123,810,124. Net proceeds from land sales, deducting expenditure on irrigation, hotels, development projects, etc., in 1916 were $68,255,803. In 1921 net proceeds from lands and town sites totalled $93,798,267, surpassing in that year the estimated value of the assets, in lands and properties, $91,962,630.

company varied widely. But generally periods of prosperity in which net earnings tended to increase were periods in which land sales were largest and periods of depression with declining net earnings were periods of declining land sales. The land situation was probably more sensitive to local conditions, but these in turn reflected general and prevailing world-wide conditions. In any event land sales are destined to be of less importance in the future.

D. TOTAL RECEIPTS

Net earnings from operation, other income, and proceeds from land sales, included in total receipts constituted a final index of the earning capacity of the road. In total receipts, fluctuations in constituent items occasioned by changes in accounting practice disappeared and the general standing of the company was most clearly revealed. Net earnings from operation were directly related to the growth of traffic. Other income because of changes in the classification of accounts became more directly related to traffic but included earnings from securities held and though these were related to traffic, fluctuations were of less significance. Proceeds from land sales fluctuated violently, because of a variety of considerations, but generally reflected the importance of the west.

Prior to 1888 land receipts were largely expended in advertising campaigns and in improvements, and were consequently unimportant. Since that time large portions of these proceeds have been devoted to the same purpose, but the statistics chosen represent the net amount remaining after such expenditures have been made. These statistics have been taken from " receipts and expenditures." They do not represent the amount realized from land sales in any given year but the amount actually received after allowance for deferred payments and for expenditures for purposes stated in that particular account. Other income was not of material importance until 1892, after which date the fund guaranteed by a deposit with the Government for the payment of dividends was exhausted. The first decade of the company's history was particularly subject to the uncertainties of early expansion, and was consequently of slight importance from the standpoint of total receipts.

From 1888 to 1892 total receipts [1] increased steadily as a result of the increase in net earnings, and to 1894 declined to a marked extent with a decline in net earnings, and despite a slight increase in land receipts and a marked increase in other income. Throughout the remainder of the decade, total receipts increased steadily with a similar increase in net earnings, despite a decline in other income to 1897 and in land receipts in 1895. Land receipts increased slowly during the first two years of this period, and with other income very rapidly in the last two years. In 1901 a decline in net earnings, a decline in other income, and an increase in land receipts, brought a decline in total receipts, and to 1903, an increase in all the constituent items, an increase in the total. In 1904 a decline in land sales and in net earnings led to a decline in the total, despite an increase in other income. Total receipts and land earnings increased from 1905 to 1907 despite a decline in other income in 1906. In 1908 all these items declined. In 1909 a slight increase in total receipts followed a slight increase in net earnings, an increase in other income, and a decline in land

[1] Total receipts, 1888–1921 :

1888*. . . .	$4,175,981·10	1906	$29,458,684·73
1889	6,040,742·86	1907	35,260,475·94
1890	6,333,242·36	1908	29,036,094·25
1891	8,023,678·05	1909	29,055,280·92
1892	8,729,739·08	1910	42,372,921·31
1893	8,016,343·80	1911	42,624,303·72
1894	6,825,995·39	1912	49,383,964·34
1895	8,054,181·13	1913	58,640,003·08
1896	8,835,688·46	1914	52,142,975·29
1897	10,861,563·66	1915	44,918,509·14
1898	11,132,336·59	1916	62,273,257·91
1899	13,780,972·31	1916 (6 months)	38,837,198·50
1900† (6 months)	6,289,305·50	1917*. . . .	63,848,058·72
1901	13,709,928·71	1918	48,465,193·16
1902	16,614,640·53	1919	46,636,890·65
1903	20,031,686·74	1920	47,971,869·18
1904	18,607,426·75	1921	47,168,426·32
1905	20,362,510·91		

Compiled from *C.P.R. Reports.*

* Calendar year. † Fiscal year.

These do not include contributions to pension fund. This fund was started in 1903 with an original contribution of $250,000. To 1911 yearly contributions of $80,000 were made, to 1915 of $125,000, in 1916 of $200,000, and to 1921 of $500,000.

receipts. From 1909 to 1913 total receipts practically doubled as a result of an increase of 100 per cent. in net earnings, an increase of 200 per cent. in other income, and an increase in land receipts in 1910, a marked decline in 1911 and rapid recovery in the last two years. In 1914 and 1915 a decline in total receipts followed a marked decline in land receipts, and in net earnings, despite an increase in other income. In 1916 total receipts increased as a result of an increase in net earnings, and in land sales, and a slight decline in other income. In the following year, total receipts again increased, for the first time, despite a decrease in net earnings, and with an increase in other income and in land receipts. In 1918 and 1919, as a result of a decline in net earnings and in land receipts, and despite an increase in other income, total receipts declined. In 1920 an increase in net earnings and in other income brought an increase in total receipts, despite a decline in land receipts. In 1921, for the first time, an increase in net earnings and in other income was followed by a decline in total receipts, because of the decline in land receipts. With two exceptions, 1917 and 1921, total receipts fluctuated in consonance with net earnings. The exception in 1917 was the result of the reclassification of accounts, which transferred steamship earnings from earnings from operation to other income, and strictly speaking was not an exception. In 1921 the increase in net earnings and in other income was slight, and the result of considerable economy, consequently it did not offset the marked decline in land receipts. Net earnings were therefore of dominant importance in the total receipts of the company.

Net earnings were in turn dependent on gross earnings and expenses. Expenses related to passenger traffic were unusually high, and the percentage of passenger earnings to gross earnings was much lower than that of freight earnings. Consequently net earnings dependent on gross earnings were in turn particularly dependent on freight earnings. This was especially the case since freight traffic was handled much more efficiently and since freight expenses were consequently lower. Net earnings were, therefore, largely dependent on freight earnings and on freight traffic.

Freight earnings and freight traffic have depended directly and indirectly to a very large extent on the expansion of western Canada, especially with the development of the west, and with the effect of higher rates resulting from a non-competitive situation in that area. The contributions of western Canada were evident in the receipts from land. It follows, therefore, that to a very large extent the net earnings and total receipts of the Canadian Pacific Railway have been directly obtained from western Canada.

X

Capital

PHYSICAL expansion of the road to a large extent determined, and was determined by, the growth of traffic. The development of physical property was generally reflected in capital, represented by instruments as bonds and stocks, and by accounts as surplus and reserves ; and the growth of traffic was generally reflected in total receipts, which were disbursed in the form of payment of interest on bonds, of dividends on stocks, and of additions to reserve and surplus accounts. Disbursements depended largely, therefore, on the quantity and form of the securities involved, and these in turn depended on the particular conditions under which capital was obtained, and on the policy adopted to meet those conditions. Government aid was a determining condition as to the character and extent of securities issued. Aid in land, in money, and in other privileges outlined in the charter, enhanced in value through the business astuteness of the company, was of vital importance in the construction of the main line. Of necessity it continued to exercise a significant influence over the financial policy of the company.

The business astuteness of the company, evident in relation to the land grant and other privileges, was prominent in later negotiations with the Government leading to the final settlement of the payment of the money subsidy. After the completion of the main line, a financial controversy appeared as to the payment of interest on $9,880,912 loaned by the Government in the Act of 1885. The loan was secured by a first lien on all the unsold lands of the

company, and the company claimed [1] that since it was
secured only by the lands, interest could be paid only from
the proceeds of land sales.   At the same time the Government had in its possession $8,996,000 of land grant bonds.
Questions arose as to whether these bonds were still subject
to redemption under the terms of the land grant mortgage,
since the road was completed and the bonds therefore
earned, and as to whether the Government could collect
interest on these bonds and apply it to the interest due on
the loan of $9,880,912.   These questions were asked in a
letter dated January 22, 1886, and on January 28 the
company paid no interest [2] on the loan.   A ruling [3] was
made on February 8 in accordance with the ruling of January
7, 1885.   It was held that the land grant bonds might be
treated as earned and issued, and that the Government was
entitled to the interest, such interest to be applied to the
principal and interest on the loan of $9,880,912.   The
security for the loan was : first, $8,996,000 of land grant
bonds ; second, a first lien on all the company's lands after
the land grant bonds were redeemed ; third, the Algoma
branch and the interest of the company in leased lines ;
fourth, the company's entire revenue, and lastly, the
liability of the company.   Consequently the loan was not
secured by the land alone, and the company was obliged
to pay the interest on it.

A final adjustment of the main accounts was made in
an agreement [4] of March 30, 1886.   The company agreed
to pay the debt of $19,150,700 to the Government in two
instalments, the first on May 1, 1886, and the second on
July 1, with interest at 4 per cent.   The remainder of the
debt, $9,880,912, was extinguished by reduction of the land
grant.   On payment of the debt, the Government agreed to
cancel all the land grant bonds in excess of $5,000,000
held as security for the construction of the road, to return
$300,000 of debenture stock of the Ontario and Quebec
Railroad, [5] deposited with the Government as security for
the loan, and to authorize the company to mortgage the

[1] *Sessional Paper*, No. 35, 1886, p. 19.
[2] *Ibid.*, p. 22.   [3] *Ibid.*, p. 23.
[4] 49 Vic. C9.   [5] 47 Vic. c. 61, sect. 1.

Algoma branch to the same amount per mile as the charter of the company authorized for the main line. The company was given power to issue land grant bonds on the remainder of the land grant, though not in excess of $2 per acre, and after provision had been made for the bonds already outstanding. Of these the public held $3,612,500, and against them the company had interest bearing obligations for lands sold on deferred payments, $1,579,708 and 14,734,667 acres of land. The Government accepted the new land grant bonds to be issued, after provision had been made for the outstanding bonds, in lieu of the $5,000,000 of land grant bonds held as security for construction of the road. On May 1, 1886, the company paid in $9,887,347, and on July 1, $9,163,353. The land [1] was formally agreed upon on July 22.

A minor adjustment was made later with reference to the nine miles of permanent road which had not been built in the Rocky Mountains. The engineer-in-chief held that the grade of 238 feet per mile used for the temporary road was below the standard of the Union Pacific and $460,087 of subsidy was withheld. On November 2, 1886, an agreement [2] was approved by the Government, and on November 15 signed. In consideration of the early completion of the road, and of its being opened for traffic and regular operation on June 28, and in consideration of the repayment of the loans, it was agreed : (1) that the Government should accept the road ; (2) that the company should accept the road built by the Government subject to deficiencies ; (3) that the Government should pay the balance of the subsidy ; (4) that the Government should release $5,000,000 of land grant bonds held as security, and (5) that the company should make improvements at Mount Stephen and should deposit $1,000,000 of land grant bonds with the Government to be held until they were made. On November 20, $458,058 was paid [3] to the company. To this amount, objection was made that no adjustment was provided as to the value of ballast pit rails on the Pembina branch, and of materials on the Thunder Bay branch. The Government replied [4] on December 8 that the rails were to be transferred

[1] *Sessional Paper*, No. 34, 1887, p. 105.
[2] *Ibid.*, No. 34b, p. 127.   [3] *Ibid.*, p. 128.
[4] *Ibid.*, p. 129.

to the company at cost price—cost being the amount paid by the Government in 1879, the date of purchase—and that this amount, plus the cost of materials on the Thunder Bay branch, had been deducted. A final dispute arose as to the character of the road handed over by the Government in British Columbia. Messrs. John A. Boyd, Thos. C. Keefer and Chas. C. Gregory were appointed as arbitrators by an Order in Council [1] of January 5, 1888. A claim of $12,000,000 on the part of the company gained an award of $579,255.

Aid given directly to the company by the Dominion Government was supplemented by aid from Provincial and Municipal Governments, especially through assistance given to subsidiary companies. This aid, as has been shown, was given partly in land grants. It was also given in the form of subscriptions to bonds or stock, and in cash payments. The total amount of aid given in cash by the Dominion Government was [2] $30,289,343. The cost of the road handed over by the Government to the company was $37,785,320. Provincial Governments gave directly to the Canadian Pacific a relatively small sum, $412,878, and municipalities, $464,761. Through subsidiary companies the Dominion Government gave indirectly to the Canadian Pacific in cash, $13,129,873, Provincial Governments gave $12,016,257, and municipalities, $4,632,422. Almost as much cash aid was given to the company indirectly through its subsidiaries as directly through the charter. In the acquisition of lines through subsidiary companies the company was in a strategic position. These lines, often largely built with money subscribed by various Governments,[3] were in many cases unable to meet heavy fixed charges, because of reckless expenditure in construction, encouraged by financial aid of this character, and because of ill-advised construction.[4] Operating expenses were seriously increased because of this ill-advised construction, and with low revenue a characteristic feature, the companies were involved in serious difficulties. Consequently the Canadian Pacific was in a

[1] *Ann. Report Dept. of Railways and Canals*, 1894–5, p. xvi.
[2] *Railway Inquiry Commission*, 1917, p. xvi.
[3] British Columbia was typically a province in which difficulties of construction made necessary the existence of various subsidiary companies and liberal Government support.
[4] See *Economic Journal*, vol. 12, p. 405.

position to acquire the roads at a relatively low price, and although they were inefficiently operated as separate lines, as parts of a complete system or as part of a through connexion, they were of considerable advantage. For example, the Canada Central was subsidized from Pembroke to Callander, 120 miles, at $12,000 per mile by the Dominion Government, by a municipal bonus of $75,000; and by municipal subscriptions of $42,500. As part of a through route to the west it was invaluable. Again; the South-Eastern Railway, consisting of several ill-pieced sections of road, was acquired through the foreclosure of a mortgage, and became a valuable portion of a through route to Boston and St. John. Branch lines unable to exist by themselves became valuable feeders to a complete system, as in the case of the Manitoba South-West Colonization Railway, the Laurentian Railway, or the St. Lawrence and Ottawa Railway. Charters of subsidiary companies were of a valuable character. Bonds and securities could be issued on the property of the subsidiary line without seriously impairing the security of bonds on the main lines. Loans, subsidies, and various privileges which could not be obtained directly by the Canadian Pacific could be obtained through these charters. Access to territory otherwise impossible was obtained through extension rights. The disadvantages occasioned through heavy operating expenses were, in contrast to the advantages, of relatively slight importance.

The strategic position of the company, evident in the substantial Government aid and in the acquisition of other roads under favourable conditions, was a cause and a result of the stability of the management under which the policy of the company was formulated. The management which carried through the construction of the main line with minor changes remained in control throughout the history of the road. In 1886 Messrs. Grenfell and Rose of London retired in favour of Mr. Levi P. Morton and Mr. R. J. Cross of New York, members of the firm of Morton, Bliss & Co., the American branch of Morton, Rose & Co. In the following year, Mr. H. S. Northcote retired, and the Hon. G. A. Kirkpatrick, M.P., of Kingston, was appointed. In 1888 Mr. Grenfell again became a director, as did also Mr. W. D.

Matthews of Toronto, Mr. D. McInnes of Hamilton, and Mr.
J. J. C. Abbott, solicitor of the company.   Following these
changes, in the next year, Messrs. Grenfell and Morton retired
in favour of Mr. Thomas Skinner of London.   In 1890, Mr.
Martinsen retired in favour of Mr. Samuel Thomas of New
York.   In 1891 Mr. Thomas and Mr. Kirkpatrick retired,
and Mr. J. W. Mackay of New York was appointed.   Two
years later Mr. R. J. Cross retired.   Mr. C. R. Hosmer
was added in 1899.   Mr. J. W. Mackay died in 1902.
The Hon. G. Drummond, the Hon. R. Mackay and
the Hon. R. G. Reid were added in the following year.
Mr. L. J. Forget was added in 1909. The Hon. G. Drummond
was replaced by Mr. A. R. Creelman in 1910.   Mr. H. S.
Holt was added in 1912, and Mr. A. Nanton took the place
of Mr. Creelman in 1914.   Mr. J. K. L. Ross and Sir George
Bury became members in 1915.   Senator F. L. Beique
and Sir Vincent Meredith were added in 1916, and Mr. R.
Mackay retired.   Sir George Bury retired from the directorate and the executive committee in 1918.   Mr. R. Dunsmuir
was succeeded by the Hon. W. J. Shaughnessy in 1920.
Sir John Eaton became a director on December 8, 1919,
and continued until his death in 1922.   These changes were
changes in personnel rather than changes in the interests
represented.   Mr. Sandford Fleming was a member from
1885 until the time of his death in 1916.   Mr. Donald
McInnes was a member until 1904, the date of his death.
Mr. G. R. Harris represented Blake Bros. & Co. of Boston
from 1885 to 1904.   Mr. W. D. Matthews was a member from
1889 until his death in 1920.   Mr. Thomas Skinner has been
a member from 1888.   Membership of the executive committee was even more continuous.   In 1887 this committee
was revived with Messrs. Stephen, Van Horne, Smith and
Angus as members.   Mr. R. B. Angus has been a member
since that date.[1]   Lord Strathcona was a member until
1915, the date of his death.   Sir Edmund Osler has been
a member since 1899.   Mr. D. McNicoll became a member
in 1907 and continued until 1917.   During the war period,
Mr. Grant Hall and Mr. H. Holt became members.   In the

[1] The death of Mr. Angus since this book went to press removes the last
member of the first directorate of the Company.

more important offices continuity has also been characteristic. Mr. W. C. Van Horne became president in 1890,
and Mr. T. G. Shaughnessy vice-president. Mr. Van Horne
continued as president until 1899, when he became chairman
of the executive committee. He was a member of this
committee until his death in 1916. Mr. Shaughnessy
became vice-president in 1891 and president in 1899,
continuing in that capacity until 1918, when he became chairman of the executive committee and was succeeded by
Mr. E. W. Beatty as president. From the year of its inception to 1918 the company has had three presidents, all of
whom had been with the road from the beginning. Sir
William Van Horne and Lord Shaughnessy were typically
expert railroad men, and from the standpoint of technical
efficiency the road was admirably served.

The continuity and ability of the management were causes
and effects of the dominance of individual members as
holders of capital stock. In October, 1883,[1] there were
550,000 shares of this stock held by 525 shareholders. These
shareholders were scattered through the states of the
Union, through the British Isles, and four of the leading
countries of Europe, and through different parts of Canada.
The State of New York had within its boundaries individuals
holding 290,000 shares, the province of Quebec over 100,000,
the British Isles over 90,000, Holland 57,000 and France
15,000. Shares were concentrated largely in New York
and Montreal. Morton, Bliss & Company held 32,000
shares, Mr. George Stephen 31,000, Morton, Rose &
Company 27,500, Mr. D. A. Smith 23,000, Mr. D. McIntyre
20,000, Mr. R. B. Angus, 15,000, and Messrs. J. S. Kennedy
and J. J. Hill 10,000 each. In 1915 it was stated that 13·64
per cent. of the shareholders were in Canada, 62·88 per cent.
in the United Kingdom, and 10·39 per cent. in the United
States. Assuming that slight change [2] has been made since

[1] *Sessional Paper*, No. 31, 1884, p. 225.
[2] On March 1, 1921, shares were distributed :

United Kingdom	.	.	1,242,837	..	47·8	per cent.
Canada .	.	.	460,838	..	17·73	,,
United States .	.	.	626,510	..	24·10	,,
France .	.	.	79,123	..	3·04	,,
Other holdings.	.	.	190,692	..	7·33	,

1915—a reasonable assumption in view of the stable character of the shares as securities—it would appear that 47·8 per cent. of the shares were distributed among 62·88 per cent. of the shareholders in the United Kingdom, and that control from the United Kingdom was not concentrated but rather in the hands of several smaller shareholders; that 24·10 per cent. of the shares were distributed among 10·39 per cent. of the shareholders in the United States, and that control was more distinctly concentrated, and that 17·73 per cent. of the shares were distributed among 13·64 per cent. of the shareholders in Canada—further evidence of concentrated control.[1] In 1921 eleven members of the directorate were resident in Montreal, two members in Toronto, one member each in Winnipeg, and London, England. All the members of the executive committee were resident in Montreal except Sir Edmund Osler, a resident of Toronto. This situation, of course, was rather the result of the fact that the head offices of the company were in Montreal than of any question of control. But generally control remained concentrated in the hands of a continuous management.

The liberal character of Government aid, continuity and efficiency of management, physical expansion of the road, growth of traffic, and the character of securities issued, were interdependent factors upon which depended the disbursement of net earnings. In the period prior to the completion of the main line the attitude of the Government toward the company was of considerable importance. The difficulties of the period from 1870 to 1880 in relation to Government contracts, the economic and national development of Canada which demanded the immediate construction of the road, and the difficulties of construction, made essential construction by private enterprise and necessitated liberal terms. The terms were no less liberal as a result of the experience and ability of the promoters of the private corporation shown in the success attending their efforts in the construction and operation of the St. Paul, Minneapolis and Manitoba Railway, and as a result of an appreciation

---

[1] Additional sales of stock were largely subscribed by shareholders.— *Address of Lord Shaughnessy to C.P.R. shareholders*, May 1, 1918.

of the fact that party government involved continued support to the corporation from the date of initiation of construction to the date of completion. The success of the Government was the success of the Canadian Pacific Railway.[1] As a result of this inevitable liberality [2] of the Government, the financial policy of the company during the period prior to the completion of the main line was characterized by issues of stock. The general failure of the company to finance construction through the sale of land grant bonds led to an attempt to sell stock. Earnings derived from roads acquired in Eastern Ontario were far from sufficient to warrant confidence in the company's capital stock, and a device in the nature of a guarantee for payment of dividends in the deposit of funds with the Government, to increase and stabilize the price of stock, failed. This deposit seriously reduced the company's working funds, and tended to destroy the confidence it was hoped the device would create. The payment of dividends to the extent of $2,128,000 to August, 1883, to keep up the price of stock, or to prevent shareholders from sacrificing property [3] because of attacks on the company, had an effect contrary to that intended. With uncertain market conditions, effective hostile attacks on the New York market by the Northern Pacific and on the London market by the Grand Trunk, and the questionableness of the policy itself, stock declined in price. Failure to finance construction through the sale of stock occasioned persistent demands from the Government in which loans were successfully secured at favourable rates. Moreover, governmental patronage was of consequence in stabilizing the position of the company. Objections on the part of the opposition occasioned unusual caution on the part of the Government, but the dependence of the Government on the success of the road made the loans inevitable. Aid in the form of loans from the Government was in part an explanation of

[1] The words of John Pope: " The day the Canadian Pacific busts, the Conservative party busts the day after." Skelton, O. D., *Life and Letters of Sir Wilfrid Laurier*, vol. I, p. 273.

[2] It will be understood that the word " liberality " is used to express neither condemnation nor approval. It is intended to refer only to the fact that a substantial aid was given.

[3] Circular to shareholders, December 29, 1883. *Sessional Papers*, No. 25, 1885, p. 237.

the financial policy of the company in issuing stock rather than bonds. The ability of the company to secure this aid was of natural consequence to the character of the securities issued.

As a result of the liberality of the Government, the number of bonds outstanding was relatively small. Consequently with the completion of the main line the net earnings of the company were not unduly burdened in the payment of fixed charges. In 1886 the amount paid [1] in fixed charges (including rentals) totalled $3,068,082 or $687·29 per mile. Throughout the whole period of the company's history it continued to remain of minor importance. In 1890 it had increased to $4,246,618 or $763·23 per mile, in 1899 to $6,816,676 or $973·81 per mile and in 1921 to $11,519,072 or $856·81 per mile. The percentage of fixed charges to net earnings decreased from 55·7 per cent. in 1899 to 30·7 per cent. in 1921. This favourable situation in the later years was not an immediate result of Government aid but an indirect result—through the rapid physical expansion of the road and the increase in traffic which the liberality of the Government had made possible. The rapid increase in net earnings enabled the company through the soundness

[1] 1886–1921 :

	Fixed Charges	Fixed Charges per Mile		Fixed Charges	Fixed Charges per Mile
1886*	$3,068.081·84	$687·29	1905	$7,954,065·76	$928·34
1887	3,250,263·81	640·57	1906	8,350,544·84	951·41
1888	3,544,351·00	683·44	1907	8,511,755·56	929·84
1889	3,779,132·94	751·46	1908	8,770,076·71	930·41
1890	4,246,618·00	763·23	1909	9,427,032·74	954·34
1891	4,664,493·45	808·96	1910	9,916,940·33	984·01
1892	5,102,018·09	848·21	1911	10,011,071·44	968·00
1893	5,338,597·22	843·45	1912	10,524,937·49	977·51
1894	6,581,378·82	1,038·66	1913	10,876,352·15	956·91
1895	6,659,478·32	1,033·83	1914	10,227,311·17	864·88
1896	6,708,084·42	1,035·83	1915	10,446,509·83	844·64
1897	6,783,367·26	1,032·79	1916	10,306,196·00	797·87
1898	6,774,321·24	1,013·96	1916	5,132,551·09	six months
1899	6,816,676·36	973·81	1917*	10,229,143·43	776·58
1900†	3,434,244·67	(six months).	1918	10,177,512·98	783·48
1901	7,305,835·49	965·99	1919	10,161,509·77	758·94
1902	7,334,825·09	966·76	1920	10,177,408·99	759·39
1903	7,052,197·27	910·19	1921	11,519,071·97	856·81
1904	7,586,096·24	910·47			

Compiled from *C.P.R. Reports.*

* Calendar year.   † Fiscal year.

of its position to secure capital during the later years at a comparatively low rate of interest. Application [1] was made to Parliament in 1889 for power to issue debenture stock for the purpose of consolidating obligations to the company and reducing the interest rate on those obligations. Two years later power [2] was given to raise additional debenture stock for other purposes. To enable the company to secure capital without increasing the fixed charges, the Government was asked to restore the privilege granted in the charter but cancelled in the Loan Act of 1884-5 of issuing 4 per cent. preference stock. In 1893 power [3] was given to issue stock which was non-cumulative, which was limited in quantity to one-half the common stock and which was not to affect any lien created by a mortgage debenture or bond. The depression [4] of the nineties which occasioned a decline in earnings and in the earnings of subsidiary lines, the Duluth, South Shore and Atlantic, and the Minneapolis, St. Paul and Sault Ste. Marie, made impossible the sale of preference stock at a satisfactory price and even made it necessary to reassume £300,000 of this stock negotiated before the depression. With recovery £100,000 was marketed [5] at nearly par in 1897 and £2,285,000 a year later. At the end of the decade, the company had outstanding $26,791,000 of this stock. During the period

[1] 52 Vic. c. 69. This stock is a first charge on the road, but it is perpetual and irredeemable with no right of foreclosure in the event of default.

[2] 54-55 Vic. c. 71.

[3] 56 Vic. c. 41.

[4] C.P.R. Report, 1893.

[5] Preferred stock, 4 per cent., 1893-1921 :

1893 . . . . $6,424,000·00	1908 . . . . $48,803,332·33
1894 . . . . 6,424,000·00	1909 . . . . 52,696,665·71
1895 . . . . 6,424,000·00	1910 . . . . 55,616,665·71
1896 . . . . 8,005,666·67	1911 . . . . 57,076,665·70
1897 . . . . 9,830,666·67	1912 . . . . 66,695,097·86
1898 . . . . 20,951,000·00	1913 . . . . 74,331,339·97
1899 . . . . 26,791,000·00	1914 . . . . 78,224,673·03
1901 . . . . 31,171,000·00	1915 . . . . 80,681,921·12
1902 . . . . 31,171,000·00	1916 . . . . 80,681,921·12
1903 . . . . 32,500,000·00	1917 . . . . 80,681,921·12
1904 . . . . 33,473,333·33	1918 . . . . 80,681,921·12
1905 . . . . 37,853,333·33	1919 . . . . 80,681,921·12
1906 . . . . 42,719,999·04	1920 . . . . 80,681,921·12
1907 . . . . 43,936,665·70	1921 . . . . 80,681,921·12

Compiled from C.P.R. Reports.

of rapid expansion after 1900, and the consequent improvement of the company's financial standing, additional capital was secured through the sale of this stock ensuring a low rate of interest and preventing an increase in fixed charges. The amount outstanding increased to $80,681,921 in 1915 and remained at that point to 1921. Most rapid increases were evident during the period of greatest prosperity, from 1911 to 1913, since it was only under these conditions that a security of this character could be sold. During the war it was found necessary to issue other securities.

Fixed charges were also kept at a low level by the sale of 4 per cent. consolidated debenture stocks. Through this form of security capital was again secured at a low rate of interest and with relatively slight difficulty. During the decade from 1890 to 1900 the amount of this stock outstanding increased from $4,380,000 to $54,380,000, the increase being most rapid during the years before the depression. Following the depression a steady increase was evident. With rapid expansion [1] of the road after 1900 consolidated debenture [2] stock increased to $176,284,882 in 1915 and to $238,206,432 in 1921. During the war $40,000,000 of

[1] General purposes, £2,804,873 ; China and Japan steamship, £720,000 ; Souris branch, £1,169,000 ; retirement of Canada Central bonds, £450,000 ; Pacific Coast steamers, £650,000 ; Atlantic steamship, £2,217,500 ; branch lines and acquisition of mortgage bonds, £26,593,192 ; discharge of debt to Quebec Government, £1,438,356 ; lake steamers, £180,000.

[2] Consolidated debenture stock, 4 per cent., 1889–1921 :

1889 . . . $4,380,000·00	1906 . . . $101,519,411·21
1890 . . . 12,040,606·00	1907 . . . 106,045,411·21
1891 . . . 19,770,492·65	1908 . . . 115,657,077·88
1892 . . . 34,953,008·28	1909 . . . 128,930,132·52
1893 . . . 39,819,675·00	1910 . . . 136,711,616·18
1894 . . . 41,279,675·00	1911 . . . 142,861,462·26
1895 . . . 42,353,018·33	1912 . . . 153,823,706·86
1896 . . . 45,347,843·33	1913 . . . 163,257,224·32
1897 . . . 46,055,870·33	1914 . . . 173,307,470·09
1898 . . . 48,061,866·53	1915 . . . 176,284,882·10
1899 . . . 54,237,082·53	1916 . . . 176,284,882·10
1901 . . . 60,369,082·53	1917 . . . 176,284,882·10
1902 . . . 63,532,415·86	1918 . . . 216,284,882·10
1903 . . . 67,252,252·52	1919 . . . 216,284,882·10
1904 . . . 82,355,217·66	1920 . . . 216,284,882·10
1905 . . . 89,200,549·32	1921 . . . 238,206,431·68

Compiled from *C.P.R. Reports.*

debenture stock was issued [1] as a loan to the British Treasury. The stock was purchased by the Imperial Government at 80 per cent. of its face value and the proceeds, $32,000,000, loaned at an annual interest rate of $5\frac{1}{4}$ per cent. payable semi-annually. This loan facilitated credit operations of the Imperial Government on the American market and netted the company an annual premium of $\frac{1}{2}$ per cent. In 1921 £4,800,000 was sold on the London market and $25,000,000 in New York. Consolidated debenture stock was issued to secure capital at a low rate of interest and to cancel obligations having a higher rate of interest. Its effect on fixed charges was evident. In 1921 of a total of $11,519,072 of fixed charges, $7,854,544 was due to consolidated stock.

The ability of the company to secure capital at a low rate of interest and to keep fixed charges at a low level occasioned by the rapid expansion of the road was a cause and an effect of the favourable position of the company in the issue of common stock as a security to obtain additional capital. Liberal Government aid, which to a large extent made possible the rapid physical expansion of the road, the marked increase in traffic, and the favourable position of the company from the standpoint of fixed charges, had its effect consequently on the amount of capital stock issued and the dividends paid. To August, 1893, 3 per cent. dividends were paid from a deposit of $15,942,645 made by the company with the Government in accordance with an agreement under the Loan Act, and were not therefore paid from the immediate earnings of the company. To provide for the payment of dividends after the exhaustion of the deposit at that date, a reserve fund was started. Surplus [2] of net earnings after payment of fixed charges was set aside for that purpose. In 1889 this surplus increased 600 per cent. The yearly surplus declined slightly in 1890, but the reserve fund in that year totalled $2,656,433. The

---

[1] 7–8 Geo. V. c. 8, *C.P.R. Report*, 1916.
[2] Surplus, 1886–90 :

1886	$635,444·70	1889	$2,461,708·34
1887	253,854·35	1890	2,053,082·51
1888	326,423·92		

Compiled from *C.P.R. Reports*.

rapid accumulation of surplus in 1889 was accomplished
through a decline in expenses—particularly in locomotive
expenses—despite an increase in traffic and an increase in
mileage. The slight decline of surplus in 1890 followed
an increase in fixed charges and in expenses, despite a
decline in maintenance expenses with an increased mileage
of 7 per cent. Gross earnings increased steadily during
the two years. From the fund accumulated, a dividend of
1 per cent. on February 17, 1890, and on August 17 and
February 17, 1891, was declared. In 1893 the accumulated
reserve totalled $1,261,213, but with the depression and
the expiration of the guarantee it was exhausted, and in
1895 the rate of dividends declined to 1½ per cent. During
the recovery [1] the rate steadily increased, reaching 5 per
cent. in 1899. In 1903 it increased to 5½ per cent., in 1904
to 6 per cent., in 1907 to 7 per cent., in 1911 to 8½ per cent.,
and in 1912 to 10 per cent., remaining at that point throughout the remainder of the company's history. On the stock
market C.P.R. quotations accompanied the rise in dividend
rates. Following the depression stock increased in price
from 50 to 85 in 1897, rose above par in 1901, and reached
139 in 1903, 190 in 1906, 240 in 1911 and the highest point,
276, in 1912. The expansion in traffic and in earnings during
the period was not only reflected in an increased dividend
rate and in market quotations. The favourable position
of the company on the financial market made possible the
sale of stock under fortunate circumstances and with an

[1] Dividend rate, 1884–1921 :

	Per cent.		Per cent.		Per cent.
1884 . . .	3	1897 . . .	4	1911 . . .	8·5
1885 . . .	3	1898 . . .	4	1912 . . .	10
1886 . . .	3	1899 . . .	5	1913 . . .	10
1887 . . .	3	1901 . . .	5	1914 . . .	10
1888 . . .	3	1902 . . .	5	1915 . . .	10
1889 . . .	3	1903 . . .	5·5	1916 . . .	10
1890 . . .	5	1904 . . .	6	1917 . . .	10
1891 . . .	5	1905 . . .	6	1918 . . .	10
1892 . . .	5	1906 . . .	6	1919 . . .	10
1893 . . .	5	1907 . . .	7	1920 . . .	10
1894 . . .	2·5	1908 . . .	7	1921 . . .	10
1895 . . .	1·5	1909 . . .	7		
1896 . . .	2	1910 . . .	7·5		

Compiled from *C.P.R. Reports.*

increase in dividend rates came an increase [1] in capital stock. In 1902 an issue of $19,500,000 was authorized and largely sold to shareholders at par. Again in 1904 at the same price another issue of $25,500,000 was sold and largely subscribed by shareholders. In 1913 capital stock had increased to $260,000,000 and on sales a premium had been realized of $45,000,000. From the beginning of the century to 1913 the company had received $240,000,000 from sales of capital stock. Capital was secured from the sale of common stock, particularly during a period of prosperity.

With the depression beginning in 1914, the difficulty of securing capital by the sale of debenture stock at low interest rates led to the issue of $52,000,000 of 6 per cent. note certificates due in 1924 against deferred payments and securities on land to the extent of $57,131,199. During

[1] 1890–1921 :	Low	High	Average	Common Stock
		Price of Stocks		
1890 . . .	67	84	75·5	65,000,000·00
1891	72	91	81·5	65,000,000·00
1892	86	94	90	65,000,000·00
1893	66	90	78	65,000,000·00
1894	58	73	65·5	65,000,000·00
1895	33	62	47·5	65,000,000·00
1896	52	62	57	65,000,000·00
1897	46	82	64	65,000,000·00
1898	72	90	81	65,000,000·00
1899	84	99	91·5	65,000,000·00
1900	84	99	91·5	65,000,000·00
1901	87	117	102	65,000,000·00
1902	112	145	128·5	65,000,000·00
1903	115	138	126·5	72,624,162·00
1904	109	135	122	84,500,000·00
1905	130	177	153·5	98,738,240·00
1906	155	201	178	105,995,190·00
1907	138	195	166·5	121,680,000·00
1908	140	180	160	141,534,436·00
1909	165	189	177	150,000,00·000
1910	176	202	189	173,530,085·00
1911	195	247	221	180,000,000·00
1912	226	283	254·5	196,806,621·00
1913	204	266	235	200,000,000·00
1914	153	220	186·5	260,000,000·00
1915	138	194	166	260,000,000·00
1916	162	183	172·5	260,000,000·00
1917	126	167	140·5	260,000,000·00
1918	135	174	154·5	260,000,000·00
1919	126	171	148·5	260,000,000·00
1920	109	134	121·5	260,000,000·00
1921	101	123	112	260,000,000·00

Compiled from *C.P.R. Reports* and files of the *Commercial and Financial Chronicle*.

the war similar conditions prevailed and on January 1, 1915, the company issued $8,930,000 of Victoria Rolling Stock and Realty Company equipment trust 4½ per cent. certificates. In addition to capital obtained from these securities, adjustments were made in surplus and reserve accounts to meet necessary expenditures on capital.

The disbursement of total receipts was determined by the character and number of the securities issued. Fixed charges were to a large extent [1] dependent on the issue of consolidated debenture stock and a relatively small proportion of total receipts was absorbed in this item. Dividends on preferred stock [2] were an even smaller proportion of total receipts. In 1921 dividends on this security were less than one-third of fixed charges. Dividends on common stock [3] have taken an increasing share. Prior to 1908

[1] In 1921, of a total of $11,519,072, rentals totalled $1,862,131 and interest on bonds $1,802,397.

[2] Dividends, preferred stock, 1894–1921 :

1894	$256,960·00	1909 . . . . $2,029,999·97
1895	128,480·00	1910 . . . . 2,156,533·30
1896	281,293·33	1911 . . . . 2,224,666·66
1897	327,526·66	1912 . . . . 2,399,866·63
1898	432,160·00	1913 . . . . 2,807·288·47
1899	656,182·50	1914 . . . . 3,031,653·59
1900 (six months)	599,086·67	1915 . . . . 3,169,906·26
1901	173,399·34	1916 . . . . 3,227,276·84
1902	1,246,840·00	1916 (six months) 1;612,638·42
1903	1,273,420·00	1917 . . . . 3,227,276·84
1904	1,303,406·65	1918 . . . . 3,227,276·84
1905	1,455,733·31	1919 . . . . 3,227,276·84
1906	1,562,799·99	1920 . . . . 3,227,276·84
1907	1,711.894·88	1921 . . . . 3,227,276·84
1908	1,819,073·76	

Compiled from *C.P.R. Reports.*

[3] Common stock, dividends, 1890–1921 :

1890	$1,300,000	1907 . . . . . $7,300,800
1891	1,300,000	1908 9,508,800
1892	1,300,000	1909 10,500,000
1893	1,300,000	1910 18,600,000
1894	3,250,000	1911 18,000,000
1895	1,231,960	1912 19,000,000
1896	1,625,000	1913 23,000,000
1897	1,625,000	1914 26,000,000
1898	2,925,000	1915 26,000,000
1899	2,600,000	1916 26,000,000
1900 (six months)	1,625,000	1916 (six months). 13,000,000
1901	5,200,000	1917 26,000,000
1902	3,250,000	1918 26,000,000
1903	3,737,500	1919 26,000,000
1904	5,070,000	1920 26,000,000
1905	5,070,000	1921 26,000,000
1906	6,084,000	

Compiled from *C.P.R. Reports.*

fixed charges absorbed a larger share of total receipts than dividends on common stock, but since that year, following the marked expansion of the road, dividends have rapidly increased.   An increasing dividend rate and larger issues of stock led to a marked increase in dividends from $9,508,800 in 1908 to $26,000,000 in 1914.   Since that year dividends have remained at the latter figure.   The remainder of total receipts after the payment of fixed charges and of dividends on preference stock and on common stock accumulated as surplus.   As a tribute to the increase in the earning capacity of the road despite an increase in dividends and in fixed charges, surplus has steadily increased following the recovery of the nineties.   In 1899 it had increased to $9,614,528, in 1914 to $79,711,092 and in 1921, despite the difficulties of the war, to $128,481,120.   In addition in the latter year reserves had been provided for equipment replacement $10,780,420,   for   steamship   replacement $19,185,402 and for contingencies and taxes $46,638,048. Finally the company had over $5,000,000 of cash on hand, and in Government securities (Imperial, Dominion, Provincial and Municipal) $29,327,396.

Total receipts, which depended primarily on net earnings and to a large extent on freight traffic, and the situation in western Canada, were disbursed primarily in dividends on common stock and in the accumulation of surplus.   Dividends above a normal return on common stock have, therefore, existed as the result of the expansion of the road in western Canada and have largely been paid from the economic development of that area.

XI

Conclusion

THE history of the Canadian Pacific Railroad is primarily the history of the spread of western civilization over the northern half of the North American continent. The addition of technical equipment described as physical property of the Canadian Pacific Railway Company was a cause and an effect of the strength and character of that civilization. The construction of the road was the result of the direction of energy to the conquest of geographic barriers. The effects of the road were measured to some extent by the changes in the strength and character of that civilization in the period following its construction.

The strength and character of western civilization in North America were the results of the qualities and numbers of its population. The adaptability and virility of this population were evident in the rapidity and directness with which institutions brought from Europe were abandoned or adjusted, or with which new institutions were created to meet effectively conditions imposed by a new environ-. ment. For the French, institutions in many cases proved inadequate on account of the difficulties of environment, due to harshness of climate, the inhospitable character of the soil, and the hostility of the natives and other nationalities, and the civilization concerned disappeared. Eventually with an increased knowledge of new conditions, with the necessary adaptability and with the more suitable environment characteristic of Quebec in the St. Lawrence valley, this civilization gained a foothold on the eastern shores of the continent and grew steadily and persistently. In this growth, feudalism as an institution was especially significant. Its centralizing tendencies shown in its advantages from a military standpoint were strengthened by the constant warfare of the Indians and the English, which made essential the concentration of population at strategic points along the St. Lawrence basin. The strength of this tendency toward centralization more than offset the effects of the individualism essential to the fur trade, which with the ease of penetration to the interior by waterways was especially pronounced. The opposition of these effects was evident in the number of *coureurs de bois* and in the attempts of the French authorities to prevent the population from taking to this life, but generally the *seigneurial* system, the effects of military struggle, the character of the St. Lawrence river basin, the influences of language, religion and customs promoted the development of homogeneous settlement, and the growth of a distinct national feeling.

For the English and other nationalities, difficulties of environment were also apparent in the failures of early settlements, although farther south along the Atlantic coast conditions, especially as to climate, were more favourable. But again adjustments essential to the existence and growth of settlement were accomplished. Monopolies as a part of the institutional equipment, especially of the English, and the consequent centralizing tendencies, largely disappeared because of the relatively minor importance of military exigencies. The inaccessibility of the interior, and the consequent disregard of the fur trade, and attention to agriculture, fishing, lumbering and the extractive industries in general, were conditions promoting a steady growth of settlement, a feeling of solidarity and the development of enterprise, initiative and aggressiveness.

The constant expansion westward of English settlement especially in the northern section of the Atlantic seaboard —of what is now the United States—led to increased friction with the French settlements along the St. Lawrence and eventually to the struggle for supremacy of the North American continent. In this struggle, lack of cohesion in the French settlements stretching from the mouth of the St. Lawrence to the mouth of the Mississippi, and effectiveness of British naval supremacy, were determining factors leading to the disappearance of French control. Following this result the aggressiveness of English colonists became more in evidence and westward expansion became more pronounced. In turn there came the struggle against control over the colonies exercised by Great Britain and the success of the colonists in territory in which British naval supremacy was of slight avail.

Westward colonization by English settlers received fresh stimulus with this victory, and settlements were established along the north shores of Lake Ontario and Lake Erie, or in the territory known as Upper Canada. Of these settlers, the majority were known as United Empire Loyalists, but essentially they were the same aggressive, enterprising type as the New England colonists. Demands on the part of these settlers for assistance from the British Government, anxious as to the outcome of expansion to the south, were met with substantial liberality. This general encouragement given to emigration for the settlement of Upper Canada led to the development of a distinct feeling of dependence on Great Britain.

These general characteristics of the settlers of Upper Canada contrasted with the characteristics of the French in Lower Canada. Solidarity developed in the centralization of the old regime especially in the struggle leading to the downfall of New France and, strengthened by devices of the British Government intended to foster their loyalty to the new authorities, was at variance with the aggressive individualism of the population of Upper Canada. Demands of the settlers of Upper Canada for an outlet by the St. Lawrence and for all the rights implied in self-government led to differences which were settled in the Act of 1791. The loyalty of Upper Canada and of Lower Canada encouraged by these adjustments of the British Government was strengthened by the necessity of co-operation occasioned by the attacks of the United States in 1812, but the variance between the attitudes of Upper Canada and Lower Canada continued. The loyalty to Great Britain characteristic of Upper Canada during this early period and the particular aggressiveness of this settlement were evident in later developments. Possibilities of advantage from the diversion of traffic of the rapidly expanding western states down the St. Lawrence made advisable appeals for aid from the British Government leading to the construction of canals. The attempts to improve the St. Lawrence occasioned difficulties with the French of Lower Canada, which were eventually settled, after Lord Durham's Report, by the Act of Union.

The attitude of dependence on Great Britain characteristic of English colonies was strengthened by the persistent appeals and the success with which they were met. The general aggressiveness of these settlers and especially of the trading interests led to the tariff adjustments of 1843 directed to the diversion of traffic along the St. Lawrence canals and through Montreal, and following the disappearance of advantages gained with the adjustments through the abolition of the Corn Laws in 1846 led to the Annexationist Manifesto in 1849. Of more significance, renewed efforts were made to capture the trade of the western states in the construction of the Grand Trunk as an offset to the competitive disadvantages of canals. To relieve the situation further negotiations for reciprocity were successfully terminated in 1854. The abrogation of this treaty in 1866, the feeling of jealousy and anxiety as to the attitude of the United States and the demand for improvements in transportation giving an outlet to the sea during the winter season (always with a view to a larger share of the traffic of the western states) led to further requests for aid from Great Britain and finally brought the construction of the Intercolonial and Confederation.

Generally, during the period prior to confederation, Upper Canada had developed a spirit of dependence on Great Britain which might be characterized, with no implication of condemnation, as unhealthy. The aggressive, individualistic character of its early settlers had been strengthened under the stress of circumstances and had developed especially in the trading and governing classes to the point of selfishness and of acquisitiveness. Frequent advantage was taken of the possibilities of securing aid from Great Britain for the purpose of constructing improvements designed to secure trade from the western states.

This acquisitive temperament was especially significant in the attitude of Canada, especially of Toronto and Upper Canada, toward the increased trade between the United States and the settlements which had grown up in the Hudson Bay drainage basin and in the Pacific coast drainage basin. Trade from the Red River settlement with the United States had increased greatly by virtue of direct communication and its potentialities were early recognized by Canada. In the Pacific coast district (now British Columbia) the discovery of the gold-mines and the consequent rapid immigration and development of the country were occasions for further alarm. The solicitude of Canada and of Great Britain as to these areas and their trade with the United States hastened an agreement with British Columbia which led eventually to the construction of the Canadian Pacific railroad.

This agreement, resulting largely from the acquisitiveness characteristic of eastern Canada, led to difficulties, since by virtue of the same characteristics eastern Canada found itself unable to give the support necessary to the fulfilment of its obligations. The refusal of the people to bear an increase in taxation to construct the road, the jealousies of Toronto and Montreal, the dependence on private enterprise and the accompanying fiasco in the Pacific Scandal, the gradual process of construction under the Mackenzie regime, the appeals to Great Britain for aid, and the liberality of the contract with the Canadian Pacific in 1881—a liberality based on a money subsidy which it was hoped could be recovered from sales of lands in western Canada, and on land grants in the same territory—were evidences of these particular characteristics of the national outlook. The terms of the contract with the Canadian Pacific Railway Company were designed to develop the trade of the northwest and of British Columbia, and to divert that trade from the United States to eastern Canada.

Under these conditions, the Canadian Pacific Railway was constructed through the long stretch of unproductive and difficult territory north of Lake Superior, and traffic was developed in western Canada by means of various devices and with the utmost possible rapidity. Private enterprise had undertaken the task, and by virtue of the liberality of the terms, the general attitude of the Canadian Government, the spread of population in the western states, the completion of the St. Paul, Minneapolis and Manitoba Railway to Winnipeg, and the knowledge gained of the nature of the task during the earlier years, the road was completed to the Pacific coast in 1886. Its completion, moreover, found the Canadian Pacific Railway Company in a satisfactory financial condition.

The addition of the Canadian Pacific Railroad to the technological equipment of Western civilization and the conditions under which it was accomplished have had many and varied effects. Settlement was advanced in every possible way. Immigration increased rapidly as a result of the efforts of the company and of the Government. Branch lines were laid out first in the territory south of the main line and later throughout the whole area. These branches were strategically located, with reference to possible competitors, to the development of traffic, and to the sale of the company's land. The marked increase in the production of grain and especially of wheat in western Canada, stimulated by efforts to develop traffic, and favoured by a world movement characterized by a general rise in the price of wheat, and its diversion over lines to eastern Canada, made necessary the improvement and increased control of transportation facilities in the latter area. According to plan, the economic development of the west stimulated the economic development of the east. The marked prosperity of Canada, especially from 1896 to 1913, paralleled the prosperity, the expansion, and the integration of the Canadian Pacific during that period. Following the general progress of Canada, occasioned by the opening of the west, advantage was taken by eastern Canada (always with an eye to the main chance) of stimulating progress still further by the construction of the Canadian Northern and the Grand Trunk Pacific. To the difficulties which overtook these roads were added the difficulties of the Intercolonial and the Grand Trunk, which have suffered losses partly as a result of the effectiveness of competition from Canadian Pacific lines in eastern Canada. Such were some of the important effects of the construction of the Canadian Pacific Railroad.

The diversion of traffic to eastern Canada by the Canadian Pacific and other roads has been accomplished successfully, but to some extent at least at the expense of Western Canada and with considerable protest from that area. The existence of a large surplus on the balance sheet of the Canadian Pacific Railway Company and the consistent payment of large dividends,[1] accomplished through a high dividend rate and relatively large issues of common stock, have been shown to be largely the result of the freight situation [2] in western Canada. The successful protests of western Canada against the monopoly clause did not materially change the situation, nor did the Crows Nest Pass Agreement or the appointment of the Board of Railway Commissioners. Nor does there seem to exist any prospect of immediate change. The general acquisitive attitude of eastern Canada, the result of its historical background, will scarcely sanction an increase in the deficits of the Canadian National Railways [3] in order to allow a lowering of rates in western Canada, nor will it agree to an increase of rates in eastern Canada. It will scarcely permit the reduction of a tariff [4] which would endanger the traffic of the National Railways, consequently increasing their deficits and at the same time diverting traffic to the United States. It will scarcely be tactless enough to increase taxes on the Canadian Pacific to reduce its dividends and its surplus

---

[1] Controversy has been frequent as to the right of the company to issue dividends in excess of 10 per cent., the limit laid down in the charter. It is claimed by the company that this limit no longer exists, following the changes incidental to the regulation of rates by the Board of Railway Commissioners (see Speech of Lord Shaughnessy to the C.P.R. Shareholders, May 1, 1918). It is scarcely probable that the dividend rate will be increased, because of the hostility this move would create. But in any case the discussion is not to the point. The existence of a large surplus and the payment of large dividends are the causes of complaints.

[2] This has been brought out very well in the House of Commons Inquiry regarding the abrogation or suspension of the Crows Nest Pass agreement (see especially the statement of Mr. E. W. Beatty, President of the Canadian Pacific).

[3] See the statement of Mr. D. B. Hanna, President of the Canadian National Railways (*ibid.*).

[4] The budget of Hon. W. S. Fielding is in point. Reductions are of relatively slight importance, and these pertain more largely to the preferential tariff. This will not be a substantial relief to the west.

because of the resulting disturbance to the financial situation in Canada, because of the well-known astuteness of that organization and because of a possible decline in morale which might result.

On the other hand, the tax which has been paid by western Canada as a result of the particular attitude of eastern Canada has provoked a movement the strength of which is difficult to estimate. The land situation involving the holding of alternate sections by the Canadian Pacific seriously hampers social development. With tax exemption, the construction of schools is restricted. The taxation problem, in general, has been seriously increased because of tax exemption privileges. The immigration problem has followed, and will follow, the necessities of the railroads. The question as to whether the prairie provinces shall control their own natural resources has become increasingly difficult. The rise of the Progressive party, its increasing strength with increasing population in western Canada—a population with characteristics similar to those of eastern Canada—with its attitude toward the railway rate problem, toward the natural resources question, and toward the tariff, will become increasingly significant, but prediction is dangerous. On the whole, important as the movement in western Canada must become for the future development of the country, the dominance of eastern Canada over western Canada seems likely to persist. Western Canada has paid for the development of Canadian nationality, and it would appear that it must continue to pay. The acquisitiveness of eastern Canada shows little sign of abatement.

The Canadian Pacific Railway, as a vital part of the technological equipment of western civilization, has increased to a very marked extent the productive capacity of that civilization. It is hypothetical to ask whether under other conditions production would have been increased or whether such production would have contributed more to the welfare of humanity.

Appendix "A"

TERMS OF AGREEMENT OF ENTRANCE OF BRITISH COLUMBIA IN UNION

" THE Government of the Dominion undertake to secure the commencement simultaneously, within two years from the date of union, of the construction of a railway from the Pacific towards the Rocky Mountains, and from such point as may be selected east of the Rocky Mountains towards the Pacific, to connect the seaboard of British Columbia with the railway system of Canada ; and further, to secure the completion of such railway within ten years from the date of union. And the Government of British Columbia agree to convey to the Dominion Government, in trust, to be appropriated in such manner as the Dominion Government may deem advisable, in furtherance of the construction of the said railway, a similar extent of public lands along the line of the railway throughout its entire length in British Columbia, (not to exceed, however, 20 miles on each side of the said line,) as may be appropriated for the same purpose by the Dominion Government from the public lands in the North-West Territories and Province of Manitoba ; provided that the quantity of land which may be held under the pre-emption right or by the Crown grant within the limits of the tract of land in British Columbia to be so conveyed to the Dominion Government shall be made good to the Dominion from the contiguous public lands ; and provided further that until the commencement, within two years, as aforesaid, from the date of the union, of the construction of the said railway, the Government of British Columbia shall not sell or alienate any further portions of the public lands of British Columbia in any other way than under the right of pre-emption requiring the actual residence of the pre-emptor on the land claimed by him. In consideration of the land to be so conveyed in aid of the construction of the said railway, the Dominion Government agree to pay British Columbia, from date of union, the sum of $100,000 per annum, in half-yearly payments in advance." Article II, *Order in Council respecting the Province of British Columbia Statutes of Canada* 1872, p. lxxxviii.

Appendix " B "

44 VICTORIA

CHAPTER I

AN ACT RESPECTING THE CANADIAN PACIFIC RAILWAY

(Assented to February 15, 1881)

Preamble.

WHEREAS by the terms and conditions of the admission of British Columbia into Union with the Dominion of Canada, the Government of the Dominion has assumed the obligation of causing a railway to be constructed, connecting the seaboard of British Columbia with the railway system of Canada ;

Preference of Parliament for construction by a company.

And whereas the Parliament of Canada has repeatedly declared a preference for the construction and operation of such Railway by means of an incorporated Company aided by grants of money and land, rather than by the Government, and certain Statutes have been passed to enable that course to be followed, but the enactments therein contained have not been effectual for that purpose ;

Greater part still unconstructed.

And whereas certain sections of the said railway have been constructed by the Government, and others are in course of construction, but the greater portion of the main line thereof has not yet been commenced or placed under contract, and it is necessary for the development of the North-West Territory and for the preservation of the good faith of the Government in the performance of its obligations, that immediate steps should be taken to complete and operate the whole of the said railway ;

Contract entered into.

And whereas, in conformity with the expressed desire of Parliament, a contract has been entered into for the construction of the said portion of the main line of the said railway, and for the permanent working of the whole line thereof, which contract with the schedule annexed has been laid before Parliament for its approval and a copy thereof is appended hereto, and it is expedient to approve and ratify the said contract, and to make provision for the carrying out of the same :

Therefore Her Majesty, by and with the advice and consent of the Senate and House of Commons of Canada, enacts as follows :—

1. The said contract, a copy of which, with schedule annexed, is appended hereto, is hereby approved and ratified, and the Government is hereby authorized to perform and carry out the conditions thereof, according to their purport. *Contract approved.*

2. For the purpose of incorporating the persons mentioned in the said contract, and those who shall be associated with them in the undertaking, and of granting to them the powers necessary to enable them to carry out the said contract according to the terms thereof, the Governor may grant to them in conformity with the said contract, under corporate name of the Canadian Pacific Railway Company, a charter conferring upon them the franchises, privileges, and powers embodied in the schedule to the said contract and to this Act appended, and such charter, being published in the Canada *Gazette*, with any Order or Orders in Council of the Parliament of Canada, and shall be held to be an Act of incorporation within the meaning of the said contract. *Charter may be granted.* *Publication and effect of charter.*

3. Upon the organization of the said Company, and the deposit by them, with the Government, of one million dollars in cash, or securities approved by the Government, for the purpose in the said contract provided, and in consideration of the completion and perpetual and efficient operation of the railway by the said Company, as stipulated in the said contract, the Government may grant to the Company a subsidy of twenty-five million dollars in money, and twenty-five million acres of land, to be paid and conveyed to the Company in the manner and proportions, and upon the terms and conditions agreed upon in the said contract, and may also grant to the Company the land for right of way, stations, and other purposes, and such other privileges as are provided for in the said contract. And in lieu of the payment of the said money subsidy direct to the Company, the Government may convert the same, and any interest accruing thereon, into a fund for the payment, to the extent of such fund, of interest on the bonds of the Company, and may pay such interest accordingly ; the whole in manner and form as provided for in the said contract. *Certain grants of money and land may be made to the company chartered.* *Conversion of money grant authorized.*

4. The Government may also permit the admission free of duty, of all steel rails, fish plates, and other fastenings, spikes, bolts and nuts, wire, timber and all material for bridges to be used in the original construction of the said *Certain materials may be admitted free of duty.*

Canadian Pacific Railway, as defined by the Act thirty-seventh Victoria, chapter fourteen, and of a telegraph line in connexion therewith, and all telegraphic apparatus required for the first equipment of such telegraph line, the whole as provided by the tenth section of the said contract.

Company to have possession of completed portions of the railway.

5. Pending the completion of the eastern and central sections of the said railway as described in the said contract, the Government may also transfer to the said Company the possession and right to work and run the several portions of the Canadian Pacific Railway as described in the said Act thirty-seventh Victoria, chapter fourteen, which are already constructed, and as the same shall be hereafter completed ; and upon the completion of the said eastern and central sections the Government may convey to the Company, with a suitable number of station buildings, and with water service (but without equipment), those portions of the Canadian Pacific Railway constructed, or agreed by the said contract to be constructed by the Government,

Conveyance thereof to company when the contract is performed.

which shall then be completed ; and upon completion of the remainder of the portion of the said railway to be constructed by the Government, that portion also may be conveyed by the Government to the Company, and the Canadian Pacific Railway defined as aforesaid shall become and be thereafter the absolute property of the Company ; the whole, however, upon the terms and conditions, and subject to the restrictions and limitations contained in the said contract.

Security may be taken for operation of the railway.

6. The Government shall also take security for the continuous operation of the said Railway during the ten years next subsequent to the completion thereof in the manner provided by the said contract.

SCHEDULE

THIS CONTRACT AND AGREEMENT MADE BETWEEN HER MAJESTY THE QUEEN, acting in respect of the Dominion of Canada and herein represented and acting by the Honourable SIR CHARLES TUPPER, K.C.M.G., Minister of Railways and Canals and George Stephen and Duncan McIntyre, of Montreal, in Canada, John S. Kennedy of New York, in the State of New York, Richard B. Angus, and James J. Hill, of St. Paul, in the State of Minnesota, Morton, Rose & Co., of London, England, and Kohn, Reinach & Co., of Paris, France, Witnesses :

That the parties hereto have contracted and agreed with each other as follows, namely :—

Interpretation clause.

1. For the better interpretation of this contract, it is hereby declared that the portion of railway hereinafter

called the Eastern section, shall comprise that part of the Eastern section.
Canadian Pacific Railway to be constructed, extending
from the Western terminus of the Canada Central Railway,
near the East end of Lake Nipissing, known as Callander
Station, to a point of junction with that portion of the said
Canadian Pacific Railway now in course of construction
extending from Lake Superior to Selkirk on the East side
of Red River ; which latter portion is hereinafter called Lake Superior Section.
the Lake Superior section. That the portion of said railway,
now partially in course of construction, extending from
Selkirk to Kamloops, is hereinafter called the Central Central Section.
Section ; and the portion of said railway now in course of
construction, extending from Kamloops to Port Moody,
is hereinafter called the Western section. And that the
words, " the Canadian Pacific Railway," are intended to C.P. Railway.
mean the entire railway, as described in the Act thirty-
seventh Victoria, chapter fourteen. The individual parties
hereto are hereinafter described as the Company ; and the Company.
Government of Canada is hereinafter called tne Government.

2. The contractors, immediately after the organization of Security to be given by the company.
the said Company, shall deposit with the Government
$1,000,000 in cash or approved securities, as a security for
the construction of the railway hereby contracted for.
The Government shall pay to the Company interest on the Conditions thereof.
cash deposited at the rate of four per cent. per annum, half-
yearly, and shall pay over to the Company the interest
received upon securities deposited—the whole until default
in the performance of the conditions hereof, or until the
repayment of the deposit ; and shall return the deposit to
the Company on the completion of the railway, according
to the terms hereof, with any interest accrued thereon.

3. The Company shall lay out, construct and equip the Eastern and central sections to be constructed by company described.
said Eastern section, and the said Central section, of a uniform
gauge of 4 feet 8½ inches ; and in order to establish an
approximate standard whereby the quality and the character
of the railway and of the materials used in the construction
thereof, and of the equipment thereof may be regulated, the
Union Pacific Railway of the United States as the same was
when first constructed, is hereby selected and fixed as such
standard. And if the Government and the Company should Standard of railway and provision in case of disagreement as to conformity to it.
be unable to agree as to whether or not any work done or
materials furnished under this contract are in fair conformity
with such standard, or as to any other question of fact,
excluding questions of law, the subject of disagreement
shall be, from time to time, referred to the determination
of three referees, one of whom shall be chosen by the Govern-

ment, one by the Company, and one by the two referees
so chosen, and such referees shall decide as to the party by
whom the expense of such reference shall be defrayed.
And if such two referees should be unable to agree upon a
third referee, he shall be appointed at the instance of either
party hereto, after notice to the other, by the Chief Justice
of the Supreme Court of Canada. And the decision
of such referees, or of the majority of them, shall be
final.

Commencement and regular progress of the work.
4. The work of construction shall be commenced at the
eastern extremity of the Eastern section not later than the
first day of July next, and the work upon the Central section
shall be commenced by the Company at such point towards
the eastern end thereof on the portion of the line now under
construction as shall be found convenient and as shall be
approved by the Government, at a date not later than the
1st May next. And the work upon the Eastern and Central
sections shall be vigorously and continuously carried on
at such rate of annual progress on each section as shall enable
the Company to complete and equip the same and each
of them, in running order, on or before the first day of May,
1891, by which date the Company hereby agree to complete
and equip the said sections in conformity with this contract,
unless prevented by the act of God, the Queen's enemies,
intestine disturbances, epidemics, floods, or other causes

Period for completion.
beyond the control of the Company. And in case of the
interruption or obstruction of the work of construction
from any of the said causes, the time fixed for the completion of the railway shall be extended for a corresponding
period.

As to portion of central section made by Government.
5. The Company shall pay to the Government the cost,
according to the contract, of the portion of railway, 100
miles in length, extending from the city of Winnipeg westward, up to the time at which the work was taken out of
the hands of the contractor and the expenses since incurred
by the Government in the work of construction, but shall
have the right to assume the said work at any time and
complete the same paying the cost of construction as aforesaid, so far as the same shall then have been incurred by
the Government.

Government to construct portions now under contract within periods fixed by con- tract.
6. Unless prevented by the act of God, the Queen's
enemies, intestine disturbances, epidemics, floods or other
causes beyond the control of the Government, the Government shall cause to be completed the said Lake Superior
section by the dates fixed by the existing contracts for the
construction thereof ; and shall also cause to be completed
the portion of the said Western section now under contract,
namely, from Kamloops to Yale, within the period fixed

by the contracts therefor, namely, by the thirtieth day of June, 1885 ; and shall also cause to be completed, on or before the first day of May, 1891, the remaining portion of the said Western section, lying between Yale and Port Moody, which shall be constructed of equally good quality in every respect with the standard hereby created for the portion hereby contracted for. And the said Lake Superior section, and the portions of the said Western section now under contract, shall be completed as nearly as practicable according to the specifications and conditions of the contracts therefor, except in so far as the same have been modified by the Government prior to this contract.

7. The railway constructed under the terms hereof shall be the property of the Company : and pending the completion of the Eastern and Central sections, the Government shall transfer to the Company the possession and right to work and run the several portions of the Canadian Pacific Railway already constructed or as the same shall be completed. And upon the completion of the Eastern and Central sections, the Government shall convey to the Company, with a suitable number of station buildings and with water service (but without equipment), those portions of the Canadian Pacific Railway constructed or to be constructed by the Government which shall then be completed ; and upon completion of the remainder of the portion of railway to be constructed by the Government, that portion shall also be conveyed to the Company ; and the Canadian Pacific Railway shall become and be thereafter the absolute property of the Company. And the Company shall thereafter and for ever efficiently maintain, work and run the Canadian Pacific Railway. *Completed railway to be property of company.* *Transfer of portions constructed by Government.* *Company to operate the railway for ever.*

8. Upon the reception from the Government of the possession of each of the respective portions of the Canadian Pacific Railway, the Company shall equip the same in conformity with the standard herein established for the equipment of the sections hereby contracted for, and shall thereafter maintain and efficiently operate the same. *Company to equip portions transferred to them.*

9. In consideration of the premises, the Government agree to grant to the Company a subsidy in money of $25,000,000 and in land of 25,000,000 acres, for which subsidies the construction of the Canadian Pacific Railway shall be completed and the same shall be equipped, maintained and operated—the said subsidies respectively to be paid and granted as the work of construction shall proceed, in manner and upon the conditions following, that is to say :— *Subsidy in money and land.*

(a) The said subsidy in money is hereby divided and appropriated as follows, namely :— *Apportionment of money.*

CENTRAL SECTION.

Assumed at 1,350 miles :—

1st—900 miles at $10,000 per mile	$9,000,000	
2nd—450 ,, ,, 13,333 ,, ,,	6,000,000	

15,000,000

EASTERN SECTION.

Assumed at 650 miles, subsidy equal to $15,384.61 per mile   10,000,000

$25,000,000

And of land.   And the said subsidy in land is hereby divided and appropriated as follows, subject to the reserve hereinafter provided for :—

CENTRAL SECTION.

1st—900 miles at 12,500 acres per mile	11,250,000
2nd—450 ,, ,, 16,666.66 ,, ,, ,,	7,500,000

18,750,000

EASTERN SECTION.

Assumed at 650 miles, subsidy equal to 9,615.35 acres per mile   6,250,000

25,000,000

When to be paid or granted.   (b) Upon the construction of any portion of the railway hereby contracted for, not less than 20 miles in length, and the completion thereof so as to admit of the running of regular trains thereon, together with such equipment thereof as shall be required for the traffic thereon, the Government shall pay and grant to the Company the money and land subsidies applicable thereto, according to the division and appropriation thereof made as hereinbefore provided ; the **Option of company to take terminable bonds.** Company having the option of receiving in lieu of cash terminable bonds of the Government bearing such rate of interest, for such period and nominal amount as may be arranged, and which may be equivalent according to actuarial calculation to the corresponding cash payment—the government allowing four per cent. interest on moneys deposited with them.

Provision as to materials for construction delivered by company in advance.   (c) If at any time the Company shall cause to be delivered on or near the line of the said railway, at a place satisfactory to the Government, steel rails and fastenings to be used in the requirements for such construction, the Government, on the requisition of the Company, shall, upon such terms and conditions as shall be determined by the Government, advance thereon three-fourths of the value thereof at the place of delivery. And a proportion of the amount so advanced shall be deducted, according to such terms and conditions, from the subsidy to be thereafter paid, upon the settlement for each section of 20 miles of railway—

which proportion shall correspond with the proportion of such rails and fastenings which have been used in the construction of such sections.

(d) Until the first day of January, 1882, the Company shall have the option, instead of issuing land grant bonds as hereinafter provided, of substituting the payment by the Government of the interest (or part of the interest) on bonds of the Company mortgaging the railway and the lands to be granted by the Government, running over such term of years as may be approved by the Governor in Council, in lieu of the cash subsidy hereby agreed to be granted to the Company or any part thereof—such payments of interest to be equivalent according to actuarial calculation to the corresponding cash payment, the Government allowing four per cent interest on moneys deposited with them ; and the coupons representing the interest on such bonds shall be guaranteed by the Government to the extent of such equivalent. And the proceeds of the sale of such bonds to the extent of not more than $25,000,000 shall be deposited with the Government, and the balance of such proceeds shall be placed elsewhere by the Company, to the satisfaction and under the exclusive control of the Government ; failing which last condition the bonds in excess of those sold shall remain in the hands of the Government. And from time to time as the work proceeds, the Government shall pay over to the Company : firstly, out of the amount so to be placed by the Company—and, after the expenditure of that amount, out of the amount deposited with the Government—sums of money bearing the same proportion to the mileage cash subsidy hereby agreed upon, which the net proceeds of such sale (if the whole of such bonds are sold upon the issue thereof, or, if such bonds be not all then sold, the net proceeds of the issue, calculated at the rate at which the sale of part of them shall have been made), shall bear to the sum of $25,000, 000. But if only a portion of the bond issue be sold, the amount earned by the Company according to the proportion aforesaid shall be paid to the Company, partly out of the bonds in the hands of the Government, and partly out of the cash deposited with the Government, in similar proportions to the amount of such bonds sold and remaining unsold respectively ; and the Company shall receive the bonds so paid, as cash, at the rate at which the said partial sale thereof shall have been made. And the Government will receive and hold such sum of money towards the creation of a sinking fund for the redemption of such bonds, and upon such terms and conditions as shall be agreed upon between the Government and the Company,

Marginal notes: Option of the company during a certain time to substitute payment of interest on certain bonds instead of issuing land grant bonds; Deposit of proceeds of sale of such bonds. Payments to company out of such deposits. Payment by delivery of bonds. Sinking fund.

Alteration in
apportionment
of money grant
in such case.

(e) If the Company avail themselves of the option granted by clause d, the sum of $2,000 per mile for the first eight hundred miles of the Central section shall be deducted *pro rata* from the amount payable to the Company in respect of the said eight hundred miles, and shall be appropriated to increase the mileage cash subsidy appropriated to the remainder of the said Central section.

Grant of land required for railway purposes.

10. In further consideration of the premises, the Government shall also grant to the Company the lands required for the road-bed of the railway, and for its stations, station grounds, workshops, dock ground and water frontage at the termini on navigable waters, buildings, yards and other appurtenances required for the convenient and effectual construction and working of the railway, in so far as such land shall be vested in the Government. And the Government shall also permit the admission free of duty of all steel rails, fish plates and other fastenings, spikes, bolts and nuts, wire, timber and all material for bridges to be used in the original construction of the railway, and of a telegraph line in connexion therewith, and all telegraphic apparatus required for the first equipment of such telegraph line ; and will convey to the Company, at cost price, with interest, all rails and fastenings bought in or since the year 1879, and other materials for construction in the possession of or purchased by the Government, at a valuation—such rails, fastenings and materials not being required by it for the construction of the said Lake Superior and Western sections.

Admission of certain materials free of duty.

Sale of certain materials to company by Government.

Provision respecting land grant.

11. The grant of land, hereby agreed to be made to the Company, shall be so made in alternate sections of 640 acres each, extending back 24 miles deep, on each side of the railway, from Winnipeg to Jasper House, in so far as such lands shall be vested in the Government—the Company receiving the sections bearing uneven numbers. But should any of such sections consist in a material degree of land not fairly fit for settlement, the Company shall not be obliged to receive them as part of such grant ; and the deficiency thereby caused and any further deficiency which may arise from the insufficient quantity of land along the said portion of railway, to complete the said 25,000,000 acres, or from the prevalence of lakes and water stretches in the sections granted (which lakes and water stretches shall not be computed in the acreage of such sections), shall be made up from other portions in the tract known as the fertile belt, that is to say, the land lying between parallels 49 and 57 degrees of north latitude, or elsewhere at the option of the Company, by the grant therein of similar alternate sections extending back 24 miles deep on each side of any branch line or lines of railway to be located by the Company,

Case of deficiency of land on line of railway provided for.

and to be shown on a map or plan thereof deposited with
the Minister of Railways ; or of any common front line or
lines agreed upon between the Government and the Company
—the conditions hereinbefore stated as to lands not fairly
fit for settlement to be applicable to such additional grants.
And the Company may, with the consent of the Government, Selection by company in
select in the North-West Territories any tract or tracts of such case, with consent of
land not taken up as a means of supplying or partially Government.
supplying such deficiency. But such grants shall be made
only from lands remaining vested in the Government.

12. The Government shall extinguish the Indian title
affecting the lands herein appropriated, and to be hereafter
granted in aid of the railway.

13. The Company shall have the right, subject to the Location of railway between
approval of the Governor in Council, to lay out and locate certain terminal
the line of the railway hereby contracted for, as they may points.
see fit, preserving the following terminal points, namely :
from Callander station to the point of junction with the
Lake Superior section ; and from Selkirk to the junction
with the Western section at Kamloops by way of the Yellow
Head Pass.

14. The Company shall have the right from time to time Power to construct
to lay out, construct, equip, maintain and work branch branches.
lines of railway from any point or points along their main
line of railway, to any point or points within the territory
of the Dominion. Provided always, that before commencing
any branch they shall first deposit a map and plan of such Lands
branch in the Department of Railways. And the Govern- necessary for the same,
ment shall grant to the Company the lands required for
the road-bed of such branches, and for the stations, station
grounds, buildings, workshops, yards and other appurtenances requisite for the efficient construction and working
of such branches, in so far as such lands are vested in the
Government.

15. For twenty years from the date hereof, no line of Restrictions as to competing
railway shall be authorized by the Dominion Parliament lines for a limited period.
to be constructed South of the Canadian Pacific Railway,
from any point at or near the Canadian Pacific Railway,
except such line as shall run South West or to the Westward
of South West ; nor to within fifteen miles of Latitude 49.
And in the establishment of any new Province in the North-
West Territories, provision shall be made for continuing
such prohibition after such establishment until the expiration
of the same period.

16. The Canadian Pacific Railway, and all stations and Exemption from taxation in
station grounds, workshops, buildings, yards and other N.W. territories.
property, rolling stock and appurtenances required and
used for the construction and working thereof, and the

x

capital stock of the Company, shall be for ever free from taxation by the Dominion, or by any Province hereafter to be established, or by any Municipal Corporation therein ; and the lands of the Company, in the North-West Territories, until they are either sold or occupied, shall also be free from such taxation for 20 years after the grant thereof from the Crown.

Land grant.

Their nature and conditions of issue by the company.

17. The Company shall be authorized by their Act of incorporation to issue bonds, secured upon the land granted and to be granted to the Company, containing provisions for the use of such bonds in the acquisition of lands, and such other conditions as the Company shall see fit—such issue to be for $25,000,000. And should the Company make such issue of land grant bonds, then they shall deposit them in the hands of the Government ; and the Government shall retain and hold one-fifth of such bonds as security for the due performance of the present contract in respect of the maintenance and continuous working of the railway by the Company, as herein agreed, for ten years after the completion thereof, and the remaining $20,000,000 of such bonds shall be dealt with as hereinafter provided. And as to the said one-fifth of the said bonds, so long as no default shall occur in the maintenance and working of the said Canadian Pacific Railway, the Government shall not present or demand payment of the coupons of such bonds, nor require payment of any interest thereon. And if any of such bonds, so to be retained by the Government, shall be paid off in the manner to be provided for the extinction of the whole issue thereof, the Government shall hold the amount received in payment thereof as security for the same purposes as the bonds so paid off, paying interest thereon at four per cent. per annum so long as default is not made by the Company in the performance of the conditions hereof. And at the end of the said period of ten years from the completion of the said railway, if no default shall then have occurred in such maintenance and working thereof, the said bonds, or if any of them shall then have been paid off, the remainder of said bonds and the money received from those paid off, with accrued interest, shall be delivered back by the Government to the Company with all the coupons attached to such bonds. But if such default should occur, the Government may thereafter require payment of interest on the bonds so held and shall not be obliged to continue to pay interest on the money representing bonds paid off ; and while the Government shall retain the right to hold the said portion of the said land grant bonds, other securities satisfactory to the Government may be substituted for them by the Company, by agreement with the Government.

Deposit with Government : for what purposes and on what conditions.

If the company make no default in operating railway.

In case of such default.

18. If the Company shall find it necessary or expedient to sell the remaining $20,000,000 of the land grant bonds or a larger portion thereof than in the proportion of one dollar for each acre of land then earned by the Company, they shall be allowed to do so, but the proceeds thereof, over and above the amount to which the Company shall be entitled as herein provided, shall be deposited with the Government. And the Government shall pay interest upon such deposit half-yearly, at the rate of four per cent. per annum, and shall pay over the amount of such deposit to the Company from time to time, as the work proceeds, in the same proportions, and at the same times and upon the same conditions as the land grant—that is to say: the Company shall be entitled to receive from the Government out of the proceeds of the said land grant bonds, the same number of dollars as the number of acres of the land sub-sidy which shall then have been earned by them, less one-fifth thereof, that is to say, if the bonds are sold at par, but if they are sold at less than par, then a deduction shall be made therefrom corresponding to the discount at which such bonds are sold. And such land grant shall be conveyed to them by the Government, subject to the charge created as security for the said land grant bonds, and shall remain subject to such charge till relieved thereof in such manner as shall be provided for at the time of the issue of such bonds.

Provision if such bonds are sold faster than lands are earned by the company, and deposit on interest with Government, and payments by Government to company.

Lands to be granted subject to such bonds.

19. The Company shall pay any expenses which shall be incurred by the Government in carrying out the provisions of the last two preceding clauses of this contract.

Company to pay certain expenses.

20. If the Company should not issue such land grant bonds, then the Government shall retain from out of each grant to be made from time to time, every fifth section of the lands hereby agreed to be granted, such lands to be so retained as security for the purposes and for the length of time, mentioned in section eighteen hereof. And such lands may be sold in such manner and at such prices as shall be agreed upon between the Government and the Company ; and in that case the price thereof shall be paid to, and held by the Government for the same period, and for the same purposes as the land itself, the Government paying four per cent. per annum interest thereon. And other securities satisfactory to the Government may be substituted for such lands or money by agreement with the Government.

If land bonds are not issued, one-fifth of land to be retained as security.

How to be disposed of.

21. The Company to be incorporated, with sufficient powers to enable them to carry out the foregoing contract, and this contract shall only be binding in the event of an Act of incorporation being granted to the Company in the form hereto appended as Schedule A.

Company to be incorporated as by Schedule A.

Railway Act to apply.

Exceptions:

22. The Railway Act of 1879, in so far as the provisions of the same are applicable to the undertaking referred to in this contract, and in so far as they are not inconsistent herewith or inconsistent with or contrary to the provisions of the Act of incorporation to be granted to the Company, shall apply to the Canadian Pacific Railway.

In witness whereof the parties hereto have executed these presents at the City of Ottawa, this twenty-first day of October, 1880.

(Signed) CHARLES TUPPER,
             Minister of Railways and Canals.
          GEO. STEPHEN,
          DUNCAN McINTYRE,
          J. S. KENNEDY,
          R. B. ANGUS,
          J. J. HILL,
             Per pro. Geo. Stephen.
          MORTON, ROSE & CO.
          KOHN, REINACH & CO.,
             By P. Du P. Grenfell.

Signed in presence of F. BRAUN,
     and Seal of the Department
     hereto affixed by SIR CHARLES
     TUPPER, in presence of
          (Signed) F. BRAUN.

SCHEDULE A, REFERRED TO IN THE FOREGOING CONTRACT

INCORPORATION

Certain persons incorporated.

1. George Stephen, of Montreal, in Canada, Esquire ; Duncan McIntyre, of Montreal, aforesaid, Merchant ; John S. Kennedy, of New York, in the State of New York, Banker ; the firm of Morton, Rose and Company, of London, in England, Merchants ; the firm of Kohn, Reinach and Company, of Paris, in France, Bankers ; Richard B. Angus, and James J. Hill, both of St. Paul, in the State of Minnesota, Esquires ; with all such other persons and corporations as shall become shareholders in the Company hereby incorporated, shall be and they are hereby constituted a body

Corporate name.

corporate and politic, by the name of the " Canadian Pacific Railway Company."

Capital stock and shares.

2. The capital stock of the Company shall be twenty-five million dollars, divided into shares of one hundred dollars each—which shares shall be transferable in such manner and upon such conditions as shall be provided by the by-

laws of the Company : and such shares, or any part thereof
may be granted and issued as paid-up shares for value *bona* **Paid up shares.**
fide received by the Company, either in money at par or at
such price and upon such conditions as the Board of Directors
may fix, or as part of the consideration of any contract
made by the Company.

3. As soon as five million dollars of the stock of the Com- **Substitution of Company as contractors ; and when.**
pany have been subscribed, and thirty per centum thereof,
paid up, and upon the deposit with the Minister of Finance
of the Dominion of one million dollars in money or in securities approved by the Governor in Council, for the purpose
and upon the conditions in the foregoing contract provided
the said contract shall become and be transferred to the **Effect of such substitution.**
Company, without the execution of any deed or instrument
in that behalf ; and the Company shall, thereupon, become
and be vested with all the rights of the contractors named
in the said contract, and shall be subject to, and liable for,
all their duties and obligations, to the same extent and in
the same manner as if the said contract had been executed
by the said Company instead of by the said contractors ;
and thereupon the said contractors, as individuals, shall
cease to have any right or interest in the said contract,
and shall not be subject to any liability or responsibility
under the terms thereof otherwise than as members of the
corporation hereby created. And upon the performance
of the said conditions respecting the subscription of stock,
the partial payment thereof, and the deposit of one million
dollars to the satisfaction of the Governor in Council, the
publication by the Secretary of State in the *Canada Gazette,* **Notice in the *Canada Gazette.***
of a notice that the transfer of the contract to the Company
has been effected and completed shall be conclusive proof
of the fact. And the Company shall cause to be paid up,
on or before the first day of May next, a further instalment **Further instalment to be paid up.**
of twenty per centum upon the said first subscription of five
million dollars, of which call thirty days' notice by circular
mailed to each shareholder shall be sufficient. And the
Company shall call in, and cause to be paid up, on or before
the 31st day of December, 1882, the remainder of the said **And rest of $5,000,000.**
first subscription of five million dollars.

4. All the franchises and powers necessary or useful to **Necessary franchises and powers granted.**
the Company to enable them to carry out, perform, enforce,
use, and avail themselves of, every condition, stipulation,
obligation, duty, right, remedy, privilege, and advantage
agreed upon, contained or described in the said contract are
hereby conferred upon the Company. And the enactment
of the special provisions hereinafter contained shall not be **Proviso.**
held to impair or derogate from the generality of the franchises and powers so hereby conferred upon them.

Directors

First directors of the company. 5. The said George Stephen, Duncan McIntyre, John S. Kennedy, Richard B. Angus, James J. Hill, Henry Stafford Northcote, of London, aforesaid, Esquires, Pascoe du P. Grenfell, of London, aforesaid, Merchant, Charles Day Rose of London, aforesaid, Merchant, and Byron J. de Reinach, of Paris, aforesaid, Banker, are hereby constituted the first directors of the Company, with power to add to their number, but so that the directors shall not in all exceed fifteen in number ; and the majority of the directors, of whom the President shall be one, shall be British subjects. And the Board of Directors so constituted shall have all the powers hereby conferred upon the directors of the Company, and they shall hold office until the first annual meeting of the shareholders of the Company.

Number limited.

Qualification of directors. 6. Each of the directors of the Company, hereby appointed, or hereafter appointed or elected, shall hold at least two hundred and fifty shares of the stock of the Company. But the number of directors to be hereafter elected by the shareholders shall be such, not exceeding fifteen, as shall be fixed by by-law, and subject to the same conditions as the directors appointed by, or under the authority of, the last preceding section ; the number thereof may be hereafter altered from time to time in like manner. The votes for their election shall be by ballot.

Alteration of number by by-law.

Ballot.

Quorum. 7. A majority of the directors shall form a quorum of the board ; and until otherwise provided by by-law, directors may vote and act by proxy—such proxy to be held by a director only ; but no director shall hold more than two proxies, and no meeting of directors shall be competent to transact business unless at least three directors are present thereat in person, the remaining number of directors required to form a quorum being represented by proxies.

Proviso.

Three must be present.

Executive committee. 8. The Board of Directors may appoint, from out of their number, an Executive Committee, composed of at least three directors, for the transaction of the ordinary business of the Company, with such powers and duties as shall be fixed by the by-laws ; and the President shall be *ex officio* a member of such committee.

President to be one.

Chief place of business. Other places. 9. The chief place of business of the Company shall be at the City of Montreal, but the Company may, from time to time, by by-law, appoint and fix other places within or beyond the limits of Canada at which the business of the Company may be transacted, and at which the directors or shareholders may meet, when called as shall be determined by the by-laws. And the Company shall appoint and fix by by-law, at least one place in each Province or

Territory through which the railway shall pass, where
service of process may be made upon the Company, in
respect of any cause of action arising within such Province
or Territory, and may afterwards, from time to time, change
such place by by-law. And a copy of any by-law fixing *How to be notified.*
or changing any such place, duly authenticated as herein
provided, shall be deposited by the Company in the office,
at the seat of Government of the Province or Territory to
which such by-law shall apply, of the clerk or prothonotary
of the highest, or one of the highest, courts of civil juris-
diction of such Province or Territory. And if any cause *Service of process thereat.*
of action shall arise against the Company within any Pro-
vince or Territory, and any writ or process be issued against
the Company thereon out of any court in such Province
or Territory, service of such process may be validly made
upon the Company at the place within such Province or
Territory so appointed and fixed ; but if the Company fail *And if Company fail to appoint places.*
to appoint and fix such place, or to deposit, as hereinbefore
provided, the by-law made in that behalf, any such process
may be validly served upon the Company, at any of
the stations of the said railway within such Province or
Territory.

SHAREHOLDERS

10. The first annual meeting of the shareholders of the *First and other annual meetings.*
Company, for the appointment of directors, shall be held
on the second Wednesday in May, one thousand eight hundred
and eighty-two, at the principal office of the Company, in
Montreal ; and the annual general meeting of shareholders,
for the election of directors and the transaction of business
generally, shall be held on the same day in each year thereafter at the same place unless otherwise provided by the
by-laws. And notice of each of such meetings shall be *Notice.*
given by the publication thereof in the *Canada Gazette*
for four weeks, and by such further means as shall, from
time to time, be directed by the by-laws.

11. Special general meetings of the shareholders may be *Special general meetings : notice.*
convened in such manner as shall be provided by the by-
laws ; and except as hereinafter provided, notice of such
meetings shall be given in the same manner as notices of
annual general meetings, the purpose for which such meeting
is called being mentioned in the notices thereof ; and except
as hereinafter provided, all such meetings shall be held at *Place.*
the chief place of business of the Company.

12. If at any time before the first annual meeting of the *Provision if a meeting be necessary before notice as aforesaid can be given.*
shareholders of the Company, it should become expedient
that a meeting of the directors of the Company, or a special
general meeting of the shareholders of the Company, should

be held, before such meeting can conveniently be called,
and notice thereof given in the manner provided by this
Act, or by the by-laws, or before by-laws in that behalf
have been passed, and at a place other than at the chief
place of business of the Company in Montreal before the
enactment of a by-law authorizing the holding of such
meeting elsewhere ; it shall be lawful for the President
or for any three of the directors of the Company to call
special meetings either of directors or of shareholders, or of
both, to be held at the City of London, in England, at times
and places respectively, to be stated in the notices to be

Notice in such case. given of such meetings respectively. And notices of such
meetings may be validly given by a circular mailed to the
ordinary address of each director or shareholder as the case
may be, in time to enable him to attend such meeting,
stating in general terms the purpose of the intended meeting.
And in the case of a meeting of shareholders, the proceed-

Meetings always valid if all shareholders or their proxies are present. ings of such meeting shall be held to be valid and sufficient,
and to be binding on the Company in all respects, if every
shareholder of the Company be present thereat in person
or by proxy, notwithstanding that notice of such meeting
shall not have been given in the manner required by this
Act.

Limitations as to votes and proxies. 13. No shareholder holding shares upon which any call
is overdue and unpaid shall vote at any meeting of share-
holders. And unless otherwise provided by the by-laws,
the person holding the proxy of a shareholder shall be himself
a shareholder.

And as to calls. 14. No call upon unpaid shares shall be made for more
than twenty per centum upon the amount thereof.

RAILWAY AND TELEGRAPH LINE

Line and gauge of railway. 15. The Company may lay out, construct, acquire, equip,
maintain and work a continuous line of railway, of the gauge
of four feet eight and one-half inches ; which railway shall
extend from the terminus of the Canada Central Railway
near Lake Nipissing, known as Callander Station, to Port
Moody in the Province of British Columbia ; and also a
branch line of railway from some point on the main line
of railway to Fort William on Thunder Bay : and also the
existing branch line of railway from some point on the main
line of railway to Fort William on Thunder Bay ; and also
the existing branch line of railway from Selkirk, in the
Province of Manitoba, to Pembina in the said Province ;
and also other branches to be located by the Company from
time to time as provided by the said contract—the said

branches to be of the gauge aforesaid ; and the said main line of railway, and the said branch lines of railway, shall be commenced and completed as provided by the said contract ; and together with such other branch lines as shall be hereafter constructed by the said Company, and any extension of the said main line of railway that shall hereafter be constructed or acquired by the Company, shall constitute the line of railway hereinafter called THE CANADIAN PACIFIC RAILWAY.

Commencement and completion.

Other branches.

Name of Railway.

16. The Company may construct, maintain and work a continuous telegraph line and telephone lines throughout and along the whole line of the Canadian Pacific Railway, or any part thereof, and may also construct or acquire by purchase, lease or otherwise, any other line or lines of telegraph connecting with the line so to be constructed along the line of the said railway, and may undertake the transmission of messages for the public by any such line or lines of telegraph or telephone, and collect tolls for so doing ; or may lease such line or lines of telegraph or telephone, or any portion thereof ; and if they think proper to undertake the transmission of messages for hire, they shall be subject to the provisions of the fourteenth, fifteenth and sixteenth sections of chapter sixty-seven of the Consolidated Statutes of Canada. And they may use any improvement that may hereafter be invented (subject to the rights of patentees) for telegraphing or telephoning, and any other means of communication that may be deemed expedient by the Company at any time hereafter.

Company may construct lines of telegraph or telephone, and work them and collect tolls.

Subject to Con. Stat. Can., c. 67, ss. 14, 15, 16.

POWERS

17. " *The Consolidated Railway Act, 1879,*" in so far as the provisions of the same are applicable to the undertaking authorized by this charger, and in so far as they are not inconsistent with or contrary to the provisions hereof, and save and except as hereinafter provided, is hereby incorporated herewith.

Application of 42 V., c. 9.

18. As respects the said railway, the seventh section of " *The Consolidated Railway Act, 1879,*" relating to POWERS, and the eighth section thereof relating to PLANS AND SURVEYS, shall be subject to the following provisions :—

Exceptions as to such application.

a. The Company shall have the right to take, use and hold the beach and land below high-water mark, in any stream, lake, navigable water, gulf or sea, in so far as the same shall be vested in the Crown and shall not be required by the Crown, to such extent as shall be required by the Company for its railway and other works, and as shall be exhibited by a map or plan thereof deposited in the office

As to lands of the Crown required.

of the Minister of Railways. But the provisions of this sub-section shall not apply to any beach or land lying East of Lake Nipissing except with the approval of the Governor in Council.

Plans and book of reference.

b. It shall be sufficient that the map or plan and book of reference for any portion of the line of the railway not being within any district or country for which there is a Clerk of the Peace, be deposited in the office of the Minister of Railways of Canada; and any omission, mis-statement or erroneous description of any lands therein may be corrected by the Company, with the consent of the Minister and certified by him; and the Company may then make the railway in accordance with such certified correction.

Deviations from line on plan.

c. The eleventh sub-section of the said eighth section of the Railway Act shall not apply to any portion of the railway passing over ungranted lands of the Crown, or lands not within any surveyed township in any Province; and in such places, deviations not exceeding five miles from the line shown on the map or plan as aforesaid, deposited by the Company, shall be allowed, without any formal correction or certificate; and any further deviation that may be found expedient may be authorized by order of the Governor in Council and the Company may then make their railway in accordance with such authorized deviation.

Deposit of plan of main line, etc.

And of branches.

d. The map or plan and book of reference of any part of the main line of the Canadian Pacific Railway made and deposited in accordance with this section, after approval by the Governor in Council, and of any branch of such railway hereafter to be located by the said Company in respect of which the approval of the Governor in Council shall not be necessary, shall avail as if made and deposited as required by the said " *Consolidated Railway Act*, 1879," for all the purposes of the said Act, and of this Act; and any copy of, or extract therefrom, certified by the said Minister or his deputy, shall be received as evidence in any court of law in Canada.

Copies thereof.

e. It shall be sufficient that a map or profile of any part of the completed railway, which shall not lie within any country or district having a registry office, be filed in the office of the Minister of Railways.

Registration thereof.

Company may take materials from public lands and a greater extent for stations, and, etc., than allowed by 42 V., c. 9.

19. It shall be lawful for the Company to take from any public lands adjacent to or near the line of the said railway, all stone, timber, gravel and other materials which may be necessary or useful for the construction of the railway; and also to lay out and appropriate to the use of the Company, a greater extent of lands, whether public or private, for stations, depots, workshops, buildings, side-tracks, wharves, harbours and roadway, and for establishing

screens against snow, than the breadth and quantity mentioned in " *The Consolidated Railway Act*, 1879,"—such greater extent taken, in any case being allowed by the Government, and shown on the maps or plans deposited with the Minister of Railways. Proviso.

20.   The limit to the reduction of tolls by the Parliament of Canada provided for by the eleventh sub-section of the 17th section of " *The Consolidated Railway Act*, 1879," respecting TOLLS, is hereby extended, so that such reduction may be to such an extent that such tolls when reduced shall not produce less than ten per cent. per annum profit on the capital actually expended in the construction of the railway, instead of not less than fifteen per cent. per annum profit, as provided by the said sub-section ; and so also that such reduction shall not be made unless the net income of the Company, ascertained as described in said sub-section, shall have exceeded ten per cent. per annum instead of fifteen per cent. per annum as provided by the said sub-section. And the exercise by the Governor in Council of the power of reducing the tolls of the Company as provided by the tenth sub-section of said section seventeen is hereby limited to the same extent with relation to the profit of the Company, and to its net revenue, as that to which the power of Parliament to reduce tolls is limited by said sub-section eleven as hereby amended. Reduction by Governor in Council extended in like manner.

21. The first and second sub-sections of section 22 of " *The Consolidated Railway Act*, 1879," shall not apply to the Canadian Pacific Railway Company ; and it is hereby enacted that the transfer of shares in the undertaking shall be made only upon the books of the Company in person or by attorney, and shall not be valid unless so made ; and the form and mode of transfer shall be such as shall be, from time to time, regulated by the by-laws of the Company. And the funds of the Company shall not be used in any advance upon the security of any of the shares or stock of the Company. Restriction as to transfers of stock. Advances on, by Company forbidden.

22. The third and fourth sub-sections of said section 22 of " *The Consolidated Railway Act*, 1879," shall be subject to the following provisions, namely—that if before the completion of the railway and works under the said contract, any transfer should purport to be made of any stock or share in the Company, or any transmission of any share should be effected under the provisions of said sub-section four, to a person not already a shareholder in the Company, and if in the opinion of the board it should not be expedient that the person (not being already a shareholder) to whom such transfer or transmission shall be made or effected should be accepted as a shareholder, the directors may by resolution Transfer or transmission to non-shareholders subject to veto of directors until completion of contract.

veto such transfer or transmission ; and thereafter, and
until after the completion of the said railway and works
under the said contract, such person shall not be, or be
recognized as a shareholder in the Company ; and the original shareholder, or his estate, as the case may be, shall
remain subject to all the obligations of a shareholder in the
Company, with all the rights conferred upon a shareholder
under this Act.   But any firm holding paid-up shares in the
Company may transfer the whole or any of such shares to
any partner in such firm having already an interest as such
partner in such shares, without being subject to such veto.
And in the event of such veto being exercised, a note shall be
taken of the transfer or transmission so vetoed in order that
it may be recorded in the books of the Company after the
completion of the railway and works as aforesaid ; but
until such completion, the transfer or transmission so vetoed
shall not confer any rights, nor have any effect of any nature
or kind whatever as respects the Company.

Proviso : as to transfer by a firm to a partner.

23. Sub-section sixteen of section nineteen, relating to
PRESIDENT AND DIRECTORS, THEIR ELECTION AND DUTIES ;
sub-section two of section twenty-four relating to by-laws,
NOTICES, etc., sub-sections five and six of section twenty-
eight, relating to GENERAL PROVISIONS, and section ninety-
seven, relating to RAILWAY FUND, of " *The Consolidated
Railway Act*, 1879," shall not, nor shall any of them apply
to the Canadian Pacific Railway or to the Company hereby
incorporated.

Certain other provisions of 42 V., c. 9, not to apply.

24. The said Company shall afford all reasonable facilities
to the Ontario and Pacific Junction Railway Company,
when their railway shall be completed to a point of junction
with the Canadian Pacific Railway, and to the Canada Central
Railway Company, for the receiving, forwarding and delivering of traffic upon and from the railways of the said Companies, respectively, and for the return of carriages, trucks
and other vehicles ; and no one of the said Companies shall
give or continue any preference or advantage to, or in favour
of either of the others, or of any particular description of
traffic, in any respect whatsoever ; nor shall any one of the
said Companies subject any other thereof, or any particular
description of traffic, to any prejudice or disadvantage in
any respect whatsoever ; and any one of the said Companies
which shall have any terminus or station near any terminus
or station of either of the others, shall afford all reasonable
facilities for receiving and forwarding all the traffic arriving
by either of the others, without any unreasonable delay,
and without any preference or advantage, or prejudice or
disadvantage, and so that no obstruction may be offered
in the using of such railway as a continuous line of communi-

Company to afford reason-able facilities to and receive the like from certain other railway companies.

cation, and so that all reasonable accommodation may, at all times, by the means aforesaid, be mutually afforded by and to the said several railway companies ; and the said Canadian Pacific Railway Company shall receive and carry all freight and passenger traffic shipped to or from any point on the railway of either of the said above-named railway companies passing over the Canadian Pacific Railway or any part thereof, at the same mileage rate and subject to the same charges for similar services, without granting or allowing any preference or advantage to the traffic coming from or going upon one of such railways over such traffic coming from or going upon the other of them, reserving, however, to the said Canadian Pacific Railway Company the right of making special rates for purchasers of land or for immigrants or intending immigrants, which special rates shall not govern or affect the rates of passenger traffic as between the said Company and the said two above-named Companies or either of them. And any agreement made between any two of the said Companies comtrary to the foregoing provisions, shall be unlawful, null and void. *[As to rates of carriage of traffic in such cases. Reservation as to purchasers of land, and immigrants. Contrary agreements void.]*

25. The Company, under the authority of a special general meeting of the shareholders thereof, and as an extension of the railway hereby authorized to be constructed, may purchase or acquire by lease or otherwise, and hold and operate, the Canada Central Railway, or may amalgamate therewith, and may purchase or acquire by lease or otherwise and hold and operate a line or lines of railway from the City of Ottawa to any point at navigable water on the Atlantic seaboard or to any intermediate point, or may acquire running powers over all railway now constructed between Ottawa and any such point or intermediate point. And the Company may purchase or acquire any such railway, subject to such existing mortgages, charges or liens thereon as shall be agreed upon, and shall possess with regard to any lines or railway so purchased, or acquired, and becoming the property of the Company, the same powers as to the issue of bonds thereon, or on any of them, to an amount not exceeding twenty thousand dollars per mile, and as to the security for such bonds, as are conferred upon the Company by the twenty-eighth section hereof, in respect of bonds to be issued upon the Canadian Pacific Railway. But such issue of bonds shall not affect the right of any holder of mortgages or other charges already existing upon any line of railway so purchased or acquired ; and the amount of bonds hereby authorized to be issued upon such line of railway shall be diminished by the amount of such existing mortgages or charges thereon. *[Company may purchase or acquire by lease or otherwise certain other railways or amalgamate with them. And borrow to a limited amount on bonds in consequence. Not to affect prior mortgages.]*

26. The Company shall have power and authority to erect

Company may
have docks,
etc., and run
vessels on any
navigable water
their railway
touches.

and maintain docks, dockyards, wharves, slips and piers at
any point on or in connection with the said Canadian Pacific
Railway, and at all the termini thereof on navigable water,
for the convenience and accommodation of vessels and
elevators ; and also to acquire and work elevators, and to
acquire, own, hold, charter, work and run steam and other
vessels for cargo and passengers upon any navigable water,
which the Canadian Pacific Railway may reach or connect
with.

By-Laws

By-laws may
provide for
certain
purposes.

27. The by-laws of the Company may provide for the
remuneration of the president and directors of the Company,
and of any executive committee of such directors ; and for
the transfer of stock and shares ; the registration and
inscription of stock, shares and bonds, and the transfer
of registered bonds ; and the payment of dividends and
interest at any place or places within or beyond the limits
of Canada ; and for all other matters required by the said

Must be
confirmed at
next general
meeting.

contract or by this Act to be regulated by by-laws : but the
by-laws of the Company made as provided by law shall in
no case have any force or effect after the next general meeting
of shareholders which shall be held after the passage of
such by-laws, unless they are approved by such meeting.

Bonds

Amount of
bonds limited.

28. The Company, under the authority of a special general
meeting of the shareholders called for the purpose, may issue
mortgage bonds to the extent of ten thousand dollars per
mile of the Canadian Pacific Railway for the purposes of
the undertaking authorized by the present Act ; which issue

Mortgages for
securing the
same on all the
property of the
company.

shall constitute a first mortgage and privilege upon the said
railway, constructed or acquired, and to be thereafter constructed or acquired, and upon its property, real and personal,
acquired and to be thereafter acquired, including rolling
stock and plant, and upon its tolls and revenues (after deduction from such tolls and revenues of working expenses),
and upon the franchises of the Company ; the whole as
shall be declared and described as so mortgaged in any

Proviso : in
case land
grant bonds
have been
issued under
section 30.

deed of mortgage as hereinafter provided. Provided always,
however, that if the Company shall have issued, or shall
intend to issue, land grant bonds under the provisions of
the thirtieth section hereof, the lands granted and to be
granted by the Government to the Company may be excluded
from the operation of such mortgage and privilege : and
provided also that such mortgage and privilege shall not

attach upon any property which the Company are hereby, or by the said contract, authorized to acquire or receive from the Government of Canada until the same shall have been conveyed by the Government to the Company, but shall attach upon such property, if so declared in such deed, as soon as the same shall be conveyed to the Company. And such mortgage and privilege may be evidenced by a deed or deeds of mortgage executed by the Company, with the authority of its shareholders expressed by a resolution passed at such special general meeting ; and any such deed may contain such description of the property mortgaged by such deed, and such conditions respecting the payment of the bonds secured thereby and of the interest thereon, and the remedies which shall be enjoyed by the holders of such bonds or by any trustee or trustees for them in default of such payment, and the enforcement of such remedies, and may provide for such forfeitures and penalties, in default of such payment, as may be approved by such meeting ; and may also contain, with the approval aforesaid, authority to the trustee or trustees, upon such default, as one of such remedies, to take possession of the railway and property mortgaged, and to hold and run the same for the benefit of the bondholders thereof for a time to be limited by such deed, or to sell the said railway and property, after such delay, and upon such terms and conditions as may be stated in such deed : and with like approval any such deed may contain provisions to the effect that upon such default and upon such other conditions as shall be described in such deed, the right of voting possessed by the shareholders of the Company, and by the holders of preferred stock therein, or by either of them, shall cease, and holders, or to them and to the holders of the whole or of any part of the preferred stock of the Company, as shall be declared by such deed : and such deed may also provide for the conditional or absolute cancellation after such sale of any or all of the shares so deprived of voting power, or of any or all of the preferred stock of the Company, or both ; and may also, either directly by its terms, or indirectly by reference to the by-laws of the Company, provide for the mode of enforcing and exercising the powers and authority to be conferred and defined by such deed, under the provisions hereof. And such deed, and the provisions thereof made under the authority hereof, and such other provisions thereof as shall purport (with like approval) to grant such further and other powers and privileges to such trustee or trustees and to such bond-holders, as are not contrary to law or to the provisions of this Act, shall be valid and binding. But if any change in the ownership or possession of the said railway and

Evidence of mortgage and what conditions the bonds may contain.

Right of voting may, in such case, be transferred to bondholders.

Cancellation of shares deprived of voting power.

Enforcing conditions.

Further provisions under mortgage deed.

property shall, at any time, take place under the provisions hereof, or of any such deed, or in any other manner, the said railway and property shall continue to be held and operated under the provisions hereof, and of " *The Consolidated Railway Act*, 1879," as hereby modified. And if
Increase of
borrowing power
if no land
grant bonds are
issued.
the Company does not avail itself of the power of issuing bonds secured upon the land grant along as hereinafter provided, the issue of bonds hereby authorized may be increased to any amount not exceeding twenty thousand dollars per mile of the said Canadian Pacific Railway.

Provision if
such bonds are
issued before
completion of
railway.
29. If any bond issue be made by the Company under the last preceding section before the said railway is completed according to the said contract, a proportion of the proceeds of such bonds, or a proportion of such bonds if they be not sold, corresponding to the proportion of the work contracted for then remaining incomplete, shall be received by the Government, and shall be held, dealt with, and from time to time paid over by the Government to the Company upon the same conditions, in the same manner and according to the same proportions as the proceeds of the bonds, the issue of which is contemplated by subsection *d* of Clause 9 of the said contract, and by the thirty-first section hereof.

Provision as to
issue of land
grant mortgage
bonds.
30. The Company may also issue mortgage bonds to the extent of twenty-five million dollars upon the lands granted in aid of the said railway and of the undertaking authorized by this Act ; such issue to be made only upon similar authority to that required by this Act for the issue of bonds upon the railway ; and when so made such bonds shall constitute a first mortgage upon such lands, and shall attach upon them when they shall be granted, if they are not actually granted at the time of the issue of such bonds.
Evidence of
mortgage and
conditions.
And such mortgage may be evidenced by a deed or deeds of mortgage to be executed under like authority to the deed securing the issue of bonds on the railway ; and such deed or deeds under like authority may contain similar conditions, and may confer upon the trustee or trustees named thereunder, and upon the holders of the bonds secured thereby, remedies, authority, power and privileges, and may provide for forfeitures and penalties, similar to those which may be inserted and provided for under the provisions of this Act in any deed securing the issue of bonds on the railway, together with such other provisions and conditions not inconsistent with law or with this Act as shall be so author-
Name of and
how dealt with.
ized. And such bonds may be styled Land Grant Bonds, and they and the proceeds thereof shall be dealt with in the manner provided in the said contract.

31. The Company may, in the place and stead of the said land grant bonds, issue bonds, under the twenty-eighth section hereof, to such amount as they shall agree with the Government to issue, with the interest guaranteed by the Government as provided for in the said contract ; such bonds to constitute a mortgage upon the property of the Company and its franchises acquired and to be thereafter acquired—including the main line of the Canadian Pacific Railway, and the branches thereof hereinbefore described, with the plant and rolling-stock thereof acquired and to be thereafter acquired, but exclusive of such other branches thereof and of such personal property as shall be excluded by the deed of mortgage to be executed as security for such issue. And the provisions of the said twenty-eighth section shall apply to such issue of bonds, and to the security which may be given for the payment thereof, and they and the proceeds thereof shall be dealt with as hereby and by the said contract provided.

[margin: Issue of bonds in place of land grant bonds under agreement with Government.]
[margin: To include franchise as well as property of company.]
[margin: Section 28 to apply.]

32. It shall not be necessary to affix the seal of the Company to any mortgage bond issued under the authority of this Act ; and every such bond issued without such seal shall have the same force and effect, and be held, treated and dealt with by all courts of law and of equity as if it were sealed with the seal of the company. And if it is provided by the mortgage deed executed to secure the issue of any bonds that any of the signatures to such bonds or to the coupons thereto appended may be engraved, stamped or lithographed thereon, such engravéd, stamped or lithographed signatures shall be valid and binding on the Company.

[margin: Facilities for issue of mortgage bonds as to seal and signatures.]

33. The phrase " working expenses " shall mean and include all expenses of maintenance of the railway, and of the stations, buildings, works and conveniencies belonging thereto, and of the rolling and other stock and moveable plant used in the working thereof, and also all such tolls, rents or annual sums as may be paid in respect of the hire of engines, carriages or wagons let to the Company ; also all rent, charges or interest on the purchase money of lands belonging to the Company, purchased but not paid for, or not fully paid for ; and also all expenses of, and incidental to, working the railway and the traffic thereon, including stores and consumable articles ; also rates, taxes, insurance and compensation for accidents or losses ; also all salaries and wages of persons employed in and about the working of the railway and traffic, and all office and management expenses, including directors' fees, agency, legal and other like expenses.

[margin: " Working expenses " defined.]

34. The bonds authorized by this Act to be issued upon the railway or upon the lands to be granted to the Company,

[margin: Currency on which bonds may be issued.]

or both, may be so issued in whole or in part in the denomination of dollars, pounds sterling, or francs, or in any or all of them, and the coupons may be for payment in denominations similar to those of the bond to which they are attached.

And the whole or any of such bonds may be pledged, negotiated or sold upon such conditions and at such price as the Board of Directors shall from time to time determine. And

provision may be made by the by-laws of the Company, that after the issue of any bond, the same may be surrendered to the Company by the holder thereof, and the Company may, in exchange therefor, issue to such holder inscribed stock of the Company—which inscribed stock may be registered or inscribed at the chief place of business of the Company or elsewhere, in such manner, with such rights, liens, privileges and preferences, at such place, and upon such conditions, as shall be provided by the by-laws of the Company.

35. It shall not be necessary, in order to preserve the priority, lien, charge, mortgage or privilege, purporting to appertain to or be created by any bond issued or mortgage deed executed under the provisions of this Act, that such bond or deed should be enregistered in any manner, or in

any place whatever. But every such mortgage deed shall be deposited in the office of the Secretary of State—of which

deposit notice shall be given in the *Canada Gazette*. And in like manner any agreement entered into by the Company, under section thirty-six of this Act, shall also be deposited in the said office. And a copy of any such mortgage deed,

or agreement, certified to be a true copy by the Secretary of State or his deputy, shall be received as *prima facie* evidence of the original in all courts of justice, without proof of the signatures or seal upon such original.

36. If, at any time, any agreement be made by the Company with any persons intending to become bondholders of the Company, or be contained in any mortgage deed executed under the authority of this Act, restricting the issue of bonds by the Company, under the powers conferred by this Act, or defining or limiting the mode of exercising such powers, the Company, after the deposit thereof with the Secretary of State as hereinbefore provided, shall not act upon such powers otherwise than as defined, restricted and

limited by such agreement. And no bond thereafter issued by the Company, and no order, resolution or proceeding thereafter made, passed or had by the Company, or by the Board of Directors, contrary to the terms of such agreement, shall be valid or effectual.

37. The Company may, from time to time, issue guaranteed or preferred stock, at such price, to such amount, not exceeding ten thousand dollars per mile, and upon such

conditions as to the preferences and privileges appertaining thereto, or to different issues or classes thereof, and otherwise, as shall be authorized by the majority in value of the shareholders present in person or represented by proxy at any annual meeting or at any special general meeting thereof called for the purpose—notice of the intention to propose such issue at such meeting being given in the notice calling such meeting. But the guarantee or preference accorded to such stock shall not interfere with the lien, mortgage and privilege attaching to bonds issued under the authority of this Act. And the holders of such preferred stock shall have such power of voting at meetings of shareholders as shall be conferred upon them by the by-laws of the Company.

Not to affect privileges of bondholders.

Voting.

Execution of Agreements

38. Every contract, agreement, engagement, scrip certificate or bargain made, and every bill of exchange drawn, accepted or endorsed, and every promissory note and cheque made, drawn or endorsed on behalf of the Company, by any agent, officer or servant of the Company, in general accordance with his powers as such under the by-laws of the Company, shall be binding upon the Company : and in no case shall it be necessary to have the seal of the Company affixed to any such bill, note, cheque, contract, agreement, engagement, bargain or scrip certificate, or to prove that the same was made, drawn, accepted or endorsed, as the case may be, in pursuance of any by-law or special vote or order ; nor shall the party so acting as agent, officer or servant of the Company be subjected individually to any liability whatsoever to any third party therefor : Provided always, that nothing in this Act shall be construed to authorize the Company to issue any note payable to the bearer thereof, or any promissory note intended to be circulated as money, or as the note of a bank, or to engage in the business of banking or insurance.

Contracts, bills, etc., by its agents to bind the company.

Proof thereof.

Non-liability of such agents.

Proviso : as to notes.

General Provisions

39. The Company shall, from time to time, furnish such reports of the progress of the work, with such details and plans of the work as the Government may require.

Reports to Government.

40. As respect places not within any Province, any notice required by " *The Consolidated Railway Act*, 1879," to be given in the " Official Gazette " of a Province, may be given in the *Canada Gazette*.

Publication of notices.

Form of deeds, etc., to the Company.

41. Deeds and conveyances of lands to the Company for the purpose of this Act (not being letters patent from the Crown), may, in so far as circumstances will admit, be in the form following, that is to say :—

Form.

" Know all men by these presents, that I, A. B., in consideration of   paid to me by the Canadian Pacific Railway Company, the receipt whereof is hereby acknowledged, grant, bargain, sell and convey unto the said The Canadian Pacific Railway Company, their successors and assigns, all that tract or parcel of land (*describe the land*) to have and to hold the said land and premises unto the said Company, their successors and assigns for ever.

" Witness my hand and seal, this   day of one thousand eight hundred and

" Signed, sealed and delivered
in presence of   A. B.   (L. S.)

" C. D.
" E. F.

Obligation of the grantor.

or in any other form to the like effect. And every deed made in accordance herewith shall be held and construed to impose upon the vendor executing the same the obligation of guaranteeing the Company and its assigns against all dower and claim for dower and against all hypothecs and mortgages and against all liens and charges whatsoever, and also that he has a good, valid and transferable title thereto.

Bibliography

The bibliography by no means pretends to be inclusive or exhaustive. The works listed have been found useful in the preparation of the study.

I. GENERAL WORKS

Allin, C. D., and Jones, G. M.—" Annexation, Preferential Trade and Reciprocity." Toronto, 1911.

Asher, George M.—" Henry Hudson, the Navigator." London, 1860.

Atcheson, Nathaniel—" On the Origin and Progress of the North-West Company of Canada." London, 1811. (See footnote *re* authorship of this work in Davidson, G. C.— op. cit., p. 126).

Ballantyne, Robert M.—" Handbook to the New Goldfields." Edinburgh, 1858.

Bancroft, H. H.—" History of Alaska, 1730–1885." Works, vol. 33. New York, 1874–1890.

Bancroft, H. H.—" History of British Columbia." New York, 1887.

Bancroft, H. H.—" History of the North-West Coast, 1543–1846." Works, vols. 27–28.

Bancroft, H. H.—" History of Oregon, 1834–88." Works, vols. 29–30.

Bartlett, Wm. H.—" History of the American Revolution." New York, 1881.

Begg, Alexander—" History of British Columbia." Toronto, 1894.

Begg, Alexander—" History of the North-West." Toronto, 1894-5.

Beltrami, G. C.—" A Pilgrimage in Europe and America leading to the Discovery of the Sources of the Mississippi and Bloody River." London, 1828.

Biggar, Henry P.—" Early Trading Companies of New France." Toronto, 1901.

Bland, Brown and Tawney—" English Economic History, Select Documents." London, 1920.

Bliss, Henry—" The Colonial System." London, 1833.

Bonnycastle, Sir Richard Henry—" Canada and the Canadians in 1846." London, 1846.

Bouchette, Joseph—" The British Dominions in North America." London, 1832.

Bryce, George—" Remarkable History of the Hudson Bay Company." London, 1900.

Buckingham and Ross—" Life and Times of Hon. Alexander Mackenzie." Toronto, 1892.

Burpee, Lawrence J.—" Sandford Fleming, Empire Builder." London, 1915.

Burpee, Lawrence J.—" The Search for the Western Sea." Toronto, 1908.

Burton, C. M. ed.—" Journal of the Pontiac Conspiracy." Detroit, 1912.

Capp, E. H.—" The Annals of Sault Ste. Marie." Sault Ste. Marie, 1904.

Carnarvon, Earl of—" Speeches on Canadian Affairs." London, 1902.

Cartier, Jacques—" Bref récit et succincte narration de la navigation par le Capitaine Jacques Cartier. Introduction historique par d'Avezac." Paris, 1863.

Cartier, Jacques—" Relation Originale du Voyage de Jacques Cartier au Canada en 1534." Michelant, H. and Rame, A. ed. Paris, 1867.

Cartwright, Rt. Hon. Sir Richard—" Reminiscences." Toronto, 1912.

Charlevoix, P. F. X.—" History and General Description of New France." Trans. by John G. Shea. New York, 1866–72.

Chewett, James G.—" Map of the Province of Upper Canada in 1825."

Chewett, Wm.—" Map of the Located Districts in the Province of Upper Canada." 1813.

Clark, A. B.—" An Outline of Provincial and Municipal Taxation in British Columbia, Alberta and Saskatchewan." Winnipeg, 1920.

Colquhoun, A. H. U.—" The Fathers of Confederation." Toronto, 1916.

Coats, R. H., and Gosnell, R. E.—" Sir James Douglas." Toronto, 1910.

Cook, James—" A Voyage to the Pacific Ocean, 1776–80." London, 1785.

Cornwallis, Kinahan—" The New El Dorado, or British Columbia." London, 1858.

Coues, Elliott ed.—" Expeditions of Zebulon M. Pike to the Headwaters of the Mississippi River through Louisiana territory and in New Spain during the years 1805–6–7." New York, 1895.

Coues, Elliott ed.—" History of the Expedition under the Command of Lewis and Clark." New York, 1893.

Coues, Elliott ed.—" New Light on the Early History of the Greater North-West." Journals of Alexander Henry and David Thompson. New York, 1897.

Cox, Ross.—" The Columbia River." London, 1832.

Davidson, G. C.—" The North-West Company." Berkeley, 1918.

De Celles, A. D.—" Sir George Etiennes Cartier." Toronto, 1910.

Denys, Nicholas—" Description and Natural History of the Coasts of North America." Trans. and ed. Ganong, Wm. F., Publ. of the Champlain Society, No. 2. Toronto, 1906.

Dixon, A.—" A Voyage around the World, but more particularly to the North-West Coast of America, performed in 1785, 86, 87 and 88." London, 1789.

"Documentary History of the State of Maine." Portland.

Dollier, De Casson—" Histoire du Montréal, 1640–72." " Mémoires de la Société Historique de Montréal," vol. IV. Montreal, 1868.

Emmerson, John—" British Columbia and Vancouver Island, Voyages, Travels and Adventures." Durham, 1865.

Ferland, J. B. A.—" Cours d'Histoire du Canada." Quebec, 1861–5.

Fleming, Sir Sandford—" The Intercolonial." Montreal, 1876.

Fleming, Sir Sandford's, " Scrapbook." Archives, Ottawa.

Forbes, C.—" Vancouver Island : Its Resources and Capabilities as a Colony." Victoria, 1862.

Fox, Luke—" North-West." London, 1635. (Hakluyt Society, London, 1894.)

Franchere, G.—" Relation d'un Voyage à la cote du Nord-Ouest de l'Amérique septentrionale dans les années 1810, 11, 12, 13 et 14." Montreal, 1820.

Frothingham, R.—" History of the Siege of Boston." Boston, 1849.

Ganong, W. F.—" A Monograph of the Origins of Settlements in the Province of New Brunswick." *Proceedings and Transactions of the Royal Society of Canada*, 1904.

Grant, George M.—" Ocean to Ocean." Toronto, 1873.

Gravier, Gabriel—" Découvertes et Établissements de Cavalier de la Salle de Rouen dans Amérique du Nord." Paris, 1870.

Greene, F. V.—" The Revolutionary War and the Military Policy of the United States." New York, 1911.

Greenhow, Robert—" Memoir, historical and political, on the North-West Coast of North America and the adjacent territories." Washington, 1840.

Gunn, Donald, and Tuttle, Chas. R.—" History of Manitoba." Ottawa, 1880.

Haliburton, Thomas C.—" An Historical and Statistical Account of Nova Scotia." Halifax, 1829.

Ham, George—" Reminiscences of a Raconteur." Toronto, 1921.

Hamilton, P. S.—" Observations upon a Union of Colonies in British North America." Halifax, 1855.

Hakluyt, Richard—" Discourse on Western Planting." 1584. " Documentary History of the State of Maine," vol. II. Cambridge, 1877.

Hakluyt, Richard—" The Principall Navigations, Voyages and Discoveries of the English Nation." London, 1589.

Hakluyt, Richard—" Voyages of Elizabethan Seamen to America." Ed. Payne, E. J. London, 1880.

Hargrave, J. J.—" Red River." Montreal, 1871.

Harmon, Daniel W.—" A Journal of Voyages and Travels in the Interior of North America." Andover, Mass., 1920.

Harvey, Arthur—" A Statistical Account of British Columbia." Ottawa, 1867.

Hatheway, C. L.—" History of New Brunswick." Fredericton, 1846.

Haynes, F. E.—" Reciprocity Treaty with Canada of 1854." *Publications of American Economic Association*, vol. VII., No. 6. Baltimore, 1892.

Hazlitt, W. C.—" British Columbia and Vancouver Island." London, 1858.

Hearne, Samuel—" Journey from Prince of Wales Fort in Hudson's Bay to the Northern Ocean, 1769–72." London, 1795.

Hendry, Anthony—" Journal 1754–5." Ed. Burpee, L. J., in Royal Society of Canada, *Proceedings and Transactions*, series III, vol. I., 1907–8. (Journal of a journey by Anthony Hendry to explore the country inland, and to endeavour to increase the Hudson Bay Company's trade.)

Hincks, Sir Francis—" Reminiscences of my Public Life." Montreal, 1884.

Holman, F. V.—" Dr. John McLoughlin, the father of Oregon." Cleveland, 1907.

Hopkins, John C.—" Canada : An encyclopædia of the country." Toronto, 1898–1900.

Hulbert, A. B.—" Historic Highways of America." Cleveland, 1902–5.

Iberville, Pierre le Moyne Sieur d'—" Histoire du Chevalier D'Iberville, 1663–1706." Montreal, 1890.

Irving, Washington—" Astoria." In Works Philadelphia, " Jesuit Relations and Allied Documents, 1610–1791." Thwaites, R. G., ed. Cleveland, 1896–1901.

Kane, Paul—" Wanderings of an Artist among the Indians of North America." London, 1859.

Keating, W. H.—" Narrative of an Expedition to the Source of St. Peter's River, Lake Winnipeek, Lake of the Woods, etc., in 1823." London, 1825.

Kingsford, W.—" The Canadian Canals." Toronto, 1865.

Knox, John—" Journal." Champlain Society. Toronto, 1914–16.

La Salle, Robert Cavalier sieur de—" La Découverte du Mississippi." Quebec, 1873.

Laut, A. C.—" The Cariboo Trail." Toronto, 1916.

Laverdière, C. H.—" Œuvres de Samuel Champlain." Quebec, 1877.

Le Clerq, F. C.—" First Establishment of the Faith in New France." New York, 1881.

Lescarbot, Marc—" The History of New France." Champlain Society, Publ. Nos. I, VII and XI. Toronto, 1907–14.

Lewis, John—" George Brown." Toronto, 1906.

Lincoln—" Correspondence of William Shirley." New York, 1912.

Livingstone, W.—" A Review of the Military Operations in North America from 1753 to 1756." London, 1757.

Longley, James W.—" Joseph Howe." Toronto, 1904.

Lucas, Sir Charles—" Historical Geography of the British Colonies." Oxford, 1913–15.

McCain, Chas. W.—" The History of the S.S. *Beaver.*" Vancouver, 1894.

MacDonald, D. G. F.—" British Columbia and Vancouver's Island." London, 1862.

M'Donnell, Alexander—" Narrative of Transactions in the Red River Country." London, 1819.

Macfie, M.—" Vancouver's Island and British Columbia." London, 1865.

MacGibbon, D. A.—" Railway Rates and the Canadian Railway Commission." Boston and New York, 1917.

MacKenzie, Sir Alexander—" General History of the Fur Trade from Canada to the North-West." London, 1801.

MacKenzie, Sir Alexander—" Voyages from Montreal through the Continent of North America to the Frozen and Pacific Oceans in 1789 and 1793." London, 1801.

McNaughton, Margaret—" Overland to Cariboo." Toronto, 1896.

Macpherson, James P.—" Life of the Right Hon. Sir John A. MacDonald." St. John, N.B., 1891.

MacTaggart, John—" Three Years in Canada: An Account of the Actual State of the Country in 1826–8." London, 1829.

Manning, Wm. Ray—" The Nootka Sound Controversy," in *Annual Report of the American Historical Association*, 1904. Washington, 1905.

Margry, Pierre—" Découvertes et établissements des Français

330 BIBLIOGRAPHY

dans l'ouest et dans le sud de l'Amérique Septentrionale,
1614–1754." Paris, 1879–88.
Marquis, T. G.—" The War Chiefs of the Ottawas: A Chronicle
of the Pontiac War." Toronto, 1915.
Martin, Chester B.—" Lord Selkirk's Work in Canada." London,
1898.
Martin, Chester B.—" Natural Resources Question." Winnipeg,
1920.
Masson, L. F. R.—" Les Bourgeois de la Compagnie du Nord-
Ouest." Publ. avec une Esquisse Historique. Quebec,
1889–90.
Mavor, James—" Report to the Board of Trade on the North-West
of Canada." London, 1904.
Mayne, Richard C.—" Four Years in British Columbia and
Vancouver Island." London, 1862.
Meares, John—" Voyages made in the years 1788 and 9 from
China to the North-West Coast of America." London,
1790.
Milton, Viscount, Wm. F., and Cheadle, W. B.—" The North-West
Passage by Land." London, 1865.
Moberly, Walter—" The Rocks and Rivers of British Columbia."
London, 1885.
Monro, Alex.—" New Brunswick with a brief outline of Nova
Scotia and Prince Edward Island." Halifax, 1855.
Morice, A. G.—" History of the Northern Interior of British
Columbia, 1660–1880." Toronto, 1904.
Murdoch, Beamish—" A History of Nova Scotia." Halifax,
1865–7.
Myers, Gustavus—" History of Canadian Wealth." Chicago,
1914.
Neill, E. D.—" The History of Minnesota." Philadelphia, 1858.
Oberholtzer, E. P.—" Jay Cooke, Financier of the Civil War."
Philadelphia, 1917.
Ogg, Frederic A.—" The Opening of the Mississippi." New
York, 1904.
"Ohio Archæological and Historical Publications." Vol. I.
Columbia, 1887.
Oldmixon, J.—" The British Empire in America." London,
1741.
" Parkman Club Publications, 1895–7."
Pemberton, J. D.—" Facts and Figures relating to Vancouver
Island and British Columbia." London, 1860.
Pope, Sir Joseph, ed.—" Confederation Documents hitherto
unpublished." Toronto, 1895.
Pope, Sir Joseph—" Correspondence of Sir John A. MacDonald."
Toronto, 1920.
Pope, Sir Joseph—" Memoirs of the Rt. Hon. Sir John A.
MacDonald." London, 1894.

Preston, W. T. R.—" Life and Times of Lord Strathcona."
London, 1914.
Pritchard, John—" Narratives respecting the aggressions of the
North-West Company against the Earl of Selkirk's Settle-
ment." London, 1819.
Prowse, D. W.—" History of Newfoundland from English,
Colonial and Foreign Records." London, 1895.
Pyle, J. G.—" Life of James J. Hill." Garden City, 1917.
Radisson, Pierre Esprit — "Voyages, 1652–84." Boston,
1885.
Rame, A.—" Documents inédits sur le Canada. 1865–7."
Rameau, De S. R.—" Une Colonie Féodale en Amérique—l'Acadie,
1604–1881." Montreal, 1889.
Robson, J.—" An Account of Six Years' Residence in Hudson's
Bay, 1733–6 and 1744–7." London, 1752.
Rogers, Robert—" Ponteach or the Savages of America, a
Tragedy." London, 1766.
Roosevelt, Theodore—" The Winning of the West." New York,
1889–96.
Ross, Alexander—" Adventures of the First Settlers on the
Oregon or Columbia River." London, 1849.
Ross, Alexander—" The Red River Settlement: Its Use, Pro-
gress and Present State." London, 1856.
Schoolcraft, Henry R.—" Summary Narrative of an Explora-
tory expedition to the Sources of the Mississippi River,
1820." Philadelphia, 1855.
Scholefield, E. O. S.—" British Columbia from the Earliest Times
to the Present." Vancouver, 1914.
Seemann, Berthold C.—" Narrative of the Voyage of H.M.S.
Herald." London, 1853.
Selkirk, Thomas D., Earl of—" Observations on the Present
State of the Highlands of Scotland." London, 1805.
Semple, Ellen C.—" American History and its Geographic
Conditions." Boston, 1903.
Shortt, Adam ed.—" Canada and its Provinces." Edinburgh,
1914–17.
Simpson, Alexander—" Life and Times of Thomas Simpson, the
Arctic Discoverer." London, 1845.
Skelton, O. D.—" Life and Letters of Sir Wilfrid Laurier."
Toronto, 1921.
Skelton, O. D.—" The Railway Builders." Toronto, 1916.
Slafter, E. F.—" Sir William Alexander and American Coloniza-
tion." Boston, 1873.
Smalley, E. V.—" History of the Northern Pacific Railroad."
New York, 1883.
Smith, Hon. William—" History of the Late Province of New
York—to 1762." New York, 1829.
" Sources of the History of Oregon." University of Oregon,

Dept. of Economics and History—Contributions. Eugene, 1897–9.

Sparks, Jared—" The Works of Benjamin Franklin." 1844.

Stone, Wm. L.—" The Life and Times of Sir William Johnston, Bart." Albany, 1865.

Strachan, John—" A Letter to the Right Hon. the Earl of Selkirk on his settlement at the Red River near Hudson's Bay." London, 1816.

Sulté, Benjamin—" Histoire de la Ville des Trois Rivières et de ses environs." Montreal, 1870.

Synge, M. H.—" Great Britain One Empire, 1852." London, 1852.

Thompson, D.—" History of the Late War between Great Britain and the United States of America." Niagara, 1832.

Thompson, David—" Narrative of Exploration in Western America, 1784–1812." Ed. Tyrell, J. B., Champlain Society Publ. vol. XII. Toronto, 1916.

" Toronto—History of Toronto and the County of York, Ontario." Toronto, 1885.

Trout, J. M., and Edw.—" The Railways of Canada for 1870–1." Toronto, 1871.

Tupper, Sir Charles—" Recollections of Sixty Years in Canada." London, 1914.

Umfreville, E.—" The Present State of Hudson's Bay." London, 1790.

Vaughan, Walter—" Life and Work of Sir William Van Horne." New York, 1920.

Vineberg, S.—" Provincial and Local Taxation in Canada." New York, 1912.

Wallace, W. S.—" The United Empire Loyalists." Toronto, 1914.

Washington—" Journal of Colonel George Washington." Ed. Toner, J. M. Albany, 1893.

Watkin, Sir E. W., Bart., M.P.—" Canada and the States, Recollections 1851–86." London, 1887.

Weise, A. J.—" Discoveries of North America to the year 1525." New York and London, 1884.

White, James—" Altitudes in Canada." Ottawa, 1915.

Whymper, Frederick—" Travel and Adventure in the Territory of Alaska." London, 1869.

Willison, Sir J. S.—" Sir Wilfrid Laurier and the Liberal Party." Toronto, 1903.

Willson, Henry Beckles—" Life of Lord Strathcona and Mount Royal." London, 1915.

Willson, Henry Beckles—" Lord Strathcona, The Story of His Life." Toronto, 1902.

Willson, Henry Beckles—" The Great Company." London, 1900.

Wilson, F. A., and Richards, A. B.—" Britain Redeemed and
    Canada Preserved." London, 1850.
Winthrop, John—" Journal in Original Narratives of Early
    American History of New England." 1630–49. New York,
    1908.
Wolseley, G. J. F. M., Viscount—" Story of a Soldier's Life."
    Westminster, 1903.
Wood, Wm. C. H.—" The War with the United States; A
    Chronicle of 1812." Toronto, 1915.

II. Newspapers and Magazines

" Commercial and Financial Chronicle." New York.
" Economic Journal." London.
" Economist." London.
" Globe." Toronto.
" Leader." Toronto.
" London Times." London.
" Railway Age Gazette." Chicago.
" United Service Journal and Naval and Military Magazine."
    London, 1829–1865.

III. Pamphlets

Allan, H.—" The Times and its Correspondents on Canadian
    Railways." London, 1875.
Bell, Charles N.—" Some Historical Names and Places of the
    Canadian North-West "; Transactions of the Manitoba
    Historical and Scientific Society, No. 17. Winnipeg, 1885.
British Columbia—" Letters of Britannicus." Ottawa, 1876.
Bross, W.—" The Toronto and Georgian Bay Ship Canal."
    Chicago, 1864.
Ellice, Edward—" Communications of Mercator." Montreal,
    1817.
Foster, John—" Descriptions of a Wooden Railway." Montreal,
    1870.
Foster, John—" Railway from Lake Superior to Red River
    Settlement." Montreal, 1869.
Hogan, J. S.—" Canada." Montreal, 1855.
Letter from " Mohawk "—" The Canadian Pacific Railway and
    its Assailants." London, 1882.
MacDonnell, Allen—" The North-West Transportation, Naviga-
    tion and Railway Company. Its Objects." Toronto, 1858.
Meddaugh, E. W., and Raymond, A. C.—" The Canadian Railway
    Question." Detroit, 1891.
" Notice on the Claims of the Hudson's Bay Company and the
    Conduct of its Adversaries." Montreal, 1817.
" Open Letter to the shareholders of the Canadian Pacific Railway
    Company, 1st October, 1887. Ashdown, J. H., and Robinson,

J. C. Issued by authority of the Winnipeg Board of Trade and the Brandon Board of Trade.

" Railway Interests of the City of Montreal." Montreal, 1872.

Smith, T. T. Vernon—" Pacific Railway Claims of St. John to be the Atlantic Terminus." 1858.

Smyth, Carmichael—" Employment of People and Capital in Great Britain in her own Colonies." Ottawa, 1871.

Smyth, Sir J.—" Railroad Communication." Toronto, 1845.

Waddington, Alfred—" Sketch of Proposed Railroad Line Overland through British North America." Ottawa, 1871.

Wilson, J. R.—" The Oregon Question " ; *Quarterly of the Oregon Historical Society*, vol. I. September, 1900.

Wilson, Wm.—" Dominion of Canada and the Canadian Pacific Railway." Victoria, 1874.

IV. OFFICIAL REPORTS AND DOCUMENTS

Andrews, Israel D.—" Report on Trade and Commerce of British North America Colonies. Report of the Secretary of the U.S. Treasury in answer to a resolution of the Senate calling for information in relation to trade and commerce of the British American colonies with the United States and other countries since 1829." 1851.

" Annual Reports of the Board of Railway Commissioners." Ottawa.

" Annual Reports of the Canadian Pacific Railway."

" Annual Reports of the Department of Railways and Canals." Ottawa.

" Atlas of Canada, 1915." Canada, Dept. of the Interior.

" British Columbia Yearbooks." Victoria.

" Canada—Board of Registration and Statistics, 1849." Appendix to the first report. Montreal.

" Canada Gazette." Ottawa.

" Canada House of Commons and Senate Debates."

" Canada Yearbooks." Ottawa. (Statistical Abstract and Record of Canada, 1886–8, The Statistical Yearbook of Canada, 1889–1904. Present title since.)

" Canadian Archives Reports." Ottawa.

" Canadian Cases in the Judicial Committee of the Privy Council —Appeal Cases." London.

" Canadian Pacific Railway Royal Commission Report." Ottawa, 1882.

" Canadian Supreme Court Reports."

" Census of Canada." Ottawa.

" Census of Nova Scotia." Halifax, 1862.

" Collection de documents relatifs à la Histoire de la Nouvelle France." Quebec, 1885.

" Copies of extracts of any dispatches—on the subject of the establishment of a representative assembly at Vancouver's Island. London, 1857.

" Copies or extracts of correspondence relative to the discovery of gold in Fraser's River District in British North America." London, 1858.

" Copy of correspondence between the chairman of the Hudson Bay Company and the Secretary of State for the colonies relative to the colonization of Vancouver's Island." London, 1848.

" Copy of Treasury Minute dated 18th July, 1889, and of contract with Canadian Pacific Railway dated 15th July, 1889, for conveyance of Her Majesty's mails, troops and stores between Halifax or Quebec and Hong Kong and for hire and purchase of vessels as cruisers and transports." London, 1889.

" Correspondence, Papers and Documents of dates, 1856 to 1882 incl., relating to Northerly and Westerly boundaries of the Province of Ontario." Toronto, 1882.

" Correspondence relative to the Canadian Pacific Railway." London, 1874.

" Correspondence relative to the Negotiation of the Question of disputed right to the Oregon territory—subsequent to the Treaty of Washington of August 9, 1842." 1846.

" Correspondence relative to the Recent Disturbances in the Red River Settlement." London, 1870.

" Correspondence respecting the Canadian Pacific Railway Act so far as regards British Columbia." London, 1875.

" Correspondence respecting the North-West Territory including British Columbia." Ottawa, 1868.

Dawson, Simon J.—" Report on exploration of the country between Lake Superior and the Red River Settlement and between the latter place and the Assiniboine and Saskatchewan. 1858." Toronto, 1859.

" Documents relative to the Colonial History of the State of New York." Albany, 1861.

Durham, Earl of—" Report on the Affairs of British North America." London, 1839.

" Édits, Ordonnances Royaux, Déclarations et Arrêts du Conseil d'état du Roi concernant de Canada." Quebec, 1855.

Fleming, Sandford—" Report and Documents in reference to the Canadian Pacific Railway." Ottawa, 1872–80.

Fleming, Sandford—" Report on Surveys and preliminary operations on the Canadian Pacific Railway to January, 1877." Ottawa, 1877.

" Further Copies or Extracts of correspondence relative to the affairs of Lower and Upper Canada." London, 1837–8.

Hart, A. B., and Channing, E.—" American History Leaflets, Colonial and Constitutional." New York, 1892–1911.

Hind, Henry Youle—" Narrative of the Canadian Red River exploring expedition of 1857 and of the Assiniboine and Saskatchewan expedition of 1858." London, 1860.
" Interstate Commerce Commission Reports."
" Journals of the Legislative Assemblies of the Provinces."
" Journals of the House of Commons of the Dominion of Canada."
" Judgments, Orders, Regulations and Rulings of the Board of Railway Commissioners of Canada." Ottawa.
Langevin, Hon. H. L.—" British Columbia Report." Ottawa, 1872.
MacDonald, W.—" Select Documents of the History of the United States." New York, 1898.
MacMurchy and Dennison, or MacMurchy and Spence—" Canadian Railway Cases." Toronto.
" Messages and Papers of the Presidents." Vol. IX. Washington.
" Minutes of evidence taken before the Select Committee of the Senate appointed to inquire into all matters relating to the Canadian Pacific Railway and Telegraph west of Lake Superior." Ottawa, 1879.
Palliser, Capt. John—" Journals, detailed reports and observations relative to the exploration—1857–8, 9, 1860." London, 1859–63.
" Papers connected with the awarding of section 15 of the C.P.R." Ottawa, 1877.
" Papers relating to the Hudson Bay Company, 1842–70." London, 1842, 49, 50, 58.
" Papers relating to the Red River Settlement." 1819.
" Papers relative to the Affairs of British Columbia." 1859–62.
" Report and Minutes of evidence taken before the Select Committee of the Senate appointed to inquire into and report upon the purchases of lands at Fort William for a terminus to the Canadian Pacific Railway." Ottawa, 1878.
" Report and minutes of evidence taken before the Select Committee of the Senate to inquire into and report upon the route of the C.P.R. from Keewatin westward." Ottawa, 1877.
" Report from the committee appointed to inquire into the state and condition of the countries adjoining to Hudson Bay, and of the Trade carried on there." London, 1749.
" Report from the Select Committee on the Hudson's Bay Company." 1857.
" Report of the Commission appointed to inquire into the affairs of the Grand Trunk Railway." 1861.
" Report of the Ontario Commission on Railway Taxation." Toronto, 1905.
" Report of the Royal Commission appointed to inquire into

and report upon the several matters relating to the C.P.R."
Ottawa, 1873.
" Report of the Royal Commission to Inquire into Methods by
which Oriental labourers have been induced to come to
Canada." Ottawa, 1908.
Selkirk, Earl of—" Report of Proceedings at a court of oyer and
terminer appointed for the investigation of cases from the
Indian Territories." 1819.
Selkirk, Earl of—" Report of the Proceedings connected with
the disputes between the Earl of Selkirk and the North-West
Company at the Assizes at York, 1818." London, 1819.
" Sessional Papers, Federal and Provincial, of the Dominion of
Canada and Parliamentary Papers of Great Britain."
Shortt, Adam, and Doughty, A. G.—" Documents relating to the
constitutional History of Canada." Ottawa, 1907–14.
" Statistical Abstract of the United States." Washington, 1919.
" Statutes and Proclamations, Federal and Provincial, of the
Dominion of Canada."
" Statutes of Great Britain."
" United States Senate and Congressional Reports and Papers."
Wood, Wm.—" Select British Documents of the Canadian War
of 1812." *Champlain Society Publ.* vol. XIII. Toronto,
1920.

INDEX

Abbott, J. J. C., 102, 275
Abercorn, 135 *n.*
Aberdeen, the, 150
Acadia, 54 *n.*, 57 *n.*, 60 *n.*
Accidents, 231
Acme, 153
Acquisition, 111, 122, 134, 135 *n.*,
    136, 140, 141, 142, 143, 158,
    169, 199, 237, 248, 249, 255,
    273, 281 *n.*
Act, 14, 17 *n.*, 38, 39, 40, 63 *n.*,
    67 *n.*, 89 *n.*, 100, 120, 123, 174,
    179, 184, 186, 251, 255, 256,
    257, 270, 289
    British North America, 45, 72 *n.*,
    179, 180, 181
    Canadian Pacific Railway, 81 *n.*,
    83, 85 *n.*, 124, 172, 250 *n.*
    Consolidated Railroad, 172, 256
    Loan, 125, 126, 280, 282
    Manitoba, 50
    of Union, 66, 75, 75 *n.*, 76 *n.*, 290
    Quebec, 62 *n.*
    Rupert's Land, 46, 46 *n.*
    Railway Taxation, 239 *n.*
Admiralty, 139, 170
Agincourt, 156
Agriculture, 6, 7, 7 *n.*,8, 9, 16, 28 *n.*,
    29, 38 *n.*, 42 *n.*, 130, 141, 145,
    146, 147, 162, 163, 164, 183,
    185, 199, 216, 245, 260, 265,
    288
Alaska, 19
Albany, 56, 56 *n.*
    River, 23 *n.*, 24 *n.*, 25 *n.*
Alberni, 154
Alberta, the, 134
Alberta, 152, 153, 170, 191 *n.*, 255,
    264
    Central Railway, 154
    Railway and Coal Co., 139
    Railway and Irrigation Co., 154,
    191 *n.*
Aldersyde, 152
Alexander, Sir William, 55 *n.*
Alexandria, 15

Algoma Mills, 106, 107, 112, 115,
    121, 125, 134, 137, 271, 272
Alida, 153
Allan, Sir Hugh, 79, 79 *n.*, 80 *n.*,
    81 *n.*, 82, 92 *n.*, 83, 95 *n.*, 102
    Line, 170
Alleghany Mountains, 59, 61, 73
    River, 60 *n.*
Almonte Knitting Co. case, 189
Alps, 170
America, 19, 22 *n.*, 34 *n.*, 41 *n.*, 52,
    70 *n.*
America, the, 10 *n.*
American, 6, 8, 19, 32 *n.*, 49, 61 *n.*,
    62 *n.*, 64, 64 *n.*,67 *n.*, 77 *n.*, 79,
    79 *n.*, 81 *n.*, 82, 82 *n.*, 98, 100,
    134, 138, 182, 188, 189, 189 *n.*,
    191, 194, 274, 282
    Anglo-American, 44
    Civil War, 71 *n.*
    expansion, 42 *n.*, 69 *n.*, 71
    fur trade, 26
    Imperialism, 32, 35, 44
    lines, 139, 180, 181, 193, 207
    railroads, 69 *n.*, 70, 93 *n.*, 112,
    113 *n.*, 137, 139, 154, 158, 173,
    174, 179, 183, 187, 189, 191,
    192, 194, 195, 205, 206, 207,
    208
    Revolution, 61
    route, 42 *n.*, 193, 195
    traffic, 77, 78 *n.*, 80, 83
Amsterdam, 114
Anderson, 11 *n.*
Anglo-American capitalists, 44
Angus, R. B., 97, 102, 113, 114, 259,
    275, 275 *n.*, 276
Annexationist Manifesto, 68 *n.*, 290
Anticosti, 33 *n.*
Appropriation, 90 *n.*
Archibald, Lieut.-Gov., 51
Arcola, 152
Arctic Ocean, in, 2
Aroostook Junction, 143
Arrowhead, 142
Ashburton treaty, 70 *n.*

339

340 INDEX

Ashley Creek, 6 *n.*
Asia, 66 *n.*
Asquith, 153
Assessment, 80 *n.*, 81 *n.*
Assinæ Poets, 23 *n.*
Assiniboia, 153
  Council of, 29 *n.*, 31 *n.*, 47 *n.*
  Valley, 78 *n.*
Assiniboine, branch, 103
  House, 25 *n.*
  River, 23 *n.*, 24 *n.*, 25 *n.*, 28, 36 *n*
  territory, 27 *n.*
Astoria, 6, 7, 8 *n.*
Athabasca, the, 134
Athabasca territory, 27 *n.*, 67 *n.*
Athenian, the, 150
Atlantic and Northwest Railway,
  122, 122 *n.*, 135, 137, 142
  and Pacific Transit and Telegraph
  Co., 42 *n.*
  coast, 68, 70, 70 *n.*, 73, 135, 136,
  155, 169, 181, 195, 209, 288
  division, 33 *n.*
  Ocean, 1 *n.*, 3 *n.*, 18 *n.*, 26, 42 *n.*,
  55 *n.*, 62 *n.*, 69 *n.*, 70, 169, 281 *n.*
Attorney-general, 37 *n.*
  of British Columbia, 189
Austrian Government, 170
Aylmer, 112, 112 *n.*, 156

Baffin, 22 *n.*
Baggage, mail and express car, 133,
  201, 201 *n.*
  rates, 86 *n.*
Bald Range, 78 *n.*
Ballast pit, 257, 272
Baltimore and Ohio Co., 151
Banff, 204
Bank of Montreal, 92 *n.*, 97, 117
Baring, Rt. Hon. A. C., 126
  and Co., 127
Barkerville, 17 *n.*
Barnard, F. J., 88 *n.*
Barnesville, 93 *n.*
Barnet and McKay, 99 *n.*
Barney, A. H., 80 *n.*, 81 *n.*
Basins, drainage, 1, 2, 3, 74
  Arctic, 1 *n.*
  Atlantic, 1 *n.*
  Hudson Bay, 1 *n.*
  Pacific, 1 *n.*
  St. Lawrence, 52, 59
Bassano, 152, 153, 255 *n.*
Battleford, 3 *n.*, 252, 254
Bay of Fundy, 54 *n.*, 71 *n.*, 158, 169
  Quinte, 63 *n.*
  St., Toronto, 137
Bear Lake, 9 *n.*
Beatty, E. W., 276
Beaubassin, 60 *n.*

Beauharnois Canal, 67 *n.*
Beausejour, 60 *n.*
Beaver, the, 13 *n.*
Beaver Creek, 110
  Line, 169
  River, 25 *n.*, 110
  town, 259
Bedford House, 25 *n.*
Beique, Senator F. L., 275
Belle Isle, Straits of, 53
Bellevue Islands, 157
Berlin, Waterloo, Wellesley and
  Lake Huron Railway, 157
Berthier, 123 *n.*
  Junction, 123 *n.*
Berwyn, 154
Bethany Junction, 156
Biencourt, 55 *n.*
Big Bend, 15
  " Big Hill " grade, 155
Bill of Rights, Settlers', 50 *n.*
Billings, Frederick, 80 *n.*, 81 *n.*
Binscarth, 152
Birdtail Creek, 87 *n.*
Biscayan Whaling expedition, 53
Black Sturgeon district, 78 *n.*
Blake Bros. & Co., 275
Blakiston, Lieut., 35 *n.*
Blanshard, Richard, 12 *n.*, 13
Board, 95 *n.*, 188
  of directors, C. P. R., 82 *n.*
  of directors, Hudson's Bay Co.,
  48 *n.*
  of Railway Commissioners, 186,
  188, 189, 190, 190 *n.*, 191 *n.*,
  196, 209, 220, 221, 230, 293,
  293 *n.*
  of Trade, 36, 69 *n.*, 100, 176, 180
Boarding, tool and auxiliary cars,
  150, 150 *n.*, 168, 168 *n.*
Bobcaygeon, 157
Boissevain, 153
Bolton Junction, 156
Bond, 81 *n.*, 101, 107, 118, 118 *n.*,
  119, 120, 121, 123, 124, 125,
  126, 127, 135, 182, 270, 271,
  272, 273, 274, 279, 280, 281 *n.*
  land grant 98, 101, 103, 104,
  107, 108, 109, 115, 116, 117,
  118, 118 *n.*, 125, 182, 250, 271,
  272, 278
Bonus, 92 *n.*, 100, 181, 274
Boston, 4 *n.*, 62, 79 *n.*, 92 *n.*, 112,
  114, 135, 156, 157, 192, 194,
  207, 274, 275
  Lowell Railway, 135
  Port Bill, 61 *n.*
Boston Bar, 88 *n.*
Bostonian, 57 *n.*
Boulder Creek, 262